A Pictorial History of the American Carnival

LOCKERBIE FAIR
James Whitcomb Riley

O! the Lockerbie Fair! — Have your heard of its fame
And its fabulous riches, too rare for a name!
The gold of the moon of the June-time refined
To the Orient-night, till the eyes and the mind
Are dazed with the sights, in the earth and the air
Of the opulent splendors of the Lockerbie Fair.

What more fortunate fate might to mortal befall
Midst the midsummer beauty and bloom of it all
Than to beam with the moon o'er the rapturous scene
And twink with the stars as they laughingly lean
O'er the luminous revel and glamour and glare
Fused in one dazzling glory at Lockerbie Fair.

The night like a Queen in her purple and lace
With her diamonded brow and imperious grace
As she leads her fair votaries, train upon train
A-dance thro' the feasts of this mystic domain
To the mandolin's twang, and the warble and blare
Of voice, flute and bugle at Lockerbie Fair.

All strange, ever-changing, enchanted delights
Found now in this newer Arabian Nights
Where each lovely maid is a Princess, and each
Lucky swain an Aladdin — all treasures in reach
Of the lamps and the rings — and with Genii to spare
Simply waiting your orders, at Lockerbie Fair.

A PICTORIAL HISTORY OF THE
AMERICAN CARNIVAL

By Joe McKennon

Volume I

Reproduced from the Collection of the Library of Congress

Library and General Distribution
by Popular Press
Bowling Green, Ohio 43403

CARNIVAL PUBLISHERS of Sarasota, Sarasota, Florida

Dedicated to my wife,
MARIAN,
whose forbearance has
made it possible.

ACKNOWLEDGEMENTS

Chicago Historical Society
Ringling Museum of the Circus
New York Public Library
Circus World Museum
Albert Conover and Fred Pfening, Jr.
Billboard Publishing Company
San Antonio, Texas, Public Library
Canton, Cincinnati, Columbus and Dayton, Ohio, Public Libraries
Art Doc Miller and Harry Shell
Lou Dufour and Merle Evans
Amusement Business and its publisher, Walter Heeney. Irwin Kirby, editor, Amusement Business.
Earl Purtle, Nat Worman, Dick Best and L. Harvey (Doc) Cann.
Al Kunz, Fred Thumberg, Buster Brown, Patty Conklin and the Drews.

Frank Morrisey, Joe Pearl, Johnny Portemont, Col. C. C. (Specs) Groscurth.
Dallas and Houston, Texas, Public Libraries.
Shreveport, Louisiana, Public Library.
Johnny Keef, Harvey Wilson and hundreds of other carnival troupers.
Harry Frost of the Minnesota State Fair.
Clyde Propst, Jr. of the Cabarrus County, North Carolina, Fair.
Burdette Kelley of the Hillsdale Fair.
Floyd E. Gooding and his entire staff.
New York Clipper and newspapers too numerous to mention.
William T. Collins and Bill McKay of O.A.B.A.
Mrs. Harold (Bootsie Hurd) Paddock and Mrs. Johnny J. (Etta Louise Blake, Hody Hurd) Jones. And, many more which I regretfully cannot list.

BIBLIOGRAPHY

If this history had been written as a dissertation for a doctorate, I would list all of the newspapers and books that I read before I began to write. Then the text would be filled with footnotes and reference marks, so that it would be almost incomprehensible to the average reader for whom it is written. As explained in the introduction there has been no literature on the American Carnival.

For the European roots, read any one of the many Greek and Roman mythologies and acquire a comprehensive knowledge of London Town of Medieval days. Then go into any public library and read the old newspaper files and study all the back issues of Billboard and the New York Clipper. When you have done this, you will have a "press agent's viewpoint" of the American Carnival. Unless you have known those press agents and their cliches, as I have known them, you will not have a clear mental picture of the collective amusement industry. Many of the old-timers in the business get their names, dates and events mixed up, and are not reliable sources of information.

For this reason I am not including a long list of reference material. It would be useless, if accuracy is desired. I have used my own experiences in the business coupled with hundreds of personal interviews and thousands of hours of reading back issues of periodicals. After ten years of research, I sat down and wrote from my notes. For every item used herein, I discarded ten items that were noted. I regret that I cannot furnish more substantial references; but if you are not a carnival trouper, you would interpret them differently.

First Printing - August, 1972
Second Printing - October, 1972
Third Printing - November, 1972

Contents

Volume I

THIS IS A CARNIVAL "TIE-OFF." This type tie was never used on the old time circuses. Circus men used the two hitches only without the center wrap around the stake. Some of the circuses today do use this type tie-off as they guy out the tent only once during the day. Courtesy James E. Strates Shows.

INTRODUCTION

There has been no definitive literature of any kind about the American carnival, and the infrequent carnival-based works of fiction are either freak show or "Gal" show oriented. The few writers who have attempted carnival fiction have become intrigued by the plot possibilities offered by a collection of human oddities or a strip tease queen; and consequently have overlooked the more interesting stories that the dignified old lady selling tickets on the merry-go-round or the weatherbeaten, toothless old fellow operating the fun house might have to tell. The lady may have been the "cootch" dancer on the Barkoot Shows fifty years ago, and her son and grandsons probably own and operate that big spectacular riding device on the back of the present midway. As for the old man, he owned and managed his own thirty car railroad carnival for ten, fifteen, maybe twenty years.

Since there are no literary works on the collective amusement industry, the research for this volume has been slow, tedious and often frustrating. Over ten years have been spent in locating and acquiring material used. The tedium of gazing at thousands of feet of microfilm projected on flickering viewers in back rooms of libraries, historical societies and newspapers has been relieved by finding a particular bit of information that fills in the story of some show or of an old time carnival trouper.

The frustration still remains though, as it is ascertained that no one volume can ever relate the full story of the American Carnival. For each individual mentioned, thousands of others of equal importance must remain unnamed; and for each midway history traced; hundreds with sagas just as interesting must remain unmentioned. The lives of many of the rugged individualist showmen traced herein are worthy of full volume biographies, not the few hundred words allotted them in this short history.

This history of the collective amusement industry in America does attempt to give a clear and concise account of its development and growth starting with its ancient roots and bringing it up to the present. For the first time, a narrative tracing the history of carnival business has been recorded; and that in itself is a source of satisfaction to the compiler. This writer has used his many years of experience in all branches of outdoor amusement business as a foundation on which to construct the story of the midways. Ever since he, at the age of thirteen, joined his first carnival, knowledge of midways and midway people has been accumulated. That knowledge coupled with interviews of hundreds of old friends in the carnival field has been added to the available microfilmed information to produce a complete history.

The chief source of information regarding outdoor amusement business is the files of the Billboard and its successor, Amusement Business. Persons unfamiliar with the vagaries of old time carnival press agents can be misled by stories in the Billboard. Having known and worked with most of those old timers on one show or another, this compiler knows how much to discount from one of their stories. As a press agent with a three car "gilly" show had to make his show sound as important as a thirty car flat car show to potential patrons; he acquired a formula with assorted cliches which was his own trade mark in the business.

Had every carnival actually owned the number of railroad cars claimed by their press agents and in their advertising matter, the railroads of the United States would have been compelled to build extra side trackage to store them. Or, if purchase orders had been placed for all of the steel flat cars bought each winter, Pttsburgh's steel mills would have needed additions to supply the metal required to build them. And, if the winter quarters crews reported as "being busily engaged with hammer, saw and paint brush" had all been as large as claimed, industry in America would have faced an acute labor shortage — actually the country side would have been jammed for miles around the quarters with newly built show properties. Such wild reports can all be brought down to proper perspective by one who has known the individual making the report, and who also has some knowledge of the show written about.

All information included in this volume has been checked and double checked for accuracy. No doubt there are some mistakes, as such things appear in all histories written; but any inaccuracy so occurring should have little or no effect on the historical data recorded. It is hoped that this book will stimulate others to do research and possibly find the missing links that will more thoroughly connect up the narrative history of certain segments of the carnival industry. It is known that certain big midways had constant existence for twenty or more years, but so far very little of interest has been found on them. The real source of information is from "old timers" who worked on such shows, and again the seeker of carnival history must know the individual being interviewed so that he can discount accordingly. First, the old carnies are reticent with strangers;

then, like everyone else, they are likely to have blurred memories regarding events that happened over fifty years ago. Also, if they do talk, they will probably tell "tall tales" to the carnival novice. Again a certain amount of judgment is required in editing the material received.

The word carnival when applied to the first collective amusement organizations, was a misnomer for they were never carnivals according to a strict historic interpretation of that term. True, some of the early street fairs gave the appearance of the ancient religious festivals, or even a Bacchanalia; but basically they had nothing in common except the carefree mood of the participants. This state of mind has been engendered deliberately by promoters of street festivals and travelling midways ever since those sources of amusement became popular. It is doubtful that any of the early purveyors of midway amusement gave much thought to the state of mind of their patrons. They found that "local yokels" were more numerous and more apt to open the snap jaws of their purses, if certain elements were present on the midway.

Early operators provided those midway elements as a matter of good business practice. Food and drink, thrilling adventure, tests of skill, games of chance and sex were found to be necessary for the well-being of any midway. It was probably accidental that the pioneers in the collective amusement industry developed those components of their midways which created the same carnival atmosphere permeating the ancient festivals. Illiterate Rubin Gruberg never heard of the Saturnalia, so had no realization of the genesis of the prevailing mood on his carnival grounds.

This volume deals with the history of the industry without deliberately trying to be sensational. There is much in the business that could be used for sensationalism, but let those writers who visit a carnival midway for a few weeks use those things in their efforts to record a story of the midway. It is hoped that this volume will be an aid to those "Johnny-Come-Latelys" in correcting many of the common mistakes they make in those literary efforts. No one in a few weeks, a few months or even a few years can learn enough about the business to do it justice on paper. It will be said that Carnies are people. They are people, but praise be, they are different from any other people on this earth. It has been said often, "Show business is just like any other business." Not one of the individuals making that statement has made a lasting success in it.

When I was approached by a publisher and asked to do this volume for them, I knew that it would be difficult to get much of the information needed. I immediately sent out two hundred personal letters to carnival people and midway owners. I expected only ten percent to reply. One percent did answer that first mailing. I was ready to quit at first, then considered from whom I received those two answers. Buster Brown took time off from his duties as manager of the Bill Hames Shows to write a personal letter offering his aid and support. And, from the Canadian National Exhibition, Patty Conklin not only sent a personal letter but material to be used. This was done by Patty during that record-breaking eighteen day run, where the largest gross in the history of the business was made. If this volume is appreciated, the thanks should go to Buster Brown and Patty Conklin.

When I started making personal visits to carnivals, I encountered everything from enthusiastic support to outright antagonism. Fortunately, only one or two are in the latter category, and they were people I hadn't planned to mention anyway. Most everyone that I have contacted personally has contributed photographs and needed information. My only regret is that there is not enough space available to use all the material so generously provided by my old friends, and a lot of new ones.

WORLD OF MIRTH SHOW TRAIN UNLOADING, 1938. Courtesy Frank Cucksey.

Cronus, The Father Of the Carnival

CRONUS EATING HIS YOUNG. From Goya's print in Museo del Prado, Madrid. Courtesy John and Mable Ringling Museum of Art Collection.

Was He the First Glomming Geek?

The carnival has always been a lusty busty bawdy bitch. Since the earliest antiquity, she has kicked up her frolicsome heels and masqueraded under many guises and names. Space limitations of this book preclude any lengthy examination of her harlotry in the Pagan cities of Athens and Rome. Very little space can be devoted to her escapades as a Christian Festival, or to her eight hundred year tenancy on the fair grounds of England and the Continent.

This is an accurate history or account of only one of her many reincarnations. A history of the American Collective Amusement Industry, commonly and fondly called The Carnival. First conceived in 1893 back of Buffalo Bill's Wild West Show on the dirty streets of Chicago, the sturdy gem of the American Carnival survived a couple of still births, several miscarriages and an abortion or two. Finally, in 1899, fathered by a complete outsider, a town mark, she was born full-blooded and ready for action. Action that was destined to thrill and shock and change the amusement pattern of all North America as her midways were set up on the streets, the fair grounds and the cow pastures of the continent.

Now a doughty dowager of seventy-two, she vainly tries to sweep some of her mischievous misdeeds of the past out of sight under her new spectacular rides, or to hide under her full skirts of middle class respectability the full-bodied earthy charm that has made her favorite "girl friend" of so many millions. There is much life in the old Gal, and she is bound to kick up her heels now and then. Don't despair over her, she will be here a long, long time as roguish and rowdy as ever.

Before any comprehensive study of the modern carnival can be made, some knowledge of her antecedents and roots must be acquired. Is she a daughter of the ancient Greek deity, Cronus, or of Apollo's son, Karnos, who is referred to by some historians as Apollo Carneus? Or, as many think, is she the direct descendent of the Roman God, Saturn, an outgrowth of the Saturnalia Festivals celebrated by the early Romans in his honor?

Cronus, the son of Uranus in Greek Mythology, revolted against his father and castrated him. He then took his sister, Rhea, for wife. Being warned that his children would overthrow him, he swallowed them at birth; but Rhea hid one child, Zeus, and gave Cronus a stone to swallow instead. Zeus in early manhood waged war against his father and defeated him. Cronus, defeated, fled the country and was welcomed by Janus, the Roman God of beginnings, at the future site of Rome. Here Cronus founded a city. The festivals in honor of Cronus, the Kronia, celebrated by the city of Attica were very much like the latter Roman festivals of the Saturnalia.

There is uncertainty as to the origin of Karnos or Karneios, but all agree that he was the favorite of Apollo. He was killed by the Heraclidae; and the people of Sparta celebrated a national festival in his honor. This nine-day festival called the Carneia was so named because of the popular designation of Karnos as Apollo Carneus. Carneus means God of flocks and herds and the festival was both agricultural and military in aspect. Because of this military aspect there were many instances where Spartan armed forces were held back, in spite of desperate need of them, until the end of the festival. For instance, the Spartans under Agis were held until the end of the celebration before being dispatched to help Epidaurus against an attack by Argos.

Saturn, the Roman god, was considered by the ancient Romans to be of Greek origin. They worshipped him in the Greek manner with uncovered heads, and believed that he was the reincarnation of the Greek god, Cronus. His cult partner was Lua, goddess of plagues; but the Romans preferred to associate him with Ops, the cult partner of Cronus. Saturn was the god of sowing, and his temple was used as the treasury of the first republic. It is uncertain when the first Saturnalia was celebrated, but it soon became the most popular of all the Roman festivals. Very much like the Greek Kronia, it started on December 17 to coincide with the winter planting season.

Augustus decreed that December 17 and 18 be sacred to Saturn, called Saturnalia; and that December 19 and 29 be sacred to Ops, called Opalia. Caligula added a fifth day, and seven days soon became common. During the festival all distinction of rank and wealth was laid aside and all business and work was suspended. Slaves and master mingled and ate together. Gifts and presents were freely exchanged, and even before the birth of Christ, this period in December had already been established as a time of feasting and gift giving.

It is not necessary to delve too deeply into the origin of the Mardi Gras Festivals and Carnivals. As Christianity gained more and more converts among the peoples of Europe, the pagan customs of the past were put aside but not completely forgotten. An enlightened clergy, not too far from paganism themselves, found that something had to be done to relieve the tedium of daily existence of their converts. In the pre-Lenten carnival the Church made a concession to the old Pagan Festivals, and the Mardi Gras became a direct descendent of the Saturnalia. The licentious revelry of these pre-Lenten celebrations became so scandalous that Pope Sixtus V decreed that whipping posts and gibbets be set up in public places and that summary justice be dealt out to the worst offenders. There is no evidence that this decree, made late in the sixteenth century, tended to lessen the enjoyment that the masses derived from the Carnival Season. A people hungry for entertainment will have that entertainment regardless of the consequences.

Almost all of the pagan festivals were agriculturally oriented and fertility rites of some sort were performed during the celebration. As the Mardi Gras was slanted more toward the spiritual side of life, as exemplified by the Roman Church, the fertility rites being in themselves pagan were left out, and there was no place at all for the agricultural ceremonies. This left quite a void in the simple land-tied peasant's life. He knew nothing else. His whole life was encompassed by one little plot of land and his so recently acquired Christianity. It is not surprising then that every small village soon had a farmer's market or fair, sometimes as often as once a month. As the church was trying to fill all the needs of all men, it would be more surprising if it had failed to get involved in these fairs. Involved it was, and soon many of them were being held in the church yards themselves.

As the Church was universal and knew no boundaries of states and kingdoms, it was to these church fairs that the commerce of Europe was destined to turn. The traders in clothing, spices and goods often were not permitted to even enter a country; and if they were able to sell their goods, the multiplicity of high fees robbed them of any profit. But a payment of one fee to the church enabled them to dispose of their goods at a fair held in a church yard or priory.

By the beginning of the twelfth century, these church-sponsored and operated trade fairs were being held annually all across Europe. One of these, Bartholomew Fair in London, will be discussed in this chapter.

It is not known where or when the first element of the type commonly associated with the American carnival first appeared. Perhaps it was a person selling sweetmeats in Sparta, or a juggler in Attica. Maybe it was a prestidigitator, a man with a trained bear, a group of tumblers or someone with a hand puppet. Or, it could have been a Roman sharper with a pair of loaded dice. It will never be known what this first component was, but accounts of Fairs of the fourteenth century show that every integral part of the modern carnival had found its way to the fair grounds of that day. Found its way in abundance.

Bartholomew Fair was representative of scores of others operating across Europe in the Middle Ages. This fair was held every year, except for the Great Plague year of 1630, on the marshland of Smithfield for over seven hundred and twenty years. Founded by a Prior named Rahere under a charter granted him in 1133 by Henry I, the fair operated through the year 1855. Rahere had been a favorite jester of Henry I, but in 1123 he turned to religion. Henry granted him a charter to build the Priory of St. Bartholomew on the common of Smithfield.

This common was almost all marsh land and had been used mostly for execution grounds of criminals. There was one portion of high ground covered by elms which Rahere's charter did not include. With the King's aid, he soon built a priory; and started work

A DESCENDENT OF THE SATURNALIA? Courtesy Ringling Museum of the Circus Collection

MAY-DAY IN LONDON.

N. W. VIEW OF THE FAIR ON THE RIVER THAMES, DURING THE GREAT FROST 1684

from an Original Drawing by Wyke in the British Museum.

on an adjoining hospital. To insure funds for the hospital, a charter was granted for him to hold a ten-day fair inside the priory and on the Smithfield Common. This fair was to be held the ten days following St. Bartholomew's Day on October 10. This date was changed years later to the last of August as London weather in October wasn't exactly what a successful fair required.

The first fair at Smithfield established the pattern that all subsequent fairs were to follow. The trade fair with all of its goods was set up inside the priory; and the fun fair with its gingerbread vendors, amusement booths, gamblers and pickpockets worked on the muddy common outside the gates. The traders and merchants inside paid certain fees to the Prior for the right to trade there, while the operators outside paid like fees for their privileges. Almost anything could be done by the denizens of the filth-laden mud outside the gate as long as they paid their fee to the prior's collector. Should they fail to pay the required sum, they would be brought before the "Pie Poudre Court."

Every fair had its own Court of Justice, and some of them had jurisdiction extending as much as seven miles outside the Fair's walls. These "Pie Poudre Courts" could order all business to cease within its jurisdiction for the duration of the fair. Some days during later Fairs the court of Bartholomew would have over a hundred cases on its docket. Stealing from Fair booths was a capital offense, and two were executed for this during the reign of Henry III. Although executions were still held on the Smithfield grounds, none were permitted during the run of the fair for religious reasons. The Prior and the exhibitors would have been glad to have them for they always drew great crowds, but church law forbade the carrying out of any sentence on Holy

Days, and these Fairs were "A Saint's Holiday."

In 1305, the civil authorities disregarded this ban on executions during the Fair. They had a prisoner that they were afraid to keep alive, Wallace the Scotch Traitor. He was dragged onto the grounds and executed under the elm trees. This gruesome and long drawn out slaughter was avidly watched by thousands as they munched their gingerbread and fought off the pickpockets.

The martyrs of those dark days of the late sixteenth century were burned on the muddy field outside the Priory gates. Often the booths of the gingerbread man or the puppeteer would be set up in the ashes of a recently burned martyr. Last burning was held there in 1611.

In 1614, the King ordered the grounds to be paved and set aside one thousand pounds to be used for that purpose. In the meantime, the Crown had seized the property of the church. The hospital was to continue to be maintained as such; but the Priory was sold to one, Lord Rich, for use as his town house. Rich also secured the rights to hold the Fair inside the walls, but the city retained all rights for the outside exhibitors.

As the grounds were now paved, one of the most common but unusual sights at the fair was no longer seen. There was no need for the stilts that many people had been accustomed to wear, even while working, to keep them out of the filthy mud. After five hundred years the fair had changed a lot. Grounds were paved and entertainment was becoming more sophisticated. Plays written especially for the fair were being presented. Fairs were now being operated by the Rich family inside the Walls and by the City Sword Bearer outside. The latter paid the city one hundred pounds per year for all rights.

During the Plague year of 1625, Bartholomew Fair was not closed but the King did issue a proclamation saying in effect, "don't go to the fair." In 1630, he did order it not to open.

During the Reformation, the revelry at Smithfield continued without too many checks. Perhaps the marriage of one of the Rich sons to the daughter of Cromwell helped to keep the Rich's fair unfettered. After the Restoration, the diversions on the outside grounds became more uninhibited than ever. Vice and gambling were unchecked on all Fair Grounds. Finally in 1708, the courts suppressed the Fair at Westminster and cut the Bartholomew Fair to three days only. For a time, cleaner entertainment was offered on the grounds at Smithfield. Drury Lane detached a troupe of their actors to work in productions at the fair, and in 1728 Gay's Beggar's Opera was produced on the grounds. It has been reported that Garrick himself appeared in productions there, but no evidence to support this claim has been uncovered.

The last hundred years of Bartholomew's existence was marked by a continual squabble with the authorities and the courts. The latter trying to limit the annual engagement to three days, and the fair's equal determination to operate ten days or two weeks. In 1769, all plays, games and puppet shows on the grounds were suppressed. Crowds became more rowdy and easily turned into a rabble. In 1776, unruly mobs broke out most of the windows in Smithfield after the Mayor had suppressed the shows on the fairgrounds; and by 1801 an unescorted woman on the grounds was likely to have her clothing torn off by hordes of thieves and pickpockets. In 1849, all shows were forced to set up at Islington and only a dozen gingerbread stands made the three-day Fair on the Smithfield Grounds. Bartholomew Fair was proclaimed by the Mayor for the last time in 1885 and its colorful career came to unheralded end.

The closing of the Bartholomew Fair and other fairs of the same class probably saved the carnival business in England. The honest showman no longer had to carry the stigma of being engaged in a dishonorable business, and their shows were allowed and even welcomed on town commons that had been denied them only a few years before. One great showman, whose sons were to make quite a name in American Fair and Carnival business, was already touring the United

BRITISH FAIR SCENE IN 1801. Note the crude Ferris Wheel-type riding device in the background. These rides were called "Ups and Downs." Courtesy Ringling Museum of the Circus Collection.

Dwarfs

Dwarfs were regarded as comical in Medieval Days so it was natural for them to be found on the Fairgrounds as entertainers. Most all of the twentieth century European circuses have one or more dwarf clowns who are treated as members of the family by the owners. They have been on American carnivals ever since the business was founded. Many work as non-entertainers. Courtesy Ringling Museum of the Circus Collection.

OWEN FARRELL,
the Irish Dwarf

A FAVORITE ATTRACTION AT ST. BARTHOLOMEW FAIR.
Courtesy Ringling Museum of the Circus Collection.

WYBRAND LOLKES.

Kingdom with a great wild animal show. The Bostock Brothers learned every phase of the business on their father's Bostock and Wombel Show. In just a few more years, an Italian Family, the Feraris, would start touring England with a great animal Show. The apprenticeship the Ferari Brothers served on their father's show enabled them to gain and hold a dominant position in the American Carnival Field.

The British Collective Amusement Industry, called Fun Fairs, not Carnival, has never become as great as that in the United States. The one reason for this is very simple; British agricultural fairs do not have carnival midways. There is not a large carnival in America today that could exist without a fairly substantial route of so-called agricultural fairs. There are several touring fun fairs in Britain, but many of their best showmen have permanent locations at beaches such as Blackpool.

GREENWICH FAIR MID 1800's. Note carnival type shows and attractions. **Courtesy Ringling Museum of the Circus Collection.**

Fat People

THERE HAVE BEEN MORE FEATURED FAT WOMEN THAN FAT MEN. Women seem to be more prone to the glandular changes that cause obesity. Courtesy Ringling Museum of the Circus Collection.

DANIEL LAMBERT.

Published July 2, 1821 by J. Robins & C.? Albion Press, London.

MRS. ELIZABETH ARMITAGE
of the Extraordinary Weight of
31 STONE 11 LBS.
OR 445 POUNDS,
Height, Five Feet, Eight Inches.

Upper Part of Arm.	22 Inches	Waist	47 Inches
Bust	72	Calf	22½
Ancle	11½	Width of Foot	2½
Round the Wrist	7	Hips	65

AGE TWENTY NINE YEARS.

FAT PEOPLE HAVE BEEN FEATURED ON ALL IMPORTANT MIDWAYS. They are the most popular of all the human freaks of nature with the show-going public. Courtesy Ringling Museum of the Circus Collection.

THIS HOGARTH PRINT DEPICTS A SCENE COMMON TO ALL FAIRS OF THE PERIOD. Note that the performer on the rope is the only circus type act shown and he is working as a free attraction for the carnival type midway shows. Courtesy Ringling Museum of the Circus Collection.

18

Circus historians are destined to shed tears of disconcertion after reading this chapter. Most all of them, even the best, are guilty of appropriating for the circus elements of outdoor show business that were actually the roots of the American Carnival. Most all writers of circus history have used the Hogarth Print reproduced here as an example of circus acts at English fairs. Only one circus act is depicted in this print, and it is working as a "bally act" for a carnival type show.

Perhaps, before continuing, definitions of the words carnival and circus, as defined in Webster's Third New International Dictionary (unabridged), should be included. First, CIRCUS: "A large oblong or circular structure similar to an amphitheatre and enclosed by tiers of seats on three or all four sides...." "a spectacular public entertainment given usually in a large tent and made up of acts of physical skill.... and daring.... and acts with trained wild animals.... and interspersed with showing off elaborate and colorful costumes and trappings and with informally interjected comedy by clowns and <u>often accompanied by menageries and side shows held in separate tents</u> ...." (underlining by author). The Oxford Dictionary defines a circus as "A circular arena surrounded by tiers of seats, for the exhibition of equestrian, acrobatic, and other performances."

From these definitions, it is apparent that an act or attraction, even of a circus type, is not a circus act unless it appears in a circus ring or in an enclosure housing a circus; and unless a menagerie or side show does accompany a circus, it is not necessarily a circus side show or menagerie.

CARNIVAL: "A traveling enterprise consisting of such amusements as side shows, games of chance, Ferris Wheels, Merry-Go-Rounds and shooting galleries." Now, it can be seen that the carnival has as much claim on the side shows as the circus. As most writers, not knowing outdoor amusement business, tend to become bedazzled by the word circus, they are prone to use that word in connection with activities that are strictly carnival in nature. A more descriptive definition of a carnival is, "a collective amusement organization consisting of various shows, riding devices, free acts, exhibitions, and gaming and catering concessions." There is no need to confuse a circus with a carnival under any circumstances. A carnival can, and often does, have a complete circus as one of the shows on its midway. By no alchemy worked by a master of circus logistics can a circus carry a carnival. If it could be done, the organization would become a fast moving carnival.

As there has been a paucity of information regarding shows and showmen in early Puritanical America, circus historians have been eager to seize any scrap or item concerning an individual's attempt

TRAPPER AND HIS TRAINED BEAR. Probably the first carnival type showman in America. Original sketch by Marian L. McKennon.

to relieve the tedium of existence by exhibiting something unusual as an exclusive development of the American Circus. That is not so. The first trapper who brought his trained bear out of the woods could have begat a line of bear training descendants who naturally gravitated to the circus when it finally evolved. Maybe one of them was with Rufus Welch on his first of all tented circuses, and later generations maybe had bear acts with John Robinson, Adam Forepaugh, Ben Wallace or the Ringlings. But it is just as likely that this rugged individualist who dared introduce a bit of frivolity in his austere surroundings spawned a line of offspring just as individualistic as himself. Folks who preferred exhibiting their bears at picnics, celebrations and later fairs as independent attractions rather than taking the pittance doled out by pinch-penny circus operators. If so, they were bound to become carnival people, when the collective amusement industry did evolve.

The individual who exhibited the "Lyon of Barberry" along the Atlantic Coast in 1719 operated exactly as the single attraction pit or platform showmen of the late nineteenth century did at the Street Fairs and Agricultural Fairs of North America. Would this man have been satisfied to work as a cage hand on Gollmar Brothers Circus in 1910? As an independent showman, Gollmar Brothers' five dollars per week salary would never appeal to him. No doubt he would have had a pit show, maybe a five-in-one or even a ten-in-one, with one of the big carnivals like the Nat Reiss Shows or Con T. Kennedy Shows. This applies to all of the showmen who exhibited single wild animal attractions in the Colonies and the young Republic.

It is equally doubtful that Hackiliah Bailey would have been content to put "Old Bet," his elephant, on one of the circuses that were ready to appear on the highways of America. After Bet was killed by the Maine farmer in 1819 ("She was taking too much money out of town"), Bailey and his kinsmen did become involved with the "Flat Foots" in their endeavors. The "Flat Foots" themselves were originally an organization of independent exhibitors of wild animals, and were actually reluctant to add circus acts to their menageries. Most of them would never have become circus men had it not been for the heavy opposition that independent circus owners such as "Old John" Robinson gave their menageries. It was from this competition that their cognomen was derived. During a period of heavy opposition from several shows, they issued the ultimatum "we put our foot down flat, we shall play New York State." Most all the individual showmen of their organization would have been likely candidates for carnival midways, if such shows had existed.

Il Cerretano

NINETEENTH CENTURY CONTINENTAL SHOWMAN USING A SNAKE FOR "BALLYHOO." This print proves that working with snakes as "ballyhoo" has not been an exclusive American showmen's practice. Courtesy Ringling Museum of the Circus Collection.

EARLY "PEEP" SHOW. Courtesy Ringling Museum of the Circus Collection.

All circus historians know that the Great Phineas T. Barnum was never a circus man by choice. They all know that he worked on a circus early in his career; he even bought it and operated it unsuccessfully in the South. After his retirement at sixty from a lucrative career of Museum operation and lecturing, he had to be persuaded to join the circus team of Coup and Costello. He was given half interest in the show just to lend his name to an already great circus. They have recorded his inability to operate the circus himself after Coup and Costello had withdrawn from the enterprise in disgust. Probably the greatest circus man of all time, James A. Bailey, withdrew also from a later partnership because of the ineptness of his older partner in matters pertaining to the circus; and

did not buy his interest back until he was sure that the aged promoter would not interfere in any way with the operating policy of the "Greatest Show on Earth."

Then why do these same historians insist that Barnum's enterprises are part of the roots of the American Circus? They list his 1851 to 1853 outdoor show, which was managed by the "Flat Foots," as a circus. It was no such thing. Read any account of this show, "P. T. Barnum's Great Asiatic Caravan, Museum and Menagerie;" and decide for yourself. Features of this show were General Tom Thumb, ten elephants and thousands of museum items. There were no ring acts of any kind. The ingredients of three carnival type shows were consolidated under one big tent over forty years before the collective amusement industry was finally founded. This book maintains that this show was more carnival than circus; and may rightly be termed the first tented collective amusement organization. This claim is just as valid as that of it being circus.

One hundred circus seasons ago, the year 1871, there were uncounted scores of showmen, not circus men, traveling the sometimes impassable dirt roads of rural America. This was the year that Barnum lent his name to the Coup and Costello enterprise; and it is possible that this same year five brothers, aged five to fifteen, saw their first circus as it unloaded from a boat for a one-day stand in their Iowa home town, thereby getting infected with the "Circus Fever" that was to make the Ringling Brothers the "Circus Kings of All Times." C. G. Sturtevant lists 37 circuses traveling in the United States that season one hundred years ago, but no one has recorded the hundreds of independent showmen struggling to get their little attractions from one village to the next.

These showmen, the forebearers of future generations of carnival followers, were not traveling blindly as their fathers had only a few years before. "The New York Clipper," a periodical devoted to theatre, pugilism and pugilistic contests was beginning to run more and more news of the outdoor show world. From its lists of picnics, fairs and celebrations, the independent showman could now lay out a route for a profitable season. True, he could not plan to have a good spot every week as the jumps were too long for his horse-drawn vehicle, or, in some cases, his flatboat or canoe. He had to stop in smaller villages and "busk" as his father had been wont to do at most all of his play dates.

The attractions carried by these showmen were not elaborate or pretentious. A trained domestic animal, a living freak of nature, a den of snakes, an act of magic or sleight of hand, or any other single attraction that could be presented in a small enclosure for an admission of five cents. In this enclosure, usually a piece of canvas side walling, the act was presented on the bare ground. This ground level presentation was later to be named "pit show"

The MAN of the WOODS

The Surprising CAMEL

Printed for & Sold by Bowles & Carver.   The TRAVELLING SHOW-MAN.   No 69 in S.t Paul's Church Yard London.

BRITISH SHOWMAN. American showmen were exhibiting wild animals in the eighteenth and early nineteenth centuries in exactly the same manner. Courtesy Ringling Museum of the Circus Collection.

and elaborate waist-high canvas "pits" were constructed for them, but our traveling showmen of post civil war days had neither the time nor the inclination for such frivolous appurtenances. Let the circus men with their costly opposition wars increase the weight of their equipment, but the independent showman couldn't afford this. He had to travel light. Most all the independents had some sort of canvas pictorial or descriptive banner that they hung on poles outside the attraction. The showman, or a member of his family, sold the tickets and worked the outside "bally," if one was used. The word ballyhoo was not used by these showmen, as it was not coined until 1893.

The outside "bally" or "Ballyhoo" for these single attractions was simple. Oftimes it was only a noise maker of some sort or a small trick of magic. Anything was used that would draw and hold a crowd of people until they could be told of the attraction inside the enclosure. No doubt many of these shows operated as simple "grind shows", the ticket seller "grinding away" with some uncomplicated spiel, a line of chatter designed to get attention and sell the wonders of the show within. There is no record of high-powered ballyhoos being used by these shows, yet some enterprising showman probably did use stunts worthy of much greater attractions than he was able to provide. A British Fun Fairman in the early eighteenth century used an exceptionally good wire walker as an outside attraction for his fat lady show, and no doubt some American Trouper did develop outstanding ballyhoos.

As yet, no conclusive records have been discovered regarding riding devices carried by these early showmen. In the eighteenth century, British Fun Fairmen were using crude wooden man or horse powered, "ups and downs" (four-seated ferris wheel type rides), and merry-go-rounds. The authorities had to limit the height of these devices finally, as the operators for the sake of thrills, mounted them on higher and higher poles. No doubt some Yankee Showman did carry a crude riding device to outdoor dates, as a permit was issued for the erection of a Carousel or merry-go-round in Manhattan about 1825. Dentzel carried his horse drawn carousel, with carved horses for the rider, on tour in the early 1870's. By eighteen eighty, he was too busy building his "flying Jennies" for other operators to carry one out for himself. As the mode of transportation was to change for the little independent showman in this decade, he was able to build more elaborate shows; and portable rides began to appear at more fairs and festivals.

W. C. Coup, despite Old Barnum's protests, put their show on railroad cars of his own design for the 1872 season. Other circus owners followed this pioneer's example in that decade; but the Ringling Brothers tiny show which opened in 1884 did not go on rails until 1890. However, the independent attraction showmen were glad to have done with the muddy unpaved roads of their wagon show days. Many smaller circuses continued to travel overland by

MERMAID.

A MERMAID EXHIBITED IN MID-EIGHTEENTH CENTURY. Hundred of fake mermaids have been exhibited on American Circus and Carnival midways. Courtesy Ringling Museum of the Circus Collection.

wagon, horse-drawn wagons, some of them even into the middle nineteen twenties. But not the fair grounds and picnic showmen. All of them left the highways in the seventies, and none went back there until motor trucks capable of hauling heavy equipment were developed. These small showmen were not large enough to have wagon and flatcar shows like the large circuses, so a new type of outdoor show was developed by them, the "Gilly Show." A "Gilly Show" was torn down on the lot, bundled or crated, hauled (gillied) to box or baggage cars by a local cartage company and loaded in these cars for transport between towns. Process was reversed in the new town. For these small single attraction showmen this was an ideal system of transportation. No capital was tied up in railroad equipment and wagons, and more of the better spots could be played now as long jumps could be made over the weekend.

With the advent of railway transportation for his paraphernalia, the independent showmen could build larger and more elaborate shows. He could book a route of only the best fairs, festivals, and celebrations and then build a high class show to play that route. Little is known about the shows built during this period, but by the time Chicago's Columbian Exposition of 1893 changed the entire concept of fair grounds entertainment, many independent showmen had built their shows on wagons which were hauled on railway flatcars. But most of the shows and all of the concessions were of the gilly type.

A SCENE ALMOST IDENTICAL WITH AN AMERICAN
COLLECTIVE AMUSEMENT ORGANIZATION. Shows are around
the perimeter of the midway and the rides are clustered in the center.
Courtesy Ringling Museum of the Circus Collection.

1805

AN 1805 PROTOTYPE OF THE FRENCH CAROUSEL OR
AMERICAN MERRY-GO-ROUND. Courtesy Ringling Museum of the
Circus Collection.

AN AMUSEMENT SCENE. This midway could have been in Eastern Canada. Note the advanced type riding devices. Courtesy Ringling Museum of the Circus Collection.

One old showman, reminiscing in the nineteen-thirties, said that he saw three train loads of show equipment, both wagon and gilly, and all independent, converging on Raleigh, North Carolina, in the late "eighties" to play the great North Carolina State Fair. This show property came into Raleigh from many towns where fairs and festivals had been held the week before; and at the end of the Raleigh Fair, was dispersed over all the Southeastern United States at the whim of the various owners' contracts.

With railroad transportation came another variety of outdoor amusement, the street fair; and another type outdoor showman, the promoter. The promoter owned nothing except a good appearance and a suave manner. He came into a town and signed contracts with the local businessmen to produce a festival for them on their city streets. He spent about three months promoting these same merchants into buying space outside their store for exhibits, possibly more space in an exhibit tent and a float for the big opening parade. He advertised in the Clipper that he had the town and needed such and such attractions and free acts. All were safely contracted long before the festival day, and were in town set up on the main street in plenty of time for the big opening parade. The mayor usually cut the ribbon for the opening of these "Street Fairs."

These promoters, who will be discussed more thoroughly in a later chapter, were really the fathers of the American Carnival. However, none of them did anything towards organizing the independent showmen of the day into a collective amusement organization. They were getting big financial returns from their three or four promoted street fairs, picnics or celebrations each year. They were bringing the independent amusement operators together into large groups for their affairs, but were not holding them together.

Had it not been for the great Columbian Exposition of 1893 in Chicago, the collective amusement industry as it is now operated, probably would not have developed. In 1892, independent showmen by the scores came into Chicago. Nightly the streets were jammed with thousands of construction workers employed on the exposition grounds. These men with their good wages were ideal customers for the small showmen who set up on vacant lots around the downtown area. When the fair opened, many of them stayed on their old locations for a time, but most of them moved out near Buffalo Bill's Wild West Show tents, which were pitched just outside the gates on Sixty-Third Street. For the first time, a group of independent showmen were playing on the same lot for a full six month season.

LE ZÉPHIR INDISCRÈT ou LES CHARMES DES MONTAGNES RUSSES.

ANOTHER BRITISH SHOWMAN. He has a "platform" type show and is using a comic character as outside "ballyhoo." Courtesy Ringling Museum of the Circus Collection.

On October ninth, eighteen ninety-three, almost three-quarters of a million, (seven hundred sixteen thousand, eight hundred eighty-one, to be exact,) citizens of Chicago and their friends crowded and packed themselves into a space designed to comfortably accommodate less than half that number. This, the largest crowd ever to assemble at one time on any fair or exposition grounds was there to celebrate "Chicago Day" at their own "World's Columbian Exposition." An exposition that their covetous and envious friends in the cities along the Atlantic Coast had said Chicago was incapable of producing. Produce it they had, and a successful production it was. Although its final three days were to be saddened and dampened by the assassination of Chicago's Mayor Harrison on October twenty-eighth, its splendid simplicity and successful operations have never been equaled by any other so-called World's Exposition.

This hungry, thirsty, uncomfortable multitude of Chicagoans were packed into the fair grounds that day not only to celebrate "Their Day" at "Their Fair", but also to proclaim to the world that Chicago People, and by the same token, peoples of the Middle West could not and would not be downed by any adversity. For this was the Anniversary, the twenty-second anniversary, of the day after Chicago's two great fires. Just twenty-two years ago today, those same friends in the East were gloatingly predicting that the great city which then lay in ashes could never rise again. Rise it did and over seven hundred thousand of its people were out this October Day to pay homage to their own determination.

A Mexican physician, Dr. I. W. Zaremba, first proposed this world's exposition that was to do so much toward the development of the still unthought-of collective amusement industry. He proposed it in 1882 and on November 24, 1885, he obtained a license from the Secretary of the State of Illinois to form "The Chicago Columbian Centenary World's Fair and Exposition Co." Nothing came of this first license, but on August 15, 1889, a Chicago group obtained a license to open subscriptions for a proposed corporation, "The World's Exposition of '92." The next year, in spite of bids from other cities, Congress approved Chicago as the site for the Columbian Exposition. On June 12, 1890, the name was changed to "The World's Columbian Exposition" with a capital stock of ten million dollars. The final total cost of building it would reach thirty-three million, four hundred one thousand, five hundred and forty-three dollars. This money was destined to finance the building of an eye-pleasing architectural and engineering masterpiece.

In 1890, architects and engineers from all civilized countries were invited to Chicago. The Columbian Exposition was the result of their combined genius faithfully executed by the capable young architect, Daniel H. Burnham, the chief of construction. Plans were made to utilize the five hundred eighty-six acres of Jackson Park, Washington Park's three hundred seventy-one acres and a new area of eighty acres for a midway. A total of one thousand thirty-seven acres were to be transformed into a world's fair and have it all ready for dedication in only two years. This dedication was held on an unfinished fairgrounds on October 21, 1892. President Benjamin Harrison gave a rather uninspired address to some one hundred fifty thousand gathered inside the thirty-one acre manufacturers' building. This building, largest in area ever built prior to the fair, was one of the few completed buildings on the grounds.

Chief Engineer Burnham and his superintendent of construction, Dion Geraldine, accomplished minor engineering miracles daily in their two-year struggle to get everything up and ready for the May first, 1893, opening. Perhaps it would have been ready, if Geraldine had been able to continue until opening day. Like many capable men who work themselves hard to get difficult jobs done, Mr. Geraldine did not have time to be as diplomatic as some of the powerful men connected with the fair thought he should be. For instance in 1891 when he was laying a thirty-one acre floor made of two-inch thick timbers, he did not have time to socialize with some powerful people visiting the building sites. These influential snobs resented his forceful disregard of their fancied authority when he had a job to complete. Geraldine resigned on October 1, 1892, saying that he had done all that he could do on the construction. The Director General knew this man's capabilities and promptly hired him to be his own chief aid in the installation of exhibits. The forces controlling the Directors refused to confirm Geraldine for the job, and the fair lost the services of a highly capable man.

On May 1, 1893, the gates of the fair opened for a crowd of five hundred thousand with buildings unfinished, most exhibits not in place, entertainment poorly organized and poor food and drink service at outrageous prices. The only high structure on the grounds was the towers of the unfinished Ferris Wheel. It is small wonder that the newspapers of the hostile Eastern Seaboard ran such headlines as, "Fair Not Ready and No Use Finishing It." Even the Chicago Tribune had one that read, "World's Fair a Triumph of Every Industry Except Cuisine," and another "Carry Your Own Food." Small crowds all

WORLD'S COLUMBIAN EXPOSITION, 1893. Tired fair visitors resting along the promenade on the North Bank of the Main Basin. Courtesy Chicago Historical Society.

during May resulted from this adverse appraisal, and the Decoration Day Holiday crowd of one hundred fifteen thousand still found unfinished projects all over the fair grounds.

To further aggravate the problem of small attendance at the fair, the Great Depression of 1893 was making itself felt by the middle of May. This depression that was to last three full years had been nurtured by six years of low business activity in all the states west of the Mississippi. Finally on April 21, 1893, the government's gold reserve fell below one hundred million dollars and the "Money Panic" ensued. Chemical National Bank of Chicago closed its doors in early May.

As business declined across the nation, unemployment rose and the people were not inclined to spend money unnecessarily going to World's Fairs. In no month during the run of the fair did the merchants in downtown Chicago have as much

business as they had enjoyed during the two-year fair construction boom of 1891-92. Police reported that there were never as many people on the streets downtown as there had been during the two previous years. A miracle was needed if this greatest of all fairs was to continue operating until its scheduled closing date. That miracle was already in the making, and the miracle maker, George Washington Gale Ferris, was working his men long, hard hours to produce it soon.

George Ferris, then a man of thirty-two, had been born in Galesburg, Illinois. Already a successful engineer, having designed and built several bridges for the Louisville Bridge Co., in 1890 he was working for a firm in Pittsburgh. This man with "wheels in his head" approached the management of the Chicago Fair with the "crazy idea" of building a gigantic amusement wheel over two hundred feet high. The management was trying to locate backing for some high tower project for the grounds, something on the order of Eiffel's tower at the Exposition in Paris, not some "fool ride" that would likely kill a lot of people. They had signed contracts with Charles L. Easton and his World's Fair Tower Company for a five hundred sixty foot tower and restaurant. Mr. Easton failed to raise the necessary capital and his project fell through.

Ferris was then called in and contracts were finally signed for his wheel at the fair. This late signing of contracts made it almost impossible to get the project, with its completely new engineering concepts, started soon enough to get ready for opening day. On December 29, 1892, the two million six hundred pounds of finished steel required to construct this mammoth ride was still in pig iron form. It required five, thirty-car trains to haul the material after it was finished by Detroit Bridge & Iron Works. The thirty-six cars on the wheel were each as large as a streetcar, being over twenty-six feet long with chair seats inside for thirty-eight passengers.

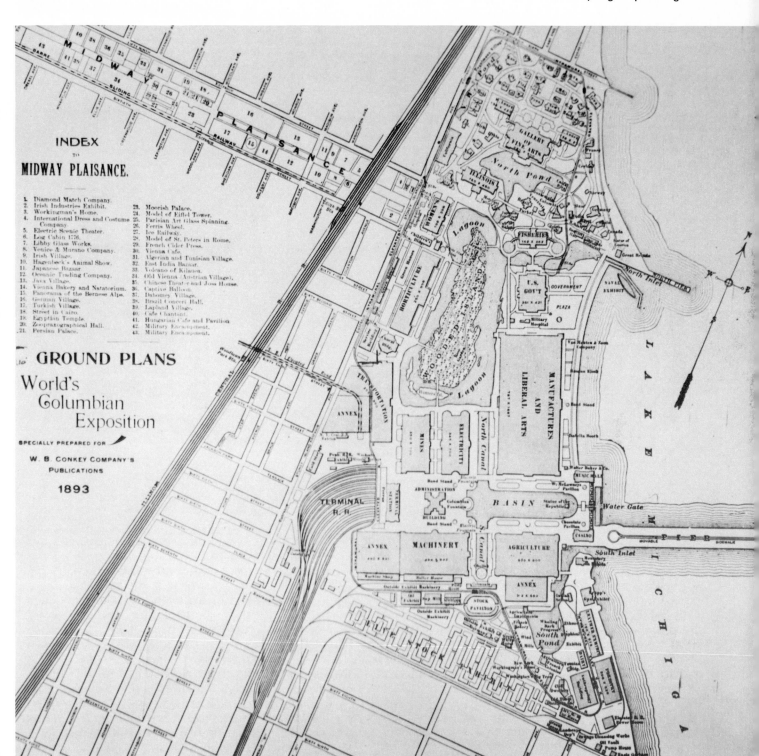

INDEX
TO
MIDWAY PLAISANCE.

1. Diamond Match Company.
2. Irish Industries Exhibit.
3. Workingman's Home.
4. International Dress and Costume Company.
5. Electric Scenic Theater.
6. Log Cabin 1776.
7. Libby Glass Works.
8. Venice & Murano Company.
9. Irish Village.
10. Hagenbeck's Animal Show.
11. Japanese Bazaar.
12. Oceanic Trading Company.
13. Java Village.
14. Vienna Bakery and Natatorium.
15. Panorama of the Bernese Alps.
16. German Village.
17. Turkish Village.
18. Street in Cairo.
19. Egyptian Temple.
20. Zoopraxographical Hall.
21. Persian Palace.
22. Moorish Palace.
23. Model of Eiffel Tower.
24. Parisian Art Glass Spinning.
25. Ferris Wheel.
26. Ice Railway.
27. Model of St. Peters in Rome.
28. French Cider Press.
29. Vienna Cafe.
30. Algerian and Tunisian Village.
31. East India Bazaar.
32. Volcano of Kilauea.
33. Old Vienna (Austrian Village).
34. Chinese Theater and Joss House.
35. Captive Balloon.
36. Dahomey Village.
37. Brazil Concert Hall.
38. Lapland Village.
39. Cafe Chantant.
40. Hungarian Cafe and Pavilion.
41. Military Encampment.
42. Military Encampment.

GROUND PLANS
World's
Columbian
Exposition

SPECIALLY PREPARED FOR
W. B. CONKEY COMPANY'S
PUBLICATIONS
1893

GROUND PLANS. World's Columbian Exposition, 1893. Courtesy Chicago Historical Society.

WOMEN'S BUILDING. World's Columbian Exposition, 1893. Viewed from front end of Midway Plaisance. Courtesy Chicago Historical Society.

Thirteen hundred sixty-eight seats for passengers on a riding device!! The wheel was planned to make three trips per hour, which it proved it could do. When the fair opened, Ferris had three months work to do before the wheel could be ready for passengers, but he had it ready and open on June 11, and the resultant publicity saved the fair.

Much testing had to be done as the wheel was erected. Ferris was out of town when the first test was made before the cars were mounted on the structure. He had assigned trusted men to every critical point of the wheel, and ordered them "turn it or tear 'er off the towers." The engineer at the huge steam engine turned the valves in the ten inch steel pipe that brought the steam from the boiler house seven hundred feet away outside the fair grounds. The engines puffed, their fly wheels slowly turned and the great wheel began to move.

The natives of the Middle Eastern countries working in Cairo Street, Moorish Mosque, Algerian, Tunisian and Turkish Villages and Egyptian Temple on the Midway Plaisance all rushed from their booths, bazaars and performance platforms as this iron neighbor of theirs began to move. This neighbor that had puzzled them for several weeks was actually moving. They began to gesticulate with their hands and shout in their native languages. Some were playing drums and native musical instruments. They were soon joined by the Chinese from the Chinese Village and the lion and tiger trainers from Hagenbeck's Trained Animal Show. They now stood in hushed awe as the majestic wheel continued on its maiden revolution. They watched with admiring wonder this thirteen hundred ton steel miracle as it slowly revolved its members over two hundred feet into the air.

WIND MILL EXHIBIT. World's Columbian Exposition, 1893. Courtesy
Chicago Historical Society.

DEWITT CLINTON TRAIN. World's Columbian Exposition, 1893.
Courtesy Chicago Historical Society.

A few days later the first trial trip was made with the cars attached and Mrs. Ferris rode the first car around the wheel. Ferris was telegraphed particulars and wired back "God bless you, my dear." On June 11, Mrs. Ferris handed her husband a gold whistle. He blew the signal to start, and as the Iowa State Band played "America," the great wheel began its endless cycles for the thrill-seeking fair-goers. These circuits were to continue without interruption or injury to a passenger until the end of October. They were to be constant until over one million, seven hundred and fifty thousand persons had thrilled and enjoyed a journey around the wheel.

The wheel grossed $726,805.50 of which the fair received $211,805.00, as 50% of admissions over cost of wheel as per the contract. After all expenses were paid, Ferris had $78,294.40 cash. The wheel had paid for itself and returned a nice sum to its creator. There is no doubt that its successful debut in June was the turning point in the fortunes of the fair. As word of this marvel of engineering skill spread across the nation, thousands of potential fair-goers were given the pretext they needed for starting toward Chicago.

Attendance at the fair increased steadily after the wheel became operative, but it took all of the month of July for the good reports from Chicago to overcome the antagonism of the Eastern press, and profitable business at the fair did not develop until late in August.

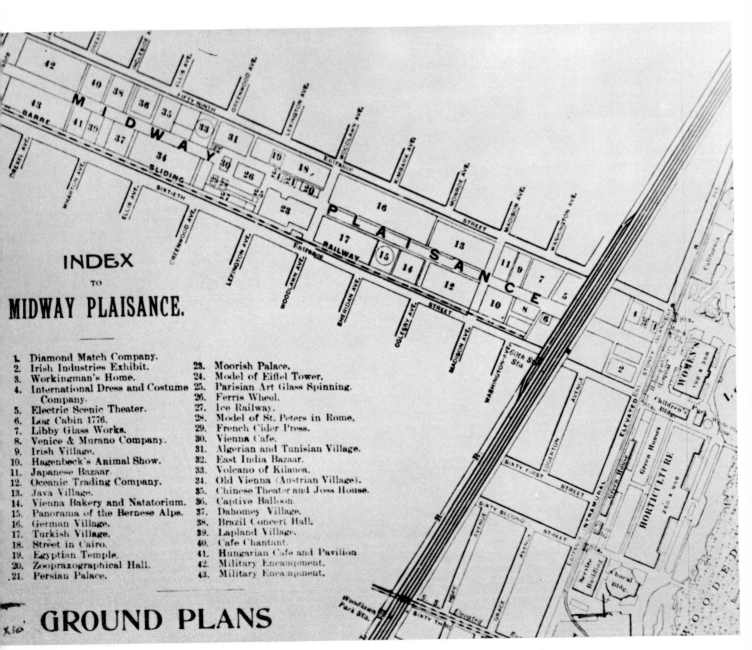

INDEX TO MIDWAY PLAISANCE.

1. Diamond Match Company.
2. Irish Industries Exhibit.
3. Workingman's Home.
4. International Dress and Costume Company.
5. Electric Scenic Theater.
6. Log Cabin 1776.
7. Libby Glass Works.
8. Venice & Murano Company.
9. Irish Village.
10. Hagenbeck's Animal Show.
11. Japanese Bazaar.
12. Oceanic Trading Company.
13. Java Village.
14. Vienna Bakery and Natatorium.
15. Panorama of the Bernese Alps.
16. German Village.
17. Turkish Village.
18. Street in Cairo.
19. Egyptian Temple.
20. Zoopraxographical Hall.
21. Persian Palace.
23. Moorish Palace.
24. Model of Eiffel Tower.
25. Parisian Art Glass Spinning.
26. Ferris Wheel.
27. Ice Railway.
28. Model of St. Peters in Rome.
29. French Cider Press.
30. Vienna Cafe.
31. Algerian and Tunisian Village.
32. East India Bazaar.
33. Volcano of Kilauea.
34. Old Vienna (Austrian Village).
35. Chinese Theater and Joss House.
36. Captive Balloon.
37. Dahomey Village.
38. Brazil Concert Hall.
39. Lapland Village.
40. Cafe Chantant.
41. Hungarian Cafe and Pavilion.
42. Military Encampment.
43. Military Encampment.

GROUND PLANS

MIDWAY PLAISANCE, ground plan. World's Columbian Exposition, 1893. Courtesy Chicago Historical Society.

GEORGE WASHINGTON GALE FERRIS. "The man with wheels in his head." His wheel, which paid for itself in the four and one-half months of operation, helped make the exposition a financial success. Ferris lost all interest in it after the fair. He died of tuberculosis in 1896, aged 37. Courtesy Chicago Historical Society.

The showmen and concession operators were all rapidly approaching bankruptcy. To make matters worse, the silk-hatted snobs who dictated the policy of the fair, issued an edict that outside "ballyhoo" could no longer be used in front of the attractions on the Midway Plaisance.

The showmen and their talkers; the latter were called "spielers" in those days, overcame this order to a certain extent by bringing everyone out on the front for bally purposes as usual and all stood mute. The spieler, (no talker in outdoor show business has ever been called a barker by fellow showmen,) would do dramatic gestures and point at his people on the bally. Then all would point to the entrance of their attraction as they moved inside. This helped "turn" a few of the onlookers into that particular show or village, but there were too few onlookers to do much to relieve the financial stress of the attraction owners. Something had to be done, or they would all be bankrupt. A meeting of concessionaires was called for the last of May. This was to be the first such meeting of outdoor showmen.

This meeting resulted in the adoption of certain recommendations and requirements that had to be met, if the concessionaires were to remain solvent. This then, was the first recorded instance of concerted action being taken by showmen for the common good. Naturally, the low daily attendance at the fair was discussed. Everyone had some idea for increasing that attendance. Some little man in the back of the room muttered, "That Dance." This individual, whose name was unrecorded, probably did more than anyone else, with the exception of George

Ferris, to save the great fair. Others heard his murmured comment, and soon suggestions were being given by all attraction people on how the new-to-America belly dance of the midway could be utilized for publicity purposes.

Utilized it was, and it alone, without Ferris' Wheel, would have increased the attendance somewhat. A leading minister of Chicago was persuaded to preach a sermon condemning the dancing on the Midway Plaisance. Then the ever-ready, blue-nosed, self-appointed arbitrators of the public morals stepped in quickly and began their campaign to close down such sinful and debauched exhibitions. All of this was newsworthy, and soon the young sports all the way from Portland, Maine to Portland, Oregon, had been informed that there was more to that Fair in Chicago than steam engines and electric lights. When they got to the Fair, they would invariably sidle up to an employee and mutter, "Where is that dance?" Being directed to the Midway Plaisance, they could take their choice of a score or more dancers. For now all attractions were featuring "the dance." However, they never found what they were seeking on the grounds itself, as the native dances done there were rather tame. Had this small-town seeker of things erotic strayed off the fairgrounds to the streets back of the wild west show, he would have found what he sought. It was out there in abundance.

There may be some ninety-nine year old, "Gay Blade of 1893," who will say "This book is all wrong, I did see Little Egypt at the World's Fair." This popular misconception that the young lady with the

FERRIS WHEEL IN ST. LOUIS. At Louisiana Purchase Exposition, 1904. Courtesy Chicago Historical Society.

FERRIS WHEEL IN CHICAGO. Front of the Egyptian Temple to the right and building housing Street in Cairo in left foreground. Courtesy Chicago Historical Society.

sobriquet of Little Egypt danced in one of the shows on the Midway Plaisance has persisted for seventy-nine years. There was belly dancing aplenty in the bazaars and imitation Middle Eastern Streets of that great midway, but none of them was a Little Egypt. For twenty-five years after the Midway Plaisance was dismantled, an undetermined number of dancing girls calling themselves Little Egypt appeared upon the midways of Street Fairs and carnivals in North America. All of them billed as being "direct from the World's Fair," and some of them possibly had danced on the Fair Midway, but not as Little Egypt.

There have been many stories of how and where this cognomen originated; and at least three different dancing girls have persisted, even on death beds, in the claim that they alone were the first dancer to use that pseudonym. This book shall not try to establish the validity of these claims. The young man in 1893 could have seen any one of a couple of dozen dancers

at the World's Fair. Maybe he saw Fatima, the wildest of them all, over at the Turkish Village. This female impersonator when last heard of in 1933 was the father of five and grandfather of seven.

Sol Bloom in his 1948 autobiography states emphatically that at no time did a female entertainer known professionally as Little Egypt appear on the Midway Plaisance. Sol should have known as he was manager for the Fair of all amusement concessions, and managed personally the Algerian and Tunisian Village. From Bloom's word choice, he may have known of a dancer using the Little Egypt title who danced on the off-fairgrounds midways. However, he does not mention this conglomerate of amusements that had been set up on the streets near Buffalo Bill's Wild West Show just outside of Jackson Park on 63rd Street.

Another amusement area had been set up just outside the gates of The Midway Plaisance itself. In his story of Ferris' Wheel in August 1893 issue of

Illustrated World's Fair, Editor John McGovern uses these words to describe this midway, "A little Ferris wheel, and still a littler one, work their unlovely motions in that vast and unlovely region that has fastened to the Fair on Cottage Grove Avenue — a huge barnacle of entertainment, avarice and sin..." McGovern did use the word entertainment, and it is right that he should have for it was in this "region of avarice and sin" that the idea for the first collective amusement company was conceived and talked about. These independent showmen outside the gates had many friends working on the Midway Plaisance, and there is no doubt that this idea for an entirely new concept in amusement business was discussed freely on all midways. These discussions and their results will be detailed in the next chapter of this book.

The Fair had nation-wide press coverage in July from an unfortunate occurrence. On July 10th, a fire was discovered in the huge barnlike Cold Storage Exhibition Building. Fair grounds fire department men and equipment were in action at the building within five minutes, and a whole company of firemen climbed to the roof via ladders. The hollow, shell-like building was adorned with a fifty foot tower projecting above the roof on the front side. The firemen climbed to the roof of this tower, planning to direct streams from their hoses down through the tower. When the first hole was broached in the tower roof, flames leaped up through the chimney-like structure and the men were trapped on that roof. One fireman slid down a hose to safety, but the hose burned through and the man following him fell to his death on the street almost one hundred feet below. Some firemen jumped from the burning tower to sure death on the street, while others leaped to surer and quicker death in the flames bursting through the roof below them. Others stayed on the tower until flames consumed them. Altogether fifteen experienced fire fighters died that day because they did not realize

THE FERRIS WHEEL. 264 feet high. 260 feet in diameter. Total weight of wheel alone 2100 tons. Total weight of wheel and all machinery 4300 tons. Powered by two 1000 horsepower steam engines. Twenty minutes to complete a ride around it. Full load 2160 passengers. Courtesy Chicago Historical Society.

EGYPTIAN TEMPLE. On Midway Plaisance. Courtesy Chicago Historical Society.

how quickly fire could spread in an exhibition building of temporary construction.

Another bit of nationwide publicity resulted from a practice of all exhibitions — that of selling exclusives to some company for its products or services inside the grounds. For instance, in 1893, a man named Aaron Nusbaum had exclusive on all temperance drinks on the grounds, except for lemonade and Waukesha water. He gave the fair 55% of his gross with a guarantee of $27,500. Nichols, Gillies and Martin had the popcorn and lemonade privilege, and Waukesha Water Co. had the exclusive for their water. Some contracts signed by large

restaurant operators forbade their "serving of any water except Lake Michigan water."

A young concert pianist who was destined to become the "strong man" of Poland thirty years later had been contracted by the Fair to play on the grounds. Paderewski used no instrument except his own Steinway Grand. The Fair had given exclusive contract to another maker of pianos. The Polish pianist gained thousands of words of free publicity as embarrassed fair officials tried vainly to get him to change his brand. Both piano companies received unpaid press notices at the expense of the chagrined board members. On the day of the concert,

Paderewski solved the problem very easily. He hired a cartage company to haul his own Steinway to the grounds and personally supervised moving and installing it on the concert stage. Fair officials thought it was bad publicity for the Fair. But was it?

Many people thought that the term "White City" applied to the midway portion of the Columbian Exposition. The midway was never referred to except as the Midway Plaisance. "White City" was the fairgrounds itself with its gleaming white architectural marvels. The exteriors of all the temporary buildings erected for the Fair were covered with sections of staff. These sections of that plaster of Paris-based material were moulded and shaped in special studios built for the purpose by some of the top sculptors of the day. Three hundred ninety-four thousand, four hundred ninety-five (394,495) pieces of this staff were utilized as exterior coverings for the buildings. Two hundred ninety-five statues were made from the same material for the grounds. From the photographs extant, it can be judged that the Columbian Exposition of 1893 was probably the most striking scene, from an architectural point of view, ever assembled and erected by man.

The Midway Plaisance was designed and built to complement the Fair itself. All villages were built and maintained as nearly authentic as conditions in Chicago would permit. There were only two or three attractions on the midway that could be likened to anything known in outdoor amusement business in America prior to 1893. Hagenbeck's Wild Animal Show was just that, but it was housed in a pretentious structure that could have passed for an office building. One peculiarity as seen from the photographs was the abundance of metal smoke stacks protruding from the buildings on the midway. As all power had to be supplied by steam, boilers for generating that steam had to be close at hand. Ferris did put his boiler outside the grounds, seven hundred feet from the Wheel, but most attractions that required power built the boiler houses in or adjoining their ride or show.

This book will not attempt to tour that mile-long 1893 midway. The accompanying sketch gives the location and listing of all attractions on the amusement zone. However, there was another attraction booked that was not listed on this midway sketch. (Conkey did list it in his programs.) It was an

FERRIS WHEEL. Scenic Ice Railroad to the right. Note smoke stacks for this attraction's boiler. Steam plant for the Ferris Wheel was located outside the fairgrounds seven hundred feet from the wheel. Steam was piped to the engines at the wheel through a ten-inch steel pipe, and condensed water was returned to the boilers through another ten-inch pipe. Courtesy Chicago Historical Society.

FERRIS WHEEL DESTROYED. St. Louis, May 11, 1906. Wheel was moved to North Clark Street, Chicago, in 1894 backed by a six hundred thousand dollar corporation. Corporation bankrupt in 1896. Moved to St. Louis in 1903 for the World's Fair; the wheel lost money during the 1904 run of the fair. No money available for dismantling it, so Ferris's wheel destroyed for scrap after thirteen years of "ups and downs." By permission of Missouri Historical Society.

MIDWAY PERFORMER. World's Columbian Exposition, 1893. Although listed as a midway performer, it is possible that this photograph was taken on Buffalo Bill's Wild West Show grounds located outside the gates of the fair. Courtesy Chicago Historical Society.

Ostrich Farm and had space on plots number thirty-eight and forty (between the Brazil Concert Hall and the Cafe Chantant.) It featured ostrich-egg omelettes. About three thousand tickets were sold to this attraction each day and at least half of the patrons paid a half dollar extra for an order of the omelette. Naturally, a few of the big birds could not lay enough eggs for fifteen hundred omelettes per day. The poultry farmer, who supplied the hens' eggs for the concession, made his deliveries just before daylight each morning.

It was on this midway that the word ballyhoo was first used. There are two stories as to the origin of the word. W. O. Taylor, a talker there, said it came from the Arabic words, "B'Allal Hoo," which he thought meant "Thou Art God." He added that many of the Middle Easterners on the Midway used the word so frequently, that the talkers began to use it also.

Jean DeKreko, a long-time carnival showman, who was also at the 1893 Fair gives it a more likely explanation. All talkers had to use interpreters in order to communicate with the people on their next attraction. All of the Middle Easterners used Arabic as a common language. A spieler would tell the interpreter to get the performers out front to attract a crowd. The interpreter would yell back to the attraction's personnel, "Dehalla Hoon," an Arabic word meaning "Come here." If the interpreter was away and the talker wanted his people out front, he used that word himself. He pronounced it a little differently, though. To his Western ear it sounded like "Ballyhoo." All outdoor showmen use it or its contraction, "Bally," for calling performers out front. And, the little free entertainment given outside is called a Bally.

DUNN'S BRIDGE, INDIANA. This bridge across the Kanakee River forty-five miles south of Chicago constructed from sections of the Ferris Wheel. Courtesy of Chicago Historical Society.

MIDWAY BYSTANDERS. World's Columbian Exposition, 1893. Were they looking for THAT DANCE? Courtesy Chicago Historical Society.

CAPTIVE BALLOON. Midway of World's Columbian Exposition, 1893. For a two-dollar fee, passengers were given a fifteen minute ride up to fifteen hundred feet in the air. Courtesy Chicago Historical Society.

NOTE

I have written this from the viewpoint of a 'carny' and have used expressions that he would use and words that he understands, so it is suggested that you read the glossary of carnival words in the back of this manuscript. (Perhaps before you read any further.)

Also remember that we outdoor showmen, circus or carnival, have a certain perverted sense of humor. We all agree that you have to be 'nuts' to get into the business and stay. We all laugh at our misfortunes and those of our fellow workers. When we are 'cutting up jackpots' with great glee, we are probably discussing an unfortunate season or occurrence on a midway. Some of this psychological deviation does show in a few places in the text. For instance the incident where the professional snake catcher got bitten by a rattler and died in Mexico. That was his profession. If he was lax in taking precautions against a hazard of his profession, he died. We were sorry, but not nearly as sorry as we would have been had he died in bed.

I do not use as many ''thes'' as some professors of rhetoric might think necessary. I have no objection to that little space filler, except most people use very few of them in conversation. Many explanations in the manuscript are made as a showman would make them. The change of a word as preferred by that rhetorician in all probability would change the meaning of the sentence. Thanks.

LITTLE EGYPT NEVER DANCED HERE. Cairo Street, World's Columbian Exposition, 1893. Building in background was outside the grounds on Lexington Avenue. Courtesy Chicago Historical Society.

Chicago's great White City was now only a deserted memory. The Midway Plaisance, its strange people long departed for their native lands, was rapidly under the wreckers' hammers assuming the appearance of a storm-torn village. Ferris' big wheel was being dismantled for its short move across town to North Clark Street and at night the notes of some wild bird's song ringing across the deserted wreckage had replaced the noise and din of last year's midway. But the spirit of that midway had not died. From that first meeting of all the concessionaires, the first time independent showmen had ever met together for a concerted action, an idea had been born.

In this meeting, called to work out a solution to their common dilemma, something much greater than this solution had evolved. If Independent Showmen could meet together in harmony to work our common problems, why could they not collectively travel and exhibit in multiple show units? Why not organize the independents into traveling Midway Plaisances and carry them to the smaller cities? These questions were asked and discussed everywhere showmen assembled whether it was on the Midway Plaisance or on its noisome offsprings outside the grounds.

It was probably discussed more earnestly outside on the streets than on the fairgrounds for the independents outside needed the protection that collective operations could assure them. Although the Chicago Tribune in its summer-long front page crusade against the "Highway robbery" and "vice" outside the gates left the impression that there could be nothing good out there, many decent show people were trying to make an honest living on those outside midways.

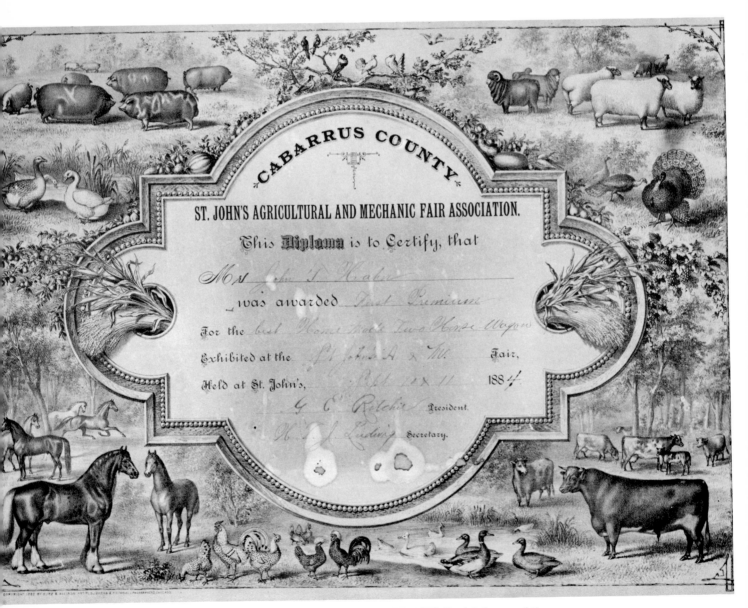

ST. JOHN'S FAIR PREMIUM AWARD, 1884. St. John's, one of the oldest Lutheran Churches in North Carolina, is six miles East of Concord. Courtesy Clyde Probst, Jr., Manager Cabarrus County Fair.

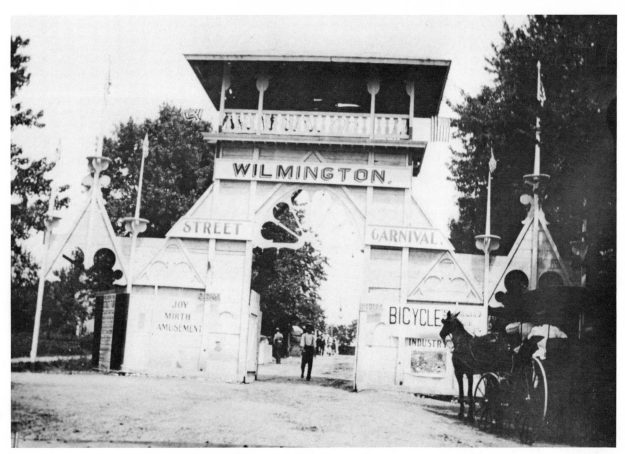

WILMINGTON STREET CARNIVAL, 1899. Bostock Carnival Company played this Ohio date. The temporary front pictured was built by the local sponsors. Courtesy Albert Conover.

These people would welcome any change that could give them profitable show dates, and free them from the stigma of being associated with the thieves and vice they were likely to find on any grounds they pitched their tents. The discussions had been lively all summer and fall. Many schemes of operations and ideas for new shows and attractions had been brought out, but no outdoor showman had initiated a plan for consolidation of shows. A new season was now starting and the independent showmen all remained just that — independent and unorganized. A plan for an organized midway was being implemented right then in Chicago, but not by an outdoor showman.

All during the fair and after, a scenic artist of a local theater had frequented the places where showmen were apt to be. He said very little, this Germanic Character, but he listened to all the discussions. This man, Otto Schmidt, persuaded the former owner of the theater, Joe Bayless, to finance a trial traveling midway. Before the summer was over he had opened it in Toledo, Ohio, and moved it to St. Louis, Missouri. He split it into two sections going out of St. Louis. One section went into the Southeast for two dates and the other into Texas. They were to reunite in New Orleans for a big date. The first unit got into New Orleans from Georgia broke, and the other one had broken up in Texas. Schmidt did not get anything open in New Orleans.

This disaster didn't stop Mr. Schmidt, as he was now a true outdoor showman. When he got back to Chicago, he obtained thirty-five thousand dollars more from his backer, Joe Bayless. This time he framed a real show for 1895. It was called the "Chicago Midway Plaisance Amusement Company" with Bayless listed as owner, H. B. Thearle as president and Schmidt as manager. He booked the New York State Fair at Syracuse as first date on his route, and left Chicago on a special train of seven loaded flatcars, six boxcars and coaches enough for 540 people.

As there is no record that he had any wagons at all, show paraphernalia was evidently piled onto those flatcars like so much loose hay. There is no information available regarding that first move from Chicago to Syracuse, but there is an account of the second move from Syracuse to Oswego, and the informant reported that the train had to stop frequently on this short move as equipment was blown from the flatcars.

Syracuse was a winner financially, but Oswego was a "blank," and Providence, Rhode Island, the next spot, was no better. Most accounts regarding this show have it breaking up here, but the show's secretary, Howard F. Jones, writing in the Billboard (June 13, 1925) said that the show made four more fairs under Schmidt's management before Bayless came on and closed it in Brockton, Mass. Bayless was now loser of sixty-two thousand dollars. Jones reported that he and the show's agent, Charles McDonald, took over the equipment and played several more fairs south of New York without any great financial returns. Schmidt seems to have retired from the outdoor scene after this 1895 fiasco as no other record of his activities has been found. (An ad in The New York Clipper does list him as manager of "Camp 48" at St. Louis Fair later in 1895.) Several showmen from this aborted effort, among them two of the DeKreko Brothers, later became well-known carnival operators.

This show of Otto Schmidt's was not destined to be a success, for it was not framed so that it could make money. Armies of carpenters were secured in each town and the midway was built up on the show grounds. Rows of two-by-four inch timbers were erected on each side of the carnival street, and Schmidt's showmen fastened long canvas banners to them, as the carpenters built up the exhibition platforms behind the banners and the bally platforms out on the midway itself. These banners painted by scenic artist Schmidt himself were rather crude, and having been painted by the same hand gave the impression of sameness down both sides of the street. Canvas was left on the timbers when the show was dismantled and was wrapped and wadded around them in huge bundles. It was these bundles of unwieldy proportions that persisted in unloading themselves from the flatcars on the moves. Because of this process of

BOSTOCK CARNIVAL COMPANY. Wilmington, Ohio, 1899. The Hagenbeck Zoo pictured here had no connection with the Carl Hagenbeck Trained Animal Show. Bostock used the title to give the impression that he had shows from the Midway Plaisance. Courtesy Albert Conover.

BOSTOCK AND FERARI WAGONS ON LOT. Wilmington, Ohio, 1899. First wagons used on an organized carnival midway. They were brought from England by Bostock and the Ferari Brothers in 1894 for use at Coney Island and at fairs. Courtesy Albert Conover.

PAN LAMPS. These torches were used by outdoor shows for lighting. They burned kerosine and gasoline. Courtesy Albert Conover.

GOLDEN CHARIOT RIDING DEVICE. On Bostock's midway at Wilmington, Ohio, in 1899. Note the "high dive" free act ladder in left foreground. Courtesy Albert Conover.

building up in each town, the show was forced to lay off one week for each show date. It was for this reason, coupled with the fact that he never completed a full season in either of his aborted attempts, that Schmidt is not credited with being the first full-fledged carnival operator.

Most reporters do not credit Schmidt with having much of entertainment value when he opened in Syracuse, but Wilson, who was there, lists thirteen pay attractions, five free acts, three bands of music, eight or ten sales concessions, a long-range shooting gallery and five talkers from the Midway Plaisance itself. Shows listed were Streets of Cairo, Persian Theatre, Irish Village, Living Pictures (Posing Show), one-ring circus, Bostock's Trained Animal Arena, three illusion shows, Old Plantation Minstrels, Bosco's Pit Show, Smith's Operatic and Beauty Show and Lee's Congress of Wonders. Minstrel show had a colored band, Oriental Show had its own band and there was a white concert band for ballyhoo purposes on the remainder of the midway. There were no riding devices on this first attempt to operate an organized carnival, and the long lines of uninspired canvas paintings lighted by flickering kerosene torches and gasoline pan lamps would be laughable by present-day standards; but in 1895 it was so big that no arena could contain it, not even James A. Bailey's huge canvas Big Top.

This illusion of unfettered hugeness, of being too large to fit in any arena or under any big top canvas, of being forced to erect its own perimeter with only God's blue sky canopy being sufficient to cover it, is probably the psychological key to the success of the collective amusement business. An industry, often called "the Poor Man's Entertainment," which attracts more millions to its brightly lighted raucous and racy midways than any other form of live entertainment pulls to its theatres, stadiums, arenas or race tracks. In 1969, one of the over six hundred carnivals in the United States sold over fifteen million single admission tickets on its midway; and up in Toronto, Patty Conklin's Canadian National Exhibition Midway grossed almost one and three quarter million dollars with its rides and shows during the less than three week run of this great fair.

"Fairy Tale Grosses," "Unbelievable," "Impossible" would have been the comments of a group of British Fun Fair Men who landed in New York in 1894 had they been told the receipts of any one of the smaller 1969 shows. W. O. Taylor's description of these seasoned showmen published in the Billboard on February 10, 1934, is worth repeating.

"Another step in the formation of the American Carnival idea occurred in 1895, when a tramp steamer unloaded a queer mess of show stuff at Coney Island, N.Y. There was a small but gaudy animal show known as Noah's Ark in which a boxing kangaroo; Jolly, the elephant; Wallace, the untamable lion; a tatooed yak; some performing lions and 'whatnots' were exhibited. This outfit was manned by a bunch of Englishmen with the broadest accents."

These Englishmen, Frank Bostock and the Ferari Brothers, were destined to contribute much towards the development of the carnival industry. Bostock, the product of two generations of English Animal Showmen, and the Ferari Brothers, the sons of generations of Italian Animal Show People and now British citizens, have "queer ideas" of show operations, but many of their ideas became basic operating procedures as the industry moved quickly towards collectivation of its smaller enterprises. For instance, they brought their own wagons, many of them ornately hand-carved, and it was from them, not the American Circus, that the American Carnival Operators learned to move their shows by wagon and flatcars. The Englishmen also learned much from the Americans. They refused to use the "Narsty" ballyhoo of their "Yankee Friends" until lack of business on their own shows forced them to adopt this ignoble means of attracting attention.

CAMEL AND RIDER ON MIDWAY. Bostock Carnival Company, Wilmington, Ohio, 1899. They give the midway "the 1893 Fair Look." Courtesy Albert Conover.

SPECIAL EXCURSION TRAIN TO HILLSDALE FAIR. Railroads ran these excursion trains to most fairs. The larger railroad transported circuses also had special excursion trains to their show dates. Courtesy Harry B. Kelley, Hillsdale Fair.

"Frank Bostock looked good in a uniform in a cage of lions and Francis Ferari looked like a Spanish Don with the commanding air of a sea captain," wrote Taylor. These capable showmen were not to stay long at Coney Island. Bostock had his trained wild animals with Schmidt at Syracuse and possibly made other fairs with him. He had too much mobility to stay long with a show that took a week to move and set up, and he and the Feraris were soon moving about on their own. They had brought over several British riding devices including an elaborate carousel and could furnish a large portion of the midway for the larger fairs and expositions. In the fall of 1896, Bostock with George Jabour and other independent showmen organized a company to play several New England Fairs.

These first attempts to organize collective amusement units were most always booked for routes of fairs; and it seemed then, that the inevitable destiny of the yet unborn industry would be to supply entertainment on the fairgrounds of North America. Yet, the first organized carnivals did not play established fairs of any sort for several years after their formation. A potent new force had quietly entered the amusement field, and the carnivals were to develop along with the Street Fair and the street fair promoters.

Many of the agricultural fairs in the United States had been operating annual exhibitions for more than fifty years when Chicago's Columbian Exposition opened. Hundreds of new agricultural fairs were being formed each year, many of them for that year only. Almost all of the new fairs were organized and operated by a promoter who came into town for a few months, made all he could from the fair and went to another one the next year. In 1896, "Col." A. B. deFrece bragged that he had managed over one hundred fairs with a gross in excess of three million dollars. It was this same year in August that the manager of a well-established southern fair suggested to a regional meeting of fair secretaries and managers that they all install horse and vehicle checking posts on their grounds to help stop the stealing of buggy whips. The suave promoter with his showy dress, flashy jewelry and gracious manner represented the height of big city sophistication to the would-be fairmen of the small towns and villages; and like their present-day counterparts even in larger city chambers of commerce, these outside "experts" must be called in and their advice followed.

BOSTOCK CARNIVAL COMPANY AT WILMINGTON, OHIO, 1899.
All views of the event have been discovered recently by Albert Conover,
Circus Historian of Xenia, Ohio. Courtesy Albert Conover.

The depression years of 1893-95 were ruinous for many established fairs and fairgrounds' promoters, and one well-known promoter reported in the fall of the following year that "1896 is the most disastrous year I have ever seen in the fair business." Several men had been promoting the merchants of cities to sponsor free street fairs in front of their stores on main streets for several years. Somehow, these street fairs were not hurt as badly as the agricultural fairs by the business conditions. Then the Elks began to charter new lodges whose members were composed mostly of downtown business and professional men in every town of any consequence in the midwest. These lodges were quick to sponsor any money-making exposition which could possibly help to fill their treasuries. With this situation prevailing most all of the established promoters and many new ones moved into the Street Fair field. By 1900 Billboard listed as many as two hundred of these celebrations in preparation.

By 1898, considerable rivalry had developed between the older promoters. W. W. Babcock stated that he had been in the fair business nine years, and I. N. Fisk replied that he was "the originator of the American Street Fair." George D. Benson of La Porte, Indiana retorted that he, not Fisk, was "the originator of free street fairs" (first one in 1887); while Will Heck, George L. Hutchins and Harry W. Wright were too busy with their dates to reply.

In 1899, "Rod" J. McDonald, "the Prince of Street Fair Promoters" settled the question for all of them. McDonald, who had won against all comers in the Scottish Dancing Competition at the Philadelphia Centennial of 1876, said he promoted the first street fair in North America in 1871 in his home county, Glengarry County, Canada. This former teacher of highland dancing, had been promoting such events every year since then; and reported that his 1899 Street Fair in Moline, Illinois, had been a great success.

H. F. McGarvie, promoter of big expositions had now completed his work at the six-month "Trans Mississippi and International Exposition in Omaha, Nebraska," and was preparing for his next big exposition. "Col." DeGarmo Gray, "well-known fair manager," who was to change the "Col." to "Prof." and become the founder and president of an association of horsemen and horse show owners a few years hence, was on his way to visit the Paris Exposition but could be induced to promote another fair before leaving. "Col." Gray claimed that he had spent six years in the south of France promoting the Exposition at Nice and elsewhere.

This was the chaotic state of affairs in the street fair business when some unknown promoter induced the Elks of three Ohio cities, Akron, Zanesville and Canton, to produce enclosed street fairs on the streets of those towns. "The Elks' Mid-summer Street Carnival, Art and Industrial Exhibition" was the last of the three. Starting with the July 13, 1898, issue, The Canton Repository, founded in 1815, ran some eighteen or twenty news stories on this event. These stories, most of them on the front page, gave a complete and accurate word picture of the organizational work involved and of the carnival itself.

On July 13, it reported that Elks' Carnival Committees had been formed and that a prize would be given to the township sending in the best-looking wagonload of girls under age of eighteen. July 26 it stated that the advertising wagon for the event had started making its rounds; and the next day carried a story that the midway committee was going to visit Coney Island to book shows for the Carnival. The chairman of this committee, hotel keeper Frank W. Gaskill, no doubt did visit Coney Island, but this newcomer to Canton booked most of the attractions playing the other two towns.

It stated on August 8 that Wallace, the man-eating lion and the London Zoo of Hagenbeck's would be at the Carnival. London Zoo was Bostock's title and he had Wallace, so Hagenbeck's name was being used illegally because of his Columbian Exposition connections. A congress of beauty and excursions from Cleveland and other cities were announced three days later. August 14th and 21st issues carried one-third page ads about the big carnival, and the August 22nd issue ran the full program of events and a listing of the attractions. Stories were run almost every day the week before Labor Day, an entire front page being devoted to the fair that Monday morning. During carnival week stories were in every issue praising the celebration and the Elks. However, the street fair lost the front page on September 8 as Canton's own 8th Regiment returned home from Cuba that day, and naturally news of the soldier boy homefolks was more important to their friends and relatives than that of the carnival.

The Street Fair opened on Labor Day, September 5, with a huge parade. One hundred fifty local business people had pledged to have wagons in this home-produced spectacle and one hundred forty-five did participate. This parade was divided into three divisions. Leading the first division was the Canton Troop Grand Army Band followed by various uniformed ranks of fraternal organizations. The Canton Fire Department was followed by the American Mechanics and Visiting Elks Organizations. Second division consisted of horse-drawn floats entered by one hundred one merchants, forty manufacturers and four express companies. Some of the participants had as many as twelve floats on the march, so there were several hundred horse-drawn vehicles in this interesting display of merchandise and wares.

GOLDEN CHARIOT

EARLY RIDING DEVICES. First riding devices at fairs were crude Merry-Go-Rounds, either horse-drawn or powered by steam engines. Bostock-Ferari's Golden Chariot was such a success that others imitated it with a much lighter-weight ride called the Ocean Wave. This ride did not do as well as it should have because Parker's (and other manufacturers) new jumping horse Merry-Go-Rounds were getting most of the patronage from thrill-seeking midway-goers. Conderman put out a heavy Ferris Wheel type ride that did good business, but was difficult to erect and tear down. In 1900, W. E. Sullivan of the Eli Bridge Company in Southern Illinois put out a light-weight wheel that was more easily handled. Most carnival owners either bought or booked one of these wheels on their midways. Next important ride was the Whip put out by W. E. Mangels in the mid-teens. As late as 1919, most big carnivals carried only three rides; a Whip, a Big Eli Wheel, and a Merry-Go-Round. Photograph courtesy Albert Conover.

Such diverse items as loads of cattle feed from a feed mill to an exquisitely gowned manikin from the ladies' wear store, a steam laundry display to a float from the confectionery store, a load of produce from the green-grocer to a new-fangled sewing machine from the Singer Factory or a billiard table from the new pool hall to a load of tomatoes from one of the grocery stores. There were ten loads of tomatoes in this parade. Almost anything that could be imagined was displayed on the wagons. The local undertakers had their new shiny metal and glass-trimmed hearses in the line of march. Hearses pulled by beautifully matched sedate teams of horses driven by somber drivers in their funereal black and high silk hats.

Third division was headed by the American Theater Band and consisted mostly of people from the midway with their camels and other animals. Captain Stolberg commanding, fifty bicyclers in costume was the final unit to pass the reviewing stands. As the parade ended, the thousands of spectators went up the street to the main entrance and paid their ten cent admission fee to the closed area. They inspected the display of goods that the merchants had in booths erected on the sidewalks in front of their stores. They watched the free acts on the midway in the center of the street and the shows erected on side streets with fronts on the main midway, and they were entertained by the special events. Many of them paid their extra dimes to go into one or more of the midway shows set up on the streets. It was here on this Canton, Ohio street that the spark was ignited in the man who was to father the first successful collective amusement company.

The special events on the streets that week ranged from an Elks' Minstrel Show to a public wedding, from band concerts and contests to gymnastic drills; and from a colored cake-walkers contest to the choosing of the most beautiful lady at the Street Fair. On Wednesday, the Beauty Contest Day, all guards, police, gate-keepers and workers were women. The carnival closed on Saturday with a Masque and dancing on the streets. The midway with the London Zoo, the congress of beauties, the projectoscope, a 715-pound man, the Hindu and Japanese Theatres, Turkish Dancing Theatre with Little Egypt, Streets of Cairo, A German Village and camels and elephants did big business all week. A two-column front page newspaper story on Sunday, September 11, stated that fifty thousand people had attended and that the Elks had made a "substantial profit."

Courtesy Albert Conover

52

The profits were so good that both Midway Manager, Gaskill, and Exalted Ruler of the Elks, Chartier, decided that they would put out Midways in 1899. Gaskill, however, didn't wait until next year to test his idea. This "First of May" in show business with no previous experience went to his old home town of Alliance, Ohio, and promoted a late fall festival on the streets. He sold only one block of space to the merchants, booked in four or five shows, and produced two or three more himself. Carnival week came with a rainstorm, and it rained all week. Gaskill made some money from it anyway. He went back to Canton and started to build a carnival. He said, "If I can make money in a bad town with a bad show in bad weather, what can I do in a good town with good weather and a good show?" Harold Bushea, his first contracting agent, went out and contracted a route for the full 1899 season. George F. Dorman and Joseph J. Conley built this first midway, the Canton Carnival Company, that winter in Canton.

Gaskill's Canton Carnival Company opened its first stand on May 30, 1899, in Chillicothe, Ohio. This first collective amusement organization opened its front gates just two weeks before George Chartier's Exposition Circuit Company got started. The Canton Carnival Company, owned and operated by a "First of May" showman, was a success at its Decoration Day opening and continued to be profitable until the end of its twenty-two week season on October 28th in Savannah, Georgia. This show that had left Canton in one baggage car came back home that fall in a special train of cars.

Although this first successful traveling collective amusement company built up each week in the same manner that Schmidt's earlier shows had done, Gaskill contrived to keep it moving and showing each week. This was done by sending Joe Conley one week ahead of the show as advance superintendent of construction. It was the duty of the show's sponsor in each town played to furnish material and manpower for the erection of frames for front banners, platforms and stages. Conley supervised this construction and had it all ready for the attachment of banners and canvas when the show got into town on Sunday afternoons. Showmen took down their properties and canvas on Saturday night and loaded them into the railroad cars. In the next town they unloaded and set up and attached to the waiting superstructures in a few hours, and were ready to start grinding and ballying in the coins of the amusement-hungry natives.

This first show of Gaskill's carried no riding devices and had only one concession. This was a tin-type gallery, called by later showmen a "mug joint." This photographer with his one tin-type camera never seemed to be able to make enough to pay the ten dollar "privilege fee" Frank Gaskill assessed him. According to Mrs. Gaskill's article in March 21, 1925, issue of the Billboard, this unpaid "privilege" covered his transportation, lights, hauling and location on the lot. Perhaps this man was the late Whitey Murray, last of the tin-type men to work Circus lots (Haganbeck-Wallace in early thirties), as Mrs. Gaskill's description sounded much like him.

A visitor to Gaskill's Canton Amusement Company's midway in 1899 would have first encountered young George F. Dorman, who later became a big-time carnival owner, selling tickets at the main entrance. Inside the gate, he would have been accosted by a concession salesman with a badge board and another one selling whips. Across the midway to the right was a long range shooting gallery and on the left was a jewelry sales booth. The tin-type camera was set up in center of the midway a few feet from the gate, but it was easily moved by the purveyor of the product of this forerunner of Polaroid. This "mug joint" operator was dressed for action with his long billed cap turned to the rear, as baseball players were wont to do, for easier peering into the apparatus. There were no other concessions. No bottled drinks, no hot dogs, no ice cream cones, the latter would not be invented for another five years.

On the main midway, Achille Phillion was coming down his spiral tower perched on his revolving ball as fireworks burst from the top of the tower. After the free act, the six-piece colored band on the front of the Japanese theatre at back end of midway began playing. As the visitor walked down toward the music, he would pass the Wild Man of Borneo, American Theatre and the Streets of India. If he had looked closely he would have seen big Frank Gaskill with his genial general agent, Harold Bushea, discussing a route change as they stood under the small office tent. Doc Waddell, the show's young new press agent, was standing near them with his ever-present buggy whip. Coming up the other side of midway, the Moorish Palace, Oriental Theatre, and Wild Animal shows would be passed. On the latter, silver-tongued talker George

Courtesy Chicago Historical Society

54

STREET FAIR SHOW. Jamestown, Ohio, 1914. Corutesy Albert Conover.

Johnson would be beating the banners over the doorway with his buggy whip to emphasize the importance of the attractions portrayed thereon. Perhaps he had the show's two elephants outside to help on bally. Anyway, that was all the 1899 visitor would have seen on that first carnival midway, unless he had gone inside one of the shows to see the dancing girls.

In May, Gaskill himself had tried to book Canton for a July date, but nothing had been done by the Elks toward contracting him. It was just as well that he didn't play his winter quarters town that year, as the Repository was running news stories from other papers of the activities at street fairs. Stories like the one from the Pittsburgh Times of June 8th headed, "New Castle Elks Pleased With Toning Down of Street Fair," continued with, "All gambling places closed and dancing girls must wear long skirts."

New Castle was not a Gaskill spot, but the story from Columbus on July 7th did cover two of his towns, Dayton and Columbus. This story said that the W.C.T.U. was protesting to everyone who would listen about the performances given on the midway of the Elks' Fair, and that they were going to warn the people of Cleveland about the shows coming there. They said that the temperance workers of Dayton had informed them that some of the shows had not been permitted to work at the Dayton Street Fair. Chartier's Show was sharing midway honors with Gaskill at Columbus, and he, not Gaskill was going to the Cleveland Street Fair; but Gaskill had played the Dayton spot on his own, so his shows must have tried to work "strong" there. The Elks' chairman at Columbus was a young man named Al G. Fields. He later became the leading white minstrel show operator of America.

In the Columbus story there is no mention of gambling, and there is no record that Gaskill carried any games at all on that maiden tour. If he had no games, crooked ones, he was an exception in the outdoor amusement field. Almost all of the circuses, with the exception of the Ringling Brothers, that first great "Sunday School Show," carried "grift" as a matter of course. The "Shell Workers" and "Broad Tossers" moved many a circus when the front door didn't take in enough to do it. The agricultural fairs were not "Sunday School" either as these ads will attest. In August 1898, Mr. Fred S. Hellanbeck of the Hudson (N.Y.) Fair "wants to hear trom Grafter and Fakirs, Everything Goes." One of the first fair ads carried by the new publication, the Billboard, ran in August, September and October issues of 1895 as follows: "WANTED!! — Privilege men in all branches. EVERYTHING GOES THIS YEAR. The Central Ohio Fair, Orrville, Ohio. Prices reasonable and fair treatment. Oct. 8 to 11. Proctor E. Seas, Sec. and supt. Privileges." Another fair manager of the period advertised for grafters saying "if you have a new device our people are ready to try it." As the so-called "Lucky Boys" of the period were persistent, even resorting to strong arm methods, in their efforts to set up their "no chance of the sucker winning games" anywhere that "sucker" was apt to congregate in numbers; Gaskill was indeed a strong character if he did keep them off his midway for the full season.

Gaskill and Chartier did not have this new field to themselves very long. Victor D. Leavitt, who was with Bostock at Coney Island heard of these new shows. He investigated and he and Bostock formed the Bostock Mighty Midway Company. As they had no dates of their own booked, they played the big dates that the other two shows had booked and promoted. They would rent a vacant lot abutting onto the other show's midway and operate with a free admission on their front gate. Coupled with the fact that they had much better shows and attractions than either of their competitors, they were able to show to big business without much expense.

Season was almost over before Gaskill and Cartier were able to get "shut out contracts" in the cities they had booked for their respective shows. As the nineteenth century ended, the collective amusement industry consisted of three lusty infants scratching and clawing to obtain subsistence from their mother, the American Public. A mother who had ample means of nourishing four hundred such infants, as she was doing in less than four decades.

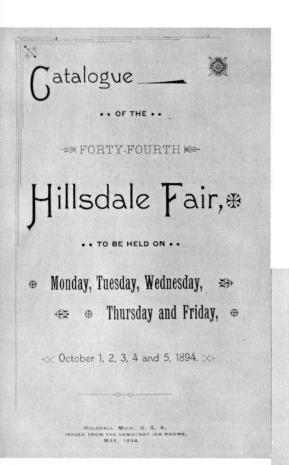

ROOM FOR TEAMS.

Another great convenience to be appreciated by the public is the ample room provided for hitching of teams upon the grounds. There are over five miles of good substantial hitching rails conveniently accessible. By a little computation it is seen that there is ample room to securely hitch four thousand and five hundred teams on the grounds, and it is confidently predicted that a very little observance will show that this immense amount of hitching space will be completely occupied on the principal days of the fair.

Courtesy Harry B. Kelley, Hillsdale Fair

Gaskill begat Rice, Munday and Dorman. Bostock begat Ferari, Leavitt, Potter and Kilpatrick Brothers. Parker begat Con. T. Kennedy, Darnaby and Raver, Edwards and the Velare Brothers. If this genesis of the carnival business was being written by one of King James' scribes there would likely be some eight or ten pages of "begats," as almost all of the showmen and promoters on those early carnivals organized shows of their own in the first decade of the Twentieth Century. It is not proposed that this narrative become enmeshed in useless verbiage, so this and subsequent chapters will deal as briefly as possible with the leaders and builders of the carnival industry in order to present an interesting and accurate history of their activities.

During their second year, two of the three original fair companies had disastrous business. Only Frank C. Bostock survived unscathed. At the beginning of the season of 1900, Bostock took in Francis Ferari as a partner; and the Bostock-Ferari Mighty Midway with the hand-carved wagons and meritorious attractions had a good season.

Both Gaskill and Chartier were broke at the end of the season, and the latter never had another show on the road. Gaskill had carried his show into the Northeast where the natives hadn't been "sold" on the street fair concept. The show folded in Albany, N.Y. He acquired a residence in Watertown, N.Y., where he took advantage of the bankruptcy laws. Before his death, however, he had paid all of his creditors, in spite of not being required to do so.

During the year Jim Sturgis had gotten a small outfit together and kept it out all the following winter in the deep South. DeKreko Brothers, while playing Salt Lake City's Salt Palace in 1899, had formed their Oriental American Carnival and Midway Company, and had taken P. J. Munday with his animal show as a partner. They toured the Southwest in the spring and summer of 1900 and went into Mexico for the winter. Percy Munday had left them before they entered Mexico and played some fairs on his way back East.

In 1900, Bill Rice, Harry R. Polack, George Dorman and Harry Sourbeck started a show that Rice in later years called his "Mail Order" carnival because he had done all the booking of towns and attractions by mail. In the spring Special issue of Billboard, March 22, 1919, Harry Polack wrote the following about that show:

"The following year I met George Dorman, Harry Sourbeck and Bill Rice in Toledo, they all having left the Gaskill Show, being ambitious to own their own troupe and deciding to go in for themselves. Their principal assets were healthy appetites and plenty of nerve and ambition. They had a contract under auspices, and, as I had the same amount of assets as they, we immediately pooled our resources and started the American Amusement Company."

"We booked a lot of independent attractions and concessions (principally grift) and had a pretty successful week — that is, for the American Amusement Company. If my memory serves me right the Lodge lost its charter for playing the show."

"We went along fine after this for a few weeks until the blowoff came at Crown Point, Indiana. There we had sold the committee a number of free attractions including a balloon act. We very carefully wrapped up an old piece of sidewall and showed this to the committee as evidence that we really had a balloon, but explaining that an ascension would be impossible, as the aeronaut had been suddenly called home on account of the serious illness of a near relative and would not be back till Friday — and the celebration closed on Thursday."

"As we had been stalling the troupe for weeks figuring to pay them with the money we were going to get from the free acts, some smart guy tipped it off to the committee about the sidewall. All of us immediately had business in other and distant parts of the United States."

(Mr. Polack, who was then a "Sunday School Showman" died the week this story appeared in Billboard.)

Many of the big outdoor shows of the early 1900's were started in this manner. Both circuses and carnivals were started "on a shoestring" by "suitcase promoters." Some had successful opening weeks and continued to operate, while a few grew into big shows. All a promoter needed was a suitcase and "Nerve."

AD IN BILLBOARD, 1901. Note small Conderman Pleasure Wheel ad with caution against infringement of patents. Courtesy Billboard Publishing Co.

Winter and spring of 1901, Gaskill framed a new show and booked Munday's animal show as a feature. Munday had purchased this show from Bostock before going to the Salt Palace in 1899. This 1901 season had on tour the Gaskill Carnival Company, Bostock and Bostock-Ferari Midway Carnival Companies, Sturgis Carnival Company, Wright (Harry) Carnival Company, DeKreko Brothers Oriental Carnival Company and Robinson (Dan) Amusement Company. All of them, and most of the small shows, had big business all year. This season, a young ex-coal miner from Pennsylvania ran one ad saying that John J. Jones was general manager for the Jones Combination playing the Elks' Street Fair in Erie.

There were more street fairs than ever before; and the established carnivals, as well as the promoters of street fairs, closed their seasons with plenty money in their office tents or wagons. It was in May of this year that the Georgia State Convention of the Elks condemned noted revivalist, Sam P. Jones, for his "profane," "vulgar" and "blasphemous" attack on Elks' Street Fairs during his Waycross revival meetings.

This second year of the new century was a profitable one for Bostock, in spite of heavy losses he sustained when one of his zoos burned in Baltimore. In this late January fire, he lost seventy-four lions and over ninety other animals. He almost lost one of his trainers, Mme. Gertrude Planka in this same fire. This brave young lady went into the blazing arena building and tried to coax the six lions composing her act into shifting dens so they could be rolled out to safety. Crouching in fear, they wouldn't move for their trainer. As burning debris fell into the ring, she tried vainly to lift her huge charges and bodily carry them from the building. The head trainer, seeing that the big cats were doomed, tried to get his fellow worker out of the arena. She refused to leave her pets, and clung to one of her biggest lions as he trembled in fear. Two cage hands finally forcibly pulled her away from the big cat and carried her sobbing from the building as the roof crashed in behind them, stilling the cries and screams of the dying wild animals.

Bostock himself did not travel with either unit bearing his name. He spent all season with his huge wild animal show on the midway of the Pan American Exposition in Buffalo, New York. Gaskill's

FERARI BROTHERS NEWSPAPER AD, 1904. The brothers dissolved their partnership two years later. Courtesy Circus World Museum, Baraboo, Wisconsin.

Beloit's Big FREE Fall Festival
1 WEEK! Beginning Sept. 19th, Ending Sept. 24th. **1 WEEK!**

THE GREAT FERARI BROTHERS' SHOWS UNITED

12 ═══ Grandly Interesting and Novel Shows! ═══**12**

1904

DIAVOLO
At every performance

Oliveto's Royal Italian Band!
50 Expert Musicians

Mysterious Asia
Minnie Ha! Ha!
HUMPTY=DUMPTY!
The Stadium (Circo Grande.)

Creation!
Theatre La Orient
FERARI BROS.'
Dog, Pony and Monkey Show!

MAMIE, "Queen of Fire"

Speedy, The World's Champion Highest High **Diver!**
Diving 125 feet head foremost into a tank containing three feet of water.

Magic Pool! Old Mill!
Ferris Wheel, Gondolas!

SPECIAL FEATURE
Ferari Bros.' Famous Animal Arena
45 MONSTER, MASTERFUL PERFORMING LIONS!
More Mixed Groups; More Educated Wild Beasts; More Daring Trainers; More Feature Acts than any other traveling institution on Earth; 200 Lions, Tigers, Pumas, Bears, Wolves, Hyenas, Jaguars, Etc.
THE BIGGEST, PORTABLE STEEL ARENA IN THE WORLD.

COOPER'S AERIAL CYCLE SENSATION!

5 ═══ Sensational Free Acts! ═══**5**

MILLE DE VOU LON "Leaping the Gap!"
Riding a Bicycle down an incline 150 miles an hour and jumping 50 feet through space. The veritable cap sheaf of all hazardous exploits; the culminating climax and crucial test of Human Cool Courage.

Special Excursion Rates on all Railroads

press agent with the buggy whip, Doc Waddell, was Bostock's publicity man at Buffalo. Doc, who called himself "the greatest press agent in captivity," took great pride in having a story on the show appear in the papers every day. One time he offered to bet that he could get a front page story every day for ten days about a snake. He had a twenty-two foot boa constrictor in one of the back rooms and announced that it had escaped. After the sixth day, interest began to drop, so a farmer near town brought in a half-eaten calf from his farm. Neither Doc, the farmer, nor the newspapers knew that the big reptiles swallowed their prey whole, so the stories stayed on the front pages. On tenth day, Doc paid a boatman ten dollars to "find" this sizable ophidian where it had been hidden alongside a deserted wharf earlier that same morning. The story got an extra day on all front pages.

Doc probably got the idea for the snake publicity stunt from a story that had broken just a few months before. In December, the Gibbs Olympic Show had come back to their Wapakoneta, Ohio, winter quarters and found a nineteen foot boa constrictor that had disappeared in the building two years before. She was only twelve feet long when she was lost. They now knew that she was female because she had eight of her year-and-a-half old, healthy,

thirty to thirty-five pound babies with her. This story was never disproved, and she did kill a two hundred fifty dollar trained Great Dane before they could get her tucked away in a strong box.

September 7, 1901, issue of the Billboard ran a story that Carrie Nation, the "Kansas Joint Smasher," had been liberated and was now delivering lectures... at fairs in New York State and Pennsylvania. Story stated that "She is an interesting talker with a voice like a trumpet." Poor Carrie had to earn money to pay her debts incurred during her crusade against the "Demon Rum." Late in the season, H. L. Leavitt (no relation to Victor), who started with Gaskill in 1899, announced that he was manager of the New England Carnival Company which he was taking to the West Coast.

Season of 1902, there were seventeen organized carnivals on tour. All of them were playing street fairs and "promoted dates" exclusively. This year the Gaskill Show was called the Gaskill-Munday Carnival Company and featured beautiful new handcarved wagon fronts on all its shows. There were two Bostock-Ferari Midway Carnival Companies, and John J. Jones was calling himself Johnny J. Jones. He had taken a partner in the Jones and Adams Carnival Company. James Patterson had a new show with his partner Brainerd, and Nat Reiss got one open middle of the summer. Jabour opened in Minnesota with a new idea — fifty cent front gate and all shows free inside. He didn't do too well with this show. Biggest news of the season was the entry of C. W. Parker, amusement property builder, into the ranks of active carnival owners and operators. Everybody made money that season although the supreme council of the Elks put a ban on all Elks' street fairs and carnivals.

It was reported in midseason of 1902 that the Charleston (S.C.) Exposition was doing well now that H. F. McGarvie had taken over management, and that the Jabour Carnival was in financial trouble in Los Angeles. In November, Doctor C. DeGarmo Gray was promoting the St. Louis Horse Show. Evidently Gray had found the professional appellations of "Professor" and "Doctor" more suitable to the rarefied atmosphere of the horse show arenas than his old exposition grounds military title of "Colonel." Will S. Heck's Carnival Company had closed its season in Mexico, Missouri, but the Gaskill-Munday Show was still on the road in Texas. It was playing Waco week of December 22nd and moved to San Antonio out of Waco. It played El Paso after San Antonio.

First news of the 1903 season stated that Munday was building twelve new fronts in Dallas and that Gaskill was at his home in Cleveland, Ohio. The carnival industry was shocked by the news that the Kansas State Senate had passed a bill prohibiting the exhibition of "Glomming Geeks." Of course, the sunflower state lawmakers called them "persons who ate live snakes, rats or other small animals." Such laws never really ended the practices aimed at. Twenty-three years later a small show in Texas made thousands of dollars with a "Geek" who ate

1903 BILLBOARD AD. Leavitt was with Gaskill one season only. Munday was with him the seasons of 1902 and 1903. Courtesy Billboard Publishing Co.

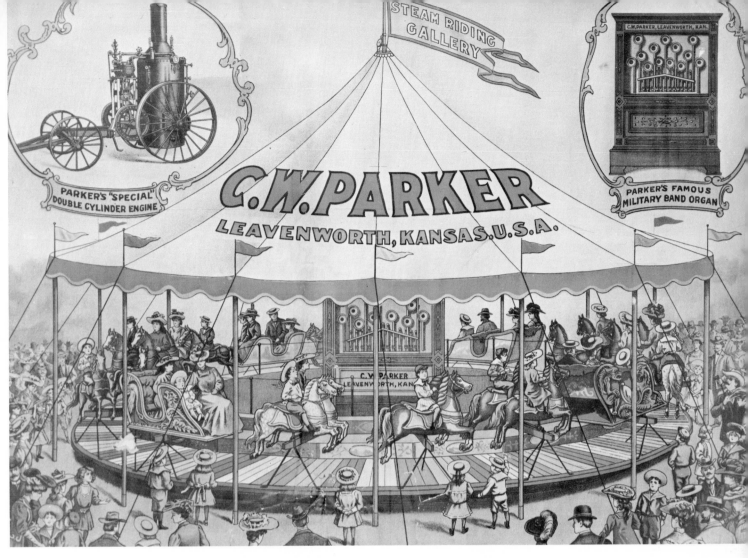

C. W. PARKER FACTORY AD. For his early steam-driven Merry-Go-Rounds. Courtesy Circus World Museum, Baraboo, Wisconsin.

squealing, squirming live rats. Bert Hoss announced that he and the little fellow with the big hat and long mustaches, Johnny J. Jones, were partners in the Columbus Carnival Company and would open the season June 8th. First week in June the Gaskill-Munday Carnival didn't get open all week in East St. Louis. All the able-bodied people on the show worked on the levee alongside the townspeople. The levee broke anyway.

There were twenty-two organized carnivals in the United States this season. All of them were traveling by railroad. Although W. C. Coup had put the first circus on rails in 1871, many of the one-nighters were still traveling over country roads with wagons and teams.

There is no record that any organized carnival ever traveled as a "Mud Show." Gaskill started out by rail and all others used railroad transport until trucks were proven to be successful in moving heavy loads between towns. True, not all of the carnivals had wagons and flatcars. Many of them were "Gilly Shows" and loaded their equipment into baggage or box cars for their moves. This "gilly" system of

operation entailed quite a lot of extra labor. All equipment had to be crated or bundled for loading, and every piece had to be handled four times on every tear-down, move and set-up.

Big news of that spring of 1903 was from Abilene, Kansas. C. W. Parker, the shooting gallery and merry-go-round builder, who had put out a small show in 1902, was putting his show on twenty-six cars. He was using a steam engine tractor to pull his wagons between train and lot, five or six wagons on each trip. This same engine was used as motive power for the show's own lighting plants. Another engine was mounted on the "run," or first flatcar on the train to pull the loaded wagons up the "runs" or "chutes" onto the car when loading out on Sunday mornings. The Velare Brothers Trio, an acrobatic act, was with Parker that season. Parker, a 32nd Degree Mason, was to become the biggest man in this new industry within the year. His show was one of the first big shows to carry a carousel. He carried one with a crew of twenty uniformed men, and every man was needed as the patrons swarmed onto the ride from early morning until closing time.

PARKER'S WOODEN HORSE RANCH. Scene outside the Parker factory at Abilene, Kansas. Hundreds of wooden Merry-Go-Round horses grouped in front of newly built carnival show fronts. From a glass negative courtesy Harry Field.

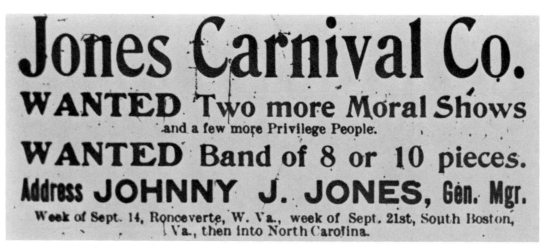

Jones Carnival Co.
WANTED Two more Moral Shows
and a few more Privilege People.
WANTED Band of 8 or 10 pieces.
Address JOHNNY J. JONES, Gen. Mgr.
Week of Sept. 14, Ronceverte, W. Va., week of Sept. 21st, South Boston, Va., then into North Carolina.

BILLBOARD AD, 1903. First ad from Johnny J. Jones in which he used the Johnny J. Jones title. Courtesy Billboard Publishing Co.

Jones and Hoss broke up the middle of this 1903 season. Hoss continued to operate the Columbus Carnival Company, but Johnny J. advertised that he had practically everything and everybody that had been on the partnership show. A press report from New York, in September, reported that the high wire walker at Coney Island was having much trouble with pigeons during his act. One end of his wire had been attached to a building in which they nested, and when their young were hatched, the parents seemed to think his dancing on the wire was a threat to their children. In October, Ali Baba, the Hindu Sword Swallower, reported that he almost bled

to death as a result of having to cough before he could remove the sword from his throat. In Gainesville, Georgia, the mayor kept the Robinson Amusement Company closed until after prayer meeting; and a Ft. Worth, Texas, man was given a $2,000.00 fine and four years in jail for making himself "obnoxious" to women on a carnival grounds. The Gaskill-Munday-Leavitt show went into receivership in Austin, Texas, at the end of their season.

This receivership was not for financial reasons, as the show had enjoyed a highly prosperous season. Victor Leavitt, the new partner, was not happy away from the Ferari Brothers, but the chief contention was between Gaskill and Munday. The break-up came when Munday objected to Gaskill's picture being on all the show's advertising paper. Gaskill retorted that Munday did have his picture on the big twenty-sheet wild animal act poster. Munday replied heatedly that no one recognized him in there with all the cats and that his name wasn't under the picture. The receivership was then set up for the purpose of dividing the property. After the division, Gaskill moved his equipment and animals to San Antonio for the winter where he set up a large zoo.

On January 11, 1904, the San Antonio Daily Express reported that Frank W. Gaskill, proprietor and manager of the Gaskill Carnival Company was in town for two days to sound out the business men in regards to holding an immense Spring Carnival in conjunction with the San Jacinta Day Celebration in April. Gaskill told them that carnival business had settled down on a real business basis.

A March 8th news story stated that the Great Munday Amusement Company and Kilpatrick

PREFACE TO THE 1906 ICE CREAM CONE MAKING MANUAL. Courtesy Concession Supply Company.

FRONT PAGE OF ICE CREAM CONE MAKING MANUAL, 1906. First ice cream cones were sold at St. Louis World's Fair in 1904. (First bananas sold in United States were sold at the Centennial in Philadelphia in 1876.) Book courtesy Concession Supply Company.

Brothers' Shows had contracted with the Daughters of the Republic of Texas to play this April 18—25 date; and that the proceeds from the carnival would go into their "Save the Alamo" fund. The ladies also discussed the holding of a "Flower Battle" during the celebration. Although he had lost out on the contract, Gaskill's show did play this FIRST San Antonio Battle of Flowers Celebration along with the other two shows.

Frank Gaskill died that spring in Pittsburgh, Kansas, on May 24th. This forty-five year old ex-grocery store owner and hotel keeper had founded a new business, and in five years he had moulded and shaped it into the operational pattern it would continue to follow. His funeral in Pittsburgh was impressive. Conducted by the Pittsburgh Elks, Eagles and the Gaskill Carnival people, it started at five P.M., May 26th. The Roberts Quartette sang several numbers, the Presbyterian Ministers gave an eulogy on Gaskill's life, and the carnival's band played "Free As a Bird" as the show folks filed by the boss man's coffin. The pallbearers, William Hanna, Oscar

FISK & SNYDER AD IN BILLBOARD, SEPTEMBER 1902. Carnival owners ran ads in Billboard not only to secure people and attractions but also to advertise their success. If a big midway had little, or no, advertising in the Billboard, all showmen knew that the show wasn't doing very well. Courtesy Billboard Publishing Co.

Babcock, Abdallah, W. C. Clark, Thomas and Harry Hurd, then carried the casket to the funeral car and deposited it therein. This car, Gaskill's private car, carried the body to Alliance, Ohio for burial.

Meanwhile, Bert Hoss had formed a partnership with Chris M. Smith; Hoss and Smith Carnival Company, and the Great Munday show's train was wrecked in Wynadott, Arkansas, enroute to Birmingham, Alabama. Mrs. Victor Leavitt was hurt in this wreck, and Harry L. Leavitt announced that he was closing with the Nat Reiss Shows on the West Coast. Peoria, Illinois, Elks' Club lost its charter because it held a street fair after such things had been proscribed by the Supreme Authority of their Order. Bostock now had zoos at Coney Island and in Paris, France, and the Hatch and Adams' partnership was dissolved. Young General Agent, J. George Loos had gone to Wright's Mighty Midway from the Munday shows, and the 3 Velare Brothers were in the stadium show at the Hamilton, Ohio, Street Fair.

Out in Abilene, Kansas, two hundred twenty men were working in the Parker factory finishing the new number two show for its scheduled August 22nd opening. Material was already in the plant for building two more complete shows for the 1905 season. Parker built all of his own equipment in this factory — wagons, carved fronts, tents, rides, flatcars and properties. In addition to his own equipment, the plant had delivered since first of the year, nine merry-go-rounds, twelve mechanical shooting galleries, eleven military band organs, fourteen automatic pianos and two jumping horse carry-us-alls. All this equipment had been built new and delivered to Parker's competitors. It was in this Abilene factory that a young fellow named Ike Eisenhower earned some of the first and only money he ever acquired away from the public payroll. He sandpapered wooden horses in the Merry-Go-Round factory.

Johnny J. Jones acquired another partner for a Jones-Adams Exposition Shows; and the Louisiana Purchase Exposition in St. Louis did not open on Sundays, so the carnival people on the independent midway off the grounds did very well for themselves on the Sabbath. Harry Leavitt organized the New England Carnival Company in Los Angeles, and Victor Leavitt went back to Ferari Brothers with his Crystal Maze. The Gaskill show played the Minnesota State Fair in St. Paul, the first fair date ever played by an organized carnival in the United States. Jabour carried the first carnival to any fair, when he played Winnepeg in 1903. Munday played this Canadian Fair in 1904.

These first fair dates for organized carnivals started no rush among other showmen to move onto agricultural fairgrounds. They were still making too much money playing street fair promotions, where

S. W. BRUNDAGE SHOWS BAND, 1909. Fifth man from the left is Merle Evans who directed the Ringling Brothers and Barnum & Bailey Circus band for fifty seasons. Courtesy Merle Evans.

First Organized Carnival To Play a Fair In The United States

Gaskill Carnival Company at Minnesota State Fair season of 1904. This
was after Gaskill's death. Courtesy Harry Frost, Minnesota State Fair.

LOADING A CARNIVAL TRAIN. C. W. Parker Shows. The steam engine being used to pull wagons onto the flat cars was also used on the show grounds as motive power for the Merry-Go-Round. (Parker called them "Carry-Us-Alls.") Photograph from "A Pictorial History of the Carousel" with permission of the author, Frederick Fried.

they did not have to submit to the strict regulations that many of the reputable fair managers were now enforcing.

Of course, there were many "fire ball" operators in the street fair and carnival business and more and more good towns were being closed to all such affairs. When a town had been "burned up," the honest showman was closed out with the crooked ones. All tented shows looked alike to natives of any town. If they had been "burned" by one show, they were likely to shun all of them.

The twenty carnivals of 1904 increased to forty-six for the 1905 tour. Mrs. Gaskill wintered her show in Augusta, Georgia, and Parker played San Antonio's Spring Carnival and Flower Battle. H. L. Leavitt changed the name of his New England Carnival Company to the California Fiesta Amusement Company, and Oscar Babcock was keeping his Loop-the-Loop free act on the Gaskill Show another year. Bert Hoss had a new partner in the Hoss & Pilbeam Shows, but Pilbeam pulled out in April and started the Pilbeam Brothers Shows. The Lewis and Clark Exposition was open in Portland, Oregon, and Johnny J. Jones still had Adams for a partner.

The Great Train Robbery motion picture was the featured carnival show that 1905 season. A friend of Otto Schmidt, a fellow worker in the theatre, carried a motion picture machine to Syracuse with Schmidt's 1895 show. His white tent wasn't suitable, and when he blackened it inside, the blacking rubbed off on his customers. His tent was also too small and the heat of the machine made it unbearable for the few people he could get inside. Now, the carnival showmen had special black tents made especially for motion pictures and electric spectacle shows. The townspeople came out early in the morning and lined up in front of the motion picture tents. Some of them would see the Great Train Robbery over and over again, paying admission each time. One carnival carried five moving picture shows that season, and all of them showed the Great Train Robbery. These outdoor showmen who had so recently created a form of mass entertainment for the common working people were now introducing and tenderly nursing another new form of amusement that would almost put them out of business a few years later.

Carnivals were leaving their Columbian Exposition type Oriental Dancing Girls Shows in winter quarters now. Several of them had dancing girl shows titled "Peggy From Paris," and one, to be different, called his show, "Rosalee From Paris." Another called his "Miss Brown From London Town." Most colored minstrel shows were still being called Old Plantation Shows, but some progressive showmen were using the word minstrel which

HERBERT A. KLINE SHOWS AT MINNESOTA STATE FAIR, 1908.
Courtesy Harry Frost, Minnesota State Fair.

heretofore had been used only on all-white shows with blackface comedians for end men. As late as mid-thirties some lot men were still marking location stakes for the colored show as "Plant" or "Plant Show."

This year there were four times as many street fairs as in 1900. Half a dozen or so inexperienced working boys were killed trying to be performers on the Loop-the-Loop Free Act rigging; and Prince Youturkey, the Japanese high wire walker, was wanted by all the big shows. Bert Hoss's partner of last year, Chris M. Smith, had his own show this season, the Greater Smith Amusement Company; and Hoss had taken his second partner of the 1905 season to form the Hoss & Nauman United Shows.

In the spring of 1906, Bill Rice closed his Great Alamo Shows after playing a sixty-three week season, and announced that he was quitting carnival business as it had no future. Some defenders of the carnivals said that the critics were wrong when they predicted that the business would decline as fast as it had grown. There were forty-four shows on the road that year, and most of them expected to have a good season. The new ice cream cone from the St. Louis Exposition was being introduced on the midways, and Munday was using the title "Society Circus" for his animal show. Parker was building a sixty foot high structure for Jack Velare's new free act; and Bert Wheeler, comic from the Whirling Wheelers, was back on the show for his third season. That great carnival builder and superintendent, John B. Rhodes, later known as "Chew of Tobacco Jack" was master of transportation for Dan Robinson Amusement Company; and another great builder, Fred Lewis, was general superintendent of Ferari Brothers Shows.

Spring of 1907, C. W. Parker had four shows on the road transported on eighty-three railroad cars and carrying a total of eight hundred seventy-six people. Francis Ferari had a big wild animal show on the Jamestown, Virginia, Exposition's "Warpath," and Bostock had a big one on the grounds outside the Exposition. Guy Dodson was secretary of the Wonderland Shows, and Con T. Kennedy continued to manage the number one Parker Show. J. George Loos and Dave Lackman put out the Lackman-Loos Carnival Company; and former outlaw, Cole Younger of the Younger Brothers, in partnership with Col.

HIGH DIVER FREE ACT. Bostock Carnival Company, Wilmington, Ohio, 1899. Courtesy Albert Conover.

FIRST BIG ELI WHEEL, serial number 1, 1900 Model. Operated for the first time on May 23, 1900. This wheel was "trouped" with midways for over thirty years before it was brought back by Eli Bridge Company. Still in operating condition, it now stands in the factory yard. Courtesy Lee A. Sullivan, Jr., president, Eli Bridge Co.

Nichols operated the Cole Younger & Col. Nichols Amusement Company. Johnny J. was now sole owner of the Johnny J. Jones Exposition, and total number of shows was down to thirty-three.

That fall, J. A. Darnaby, Manager of the number two Parker Show, said, "This has been the worst season I have known in seventeen years." The money panic and depression of that year closed several shows forever, but others took their place, and the next spring there were thirty-six recorded collective amusement organizations on the road. This number remained constant next two seasons. Then in 1911, forty-five shows took to the road and increased to fifty-five in 1912. That year, for the first time, there were more carnivals touring than circuses. Circus numbers, at an all time high in the 1890's, began decreasing about the time of Otto Schmidt's abortive attempts to start a carnival; and this reduction in the number of one-nighters under canvas continued year by year as the number of traveling midways increased.

Starting in 1907, carnival business entered a period of "blackouts." Of this four-year "Dark Age" of midways, there remains very little record. In 1908, Con T. Kennedy's Great Parker Amusement Company wintered in Galveston, Texas; and Guy

Dodson organized his Dixie Shows. On April 23rd, the Wright Exposition was enroute by steamboat up the Mississippi from Helena, Arkansas, to Caruthersville, Missouri. A cyclone struck the boat and turned it over in midstream. Survivors clung to wreckage as the river currents carried them down river towards Memphis; after several hours they were rescued. Sixteen were drowned and the show was a total loss. That same day another cyclone struck H. M. Thompson's Alabama Carnival Company at Amite City, Louisiana, and completely destroyed it. Thirty-one show people, without food or funds, were brought to Memphis from Amite City by the Illinois Central Railroad.

In both 1908 and 1909, Frank P. Spellman's Shows had the Southern Circuit of agricultural fairs; and the Sutton and Hudspeth Amusement Company was operating through the central states. Mid-season of the latter year, Hudspeth broke up the partnership and continued alone, while Sutton took another partner in the Great Sutton-Williams Shows.

On May 5, 1909, two male lions escaped on the Great Patterson Showgrounds in St. Charles, Missouri. They proceeded to the horse tent and killed one pony before the trainers and cage hands could get organized for recapturing them. A trained Mastiff

GASKILL CARNIVAL COMPANY RAILROAD WRECK, June 23, 1905. Courtesy Fred D. Pfening, Jr. Collection.

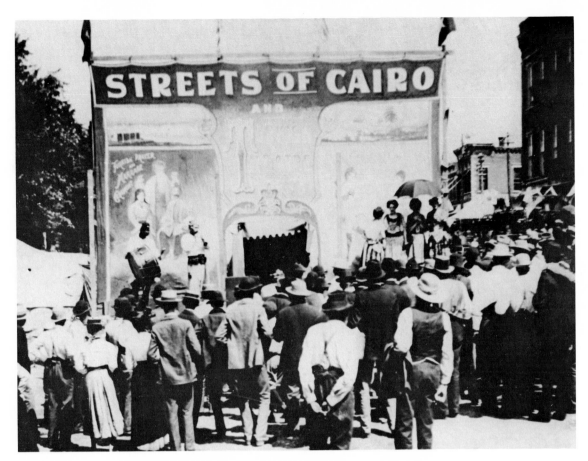

STREETS OF CAIRO. Lackman & Loos Shows, Bedford, Indiana, 1907. Courtesy Albert Conover.

charged them and got them back outside the tents where working men surrounded them with canvas sidewalling held up shoulder high. One of the cowboys from the wild west show then lassoed them one at a time, and they were dragged back to their cage. This free show was enjoyed by many of the townspeople from their safe refuge on a railroad trestle alongside the lot.

Johnny J. Jones opened his winter season at the Florida State Fair in Tampa, and the Great Patterson Shows were to go out on twenty-two cars and carry four baby elephants. Kennedy's Great Parker Shows were on twenty-eight cars, and Percy Munday sold all his animals and equipment to Dan Robinson's Amusement Company. Bert Hoss didn't report his activities for a couple of years, and Graybill opened for his fourth season in 1909. He had twelve pay attractions and no free acts. He never carried free acts.

Loop-the-Loops were still considered the best free attractions, when a sufficient supply of foolhearted youngsters could be found to make the rides. After all, there was only one Capt. Oscar Babcock. Balloon ascensions were on the wane, but some shows would have them for several years yet. J. Harry Six and Capt. David Latlip were in the wings

waiting for their cues, and in a few years all the shows would have imitators of their high dives as midway free acts. These dives, from ladders ranging in height from forty to one hundred ten feet, into nets or shallow tanks of water were to remain carnival attractions for nearly forty years.

On the last Christmas Day of this first decade of carnival business, some twenty-five midways were still on the road. This "winter trouping" was unpleasant and very little financial gain was ever realized from it. The brutal fact of the matter was that the show owners were afraid to close their shows. If they did close, they would never be able to hold them together and open again. Possibly some of them hadn't had a payday all season. If they closed, some of the help might want nonexistent cash and attach the show property for the same. The independent showmen on the midway were just as broke, and faced the same situation with their own help. These showmen, having no other place to go, stayed on hoping for that "Red One" in the next town, or the next. Meanwhile they were all cold and hungry. All cold and hungry together, eating from a common stew pot, if and when a few hardy townspeople visited the bleak midway and spent enough to provide the necessary components for the stew. For the next decade these

NEW PARKER AMUSEMENT CO'S

C.W. PARKER
FOUNDER

RAVER
AND
DARNABY
OWNERS

"WORLD'S FAIR ON WHEELS"

RAVER & DARNABY'S GLITTERING ORIENTAL EXTRAVAGANZA
THE SINGING GIRLS OF BAGDAD

"winter tours" were to continue, some of them in states as far north as South Carolina and Tennessee.

By then, some carnival genius had invented BRASS. Brass money with which to pay their help. These coin-sized pieces of brass with the denomination and show's name stamped thereon were destined to establish the carnival industry on a much stronger fiscal basis. Paydays were skipped no more. Everyone was paid in brass, or "white money" if United States legal tender was available, each payday. True, the brass was of no value at the downtown stores; but why should the employees eat downtown and buy from local merchants when they could get everything they needed on the showgrounds. When a show had good business, the employees might be paid in all "white money" or half brass and half white.

As this first decade of Collective Amusement Business ended, many of the men who were to guide it for the next thirty years already had their own shows. Most all the others, who were to own and operate the big carnivals of the twenties and thirties, were already working on midways. Fred Beckman was still with Wild West Shows and Circuses; but the Velare Brothers, Rubin Gruberg, Wilbur S. Cherry, Ed Foley, Ed Burk, and most of the others were gaining carnival experience every day as concessionaires, free acts, office men or agents. The time for the industry to expand along with the developing economy of North America had come, and there were plenty of capable and experienced carnival showmen waiting to share in that expansion.

ALAMO SHOWS BAND. Author's collection.

The Terrible Tempered Col. Francis Ferari

The Story

Col. Francis Ferari was extremely superstitious, particularly of the number thirteen. On one of their early street fair promotions, agent Victor C. Leavitt told the local committee that Col. Ferari always wanted that number on the front gate ticket box. The "set-up" had been slow in this town and Col. Francis had not had time to check the front gate until time to open. When he saw the number thirteen, he yelled, "This bloody spot is jinxed! Nothing 'as gone right today! Blimey if hi'll stand for it. Hemma," he screamed to his wife Emma, "Bring me a bloody haxe. Hi'll shop the bloomin' thing to 'ell!" She brought the axe and he splintered the ticket box as he raved on in Cockney English. Original sketch by Marian McKennon.

The North American Carnival had lost none of her rambunctious rowdiness when she entered the second decade of the Twentieth Century. In spite of reformers, both inside and out of the industry, her midway shows were as unrestrained, her "sure thing gambling privilege men" were as voracious for illicit gain and her general agents were touting her doubtful virtues to possible sponsors as deceptively as ever. True, pressure from the prevalent reformatory elements of the era was causing many city administrations to "close" their towns to her midways. But the persuasive general agent of another of her shows could usually get the town "open" for the midway he represented.

Reformers within the business, such as C. W. Parker and Johnny J. Jones, were ignored by many of the fly-by-night operators. These men owned very little equipment themselves, and they were good promoters. They could always line up a few dates for a non-existent show, and then assemble a midway to play the dates. Independent showmen, ride owners and concession men with their own equipment were constantly changing from one midway to another. One good ad in the Billboard could get everything needed for a new carnival, if the manager of the same had some good dates to play.

As this book can occupy itself with only a few of the over two thousand carnivals that have "trouped" in North America, it will try to record the history of those shows and showmen who did the most, using honorable methods, to develop the industry. The others, if mentioned at all, will be referred to briefly in the development of this narrative. Even then, it will be impossible to name the thousands of honest showmen who have helped to build the carnival industry. Those named herein will be representative of those uncounted devotees of a frivolous mistress who have served her with undeviating loyalty all these years.

Of the twenty-five shows still on the road on New Year's Day 1910, only one or two had routes that would produce grosses large enough to be profitable. Johnny J. Jones had now established a "string of dates" in Florida that were lucrative. This little Welshman with the big mustache had an unhappy New Year's though, as Mrs. Johnny J. Jones, his long-time ailing wife, died on December 31, 1909. Late in January, C. W. Parker announced that he had purchased a French Airplane while in Los Angeles. This seventy-five hundred dollar plane would be a feature free attraction with his own midway the coming season. Polack Brothers had a vaudeville booking office in Pittsburgh, Pa., and Capt. David Latlip was building his new high dive rigging ninety feet high. Prof. James Wright announced that he had made one hundred fifty-seven successful balloon ascensions in 1909, and H. H. Tipps still had the Royal Amusement Company.

On April 23rd, Rubin Gruberg, one of the big concession operators on the K. G. Barkoot Shows, was married to Miss Annie Tippich by the Rabbi in Cedartown, Georgia. "Miss Annie," as she was to be affectionately referred to for the next thirty-odd years on American Midways, was a successful businesswoman in Cedartown. She disposed of her mercantile interests in Georgia, and joined the carnival with Rubin. No doubt her business acumen helped the illiterate Rubin to gain the great successes he was to enjoy in the outdoor amusement field. They were one of the first man and wife teams in carnival business and they endured longer than any of the others.

A week later a new fourteen-car show was announced. A show to be owned by Clarence A. Wortham and Tom W. Allen. The "Little Giant" of carnival business, C. A. Wortham, was getting his baptism as a midway owner. J. George Loos had his Plantation Show on Young Brothers Carnival, and the Great Sutton Shows opened with five shows and a merry-go-round.

That same week the Fairmen met in Chicago to form an organization. An organization which they hoped would help them to clean up the midways of these collective amusement operators they were now booking for their fairs.

J. C. (Jimmy) Simpson was managing the number two K. G. Barkoot Show, and J. A. Darnaby had his Old Japan Show on the Great Parker Shows. Darnaby had thirty people with this show, nine of them Japanese. Middle of the season, Fred S. Kempf's model City mechanical show moved from the Parker Shows to the Herbert A. Kline Shows; and Tom Hasson's Streets of Cairo was booked with J. Frank Hatch's Shows.

On July 2nd, the Great DeArto, who did a slide for life with his body in flames, had a mishap that could have killed him. An assistant handed him a bottle of benzine instead of alcohol. DeArto doused himself quickly and lighted the human torch. Pain from the burning benzine caused him to lose his grip on the slide apparatus and he fell seventy feet, his fall broken by some high voltage electric lines. No bones were broken, and he considered himself fortunate as he could have been burned to death, killed by the fall, or electrocuted.

Juvenal's Famous Stadium Shows had four pay shows, eight concessions, four free acts and a ten piece band. This show featured its stadium. Most all carnivals were calling their wild animal shows, horse shows or circuses, stadiums now. Tom L. Hurd was talking on the Big Otto Wild West Show, and Ben Krause of the Krause Greater Shows was partnered

"FRONT END" OF A MIDWAY. Without a crowd of people, this photograph imparts the same feeling that you can get by entering an empty theatre the next morning after a "hit show" performance.

Everything is still there except the magic excitement of a crowd of human beings being entertained. Courtesy J. W. Patty Conklin.

with Dave Lackmen of the Lackman Greater Shows. Bert Hoss was not active this year as a show owner, and Nigro & Loos Shows had been formed with eight pay attractions. Johnny J. Jones had now played every week for three years without closing. C. G. Dodson closed his new show on October 20th. Thomas O. Littlejohn's United Shows were playing in Georgia at end of season.

Wortham and Allen Shows booked the Illinois State Fair at Springfield for 1911, and announced from their Danville, Illinois winter quarters that they were building a completely new carnival. J. C. Simpson bought the Barkoot No. 2 Show and renamed it J. C. Simpson's Greater Shows. C. C. Velare was with Barkoot No. 1 Show, and Etta Louise Blake (Mrs. Happy Holmes) was on J. Frank Hatch's Allied Shows. C. W. Parker was moving his headquarters from Abilene to Leavenworth, Kansas; while W. H. (Bill) Rice and Harry Dore had booked their attractions with Hatch's Water Circus; one of these attractions was a Rat Circus with five hundred trained mice. Smith Greater Shows opened their season in Augusta, Georgia; and C. G. Dodson took his Dancing Girl Revue to the Great Empire Shows. Ben Krause took some of his equipment to J. C. Simpson's Greater Shows, while O. J. Bucklin had booked his three riding devices on the Wortham and Allen Midway. One of these rides was a new Parker-built Carry-Us-All. The Billboard reported that Bert Hoss had been heard from, but no particulars were given.

Early in the season, Bill Rice reported that his wolf dogs got loose in the Rat Show tent and ate all five hundred performers. In June, a "town mark" named Fred Chappel sued J. C. Simpson's United Shows for three hundred dollars. The "snake charmer" in the geek show got too excited during the act and threw a live snake out into the audience. The reptile bit Chappel. J. M. Sheesley ordered a new Allen Herschell Merry-Go-Round to book with the New Olympic Shows, and Ben Krause opened his own carnival with George Dorman as his secretary-treasurer. Wortham and Allen were traveling on eighteen cars with Barney Gerety, Wortham's long-time friend, as secretary and treasurer. Two C. W. Parker Shows were on the road as was Col. Francis Ferari's Carnival Company.

In September, Harry Six had his diving Girl Show booked with Francis Ferari. All carnivals would feature diving girl shows for several years in the teens. Some of these "water shows" survived the changes of the twenties and were still active on Midways in late Thirties. In 1911, high divers were the favorite free acts on the carnival midways, and dancing girl revues were replacing many of the Oriental "cootch shows." By putting the high divers' tank inside an enclosure with seats around the tank, patrons who paid extra could get a close-up view of the diver hitting the water. At the same time, the patrons on the midway would see the dive itself. By adding shapely young ladies in one-piece bathing suits, that sexual allure that had always been the underlying force on all midways was accentuated. Even the wildest of the girl revues and belly dancing cootchs of that day covered up more than those one-piece bathings suits.

Both Hatch's Water Circus and his Allied Shows were on the "Pike" of the Minnesota State Fair, while Wortham and Allen had twenty-two paid attractions at the Indiana State Fair. Bill Rice's attractions were now with the latter show. Tom Hurd was manager of the Little Lord Robert attraction on the twenty-four car Greater United Shows; and builder Jack Rhodes was lot superintendent and train master of the Aiken Amusement Company. Joseph G. Ferari had a small show playing independently at fairs, as the Dodson Brothers combined their equipment for other fairs. DeKreko Brothers had booked their Oriental Show with J. Frank Hatch, and Morris Miller was directing the midway at the Appalachian Exposition in Knoxville, Tennessee, for K. G. Barkoot. C. H. (Doc) Starns had talked on front of Francis Ferari's Animal Show for twelve seasons, and Wilbur S. Cherry was still general agent of the Smith Greater Shows.

RUBIN GRUBERG. Courtesy Joe Pearl.

MRS. ANNIE TIPPICH GRUBERG. Courtesy Joe Pearl.

That fall, an old-time general agent complained that some of the big shows were still "burning up towns" by not paying their bills. He said, "One of them didn't even pay for the coal they used to fire the Merry-Go-Round engine last season." Drought in Kansas caused Con T. Kennedy to close his Great Parker Show unit for a few weeks, but business was good after he reopened for fairs. F. S. Wolcott, who was later to make a fortune with his Rabbit Foot Minstrels in later years, had ten paid attractions with his F. S. Wolcott's Model Shows. Mrs. Anagnosticos, better known as Mable Stark the tiger trainer, was on the Parker Carnival Company after leaving her husband. C. Guy Dodson won a five-passenger automobile in a watermelon seed guessing contest at the Lawrenceburg, Indiana, Fair. He guessed nine hundred twelve seeds. There were nine hundred fifteen.

In October, Rice and Woods Alamo Shows opened in the South on fourteen cars. Dore had his 7-in-1 freak show on their midway. In San Angelo,

77

DANCING GIRL SHOW. Jamestown Ohio, 1914. Note high diver's net in left foreground. Courtesy Albert Conover.

Texas, first week in December, Rice sold his interest to Woods. Next week, the Rice & Dore's XX Shows opened in Brownwood, Texas, with almost all the attractions that were on the former show. That fall, almost all of the big shows had closed and gone into winter quarters as they all reported big financial returns from the season. Only fifteen shows were listed as being out on Christmas Day, among them the Sheesley Amusement Company owned by John M. Sheesley.

No serious railroad wrecks were reported by any show season of 1911, but two shows were blown away by windstorms. On June 21st, the black top for the electric show burned to ashes on the Brown's International Shows; and that same afternoon, the remainder of the midway was blown to bits by a storm. Only the Lunnette Show and the Merry-Go-Round were saved. August 21st, Macy's Olympic Shows had a complete blowdown in Marshfield, Missouri. Dan R. Robinson, one of the pioneers in collective amusement business, was unable to pay salaries and his show was attached and sold for debts. Dan R. himself had a nervous breakdown and was back in Cincinnati.

At the end of the 1913 season, Wortham and Allen announced that they were dissolving their partnership. The Little Giant, Wortham, would have several "partners" in future operations, but they would actually be working for him. He and Allen had started in 1908 with four boxcars. When they divided their property in fall of 1913, they owned twenty-eight double length cars with all equipment and wagons for same. At the time, this was a mammoth show; but Wortham would have five shows operating at once before the end of the decade. His influence would be felt throughout the industry as other showmen tried vainly to "keep up with Wortham." The soft-spoken little Welshman, Johnny J. Jones, had to bestir himself to keep his show at least equal to that of Wortham, and the great Johnny J. Jones Exposition was the result of this competition.

This battle for supremacy in the collective amusement field would be waged between these two great showmen for nine years. The two "carnival kings" were both small men in stature but giants in their chosen field. Both were uneducated in academic subjects but were the equals of any master or doctor in their knowledge of human relations and of business administration, on or off of their midways. Neither of them needed a hundred thousand dollar computer nor a corp of "experts" to tell them whether one of their shows or rides was profitable or not. Both knew their business, every phase of it; and the competition between them would force their industry into a greater magnitude than ever dreamed of by any showman before this battle for supremacy was joined. Wortham's shows never invaded Jones' Eastern stronghold along the Atlantic Coast, but Jones could no longer contract any fair he wanted to play in Western Canada and in the Midwest.

The Robinson Amusement Company was reorganized for the 1912 season, but was harassed by financial problems all season until it finally disbanded in late fall with all its people broke and stranded. Dan R. Robinson, founder of this pioneer show, was committed to a mental institution on September 8, 1915. If sane, he faced long prison terms on fraudulent check charges.

Most shows reported good business on their 1912 and 1913 tours, and many of them expanded in size. B. R. Parker leased and operated his father's Great Parker Shows. Con T. Kennedy put his own name on the Parker Show that he had owned and operated for ten seasons. Nat Reiss brought his big show back from the West Coast where he had exhibited for several years, and "Captains" David Latlip and John M. Sheesley each started his own carnival. The new Foley and Burk Shows were open on the West Coast, and Sam Soloman partnered with George Dorman with their Liberty Shows. In 1913, Rice & Dore's Water Carnival featured a new Motordrome built by Joe Conley while a new riding device, the Ocean Wave, had been booked by a few shows in 1912. Nigro & Loos Shows had been on the road four years with only six weeks off, and W. S. Brundage continued to do good business with the show he founded in 1899. In 1913, Polack Brothers framed and operated their new Rutherford Greater Shows; and the Ferari Brothers had already split up

"WATER SHOW," 1919. C. A. Wortham Shows. Note high dive ladder in left foreground. Author's collection.

RICE & DORE. Owners of Rice & Dore Water Carnival. This was a regular carnival that featured a big water show. Bill Rice was partial to Water Shows and carried one on a tour of the Orient Courtesy Bill Rice, Jr.

after their 1912 reconciliation and partnership.

On March 8, 1912, carnival owners and managers met at the Wellington Hotel in Chicago where they formed the Carnival Managers Association of America. This association, which was to become the Showmen's League of America within a year, was formed for the avowed purpose of cleaning up carnival business. C. W. Parker was elected president. Other officers were J. George Loos, secretary; S. W. Brundage, treasurer; and Tom W. Allen, first vice president.

In July of 1912, Bob Younger, nephew of former outlaw Cole Younger, teamed with Dave Lackman to put out the Younger-Lackman Greater Shows. This show closed in Malvern, Arkansas, first week in December. On December 5, 1912, Bob Younger, accompanied by some of the people from his show, was riding a regular passenger train between Malvern and Little Rock when the train was held up by train robbers. Younger resisted them and was shot three times. He died in Little Rock later that day. His murderer, "Joe Willis," who was captured a few weeks later, was given a sentence of eighteen years in the Arkansas State Prison.

High divers made headlines in 1912, while snakes took the featured spots in 1913. On May 4,

1912, high diver Oddie Gifford shot himself and died from the wounds in Ashtabula, Ohio; and on July 6th, Wade Cook was killed while diving on the midway of the Barkoot Shows. Cook was the second diver killed while diving that year. A month later, a diver was badly hurt while making the plunge in St. Louis. This one followed another diver too closely and was thrown off course by a slight sway in the ladder. In September, Joseph Flory, a diver on the Rice & Dore Water Carnival was shot and seriously wounded by his wife, who was also a diver. Then in October, C. A. Warbutton, high fire diver, lighted himself off too soon on his dive into the Mississippi River from the Keokuk, Iowa, bridge. He died of the burns. Then in December, Charles Strohr, diver with Parker Shows, died of natural causes in Kansas City.

Snakes started making news in July 1912, when John Wilson let all his reptiles loose in downtown Tecumseh, Nebraska. He had been served a writ of attachment on the snakes because of a complaint of a former employee for back salary. Wilson liberated the denizens of his pit show. The irate citizenry of Tecumseh were boiling tar and gathering feathers when Wilson made a percepient and hurried move out of town. In June, 1913, Rattlesnake Frank Hoxie was bitten by a Gila Monster. He was out of danger next day. In August, Hifario, one of the snake catchers on W. A. "Snake" King's Snake Ranch at Brownsville, Texas, was badly bitten by a big rattlesnake while catching some big specimens to fill recent orders. He recovered.

In November, King issued a challenge for a snake-catching contest to be held during Midwinter Fair in Brownsville. "Snake" couldn't lose this contest as the contestants all gave their catches to him after the event. Then, he was sure to win the contest anyway as no one could beat him catching live rattlers with the possible exception of Bosco, the famous "glomming geek." For many years Bosco took snake catching expeditions into Mexico to capture replacements for his voracious and unusual appetite upon which he capitalized.

Jack and Jill, the Karns Brothers, had now been with Walter K. Sibley as fat boys for eight years. Last of May, 1912, Jack J. Wayland, a talker with Sibley's Water Circus was run over by an automobile and killed in Saginaw, Michigan; and in October, J. W. Hampton had to close his Great Empire Shows early because of a broken arm sustained while cranking his auto. Bally Girls and Diving Girls were advised by a contributor to the Billboard not to chew gum while they were out before the public on the bally platforms. Frank C. Bostock died in London on October 8, 1912; and a few months later, Joseph Ferari, Jr., son of Bostock's former associate, died of pneumonia. Twenty-one year old Ferari was with his father on the new Patrick-Ferari Shows.

In 1913, Johnie Ward, bantam-weight boxer from Memphis, joined Sailor Jack's Athletic Show on the Moss Brothers Greater Shows. Another future carnival owner was now learning the business from the viewpoint of an "At Show" mat. Several other

TYPICAL "GAL SHOW" FRONT AND PEOPLE. Each carnival midway carried a concert band of twelve to thirty pieces. After the daily concert at front gate, the band split into two ballyhoo bands. One or the other of these bands played for the opening "bally" of each midway show as they worked to the back end of the midway. Once all shows were open, one band stayed with the feature show; circus, water show, girl show, wild west, etc. The other continued to circulate around the midway playing for "ballys." In some cases the second band stayed with another of the big shows, but it usually worked around the midway. There was no canned music or loud electronic amplification systems on those midways. Courtesy L. Harvey Doc Cann.

future midway greats were to get their training for carnival careers on Athletic Shows before this decade was over. Wollcott & Murphy now had three of their motordromes booked on carnival midways with two more being built for them.

Reports came in each winter that a colored performer on a Plantation Show with one or another of the winter shows playing in the deep South had been killed by town toughs. Johnny McGrail reported in 1912 that he had to cancel out Marianne, Arkansas. "Couldn't play opposition to a lynching bee."

"Sheik" Clarence A. Wortham was the most active man in carnival business the last half of this second decade of the twentieth century. True, C. W. Parker owned more equipment than Wortham for several years, but he no longer traveled with the one show that bore his name. In 1916, Parker owned nearly two hundred railroad cars; however, only about fifty of them were being used on family-owned carnivals. All the others were leased to other showmen by the Kansas amusement device manufacturer. His son still operated the Great Parker Shows, and his son-in-law, Tom W. Allen, managed the show carrying the Allen title.

C. A. Wortham, or Mr. Wortham as he was still referred to by his long-time friend, employee and confidant, Barney S. Gerety, almost fifty years after the Little Giant's death, had more dealings in one six-year period, with more shows, showmen and fairmen than many successful carnival owners have crowded into a full lifetime. Sheik (as all carnival owners were now being referred to) Wortham never took time to have a suit cleaned. When he noticed that the suit he was wearing was becoming disheveled, he would send one of his agents downtown to buy a new fifteen dollar suit. He gave the old one away and wore the new one until it needed replacing.

He had the knack of selecting the most capable men in the collective amusement field and of relegating authority to them. He sat in one or another of his several offices giving instructions and orders to the top builders, agents and managers in the carnival field. These men, all destined to be top names in their respective jobs, translated his instructions into the successful operation of as many as five huge midways simultaneously.

THIS IS IT!
ODD FELLOWS
CARNIVAL
THE GREATEST EVENT OF THE SEASON
A Solid Week of Hilarious Fun!
6 BIG DAYS 6
NIGHTS

A Galaxy of Sports. An Illumination of a Grand and Glorious Midway one mile in extent, presenting the World Famed

JOSEPH G. FERARI SHOWS

Recognized the World over Absolutely without a Peer.

The Largest, Grandest, Most Costly Carnival Company on the American Continent.

10·BIG SHOWS·10

A $10,000.00 MERRY—GO—ROUND
A MONSTER EVER REVOLVING ALL STEEL FERRIS WHEEL

FEATURING
CAPT. JOSEPH G. FERARI'S
INTERNATIONALLY CONCEDED WORLD'S LARGEST
TRAINED WILD ANIMAL ARENA

More Lions, Tigers, Leopards, Jaguars, Panthers, Pumas, Congars, Hybrids and Bears than any show in the World.

CAPT. WILSON
ENTERS THE LIONS DEN AT EVERY PERFORMANCE AT THE RISK OF HIS LIFE. YOU WILL NEVER FORGET THIS PERFORMANCE

This is the Daring Intrepid Trainer, who dare face that terrible Savage Monster Lion of the forest, "NERO," who killed his trainer, Capt. Gene CARDONA, one month ago. June 8th, in Binghamton, N. Y.

More Fun at Our Carnival than a Barrel of Monkeys
COME OVER TO
TONAWANDA
WEEK JULY 13th TO 18th
And Have The Best Time of Your Life.

THE BIGGEST WEEK IN THE HISTORY OF
TONAWANDA
BROUGHT HERE AT TERRIFIC EXPENSE
JOSEPH G. FERARI SHOWS
THE FINEST, CLEANEST AND BEST CARNIVAL COMPANY IN THE WORLD

25 —— CAR-LOADS ——25
OF WAGONS, PARAPHERNALIA AND EQUIPMENT
400·PEOPLE·400
10·BIG SHOWS·10

Thousands of Electric Lights transfixing night into Day. The one carnival destined to make the old feel young, and the young feel gay. The event of the season.
COME—And Have The Time of Your Life—COME

SEE THE **Great Dog, Pony and Monkey Circus**

AN AVALANCHE OF SPLENDOR

A GRAND CONGRESS OF ARENIC NOVELTIES

Ride the Merry-Go-Round
SEE "MINNE HA-HA"
Only living and surviving member of the now extinct Australian Bush Race. Minne Ha-Ha is a great favorite with the ladies and children.

SEE MILLE. ANITA
AND HER HAPPY FAMILY GROUP OF
PERFORMING LEOPARDS AND JAGUARS

SEE
LOFTY ROCHETTE
World's Highest Salaried
HIGH-DIVER
Free Twice Daily,
4.30 Every Afternoon
10.30 Every Night
Diving 110 Feet into a Tank of Water but Five Feet Deep.
IT'S THRILLING, WONDERFUL, AWE-INSPIRING.

SEE WONDERLAND
Beautiful Splendora
Athletic Show
Dog and Pony Show
Wild Animal Show
RIDE-The Ferris Wheel

SEE Sports and Pastimes of the Orient
Trip to Mars
Motordrome
Minne Ha-Ha
RIDE-The Big Merry-Go-Round

Come Early! SEE IT ALL! **Stay Late!**
TONAWANDA, WEEK JULY 13th TO 18th
AUSPICES
NIAGARA RIVER LODGE NO. 527 I. O. O. F.

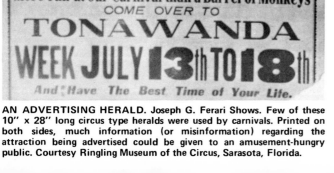

He had only one show under the C. A. Wortham title in 1914 and 1915; but owned half interest in another Wortham and Allen show the latter season. He opened the 1916 season with two shows, the C. A. Wortham Shows and the Great Wortham Shows. In August of that year he put out another big show, the Great Alamo Shows. And, a month later, the fourth one, the Little Giant or Wortham's Independent Shows, was formed.

This last show was organized in a few minutes and sent on the road in less than twenty-four hours. The C. A. Wortham Shows was playing a small fair in Iowa before going into Des Moines for the State Fair. Many managers of fairs from Iowa, Minnesota and Wisconsin visited that week. One day, several of them demanded that Wortham send a carnival to play their respective dates. In five minutes he had their names on contracts, and twenty-four hours later a small show was on its way to play the first of these fairs.

In 1917, Fred Beckman took over the management of the Great Wortham Shows which was in the Pacific Northwest that fall, and the Alamo title was changed to Wortham Brothers. C. A. Wortham's brother, John T., owned the whip on this show, and his brother-in-law, William Snapp, owned the other riding devices.

Season of 1918, Fred Beckman kept the Great Wortham Shows on the West Coast until after Christmas. Wortham's Exposition Company and the Wortham and Rice Shows played the big midwestern dates. Wortham's Alamo Shows was routed into Southern California from San Antonio, Texas, winter quarters. He announced late that season that he would have only two super midways on the road in 1919. Beckman routed the C. A. Wortham's World's Best Shows back to San Antonio and C. A. Wortham's World's Greatest Shows was ready for the road in winter quarters there. Wortham purchased and outfitted two circus-type advertising cars for this season and "billed his shows like a circus." A third show, the Greater Alamo Shows, in which he disclaimed any ownership, continued to operate in 1919. However, John T. Wortham and William Snapp had their rides on this show.

On October 26, 1919, C. A. Wortham's World's Best Shows started unloading and moving onto the Cotton Palace Grounds in Waco, Texas. Recent rains had turned the lot into a quagmire. The show's teams of horses under direction of the lot superintendent, were having difficulty getting the heavy wagons onto the soft showgrounds. A detail of Army Tanks was on the grounds also. These tanks had been exhibited at several fairs that this carnival unit had played and the officers and men knew the show people. Orders were given, the tanks were started, and the army put the show on the lot that day. This was the first time that a track laying vehicle was used to put a carnival on the lot.

Wortham's World's Best played eight days of the fifteen-day event. On the second Sunday night, Fred Beckman gave the orders; and the entire show was torn down, loaded and moved to the show's next date

Courtesy The Billboard

in Corsicana, Texas. Meanwhile, C. A. Wortham's World's Greatest Exposition Shows had torn down in Texarkana, Texas, and had moved to Waco. As one show pulled off the grounds the other one pulled on. When the Cotton Palace Exposition opened its gates for its second week, an entirely new show was on the midway waiting to give the amusement seekers something different for their second visit.

In January, 1914, Guy Dodson cranked his new automobile without disengaging the gears. It started and pushed him through a department store window. His brother, Mel, didn't enjoy the ride. The Reithoffer Amusement Company wintered in Sulphur Springs Park in Tampa that winter, and the Smith's Greater Shows were in their long-time quarters in Augusta, Georgia. The first half of the season was "frightfully bad," the Billboard reported. All shows reported wind and rain, and the Herbert A. Kline Shows folded in Joplin, Missouri, on July 5. The Hatch Motordrome Company had twelve dromes booked on shows in midseason, and Milton Norris was booking attractions for the Deep Water Jubilee in Houston, Texas, November 9—14.

A SLANT WALL MOTORDROME. This is the type "drome" in which Earl Purtle rode with the Barney Parker Show, 1914. Courtesy Earl Purtle.

Snake Oid, Cary Jones, claimed to be the oldest snake worker and said that he caught and swallowed a baby snake at a fishing camp in 1890. He gave his first public exhibition in Indiana during the season of 1891, and was still swallowing live snakes, horned toads and lizards. Bert Hoss promoted a carnival in St. Charles, Missouri, week of October 9th, and Rice and Reiss put out a Days of '49 Show indoors.

J. A. Darnaby wrote and produced the first Days of '49 in 1913 at Montreal, Canada. He used over one hundred horses and people in this production. Northam had produced a different version of this "Historical Production" at the Deep Water Jubilee in Houston. Now Bill Rice and Nat Reiss had produced a traveling show, which opened at Kankakee, Illinois; and Fred Beckman, Bert Earle, Harry Fisk and Arthur Davis produced one that opened in Peru, Indiana. These were elaborate productions with good casts; and the Panama-Pacific International Exposition in San Francisco featured another on its midway, called the Zone, that summer. Within a year, almost all of the carnivals had a Days of '49 Show on their midways. This was shortened to '49 Camp on most shows.

These '49 Camps generated more "heat" between the show people and town "marks" than any of crooked games, cootch shows or athletic shows had ever done. Most of them consisted of a bar, a dance floor, a piano and a set of drums. Soft drinks and sometimes beer were dispensed at the bar, but the town rowdies brought their own hard liquor. Sometimes on the better midways the girls did give a very good Western Honky-Tonk type dancing girl show, but in many of the Camps, their primary job was to drink and dance with the marks. Dance tickets were sold in strips, and some of the local toughs did all their carnival visiting in the '49 Camp. Under such conditions arguments were bound to start, and carnival people of that day had only one solution for an argument — slug them and fight it out. By the end of the decade, many good towns were closed to all carnivals, and the '49 Camps were not booked on the reputable shows. The reputation of all carnivals was lowered even more by these so-called shows, and the word carnival was regarded as denoting something evil, offensive and even noisome by many potential midway visitors.

Curtiss Velare had his photo gallery and penny arcade in Kansas City winter of 1914-15; and J. E. Gooding had booked a ferris wheel and an ocean wave with the Aiken Amusement Company, a gilly show. Con T. Kennedy announced that he had replaced his old No. 24 private car with a vestibuled coach. In last ten years No. 24 had gone as far north

STRAIGHT WALL MOTORDROME. First used by Doc Cann on an Eastern Show. He rode as Hal Clayton. Courtesy L. Harvey (Doc) Cann.

49 CAMP. Author's Collection.

as the railroad extended and had wintered on the Atlantic, the Pacific and the Gulf of Mexico. Fred Beckman had his first carnival in 1915, the Heinz & Beckman Shows; and C. A. Wortham played the Battle of Flowers in San Antonio that spring. Macy's Olympic Shows closed July 5th, first time since it was organized in 1910. Bill Aiken suggested that it might be profitable for carnivals to move by motor truck; and Bert Hoss was General Agent for the Harry Copping Shows. In January Joe Krause bought the first Mangels Whip to be placed on a carnival midway. He had it booked with the Leavitt-Meyerhoff Shows.

This ride, the whip, perfected and built by W. F. Mangels in his New York machine shops, was a radical development in riding devices. For hundreds of years, amusement purveyors had devised all sorts of contraptions in order to provide pleasurable motion for their patrons. They built swings, "Ups and Downs" and crude ancestors of a merry-go-round. In these devices they had incorporated all the basic movements that were possible to be built into a ride. However, the speed or pace of each had a certain sedate rhythm. Ferris' Big wheel traveled at a slow speed. The jumping horse merry-go-round now traveled faster and made use of two uniform basic motions. These "flying jennies" were being literally swamped with riders on the bigger fair dates.

C. W. Parker's crew of twenty men on his big Carry-Us-All were required to insure orderly loading of the big machines. If too many people crowded onto one side of ride before other side was equally balanced it could and would tilt to that side, sometimes causing considerable damage.

The Ocean Wave had, with its up and down dipping motion, given the riders the sensation of galloping up and down hills, but basically it was still a uniform motion. Mangels, using a basic physical principle, added another motion to his new ride, a joggle. All previous devices had utilized circular motion by aid of a circular machine. Mangels retained this circle, but divided it into equal halves separated by a straight segment like a race track. Tubs on the end of long arms were propelled by a continuous cable to which the arm was attached. This cable, powered by comparatively small horizontal bull wheels centered on the epicenters of the two half circles, carried the tubs along the straight sides at an even pace. However, the tubs being forced to travel the outer circumference of the circle at the ends of the ride were moving several times as fast. The riders were given the sensation of being hurled around the ends of the platform, as the speed of the tubs changed four times during each revolution.

Every ride inventor since Mangels introduced his Whip, has tried to get that "Joggle" which throws the riders together. Some critics have been unkind enough to suggest that this jouncing together of riders had deliberate sexual undertones. Perhaps. Has not the carnival always been a time and place where certain inhibitions have been laid aside?

The introduction of this new ride early in 1915 on the two-ride midways of America was the first sign of the transformation of those midways into the modern-day carnival. This metamorphosis would quicken in the Twenties, slow down briefly for the early Depression Days and then accelerate until the modern carnival midway consisting of scores of thrilling riding devices with only a few shows had evolved. The modern midway operator explains an "economic fact" with this characteristic statement, "you don't have to feed 'pig iron' when it's not working." Anyway carnival goers may not see so many cootch shows now, but they still have the "Joggle."

Getting back to 1915, Bootsie and Hody Hurd, "a clever little singing team," toured the South in theatres after the carnivals had closed their 1914 seasons. Their father, Tom, was general announcer for Con T. Kennedy in 1915; and the Russian Dancers on the show featured Princess Bootsie. Late that fall, the Kennedy show suffered one of the most disastrous train wrecks in carnival history. The Hurd family were not injured, but several men were killed. Spring of 1916 found the Hurds back with Kennedy. Hody was working in Max Kimerer's Miracle Show on the Kennedy Midway. Tom became ill in Grand Rapids, Michigan, and never worked again. The family left the show at Ft. Madison, Iowa, and carried Tom to Atlanta. Hody went back to the Con T. Kennedy Shows where she stayed into the 1917 season. Meantime, Bootsie was with the Johnny J. Jones Exposition where she had married the show's treasurer, F. G. Scott. In 1918, both girls were with the Jones Show, where they were to stay until the end of that greatest of all carnivals nearly forty years later.

In 1915 Harry Calvert managed Days of '49 for S. W. Brundage, and his wife, Elsie, worked in the show. Brundage's band master, Merle Evans, married Lulu Hamilton of Wichita, Kansas, who had joined the Brundage carnival the previous year. J. George Loos had completed over four hundred weeks without closing his midway; and both Mable Mack's Mules and Sibley's Diving Girls were with Con T. Kennedy. Percy Tyrrell, manager of the Gunter Hotel in San Antonio gave his annual Christmas Party for

BLOWDOWN. Lou Dufour Shows. Note details of Whip Ride. Courtesy Lou Dufour.

the hundreds of carnival people that were wintering in that South Texas City.

Guy Dodson's World's Fair Shows opened in 1916. J. C. Simpson opened season as manager of the Great Empire Shows for Mrs. Hampton after her husband's death. He enticed Harold Bushea back to the carnivals as General Agent of the show. Harold had been with circuses several years, but could never forget that he had been agent for Gaskill's first midway. Sam Soloman and Rubin Gruberg put out a new show, Sol & Rubin's United Shows; while W. S. Cherry was still general agent of the Smith Greater Shows. W. C. Fleming was now with Capt. John Sheesley's midway as a promoter, and Fred Beckman was general manager of James T. Clyde's World at Home Shows. The Clifton-Kelley Midway had sustained three blowdowns by midseason and Jack Rhoades (he had now added an ''a,'') had gone from Wortham's No. 1 Show to the Great Alamo Shows. Al Dernberger had concessions with Johnny J. Jones for the eighth year. Early in July, Nat Reiss, one of the first carnival owners, died.

These excerpts from a eulogy printed in the Billboard sum up Nat Reiss's career: ''Though he

AT SHOW WORKER. Courtesy L. Harvey (Doc) Cann.

never accumulated any great amount of money, never introduced any new or original features, methods or ideas, and never achieved any great success, he secured a name and standing that were enviable in the extreme; in fact, he just barely missed real fame.'' ''Tough luck pursued him constantly....'' ''Though he got little out of the game for himself, he provided much employment for others...''

A cyclone in Wibaux, Montana, completely wrecked the Campbell United Shows but Campbell said, ''We will show tonight;'' they did.

On June 17, 1916, Hila F. Maynes opened his ''Witching Waves'' ride on the Johnny J. Jones Exposition. Maynes' rides were the real basis of success of the little Welshman's battle to retain supremacy in the carnival field. Maynes, a mechanical genius, designed and built a new super riding device almost every year after this 1915 joining with Jones. Some of these rides were not practical, but the ones that he was able to carry with the show were far ahead of the best any of the other ride manufacturers could build. The Jones Midway had had the Hila F. Maynes rides exclusive, year after year, while other carnivals had to content themselves with smaller and lighter imitations built by other builders of riding devices.

TATTOED GIRL. Courtesy L. Harvey (Doc) Cann.

For fifteen years, those huge rides designed, built and operated by Hila Maynes gave the soft-spoken little ex-coal miner with the big mustache an edge over all other carnival owners. Jones had the Maynes Rides on his midway and no other riding devices could compete with them. Maynes and his crew of ride men were the only men capable of setting those rides up and moving them. With them as a nucleus, Mr. Jones could acquire other devices and build the greatest collective amusement organization ever put together.

In 1916, Tom Hasson and Billie Clark joined in partnership and built the Famous Broadway Shows which they operated successfully for three years. The Karns Brothers (Jack and Jill) left Walter K. Sibley after twelve years and joined Sam W. Gumpertz's side show at Coney Island. Etta Louise Blake was with Clarence A. Wortham, while Johnny J. Bejano was completing his thirteenth year with the Greater Patterson Shows. Mrs. Jim Dunlevy, whose husband was manager of the Samar Siamese Twins, gave birth to a seven and one half pound girl in Pittsburgh that September. McGarvie was in New York planning for a Bronx International Exposition to be held each year.

In 1917, Polack Brothers framed a second show with J. C. Simpson as assistant manager. Irving Polack managed this Polack Brothers 20 Big Shows while Harry Polack was manager of their Rutherford Greater Shows. Felice Bernardi opened his new fifteen-car Bernardi Greater Shows, and L. J. Heth was moving his carnival on twenty-five cars. Zeke Shumway was trick rider in the motor drome with J. F. Murphy's American Shows. Rubin Gruberg and Wilbur S. Cherry had their Rubin & Cherry Shows on the road, and Johnny J. Bejano had moved his circus side show to the Wortham Shows. Max Goodman booked three concession wheels on Sibley's Superb Shows, while Velare Brothers had their concessions and whip on Parker's Greatest Shows midway.

'49 Camp operators in Oklahoma and Texas were being arrested on charges of violating the "White Slave Laws." C. W. Parker tried to buy his own locomotives in order to beat the war time embargoes. Samuel W. Gumpertz had started a militant campaign to clean up the carnival industry. T. A. Wolfe opened his new Superior United Shows, and Bert Hoss had booked "a real route" for the Hoss-Lorman Shows.

K. G. Barkoot engaged a manager for his carnival this 1917 season, as he was too busy at this automobile accessory factory to go on the road with the show. He had patented, and was now manufacturing, a signalling device to be installed on automobiles. This device consisted of four electric signs for the rear of the vehicle. These signs were controlled by push buttons mounted on the dash. One button lighted up two inch high letters reading "STOP," another "BACK" and the other two "RIGHT" and "LEFT." This newfangled invention was considered outlandish and never sold well.

EARLY SLANT WALL MOTORDROME. Author's Collection.

WAGONS. On flat car ready for delivery from factory. They were built for one of the Philadelphia Tobbogan company's rides. Courtesy J. W. Beggs. Beggs Wagon Works in Kansas City,

GYPSY TYPE WAGON. Courtesy Frank Cucksey.

In October 1917, Tom Hasson was hit by an automobile as he stepped off the railroad station platform in Jackson, Tennessee. He was knocked down and dragged seventy feet. The driver then backed up until Tom was disengaged from the vehicle, ran over him again and drove away. Hasson had a broken arm. In March Johnny J. Jones had stepped out onto the platform of his private car and dropped through an open platform door. The train was stopped in Kissimmee and an automobile was sent back to pick up the disgruntled boss man. He had three misplaced ribs.

During the 1918 season Polack Brothers acquired their third show, the World at Home Shows. J. Simpson was their general manager for this show. C. W. Parker was building a new midway attraction in his Leavenworth factory. This Underground Chinatown show had been sold to many midway operators, and Parker had orders for more of them. W. G. Wade had the Wade Amusement Company on the road, and Private B. S. Gerety was in the army. J. H. Marks had two concessions on the Hoss & Narder Shows until this show split up in July.

On September 10, 1918, nine flatcars of the World At Home Shows piled up in a ditch in the worst carnival wreck since the 1915 Kennedy Shows wreck. Two were killed and many injured. The dining car was turned into a hospital car and the women of the show treated the injured. It was a common sight that night to see the grizzled, bloodied head of a working man resting in the lap of one of the show girls while another lady cleansed and bandaged his hurts. Finally, ambulances from Adrian, Michigan, were piloted across the fields to the wreck site, and the seriously injured were carried to Detroit hospitals.

As soon as all the men were accounted for Harry Polack began dispatching staff members and sending telegrams. The next town, Ironton, Ohio was cancelled. All wreckage was loaded upon railroad flatcars under the direction of T. W. (Slim) Kelly, World at Home train master, and the train was moved directly to Hamilton, Ohio, where some excess equipment was stored. The train was met in Hamilton by a small army of skilled men sent by Beggs Wagon Works of Kansas City, Mangels factory in New York, Philadelphia Toboggan Company, and other suppliers of carnival equipment. Show lost five days.

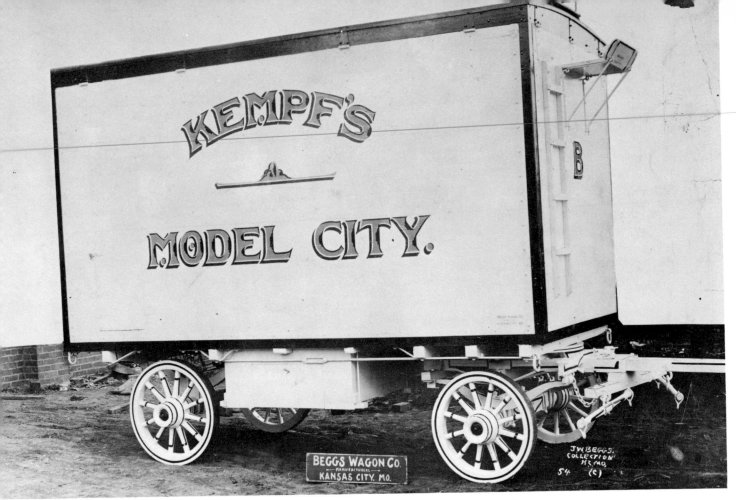

KEMPF'S MODEL CITY WAGON. Courtesy J. W. Beggs (Beggs Wagon Works).

KEMPF'S MODEL CITY. This "working world" was operated by the Kempf family for over thirty years. Courtesy J. W. Beggs.

Spanish influenza moved across the United States in October. Quarantines were imposed statewide in several states and most all towns were closed to shows. Carnivals sat on railroad sidings for six weeks before moving again. Bad weather and shortage of coal for locomotives caused many midways to go into winter quarters.

Velare Brothers had opened the season with Ziedman & Pollie Shows but moved to the Nat Reiss Shows in midyear. The Velares owned six flatcars loaded with equipment. They found winter quarters for themselves and the Reiss Shows in Hammond, Indiana. By the end of the year Elmer C. Velare had visited the Parker factory and ordered twenty thousand dollars worth more equipment to be added to that on the Nat Reiss midway.

George Bistany framed the new World of Mirth Shows for the 1919 season. Curtis L. Bockus got a new show together to play ship yard towns under Labor auspices. This Metal Trades Council Shows toured a full season playing such dates. Carl J. Sedlmayr had his circus side show on the Great Patterson Shows, and Mrs. Nat Reiss married the manager of her carnival that spring. She and her new husband, Harry Melville, kept the Nat Reiss title active for another twelve years.

Mable Mack had her mules with the Brown & Dyer Shows in 1919. This carnival had built up from four to twenty cars in one year, and was playing a week inside Camp Bragg under auspices of the army. Snake King continued his custom of sending giant Texas watermelons to the Billboard staff for July Fourth. Etta Louise Blake joined the Johnny J. Jones Exposition, and Fred Lewis was construction superintendent for Mr. Jones. Velare Brothers bought a new Frolic ride. Harry J. Polack died March 29, 1919, and Irving Polack announced that he would cut down to two carnivals as soon as the contracts for the third show were played out.

Bert Hoss was managing the Hoss-Hays Shows as the decade ended. All the big-time carnival operators for the next twenty years now had their own midways or were working with the equipment or shows that they would use to form their own organizations. Three big-time operators had died in this decade, all leaving widows who tried to keep the shows created by their late husbands on the road. Francis Ferari had died in November 1914, while J. W. Hampton of the Great Empire Shows had died in July of the same year. Their widows still had the shows touring at the end of the decade, but only the ex-Mrs. Reiss would succeed in keeping her husband's show out in the twenties.

Carnival business was now coming of age. Next year would start her twenty-second rambunctious season. She was a big girl now. Bigger, much bigger, than any of her founders ever dreamed that she could be. Some of her midways had reported fantastic grosses of fifty, seventy, even one hundred thousand dollars at just one of their big fair dates. None of her devotees knew just what the future might hold for their mistress, but they were all optimistic.

WORLD AT HOME SHOWS WRECK, September 10, 1918. This wreck occurred in Southern Michigan only a few weeks before the Hagenbeck Wallace Circus Wreck near Hammond, Indiana. The latter was the most disastrous wreck in outdoor show history. From A Pictorial History of the Carousel with permission of the author, Frederick Fried.

BIG JUNE CARNIVAL

——AND——

Base Ball Booster Week

AT NEENAH COMMENCING

MONDAY, JUNE 7

THE L. J. HETH'S UNITED SHOWS

FEATURING

10 - BIG SHOWS - 10

——AND——

Prof. C. O. Dean's Concert Band

Of 15 Soloists

SHOW PROGRAMME

Francis William's Dog, Pony and Monkey Show
Thornton's Big Circus Annex---Seven
Big Shows In One
The Blue Eyes Mystery or Show Beautiful
Tipperary Girls Big Musical Review
Hodge's Mable Show featuring the Electric Girl
The Original September Morn
McIntife's Big Molordrome or Wheel of Death
The Big Eli Ferris Wheel
The New $15,000 Four Abreast Jumping Horse
Carry-Us-All

FREE BAND CONCERTS

Up town twice daily, 12:30 and 7 p. m.

Carnival showing under auspices of the Neenah Athletic Park Association and will locate on the Fred Mayer Lots opposite the Stove Works on Main street.

1915

L. J. HETH SHOWS NEWSPAPER AD, 1915. Courtesy Circus World Museum, Baraboo, Wisconsin.

TEN COMMANDMENTS

of the

FOLEY & BURK COMBINED SHOWS

In order to maintain the high standard and reputation established by this amusement institution, we most respectfully, but emphatically, request that all attaches of the Foley & Burke organization religiously adhere to the following precepts:

1. **YOU MUST NOT MASH, FLIRT, "CHIPPIE CHASE".**
   Breach of this rule can create no end of trouble for yourself and the management.

2. **YOU MUST NOT DRINK INTOXICANTS NOR BRING THEM ON SHOW LOT.**
   "Boot-leg" breathe and "Moonshine" chatter are extremely repulsive and offensive to everyone.

3. **YOU MUST NOT USE PROFANITY OR VULGARITY.**
   If you must be profane and vulgar, do so under your breath. It will be just as effective as though the entire world were "listening in" on your mad ravings.

4. **YOU MUST NOT SMOKE DURING THE OPERATION OF SHOW OR RIDE.**
   Patrons keenly object to having clouds of second hand smoke blown in their faces; it is the height of discourtesy.

5. **YOU MUST KEEP CLEAN.**
   We will make an effort to supply the soap, water and towels, but you must supply the disposition, energy and clothing.

6. **YOU MUST NOT GAMBLE.**
   Gambling is unlawful and mighty unprofitable.

7. **YOU MUST BE POLITE AND COURTEOUS.**
   You know, it is a mistaken idea that simply because you are with a show you have to be a "rough-neck".

8. **BE LOYAL TO THE SHOW.**
   The show will always go the limit for worthy employees who are "with it" and "for it".

9. **BE ON TIME AND REMAIN ON THE JOB.**
   Do your lunching and visiting before or after shows and rides are open to the public.

10. **BE HONEST.**
    Dishonesty can lead to only one place—"the big stone house with iron bars on the bedroom windows".

Violation of rules ruins discipline, disrupts an organization and jeopardizes the employees' chances for advancement and bonus.

TEN COMMANDMENTS. Foley & Burk Shows. Courtesy Lloyd Hilligoss.

"FRONT END" OF A SMALL MIDWAY. This composite photograph taken at different times does give a good view of a complete "concession row" on a small carnival. Courtesy J. W. Patty Conklin.

FAT SHOW. Johnny J. Jones Exposition. Author's collection.

The Terrible Tempered Col. Francis Ferari

The Story

The leopard trainer was a "lush-head" (drunkard), and Col. Ferari had ordered him not to work the animals while inebrieted. The good colonel was sleeping in his living wagon which was always spotted inside the Wild Animal Show tent. While he slept, the front man had opened the show and "turned" a full house. The band playing inside the tent wakened Ferari. Looking out, he saw the drunken trainer opening the leopard's jaws preparatory to sticking his face into its mouth. The colonel burst out of the wagon in his nightgown and bedcap yelling, "Get your bloody head outa that cat's mouth. You wanta pizen 'im?" Original sketch by Marian L. McKennon.

On Decoration Day, May 30, 1920, Old Madam Carnival's youngest daughter celebrated her twenty-first birthday. There was no observance of this milestone in her career on any of her boisterous midways. It is doubtful that any one of her over twenty-thousand camp followers even remembered that just twenty-one years ago Frank W. Gaskill had opened that little show in Chillicothe, Ohio. Had superintendent Adolph Seeman mentioned this anniversary to his boss, Rubin Gruberg, Rubin's response would undoubtedly have been, "So vat, vat's in it for me?"

This "what's in it for me?" trait had already been implanted into the basic character of almost every individual midway follower. Basically a rugged individualist, each carnival adherent had to work under the most adverse conditions. Bad weather and epidemics could wipe out all hope of possible profits from a full season's hard work. Tornados, fires, floods and train wrecks could, and often did, destroy the accumulation of a life time. And being a nomad was never conducive to building lasting relationships with the inhabitants of the towns visited. The Carny, as the midway people were being referred to, became more and more dependent on himself and his fellow workers.

The carnival trouper's method of operation, the long all day "grinding in" of nickels, dimes and quarters was very likely to become a fixation with him. The "grinder" on the fun house, pit show or grab joint soon became obsessed with the idea that getting more cash out of the townspeople was the supreme achievement of each day. The talker on the bally platforms of the circus side shows, the motordromes and the other "Bally shows" had a similar obsession as did each individual on the merchandise and gaming consessions. This feeling of having to "snatch and grab" was easily transfered to the non-cash handling members of a carnival company for "if they don't get it, we don't eat" was an accepted economic fact with all of them.

These carnival people, most of them hardworking and honest family men and women, were (and are) most charitable towards a distressed fellow human being. Most of them have seen "lean times." The owner of one of the greatest amusement organizations of all times, as a wet year old, occupied a basket inside his mother's ticket box as she sold tickets for the roller skating rink in which his father attached the skates for the occasional person who braved the cold for a few rounds on the rink. That man, each year, donates and collects untold thousands of dollars for every conceivable charity. The people on his midway still "grind and bally" for

quarters and half dollars just as their fathers and grandfathers did for nickles, dimes and quarters on the midways of the past.

It is doubtful that any of the people on that first show of Gaskill's in 1899 had any idea that the Collective Amusement Business would ever consist of more than a few organizations. Many of them doubted that it would last more than a few years. Harold Bushea, Gaskill's general agent quit carnivals and went back to the circuses; and Bill Rice said the business was all done and went into another line in 1905. None of them even dreamed that in less than thirty years there would be over two hundred carnivals, each moving on from one to forty railroad cars. That each weekend over three thousand railroad cars loaded with carnival equipment would be on the move. And, that each Monday morning two hundred individual scenes of ordered confusion would be enacted as those midways grew anew on the cow pastures and fair grounds of the United States and Canada.

As the carnival industry started its twenty-second year, the Velare Brothers had three rides, three shows and twenty concessions on the Nat Reiss Shows. They also owned twenty wagons, six steel flatcars and a baggage car. Robt. L. Lohmar was the general agent for the Reiss Shows that year, and Jack Velare was also with it. Jack, who adopted the name Velare when he was understander for the brothers' acrobatic act in the 1890's, died in July of this 1920 season. C. A. Wortham's Worlds Best Shows, under Fred Beckman's management, was in Southern California, and had been going now eighty weeks without closing. The Greater Alamo Shows was in the Pacific Northwest, while Dan White, trainmaster for Rice & Dorman, was "as proud as a kid with a new pair of red topped boots" over the new equipment on that show.

Early in June, Charles Martin's Frisco Exposition Shows played on the Parade Grounds lot in Minneapolis. The Shriners, who were the sponsors of the carnival for that date, took over the Wild West Show arena one morning and transformed it into a ceremonial area. The Zurah Temple degree team, aided by Nobles Dave Lackman, Andrew Carson and George Harmon, of the Shows conferred the degree on a class of nearly five hundred candidates. The next week, Johnny J. Jones Exposition and Polack's 20 Big Shows "day and dated" each other in Duluth. Their show grounds were only five hundred feet apart. Rubin and Cherry Shows were now on thirty railroad cars, and Bert Hoss advertised that the Hoss-Hays United Shows were "Traveling on the bounding waves of success."

Minstrel Show Lady

KILL THE KATS

15 STANDARD ATTRACTIONS 15

JOS. G. FERARI SHOWS

Permanent Address:
Gayety Theatre Building
1547 BROADWAY
NEW YORK CITY, N. Y.

BENJAMIN WILLIAMS
MANAGER

Ferari Sho

Scenes,

1920 Seas

All Photos Courtesy of L. Harvey (Doc) Cann

In November, personnel of the Johnny J. Jones Exposition visited the cemetery where five ex-Jones Show Troupers were buried and scattered flowers over the graves. Among the seventy people taking part in this memorial service were the giant, the midgets, the Hurd Sisters, Mable Mack of the Mule Circus, many staff members and the Siamese Twins.

Two bad floods occurred in 1920. On April 20, Capt. John Sheesley's Midway was under nine feet of water in the ball park at Bellevue, Kentucky. Animals had all been brought out safely, but wagons and equipment were floating around inside the ball park. As the water did not go down, salvage operations were started. Boats were secured and divers went down and fastened cables to equipment. Teams of horses dragged the wagons and properties to high ground. Show was moved across town and reopened on Friday after losing three nights.

On August 27, Littlejohn's Fair Shows was hit by a flash flood in Carlisle, Kentucky. The lot was swept clean of all equipment except the rides. This property was scattered along the banks of the creek for nine miles below the show grounds. When waters receded salvage operations were hindered by a rumor that had been spread among the town people that a trunk containing three thousand dollars in cash had washed down the creek. When the carnival people got to their property, they found all boxes, trunks and containers torn, broken or chopped open and contents scattered.

In November of 1920, Velare Brothers announced that they had leased the Nat Reiss Shows from Mr. and Mrs. Harry Melville for the 1921 season. Frank West had his Bright Lights Shows, Wortham's Worlds Best played the first week at Waco's Cotton Palace and George Loos took the last week. C. D. Scott still had his Scott's Greater Shows on the road. In Cleburne, Texas, Joe McKennon, aged thirteen, started his life-time love affair with the twenty-one year old harlot by setting up dolls on Doll Rack Queen Mable's joint with the Frisco Exposition Shows. Irving Polack announced that he would have only one show on the road in 1921.

In December, the World's Best was finishing its ninety-ninth week back in Southern California while most of the big shows were in their winter quarters.

WILD WEST SHOW BALLY. Wortham Shows, 1919. Author's collection

GIRL REVUE FRONT. Brown & Dyer Shows early 1920's. Doc Cann with mustache is in ticket box to your left. Courtesy L. Harvey Doc Cann.

Tom Hasson sold his interest in the Famous Broadway Shows and planned to start one of his own. In Christmas issue of the Billboard, Bert Hoss ran biggest ad of his career. A full page for the Hoss-Hays United Shows, "Highest Class Show on Earth."

For the next two years, carnival business continued to grow in spite of the bad reputation it had acquired from its '49 camps, At Shows, crooked games and general business practices. Many towns were closed to all shows and favorite sermons for preachers, short of other material, were condemnations of carnivals and carnival people. Some hundred or more fly by night operators preyed on the public with the result that all shows suffered, since one show always looked like another to the townspeople. Some of these organizations continued to operate for twenty years, many of them without changing their titles. Their only possible excuse for existence was to fleece the show goers of the towns they played. Yet, they managed to show some of those towns every year for ten, even fifteen years. Their agents and "fixers" got permits to work, even though they had had big "hey rubes" the year before.

It is impossible to estimate the millions of dollars paid out to local authorities by show "patches and fixers" for the right to "work strong."

It would be a poor "legal adjuster" indeed who would give the "go ahead" to the girls and joints until somebody down at City Hall had been taken care of. Maybe some shows have tried to work before paying off the "right man" at the Court House or City Hall. If they did, they were operated by amateur or "first of May" showmen. Shows of today, for the most part, are one hundred percent legitimate as will be shown in later chapters, but in the early twenties many of them weren't and the business was in trouble.

In 1922, after a couple of abortive attempts by showmen to clean up the business, the Billboard took on the job for the honest carnival owners. Hundreds of letters were sent to the publishers each week endorsing this clean-up. Headlines such as this appeared in newspapers across the nation: "Iowa reported over run with grift," "Strong joints reported a t — — — — — — — — — — — — — — — — and — — — — — — — — — — — — — — — fairs" and '' — — — — — — — — — — — — — — — — — and — — — — — — — — — — — — — Fair Boards censured for allowing gambling on their midways."

Early in 1921, Snapp Brothers framed a new twenty car show in East St. Louis and Victor D. Leavitt and "Spike" Huggins opened the new Leavitt-Huggins Shows on the West Coast. Dave Lackman was with the Frisco Exposition Shows and Wright and Lindermen were co-owners of the World of Mirth Shows. Tom Hasson built the Hasson Brothers Shows in Philadelphia; and Hoss-Hays Shows were wrecked in a Pennsylvania tunnel. Leavitt and Huggins took a partner for the Leavitt-Brown-Huggins Shows. In June Sam Bailey made a good pitch to an interested "tip" at a Cicero, Illinois, picnic. Did not turn one. A total blank. Discovered later that he had set up in the deaf and dumb section of the grounds.

Bootsie Hurd Scott was given a surprise birthday party on the Johnny J. Jones Exposition in Pittsburg. Her two and one half year old daughter, Frances Iva Scott, was a lively guest at the party. On July 19, carnival King Jones sent Morris Weis and the Jones Concert Band to Gaskill's grave in Alliance, Ohio, for a service. Then in St. Louis on August 5, 1921, the quiet little showman received the following telegram: "Dear Dad———————— just arrived at Crooked Creek, Pa. Present weight nine pounds. Aunt Sue, Mother and myself doing fine. Come and see us soon as possible. Your loving son. Johnny Jenkins Jones, Jr. Yes, the little man with the big mustache and bigger show had been married for over a year. Married to that beautiful little dancer, Hody Hurd.

In 1922, Melville had the Nat Reiss Shows again as the Velare's lease was for one season only. Jim Paterson was framing only one show using best equipment from the two shows out the last season. W. S. Cherry left Rubin Gruberg and joined with Guy Dodson in the Dodson and Cherry Shows. Rubin and Cherry title was still used by Rubin as he owned show outright. Robert Gloth managed the World at Homes Shows for Irving Polack; and Al Dernberger joined the Brown and Dyer Shows. In St. Louis D. D. Murphy organized a five car show. J. W. (Paddy) Conklin, Jr., his mother and his brother, Frank, built concessions in Vancouver for the midway of the International Amusement Company. Theo Forstail was Paddy's auditor. At 12, noon, February 18, after a band concert, Starr DeBelle announced to the crowd that the twenty-five car Veal Brothers Shows was officially open.

On March 10, Honest John Brunen, owner and operator of the Mighty Doris Exposition Shows, which he started in 1916, was shot and killed by a shotgun while sitting in his Riverside, New Jersey, home. His wife and her brother, Harry C. Mohr, were arrested later. She was found not guilty by a jury in December, Mohr was convicted. Charles M. Powell testified that he had been hired by them to do the actual killing. He was convicted and received a sentence of 20 to 30 years in prison.

ILLUSION AND MYSTERY SHOW. J. L. Cronin Shows, 1929. This type show when operated by a competent magician and escape artist gave the public a very good performance well worth the admission price. Author's collection.

ILLUSION SHOW, M. J. Lapp Shows, 1920-1922. "Escape artist" is Doc Cann. From the wardrobe, it appears that Doc has just gotten to the Illusion Show after a ride on the Motordrome walls. Courtesy L. Harvey Doc Cann.

"AT SHOW," Conklin & Garrett Shows, 1928. Note the Spidoro, spider girl Illusion Show in center of photograph. Courtesy J. W. Patty Conklin.

In April the Mighty Doris Shows, owned by John Lazia, opened in Kansas City. Velare Brothers had their rides and concessions with it. Mrs. M. T. Bernardi took over all interests in the Doris-Ferari Shows and changed the title to the Bernardi Greater Shows. This was last time Ferari title was used on a major carnival.

June 16 John Veal, owner of Veal Brothers Shows, was shot and killed in Joliet, Illinois, by two negroes who attempted to hold him up. In August, C. J. Sedlmayr was general manager of the twenty-one car Siegrest and Silbon Shows. In September he announced that he was new owner of the show. Hyla F. Maynes patented a new ride and assigned the patents to Spillman Engineering Co. This ride, The Caterpillar, was a money maker on all shows that could get delivery on one.

On September 24, 1922, C. A. Wortham's Worlds Greatest Shows train moved out of Cincinnati, Ohio, leaving the Little Giant in the hospital there. Bob Lohmar stayed in Cincinnati with him. One hour after the train left town, Lohmar was sending telegrams that shocked the entire industry. Clarence

A. Wortham was dead at the age of forty. Chronic appendix and stomach trouble was the immediate cause of death. This man who owned outright two great carnivals and had financial interests in five others just did not have the physical stamina that his strong and dynamic mentality demanded. His body could not meet the requirements that he had forced on it. Memorial services were held on all seven units that he had interests in and leading showmen from all over the nation came to Danville, Illinois, for his funeral. Six hundred and forty-one floral offerings were banked around the bier at this service.

On October 31, 1922, the Wortham number one show train was going onto a side track at Adeline, Louisana, when a freight train plowed into it and killed three people. Show was enroute from Mobile, Alabama, to Beaumont, Texas, when the wreck occurred. The engine of the other train passed completely through a railroad owned coach that was being used as a caboose and on into Mrs. Wortham's private car. It killed a man and mangled his wife in the stateroom next to the Wortham bedroom. Mrs. Wortham's life was saved only because she was in

WATER CIRCUS. M. J. Lapp Shows, 1920-1922. Courtesy L. Harvey Doc Cann.

Dallas for a few days. Had Mr. Wortham not died in September, he would have been killed in that wreck as he undoubtedly would have been asleep in his bed in the splintered stateroom.

J. C. Simpson stayed in charge of the Wortham interest at the Dallas Fair Park until last of November when he was engaged by Rubin Gruberg as general manager of the Rubin and Cherry Shows. Wilbur S. Cherry sold his interest in the Dodson and Cherry Shows back to Guy Dodson and returned to Rubin as general agent. Last week in December, all equipment, wagons, rides, etc. of the Mighty Doris Exposition Shows was destroyed in a winter quarters fire at Belleville, Illinois. Owner, John Lazia, estimated the loss at one hundred twenty-five thousand dollars.

When the Wortham's Worlds Best Shows (No. 2 show) pulled into the Houston Fairgrounds a new title had been painted on the equipment. Beckman & Gerety Coney Island Shows was used for that engagement. Then Beckman, Gerety and Robinson made a deal with Mrs. Wortham for the equipment and paid her cash for same. They also obtained the right for exclusive use of the C. A. Wortham's Worlds Best Shows title for three years. Evidently they extended this exclusive right, as they continued to use the Wortham title until the end of the decade. The number one show equipment and its staff all went to Morris and Castle Shows. Mr. Wortham had owned an interest in this latter show. He also had interests in his brother's John T. Wortham Shows, in his brother-in-law's Snapp Brothers Shows, in the

Greater Alamo Shows and in the J. George Loos Shows. Mrs. Wortham never again went on the road with carnivals, but continued to operate the Dallas Fair Park rides and concessions for many years.

In 1923 all of the big shows had pledged to support the "clean-up midways" campaign. One enterprising concession supply house ran the following ad: "The clean-up campaign is on boys! Now is the time for you to clean-up with Florentine Art Marble Lamps and statues."

The Cudney & Fleming Shows, owned by Charles Cudney and Mad Cody Fleming, came out of North Little Rock, Arkansas; and F. F. Gooding's Certified Shows opened in Portsmouth, Ohio, on April 16. DeKreko Brothers were on the road with a twenty car railroad show, Carl J. Sedlmayr attained the thirty-second degree in the Scottish Rite in Kansas City; and W. H. Hames opened his Cotton Belt Exposition Shows in Pilot Point, Texas. H. H. Tipps was General Agent for Hames, Theo Ledel was secretary, Mrs. Hames sold tickets on the merry-go-round and Pearl Hames was in the Ferris Wheel ticket box. Doc Waddell came back to carnival business as press agent for T. A. Wolfe's Shows.

Waddell, the young press agent with the buggy whip on Gaskill's first show, had left the carnival field after the Pan American Exposition in Buffalo. He had disagreed with Bostock in midseason there and had gone across the midway to work for Col. Cummins on the latter's wild west show. Doc had tried many things in the intervening eighteen years but was

especially interested in social service and the uplift of the "down and outer." He came back to the carnival field in 1923 but not for long. In May 1925 he met the Reverend Howard S. Williams and joined this tented evangelist on a tour of the country. Williams, a former Hattiesburg, Mississippi, newspaper man had been converted to Christianity at a Gipsy Smith evangelistic service. He sold his holdings in Mississippi and was following the "sawdust trail" himself.

Joe Scholibo was press agent and Robt. L. Lohmar was general agent of the Morris & Castle Shows, while Harold Bushea was press agent for Lackman's Exposition Shows. Boyd & Linderman Shows, C. W. Naill's Shows and C. A. Vernon's Southern Standard Exposition Shows were touring that season. J. C. Simpson was part owner of Ziedman & Pollie Shows, while Sam Soloman was still using the Sol's Bros. title. J. L. (Peasy) Hoffman was on the Lackman Exposition Shows; and Bert Hoss was not heard from. November 23, Beckman and Gerety lost their good friend and partner, George E. Robinson. For the next twenty years a large memorial ad with Mr. Robinson's picture would be inserted in the Billboard each November by his former partners.

February 23, 1924, Daisy and Violet Hilton had a birthday party on Beckman & Gerety's Wortham Shows in Glendale, California. These English born siamese twin girls prepared the meal for their well wishers themselves. The girls were probably the most versatile of all the Siamese-like twins. They had a

headline musical act in vaudeville for several years, but always returned to the circus side show on Wortham's Worlds Best Shows for the fair season. They died in Charlotte, North Carolina, in 1969. The sixty-three year old joined-together twins were working until the week of their death, as a cashier at a Charlotte supermarket.

Fred Lewis was general superintendent of the Rubin and Cherry Shows, in 1924, while Starr DeBelle was the announcer on their wild animal circus. Curtis Velare had joined C. J. Sedlmayr in the management of the Royal American Shows; and D. D. Murphy had increased from one to twenty cars in just three years. Oldtimer, Harold Bushea, was general agent for Lackman Exposition Shows and Adolph Seeman was sent to a Chicago hospital by Rubin Gruberg. Seeman had throat cancer. Wade and May Shows opened in Detroit and Irving Polack had leased the World at Home Shows to Holland Brothers. Milton Holland was general manager for the carnival while Polack managed his new Polack Brothers Circus.

Spillman Engineering Company built an Over the Jumps Ride for Johnny J. Jones in two weeks. Capt. John Sheesley reported that the Danville, Virginia, fairgrounds was too small for his shows. He had a "tight layout" there. Bill Rice's Water Circus was one of the free acts at the Tennessee State Fair in Nashville. Felice Bernardi had the Bernardi Exposition Shows, while William Glick, Ralph Smith and M. B. (Duke) Golden had the Bernardi Greater

C. A. WORTHAM'S SHOWS. Edmonton, Alberta, Canada, 1921. Author's collection.

MONKEY MOTORDROME. Rubin & Cherry Shows, 1929. Monkeys
"rode the walls" in cars controlled by the operator. Author's collection.

Shows. Mad Cody Fleming Shows would have winter quarters in Cincinnati, but a few shows were on winter tours of the South. The oldest midway on the road, the Con T. Kennedy was in trouble.

The Kennedy Show, after the Detroit Fair ended in September, was seized by federal agents who claimed that admission taxes had not been paid. Total amount due was not reported but some estimated it as high as two hundred thousand dollars. Upon payment of two thousand dollars and promise of one thousand dollars per month, show was released and it moved on to Saint Louis.

On Monday, September 22, the Kennedy show train was enroute to Abilene, Texas, from Hope, Arkansas, when it was wrecked in the Frisco Railroad yards at Fort Worth. Four flat cars were derailed and the equipment and wagons badly smashed. All was reloaded on railroad system flat cars, but first day at Abilene was lost. On December 2, 1924, in New Orleans, Con T. Kennedy, pioneer carnival owner, died of pneumonia. His body, accompanied by Mrs. Kennedy (C. W. Parker's sister), was shipped to Miami. Body lay in state under a miniature circus big

top. The Elks and the Masons had charge of the funeral.

Mrs. Kennedy had quite a struggle getting all claims settled. She first tried to settle with government for ten thousand dollars. Officials refused. Then other creditors stepped in with their claims, U. S. Tent and Awning, Rogers Tent and Awning, Tangley Caliope Company, Venice Transportation Company and others. When all claims were presented there remained only eight wagons with clear titles. Show had been siezed by the agents immediately after Kennedy's death. Sale was set for January 3, 1925, but was postponed for fifteen days. Showmen from all over the country offered Mrs. Kennedy cash needed without security, but she let the sale go on. Dave Lackman bid eleven thousand one hundred dollars and the government gave him title to all of the equipment except thirteen cars claimed by St. Louis Rail and Equipment Company. Dave Lackman added the equipment purchased to his Lackman Exposition Shows for the 1925 season.

In 1925, the Conklin and Garret Shows, a ten car "gilly" show, was awarded the Western Canada

Class B. Circuit of Fairs. Both the Velare Brothers were with the Royal American and reported that their oil interests around Tulsa were showing a nice profit. Tom Hasson was promoting special events in Florida; and Nigro had his Great White Way Shows on tour. Jack (Dillon) Ruback was general manager of the Alamo Exposition Shows with A. Obadal as secretary-treasurer. Rice & Dorman Shows was back on the road after several years layoff, and Ben Krause announced that he was quitting the road after twenty years. He was going into the real estate business in Florida. Bert Earles, a ride owner, brought a Hey Dey Ride over from England; and J. C. Weer had a ride unit on the midway in South Bend, Indiana. O. N. Craft's Attractions were playing the California Fairs; while Lew Dufour filed voluntary bankruptcy in Brockton, Massachusetts. Elsie Calvert had the water show on the C. A. Wortham Shows; and Etta Louise Blake had a stomach operation in Detroit.

Big news of the 1925 season was the conversion of Johnny J. Jones to Christianity. This great showman had one vice, he drank too much occasionally. He admitted he was a heavy drinker. Early in October he was hospitalized in Knoxville, Tennessee, for two days. He alternately saw the pits of hell and portals of heaven. As he recovered his physician told him he needed a minister not a doctor of medicine. Jones consented and Dr. B. A. Bowers and his assistant Reverend H. H. Peacock of the Broadway Baptist Church were called and they visited the showman in his private car. He was converted, joined the church and was baptised before the show left Knoxville. He sent the following statement to the Billboard for publication:

"I thought that my time had come. At last I prayed! I prayed and prayed and all of a sudden everything brightened before me. I saw a beautiful light. You can't tell me there is no God. I know there is. I am off liquor for the rest of my life. I wouldn't take a drink for $20,000.00. I have always been fair and square in all of my dealings, but have been a boozer practically all of my life. I am through now. No more booze for me. I am supremely happy and my family are elated ovr the stand that I have taken. I expect to stick. No backsliding for me."

At the end of this season, A. H. Barkley, general agent for Sheesley, quit to take a rest after thirty-two years as general agent on circuses and carnivals. Harold Barlow was buying equipment for his Barlow's Big City Shows; and both Billie Clark's Famous Broadway Shows and the Dykman & Joyce Shows were blown down on lots in Daytona, Florida. Noble C. Fairly Shows were out late in Louisiana; but the Great Sutton midway had closed in Arkansas for the winter. Rubin Gruberg bought some of the equipment of the defunct T. A. Wolfe Shows. A. H. Barkley came out of his three weeks of retirement to sign with D. D. Murphy Shows as General Agent.

CIRCUS SIDE SHOW. A "String Show," a "Pit Show" or a "Ten-in-One." On a carnival it would be possible for it to be all of them. (See Glossary.) On a circus the side show was called the "Kid Show." Author's collection.

MODEL T FORDS AT THE CARNIVAL. Mid-twenties on the Conklin & Garrett Shows in Canada. Courtesy J. W. Patty Conklin.

The Walter Savidge Amusement Company closed its nineteenth season and went into its winter quarters in Wayne, Nebraska. This was the most unique carnival on tour and it had over thirty successful seasons. The feature show on the midway was the Walter Savidge Players, a tented repertorie company. This tent dramatic show changed plays each day, just as the six hundred other repertorie companies that were traveling independently were doing. Savidge had added some carnival shows and rides to his "rep" show, not realizing that his tent show then became just another show on his carnival midway. He always carried a repertorie of good plays and hired competent people for the company. Season of 1925, one of these people was a young actor named Lysle Talbot.

The 1926 season was a poor one for carnivals. The moving picture theatre owners were now accepted business men in every town. They belonged to Chambers of Commerce, Merchants Associations, and were even elected to city councils and sometimes mayors of their respective towns. They fought all outdoor amusements, but particularly tented dramatic shows and carnivals. And, they managed to close hundreds, even thousands, of good show towns to tented attractions. Tent dramatic shows never recovered from this opposition. The collective amusement industry still had all of its agents, those same men who had kept towns open and routes booked for their shows during the "everything goes"

era of midways. To those agents, the motion picture industries crusade against outdoor shows was only another obstacle to be overcome. They managed to keep their shows routed even though some of the dates were not as profitable as they would have like them to be. In a few years the carnivals had forgotten that they had been marked for extinction by their indoor competitors. Competitors that they had nourished on their midways only twenty years before.

Coleman Brothers did very well in Connecticut that year; but K. G. Barkoot Shows was seized by the sheriff in Dayton, Ohio, for an unpaid note of over sixteen thousand dollars. Tommy J. Tidwell had a show in Texas; and R. T. Wade had the Michigan Greater Shows. J. C. McCaffery was manager of Rubin & Cherry; and Billie Clark had closed his Famous Broadway midway. F. L. Flack reported that he had the "worst still date season in history" with his Northwestern Shows, but his fair dates were profitable. In November all shows playing Florida dates were reporting poor business. No serious wrecks or floods occurred during the year for which the harassed showmen could be thankful.

Johnny J. Jones had two big shows on the road in 1927; and Benny Krause retired from Florida real estate, bought excess equipment from Rubin Gruberg and put out a new show. Harold Bushea was general agent for the John Francis Shows; while T. W. (Slim) Kelly had carried his Coney Island Side Shows to the

CHRISTMAS GREETING . Beckman & Gerety Shows. Courtesy Harry Frost, Minnesota State Fair.

Royal American midway. On May 7, J. C. Simpson married Miss Marie Gerson in St. Louis; a mating of two wonderful people. Nat Worman was general superintendent of Bernardi Greater Shows; and "Pop" C. Smith, formerly of the Smith Greater Shows, had joined the Coe Brothers. John W. Wilson and J. J. Page had their Page & Wilson Shows out for a second season. Doc Waddell returned to carnivals as press agent for Dodson. A minister now, he began to hold daily church services in the wild west show arena.

C. R. Leggette's was the first train north out of McGehee, Arkansas, in four weeks. His show had been marooned there by the 1927 floods. All the show's able bodied men worked on the levees and were given credit by the townspeople for having helped save the town. After all personnel had been given typhoid shots, show train pulled out of town for Pilcher, Oklahoma, six hundred seventy miles away. First twenty miles, the tracks were covered by two to three feet of water. A man waded ahead of the locomotive with a long pole to ascertain if the small bridges and trestles were still intact. The pole also served to ward off the swimming water moccasin and cottonmouth snakes.

A showman observed that the reason for no water shows now was "girls on streets wear less than the diving girls." Johnny J. Jones gave a party on May 20 for the birthdays of Etta Louise Blake and Etta Louise (Hody) Hurd Jones. Dodson played to a total blank at Beaver Dam, Wisconsin. He got the lights on only one night and no one came out then. Harry Illions, now Hyla Mayne's partner, had the Bozo ride on Jones Midway at Canadian National Exposition in Toronto for the first time anywhere. James E. Strates opened his Southern Tier shows at Elmira, N. Y., April 28 on thirty trucks.

On June 8th, the Morris & Castle Shows had an almost complete blow down in Hannibal, Missouri, but the wreckage was gathered together and loaded back on the wagons. When the train was loaded, it

PERSONAL CHRISTMAS GREETINGS, from C. A. Wortham. Courtesy Harry Frost, Minnesota State Fair.

Southern Tier Shows, 1923

Courtesy Art Doc Miller

proceeded to Decatur, Illinois, where men and material were waiting to rebuild the shows. John R. (Coal Oil Johnny) Castle and R. L. Lohmar had located a high and dry lot in Decatur, and the show was unloaded and spotted on location as always, except now most of it had to be rebuilt. Under the direction of that master builder, "Chew of Tobacco Jack" Rhoades, men worked night and day restoring the equipment. The shows opened to good business five days after they pulled onto the lot.

Thomas J. Littlejohn had no carnival to play his circuit on nine Georgia fairs in 1927, so he put his Thomas J. Littlejohn's Shows back on the road in 1928 to insure his having a show for these dates. It was with Littlejohn back in 1914 or 1915 that a young man did his first full season with a carnival. This young fellow is still active in the field at this time (1972). He claims to have been general agent longer than any person now living. And he is still promoting new fairs, and successful ones too, every few years. One of the few great old-time showmen still alive, J. C. McCarter has homes in Charlotte, North Carolina, and Miami, Florida.

Mabel Mack's Mule Circus was with Ziedman & Pollie in 1927. That year she carried twenty-seven head of stock and twenty-eight people with her attraction. Rubin Gruberg bought the Ziedman and Pollie Shows at end of season to be used as a "number two Rubin Show" the following year, while Johnny J. Jones announced that he was combining his two midways. Page and Wilson dissolved their partnership in November and Page planned his J. J. Page Shows for 1928. Mr. Mathis of Warren Tank Car Company, Warren, Pennsylvania, was constantly on the move getting orders for those new seventy-two foot steel flat cars and stock cars. Every midway owner that could afford new rolling stock was ordering them.

Early in 1928, Ed Foley bought Ed Burk's interest in the Foley and Burk Shows on the West Coast. An eighteen year partnership was now ended. Ralph Miller sustained a hundred fifty-thousand dollar loss when his Miller Bros. winter quarters burned in Greenville, S. C. "Miss Annie" Gruberg stated that she bought the Ziedman and Pollie Shows for $12,650.00 to satisfy a mortgage. John W. Wilson

SEASON'S OPENING. J. W. Patty Conklin and his mother, Mrs. Jim Conklin, are pictured in front of the office tent. Conklin & Garrett, a "gilly" show, had no office wagon. Courtesy J. W. Patty Conklin

"GILLY SHOW" TRAIN. Conklin & Garrett train in the twenties.
Courtesy J. W. Patty Conklin.

SAME TRAIN. Baggage cars in which the show equipment was
transported. Courtesy J. W. Patty Conklin.

"BLOWDOWN." Lou Dufour Shows, 1923. Lou never operated with a full midway after that season. He found that he could make more money with less worry as an independent attraction owner. He still has independent attractions on the midway at Canadian National Exhibition in Toronto. Courtesy Lou Dufour.

was to be the General Manager of the New Cetlin & Wilson Shows, a "gilly" show. Ada Myers was to have the Minstrel Show with the Royal American; and Wilbur S. Cherry was taking a rest in Montgomery, Alabama.

In June, Abe Jones, Johnny J's brother, died. Rubin Gruberg announced that he would carry no more gaming concessions with his midways. One of Bill Hames' two midways had a blow down in Great Bend, Kansas. This was one of the few seasons in his long career as carnival owner that Mr. Hames carried a carnival outside the boundaries of the great State of Texas. This 1928 season was marred by numerous blowdowns, floods and wrecks. It was noted for having a president of the United States visit a carnival midway. President and Mrs. Calvin Coolidge visited the Brundage midway at the Tri-State Fair in Superior, Wisconsin. Evangelist Billy Sunday and Mrs. Sunday had lunch in Eddie Madigan's cookhouse on the Johnny J. Jones lot after Sunday had preached to a turn away crowd in downtown Hopkinsville, Kentucky. F. H. Bee had the Bee Amusement Company playing in Tennessee and Kentucky, while J. J. Colley's Shows played Oklahoma.

The old Madam's twentieth century daughter started her thirty-first year on May 30, 1929, with over two hundred of her still boisterous midways criss crossing North America. A Sunday afternoon visit to almost any railroad junction point would reward the visitor with a view of one of her show's trains enroute from somewhere to someplace. Trains upon whose flat cars nestled groups of mysterious wagons. Wagons that now seemed to be resting, gaining a brief respite from the wild pace and raucous noise of the week long activities. Tired working men resting on dirty quilts, would peer out with contemptuous leers at the poor non-trouping town "marks." As the train passed out of the railroad yards, an elephant's trunk might be seen poking inquiringly through an open stock car door. The privilege car with its lunch counter and hidden crap tables and slot machines would be followed by the sleeping cars with tousled heads peering from uncurtained windows at the pitiful people who had never enjoyed the pleasures of midway life.

Had you been an unenlightened fan, you might have said "there goes a circus." Your ignorance of outdoor show business would have been evident.

Business on carnivals this last year before the Great Depression was not as good as many would have liked. However, all the big shows survived that season. There were the usual number of small shows being framed and going broke. Wilbur S. Cherry had died in Chicago on December 16, 1928, and had been buried in the Showmen's League Showmen's Rest with Masonic honors.

Early in 1929, Frank Bergan moved his Whip and 10-in-1 to the Sheesley winter quarters. Tom Hasson and Billie Clark, after ten years apart, put the Famous Broadway Shows out again. K. G. Barkoot now called his show Barkoot Brothers; and Art Lewis was manager of the Artdick Shows. Doc Waddell gave his famous "Sawdust and Spangles" sermon over the amplifying system at the Tyler, Texas Fair. "Speedy" Babs set a record on Venice Pier, in California, by remaining on the straight up and down motor drome wall at full speed for three hours and four minutes. Karns Brothers had completed twenty-nine years in outdoor show business as fat people, while Kempt Brothers had been with their Model Cities exhibition for twenty-five years. The Al Wagners were now in the business; and Bert Hoss was set up outside the Cleveland, Ohio, city limits with three rides and fifteen concessions.

J. W. WADSWORTH. Former pit show operator who managed the Princess Olga Show in the late Twenties. Courtesy Art Doc Miller.

ON THE FERARI SHOWS IN THE "GOOD OLD DAYS." Courtesy L. Harvey Doc Cann.

There was a certain amount of mystery regarding circus trains, but never as much as provided by an old-time carnival train. Mama and the girls, even eleven year old Owen, might not know what that circus wagon housed. But thirteen year old Joe could tell them quickly, "That's got the reserved seat chairs in it, I helped unload them last year on the T and P lot." With twenty or more shows on a carnival midway, most of them owned by independent operators, loads on wagons were apt to be changed often. Even the owner of the midway could never be sure of any wagon's contents from one week to the next.

No loaded circus train, no matter how rough the tear down had been, ever looked as if it were tired and resting. Carnival trains definitely did give that impression. Carnival wagons seemed to be squatting like setting hens on the flat cars. No circus would leave a stock car door open on move between towns, and no circus elephant ever stuck her trunk out as the train moved. Here was a perfect example of the freedom of carnival people from all inhibitions. Just as the individual carny was given the right to live, without censure from his fellows, exactly as he or she desired. That elephant was given the freedom of sticking his trunk out of the car door.

HORSE RACING. Cabarrus County Fair, Concord, N.C., 1923. Courtesy Clyde D. Probst, Jr. Cabarrus County Fair.

Cabarrus

County

RUBIN & CHERRY SHOWS. Cabarrus County Fair, 1928. Courtesy Clyde D. Probst, Jr., manager, Cabarrus County Fair.

ZEIDMAN & POLLIE SHOWS. Cabarrus County Fair, 1923. Courtesy Clyde D. Probst, Jr., Cabarrus County Fair.

Fair

THE MONKEY SHOW. Conklin & Garrett Shows, mid-twenties. Courtesy J. W. Patty Conklin.

LITTLE HORSE SHOW. "Single-O Grind Show." Author's collection.

Old-time showman, Jack B. Cullen, after working the New Albany, Indiana, Street Celebration said, "It seems to me that day of locating shows and rides on the streets is a thing of the past, so long as the automobiles remain in the numbers we have them now." Ralph R. Miller, who owned four carnivals, was building a complete town in Louisana. With its own postoffice, Millerville was being built ten miles outside Baton Rouge. In October, Freckles, the trained chimpanzee was kept in the Charlottesville, Virginia, jail for a week. Freckles who was detained because of an ownership dispute was happy in jail with plenty of food and cigarettes provided by the jailers and sheriff's deputies. Only nine shows were on the road in December that year.

As this decade ended, many of the old established carnivals were not prepared to face the problems of the depression days. The owners and agents of these shows were old or tired, or both; and were not ready to adapt to new conditions. The days of starting a carnival "on a shoe string" were over; and many owners, and would-be owners, were destined to find themselves without that "shoe string." Men like Fred Beckman and Barney Gerety, Rubin Gruberg, Capt. John Sheesley, John Francis, John R. Ward, James E. Strates, Dodson Brothers, Paddy Conklin, C. J. Sedlmayr and Sam Soloman would actually gain strength during the difficult ten years ahead. All of them were capable men with resourceful and talented staff members. It is doubtful that any of them would have gone as far as they did in developing the super carnivals that were to come, had it not been for two men, who in 1969 celebrated their seventy-fifth active year in outdoor show business.

These two men, the Velare Brothers, had started as circus acrobats, moved to the carnivals as a free act, then went into concession business on established midways. They bought rides and booked rides, shows and concessions on other men's carnivals. In 1929 they were active in ownership and management of the Royal American Shows. Along with Carl J. Sedlmayr they were quietly building that carnival into a major midway. Some idea of the innovations that these men would introduce into the collective amusement field was forecast by a "wild scheme" they tried out in 1927 at the Minnesota State Fair. They had the audacity to put two ferris wheels side by side at that fair. First time it had been done. Their ferris wheel business went way up and they kept the two wheels together from then on. All competitors rushed to secure another wheel to mate with the one they had. In the thirties, the Velare Boys, would be the initiators and other showmen the imitators.

CONKLIN & GARRETT SHOWS. At one of their Canadian dates in the Twenties. Show never played the United States. Courtesy J. W. Patty Conklin.

Dragging The Midway

The Story

Old-time midway attraction owners used all sorts of tricks to entice potential patrons to their attraction's front doors. Wild Animal Showmen sent their trainers with huge chunks of raw meat on large forks to "drag" the townspeople down to the animal show tent to see the animals fed. The "Old Dago," Johnny J. Bejanno, who used a megaphone long after electronic speech amplification was introduced on midways, always tried to be the first at the front gate to start "dragging." Using his megaphone, he announced that the first free outside exhibitions would positively be given on the front of his Circus Side Show. In this sketch, we see that the wild animal trainer has gotten to the front gate first, and will "drag" the people right on by the side show and down the midway to the wild animal show tent. The "Old Dago" (this was used by his best friends as a term of affection) is seen to the left. Original sketch by Marian L. McKennon.

The thirty-first anniversary of the American Collective Amusement Industry passed on Decoration Day 1930 as unnoticed as all of her birthdays have. The industry was now accepted, even though not considered quite respectable, as a major segment of the outdoor amusement industry. Many circus troupers had been forced to join the "hamburger outfits," as they were referred to by circus people. There were fewer of the big "one nighters" each season; and circus men, even though they abhorred staying in a town longer than one day, had no other choice. It was either join a carny or quit the road. The latter was unthinkable. What circus trouper wanted to become a towner and stay in one dull town every day?

The influx of these circus men, even though few of the old-time carnies will admit it, had an ameliorative influence on the carnival business. None of them ever became owners of midways, even though several might have if World War II had not intervened. But most of them did become trusted members of carnival staffs before this decade of depressed business activity and unemployment ended. Their basic training in the "no lost motion school" of the circus served them well on the slower-moving carnivals, and their knowledge of "how to get things done" was invaluable to the midways as they struggled through the calamitous days of the early thirties.

Johnny J. Jones Exposition entered this fourth decade of carnival business as the undisputed "king of them all." Beckman & Gerety's C. A. Wortham Shows, Morris & Castle Shows and Rubin Gruberg's number one show, the Rubin & Cherry Shows, were all pushing the little man with the big mustache. All pushing him hard and often trying to get enough of his big fair dates to make a route for which they could build a midway equal to his "Mighty Monarch of the Tented World." Dodson Brothers' World's Fair Shows, Capt. John M. Sheesley's Mighty Midway, Frank West's World Wonder Shows, Mrs. Melville's Melville-Reiss Shows, to name only a few of the over two hundred midways now operating, were all struggling just as hard to improve their own position in the carnival world. Practically unnoticed, another midway, less than ten years old in 1930, was rapidly catching up with these leaders in the carnival field. In just five more years, it would supplant all of them and become the leader of the industry.

This, the Royal American Shows, owned and managed by Carl J. Sedlmayr and the Velare Brothers, would gain supremacy over all other midways by 1935. A supremacy that it has never relinquished since, except for a short time during the war emergencies of the forties. Now, in 1972, owned and managed by C. J. Sedlmayr, II, it is undoubtedly the "greatest thing on wheels." Season of 1971 it carried the greatest number of flatcars ever carried by any travelling amusement organization. It actually had several hundred feet more flatcar space than any other show in history. Spring of 1930, however, it was still struggling for its rightful place in the carnival world.

Early that year, Frank Bergan and Julius Griffel purchased William Glick's interest in the Bernardi Greater Shows. A relative of Griffel's, Max Linderman, was made general manager of the shows. Willie Glick then put out his own William Glick Shows on twenty railroad cars. Dave Stock booked all of his rides on Glick's midway. Thos. (Slim) Kelly had circus side shows (freak) on both of Rubin Gruberg's carnivals, and Gruberg stated on March 22nd, "I believe industrial conditions over the country will be materially improved during the next thirty days." Rubin was a much better carnival manager than he was prophet. That 1930 season was disastrous for all outdoor show business, although the true magnitude of this catastrophic season would not be realized until 1931.

In September the Billboard stated that C. M. Nigro, former partner of J. George Loos and owner of the Great White Way Shows, was in need of bare sustenance on his little acreage near Racine, Wisconsin, where he had hoped to start a poultry farm. That same month, Beckman & Gerety dropped the C. A. Wortham from their title and Beckman & Gerety's World's Best Shows was painted on all their wagons and rail equipment. In October, State Fair of Texas at Dallas reported business down thirty percent from previous year. Most fairs and shows failed to report their business as few showmen have ever enjoyed reporting poor financial returns.

The man who booked Frank Gaskill's route for his first carnival, Harold Bushea, died in May, 1930; and Leon W. Washburn, one-time owner of a large midway followed him to the always dry and green show grounds in November. Then on Christmas Day, all Carnivaldom was stunned by the message sent from Florida to showmen across the nation. Johnny J. Jones was dead. This greatest of all carnival showmen, this mild little man who had never knowingly been unkind to any person, was gone. His over-indulgence in his only vice, a vice that he had so hopefully renounced a few years ago, had made him an easy prey for the director of that bourne from which no traveler ever returns.

January 12, 1931, Andre K. DeKreko of Oriental Show fame died, and in April Bert Hoss

A DEPENDABLE INSTITUTION

E. LAWRENCE PHILLIPS
Presents
Johnny J. Jones Mighty EXPOSITION

The Show Beautiful

Wint...
Augu...

Perman...
511 C St., N. E...

Our Recently Concluded Season was one of Record-Breaking Grosses

THE JOHNNY J. JONES EXPOSITION—illuminated with twelve mammoth lighting towers of the latest design and trimmed in neon and "jewel lighting" splendor will take to the road in 1939 incomparable in its field! With unbounded confidence in the integrity of our enterprise—carrying on in the best traditions of our founder and rising to new heights of achievement we are proud to offer this 1939 midway to the thousands who by their annual acclaim have made the name JOHNNY J. JONES EXPOSITION the greatest of all outdoor amusement organizations.

The World's Oldest INDEPENDENT Outdoor Exposition

40 ENTERTAINING AND THRILL... ATTRACTIONS

ROYAL RUSSIAN MIDGETS	TWO-HEADED BABY	MERRY-GO-ROUND
ERNIE-LEN	ALLIGATOR FARM	CATERPILLAR
DARKTOWN FOLLIES	TEMPLE des RHUMBA	HEY-DEY
CHEZ LA FEMME	GLOBE-A-DROME	FOUR FERRIS WHEELS
LOOK	MARINE EXHIBIT	LINDY LOOP
FAT GIRL TWINS	PENNY ARCADE	FOUR KIDDIE RIDES
FREAK MUSEUM	OLGA	RIDEE-O
PALACE OF ILLUSIONS	EVER SINCE EVE	AUTO SKOOTER
	INTERNATIONAL CASINO	AUTO SPEEDWAY

V. C. FLEMING *Director General*	J. C. SIMPSON *General Representative*	J. C. THOMAS *Special Agent 1938* *General Representative 1939*	TOM M. ALLEN *Manager*	RALPH LOCKE... *Secretary*
	JOE SANDERLIN *Superintendent of Tickets*	JOE McKENNON *General Superintendent*	ERNIE DeFORT Canadian Double-Bodied Boy MRS. F. DeFORT, MOTHER A Pleasant Season With the J. J. Expo.	20TH SEASON AND STILL W... Clothes Pin Pitch Til You W... Mr. and Mrs. Ernest Dell... GEORGE DIXIE, WOODROW... Agents
3 Good Shows and a Winter One Regards to All Personnel CARL J. LAUTHER	HARRY L. WILSON HARVEY T. WILSON Going Big — Thanks to E. Lawrence Phillips	EVER SINCE EVE MOE EBERSTEIN, Mgr. Richard Livingston, Lecturer, Irving Strang, front. The finest Front and Backend Midway in my experience.	Thanks to the Johnny J. Jones Expo. for a wonderful season. MR. and MRS. J. LEE CUDDY	Caterpillar Rid... With E. Lawrence Phillips fr... start. 1938 Top Season... PEARL RINGER, Own... BILL KEYS, Mgr. Scotty, Al, Red, Smokey and...
INTERNATIONAL CASINO in the top money and a top season. MR. and MRS. BOB EDWARDS	RUBE NIXON'S MONKEY CIRCUS Back with "The Show Beautiful" and glad to be with it.	CHEZ LaFEMME MR. and MRS. HUGHIE MACK THE HORNER TWINS PAUL SPRAGUE, Announcer	12th Season No praise can be too high accorded The Johnny J. Jones Exposition. FRED MAURICE and GANG Col. H. M. Thompson, Lecturer	
A Top Money Show BRANSON'S GLOBE-A-DROME Eddie Phillimore Mary Binger Chuck Thomas Speedy Bowers Freddie Sims	DARKTOWN FOLLIES Thanks to E. Lawrence Phillips For a Nice Season, a Good Route and a Winter Bank Roll EDDIE JAMEISON	A Wonderful Season With the MIGHTY MONARCH Thanking Mr. E. Lawrence Phillips. Will see you next year. ROYAL RUSSIAN MIDGETS	A Wonderful Season with the AUTO SKOOTER AUTO SPEEDWAY STRATOSHIP R. E. HANEY, Owner	15th Season Under the Old a... JOHNNY J. JONES Bann... ROCKY ROAD TO DUB... PENNY ARCADE MRS. BERTHA (GYP) McD...

ANNUALLY SINCE 1899

Thanking Committees,
Fair Secretaries and Officials
for this Pleasant Season

NOW BOOKING FOR 1939

Fair Secretaries and Committees Are Invited To Inspect Our Offering Before Contracting Their Midway

Courtesy Albert Conover

Courtesy Albert Conover

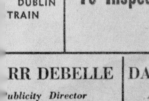

Courtesy Albert Conover

1930 — Wheeling WVA

MELVILLE-REISS SHOWS, 1930. Earl Purtle and Harvey Wilson, well-known operator of fun and glass houses, were both with this show. Courtesy Earl Purtle.

followed his first partner, Johnny J. Jones. In May J. L. Cronin, former midway owner was found dead in his hotel room, and on June 21st August Greenburg, owner of Greenburg Amusement Company died in Denver, Colorado. Owners and former owners were dying off fast but shows themselves were due to go as quickly this season.

J. L. Flack's Northwestern Shows closed after only nine weeks on the road. All the carnivals were thankful to get back in winter quarters at the end of that season. Two major shows were beset by misfortunes all season, the Johnny J. Jones Exposition and the D. D. Murphy Shows. This 1931 year of hardships would be last one for the latter show.

D. D. Murphy Shows started their fair season at the Anderson, Indiana, Free Fair. Business was down; but show manager Brophy, like many other managers, hadn't cut the show expenses to the level of anticipated grosses. Most managers had thought that the depression would be over in a few months, and only a few had managed shows during the last big money panic in 1907. Few of them were prepared

psychologically for the conditions they now faced. Mr. Brophy had done very little to get Mr. Murphy's shows ready to meet the almost daily crises the show encountered. Every week, paydays were met with "brass money" and savings were dug into for "white money" to pay the railroad move.

Finally, Labor Day Week at the Ohio State Fair in Columbus, none of the midway shows were allowed to set up on the fairgrounds. Hagenbeck Wallace Circus which was playing as the grandstand attraction for the fair had exclusive for shows on the grounds. Its huge, eight center-pole menagerie tent was set up on the midway and the Hagenbeck animals and all side show acts were combined into one big twenty-five cent show. The Murphy Shows rides did not gross enough to pay the carnival's expenses that week. Next week in Indianapolis at the Indiana State Fair the midway made enough to get the show train to the Kentucky State Fair at Louisville.

According to Tom Sharkey, who was with the show that season, Brophy had enough money in the wagon to get the equipment all back into St. Louis winter quarters, if they had ended the season in

Louisville. But he had three more fairs booked and he was determined to play them. He used the last of their savings to move the show to the Knoxville, Tennessee, Fair. It was almost a blank and the next week at the Chattanooga Fair was worse. Sharkey was sent into Atlanta to secure a quarters as it would now be impossible to get the train back to St. Louis. Last week of season in Atlanta was another blank, and the show closed without any hope of ever opening again. Brophy and Arthur Daily did play Anderson, South Carolina, Fair with part of the rides but just barely made expenses with them.

The Johnny J. Jones Exposition, without the genius of its founder, lost thirty-four thousand dollars that 1931 season. Troupers on the great show, which was being operated by trustees under a court order, thought that the bottom had been reached; but the next two years would be much worse. Melville-Reiss Shows had not come out of quarters that spring because of the illness of manager Harry G. Melville. On December 12th the equipment was sold for debt at the Charlotte, North Carolina, winter quarters. Harry Melville died just a week before the sale.

In April, it had been announced that John R. Castle and a man named Payne had bought Milton Morris' interest in the Morris & Castle Shows. No sum of money was reported. Milt Morris left quarters as did Mrs. John R. Castle. April, 1932, the wedding of Milton Morris and Ida Belle Vaught was reported. Miss Vaught was the former Mrs. John R. Castle. "Coal Oil Johnny" Castle did not do so well with the

show in 1931, as it was sold to the First National Bank of Shreveport, Louisiana, at a sheriff's sale on December 12th.

In addition to other trouble, the motion picture theatre owners renewed their drives to close as many towns as possible to outdoor amusements. In spite of all their problems, some showmen, like Sam Soloman, reported that they had made some money that season. This was the first year for Sam to have his Sol's Liberty Shows on trucks.

In April, press agent William J. Hilliar was riding in the observation car of the Illinois Central's "Seminole" passenger train enroute to the Rubin & Cherry winter quarters in Montgomery, Alabama. In a railroad yard in Mississippi, a freight train pulled in alongside this crack passenger train. Several grimy-faced "hoboes" were riding in an open coal car as it passed the observation car. One of them nudged the others. They all waved and yelled, "Hi Bill, we're on our way to Montgomery too."

In November, John J. Slangler, a former trouper who had retired to Tennessee visited a little carnival in his home town. One of the talkers had an extra large "Tip," or crowd, in front of his bally, and he was giving them an eloquent spiel. Slangler climbed onto the bally platform and asked if he could "Jam." Being assured that he could, he made about two hundred signs with his fingers and hands, and "turned" almost all of the "tip" in to see the show. The only known instance of "Jamming" to a deaf and dumb group.

MAIN ENTRANCE, Conklin All-Canadian Shows. Courtesy J. W. Patty Conklin.

Harry Frost   Courtesy Harry Frost, Minnesota State Fair

waiting for the cut rate ticket sales. Most carnival offices adopted rules that no "Jamming" would be tolerated on any shows except the "string shows"; but some members of the staff had to patrol the midway to enforce it. Any talker who had two priced tickets for his show could "jam" at will, if not watched.

In 1934, Johnny Castle asked Joe McKennon, who was ticket auditor for the midway, "Are they jamming back there?" Joe's instant reply was, "You know damned well they are. It would take ten men to stop it." Show had a no-jamming rule with ten bally shows.

In January, 1932, L. J. Heth's creditors had a meeting after he was adjudged bankrupt. His big railroad show never went on the road again. He did get a new show out on trucks in a couple of years. The fair manager at Largo, Florida, Fair carried eleven dollars worth of Jack Murray's "brass" to Johnny J. Jones office and got "white money" for it. Murray was now co-owner and manager of the show. The "brass" had gotten mixed in with the fair's percentage of the proceeds, which was always paid in "white" money. Jones Shows halted its tour and went back to quarters until time for the big dates in the North. Maynes-Illions rides were not to go out with Jones Shows until fairs started.

T. W. (Slim) Kelly claims to be the first talker to ever use a "Jam" on the front of a show. He says he used it first time in Washington, D.C. in 1918. A "Jam" on a show front has always gone something like this: "Now, Ladies and Gentlemen, the established price of this attraction has always been twenty-five cents, but for the next three minutes I am instructing the ticket sellers to lay aside their quarter tickets and let everybody in on a child's ticket for a dime." This "jamming" was a good practice for long "string shows" with their open fronts and long lines of canvas banners.

Most all so-called side shows or freak shows were of this open front "string" show type and some means was needed to get a crowd inside quickly when the tent was empty or near empty. Nothing pulls other humans into a show as well as seeing lots of their fellowmen inside enjoying themselves. A "jam" could be used and fill the tent. Then the talkers and ticket sellers could "grind away" for some time at the established price. Talkers on all shows adopted the practice, however, and soon no regular admission tickets were being sold as the townspeople were

CARNIVAL ELEPHANT. Dodson's World's Fair Shows. Many carnivals have carried elephants. Courtesy Albert Conover.

124

MORRIS & CASTLE SHOWS. Dallas Fair, 1928. Race track shown was on the area now occupied by the Cotton Bowl. Courtesy Fred D. Pfening, Jr.

In April, Lackman & Carson Show Company was adjudged bankrupt at El Reno, Oklahoma. In July, the Eugene Murphy Shows were closed by attachments in Connecticut; and Dave Lackman opened his Lackman Amusement Company in the Southwest. Dodson reported business bad every week, while most show owners or press agents reported "show's receipts are consistent with the times." Only seventy-six midways were open by May first. A few others did open to play their fair dates.

The Jones Shows had been reorganized, and opened with Mrs. Jones, Eddie Madigan and Jack Murray as co-owners. Madigan and Murray were in on ownership because of notes they held which had been signed by Johnny J. Jones before his death. These notes covered sums advanced to the little man during the last year of his life. Money that he used to keep the carnival on the road during the almost non-existent business of that season. Robert S. Bigsby, superintendent for Mr. Jones since 1916, was relieved of his duties as trustee by the reorganization. It was well that he was relieved as he was called to join his old boss on the big grassy lots in July. Jones Shows' business was below expectations at all its fair dates, and its dejected train slunk into winter quarters at Savannah, Georgia. (Those are the only words that

could aptly describe a show train of a bankrupt show. The writer has been on a few.)

Marjorie Kemp, featured rider in her brother Walter's lion motor drome with Beckman & Gerety Shows was badly mauled by lions, Sultan and Prince during her act in the drome. Walter was also badly clawed as he beat them off her. In October, John R. Castle married again. His new wife came on the midway with Russell's Penitentiary Portrayal, a crime does not pay show, in 1930. This tall blonde beauty was living proof that opposites do attract. She was much taller than her little, quick-tempered Irish husband. She made him a good loving wife, and her "Crime" shows contributed to his support in later years.

J. C. Simpson left the Rubin & Cherry organization. Rubin still managed to keep two big units operating. As an anchor, he had kept the great Canadian National Exhibition in Toronto for several years. The net from that one big exposition was sufficient to make it worth while to maintain a show of the caliber required to play it. Bill Hames was a multi-show unit operator again that year with three midways in Texas and Oklahoma. Eddie Madigan left the Jones Show after fifteen years and joined the Castle-Erlich-Hirsch Shows in Shreveport, Louisiana, winter quarters.

NAVAL SEARCHLIGHTS. Royal American Shows, Minnesota State Fair, 1932. These lights were the second step in the Royal American's climb to the greatest of them all. Courtesy Harry Frost, Minnesota State Fair.

In 1933, many of the smaller "gilly" carnivals started moving on their own motor trucks. Lew Dufour reported that his "Unborn Shows" had showed to two and one half million paid admissions in last four years. Only eleven of these "Pickled Punk Shows" were on midways in 1932, but he had sixteen of them booked season of 1931. These shows consisted of large specimen bottles each containing a human fetus ranging from a few weeks to a full term nine month baby. These "pickled punk shows" grossed untold millions of dollars for their operators over a thirty-year period.

The World of Mirth Shows opened at York, Pennsylvania, under the management of Max Linderman, first week in May. Victor D. Leavitt, Bostock's agent in 1899, died in Seattle, Washington, on May 8, 1933. Mrs. Leavitt said that she would continue operating his new Pacific States Shows. Milton Morris left the Rubin & Cherry Shows after two years. Clifford (Specks) Groscurth was business manager for the Southern Flyers Air Show. Doc Waddell was back with Dodson this year, his sixtieth year on road. Mrs. Bertha (Nat Reiss) Melville booked six rides with T. L. Dedrick's New Deal Shows, and Baba Delgarian had his Garden of Allah Show with the Castle-Erlich-Hirsch Shows.

Walter White, manager, organized the "number two Rubin Shows," the Model Shows of America, moved from quarters and opened in just a few days. It opened at the State Fair of Illinois at Springfield. In the meantime, Rubin was billing his Rubin & Cherry Shows as Model Shows of America at all of his Canadian Fair dates. He closed this show early, after playing the New Jersey State Fair at Trenton. He left it in quarters on the Trenton fair grounds. The plight of the Johnny J. Jones Shows had the sympathy of the entire industry.

Mrs. Johnny J. (Hody Hurd) Jones now had full control of the title and the remaining equipment. This young woman, barely thirty years old, fought a valiant and futile battle to save for her son the heritage that his father had spent a lifetime accumulating. Hody Jones was no "town mark." She was born in a carnival wagon alongside Percy Munday's Animal Show with the Gaskill-Munday Carnival Company.

Her mother was a wild animal trainer and her father one of the greatest spielers or talkers of his day; this meant that little Hody, like thousands of carnival children since then, had a whole magic midway as her playground. Her older sister, Bootsie, was her tutor. Bootsie knew where all the best places to play were to be found. They were sternly warned away from the wild animal arena and cages, as their older brother had been killed by one of the big cats when he was just an infant. His nursemaid left him too close to a cage. But they could play almost anywhere else on the midway. They were a little afraid of the bearded Abdullah over in the Streets of Cairo, but his Turkish wife slipped them sweet meats frequently and they did like to watch the belly dancers do their acts. Bootsie could do a fair imitation of those dancers, but she had to be careful where she danced as their father, Tom, didn't exactly approve of her doing it.

There was one big disadvantage to being a carnival child. You had too many parents. Every adult on the show, from the ride hands on the merry-go-round and the canvas men on the society circus to the "mitt readers" on the "mitt camp" (palm reader on fortune-telling booth), and the owners of the carnival all felt that it was their right and duty to help rear a midway child. Bootsie and Hody enjoyed the life and freedom of carnival children, even though they did get frequent spankings from one or another of their three hundred self-appointed foster parents.

Now, in 1933, Hody used all the knowledge gained from a lifetime on carnival midways, but two years of poor management had left the great show so debilitated that no one could save it in this third year of depression. First eight weeks of the season, the

show, now on only twenty railroad cars, was beset by rain and more rain with the resultant lack of business. General manager Camaloa was replaced by highly capable Jack V. Lyles as the show moved into Washington, D.C. for its fourth week of rain and bad business. Three weeks in Baltimore resulted in only one profitable week. Finally, on June 17th, the once-great carnival was tied up by the "Auspices" in Wilmington, Delaware. The midway did not gross enough on this ninth week of the season to pay them the amount guaranteed in their contract. Hody was taken to the hospital completely exhausted by the weeks of worry and hard work.

During the week of the long tie-up in Wilmington, Bootsie, assisted by Mrs. W. F. Korhn, Frances Shean and Fay Hearn, took over the job of feeding the hundred or more employees of the show itself. They prepared two meals a day, late breakfast and early dinner, in the galley of Mrs. Jones' private railroad car and served the show hands in relays from this improvised kitchen. After a week's layoff, arrangements were made to get the show train to Lancaster, Pennsylvania, for a week of fair business. Mrs. Jones was back on the show, but she was too ill to leave the private car. The next week, the show did fairly good business in Sunbury, Pennsylvania. It was here that the show began to feed all employees in a circus-style cook house. For nine days ending July 22nd, the show played a complete blank in Newtown, Pennsylvania. Then the train was moved over to

WHITE WING. Royal American Shows during the Thirties. He patrolled the midway with a pointed stick, a bag and a whistle. When he saw a piece of paper on the ground, he pointed the stick and rushed wildly toward it blowing the whistle loudly as he rushed. The pick-up was accomplished as scores of carnival patrons watched. Courtesy Harry Frost, Minnesota State Fair.

FOUR BIG ELI WHEELS IN A LINE. Tampa Fair, 1935. Royal American first grouped four wheels together at the Minnesota State Fair in 1933. This was their third step in the climb to outdo all competitors. Courtesy Lee A. Sullivan, Jr., president Eli Bridge Co.

Lewistown where the show laid off a week and "painted up" for the fair dates. With paint brought from winter quarters, all the rides and show fronts and properties were repainted.

The Jones route of fairs gave very poor financial returns to the show. Each week and each fair brought forth another series of emergencies and dilemmas. Mrs. Jones was now recovered enough to take charge of the operations, but there was no cash reserve left to keep it going. On October 11th news came from Norfolk, Virginia, "Jones Exposition Stranded." Southern Railroad had seized the show train for unpaid moving charges. One ride and two tents were still standing on the lot as were all the loaded wagons. A small tent was being used as a cook house for the few show hands who remained with the stranded equipment. Then on November 11th, news came from Norfolk that E. Lawrence Phillips, the one-armed promoter and motion picture theatre owner from Washington, D.C., had bought the Johnny J. Jones Exposition in its entirety. Phillips, a long-time friend of Mr. Jones, had come to the rescue of the show.

In September, Felice Bernardi had reported that his entire Bernardi Exposition Shows had been destroyed by fire while showing in the streets of Heppner, Oregon. "Nothing left but the iron tent stakes," he wired. In November, Bill Rice had both knees fractured in a Moultrie, Georgia, automobile accident; and in December, Max Linderman made headlines in York, Pennsylvania, newspapers by returning to York and paying all bills left unpaid when the World of Mirth Shows left in the Spring. The show was now in Richmond, Virginia, winter quarters.

The Velare Brothers and Sedlmayr were now forging ahead with their Royal American Shows. In 1932, they had purchased huge surplus Naval Searchlights from the government. Installed on the show grounds, the roving beams from these lights could be seen for a distance of forty to sixty miles. Many of the other shows were now trying to locate other surplus searchlights. Then at the Minnesota State Fair The Royal American unveiled their new idea for Ferris Wheels. This 1933 Fair season, they had four Big Eli Wheels in a row. These wheels were made by the Eli Bridge Company of Jacksonville, Illinois. Then they signed with the Western Canada Circuit to play the Class A Circuit on their 1934 tour. These July and August Fairs always were good for five weeks of top grosses.

Castle-Erlich-Hirsch, who had played those dates in 1933, were dumbfounded. John R. Castle and William R. Hirsch, owners of that successor to the Morris & Castle shows, decided that something drastic had to be done with their midway, if they were to continue as leaders in the carnival field. They announced that they were discarding all of their old carnival type shows and would build a new super midway for the 1934 season. Bob Lohmar was taken in as equal partner, and he designed ten new fronts for this new concept in carnival shows. Circus builder,

Joe McKennon, went to the Shreveport, Louisiana Fairgrounds from the Hagenbeck Wallace Circus to assist Lohmar in building this new midway.

Superintendent, "Chew of Tobacco" Jack Rhoades and his crew repaired and rebuilt the wagons and rolling stock, while trainmaster Grant Chandler used his train crew to get the train ready for a new season. Lohmar and McKennon used a big crew of men to build all of the new fronts. These fronts were built and set up that spring on the area on which the William R. Hirsch Memorial Coliseum now stands. Nothing like them had ever been attempted before by any traveling collective amusement organization.

A new title for this carnival was devised, the United Shows of America, which was promptly shortened to USA Shows by most people in the

SCROLL OF LIFE FRONT. New York World's Fair, 1939-1940. This "Life," "Unborn," or as commonly called by midway people, "Pickled Punk" Show was originated by Lou Dufour in the late Twenties. At one time, he had over twenty of these attractions booked on midways. These displays of human fetuses in bottles of preservatives have grossed untold millions of dollars on American carnivals. On some shows, they have outgrossed attractions with fifteen or twenty live performers. Courtesy Lou Dufour.

DIRECT FROM
A CENTURY OF PROGRESS
CHICAGO, ILLINOIS

MAJORIE KEMP AND HER FRIENDS. Royal American Shows. As
Majorie rode with lions in the Royal American Motordrome, Ethel
Purtle was carrying a big cat as passenger in the World of Mirth Shows
drome. Courtesy Harry Frost, Minnesota State Fair.

midway field. Season did not open until June 26th at
the Grand Forks, North Dakota, Fair. The season of
eighteen weeks had only one "still date." The other
seventeen weeks were profitable for the show.

Its feature attraction and show on the midway
was the Louisiana Lou Showboat Revue, a colored
minstrel show consisting of over thirty performers
and musicians. This performance was given in a
tented theatre set up behind a twenty-six foot high
front. A front that was the exact replica of an
old-time side wheel riverboat with its twelve foot high
paddle wheels turning in real water. The bally
platform for this one hundred forty foot long

riverboat front was the boat deck twelve feet above
the ground level. During the season, both Lohmar and
McKennon stopped often for admiring glances at
their handiwork. The genius of the former and the
skill of the latter had created a show front that was in
itself a midway attraction.

Before leaving winter quarters, all ten shows had
been gotten together. Two of them deserve special
mention. The first of these was the "Fat People"
show built and operated by the Karns Brothers of
"Jack and Jill" fame. This year seven hundred pound
Eddie managed the show and five hundred pound
Cliff sold the tickets as they had a better attraction

than themselves inside. Mrs. Clifford Karns, weight over seven hundred pounds, gave birth to a baby girl in a Shreveport hospital a few weeks before the season began.

Mrs. John R. Castle was planning a super "Crime Does Not Pay Show," when Clyde Barrow and Bonnie Parker were killed in an ambush near Shreveport. The death car disappeared a few days after this ambush. Everyone, including the sheriff of the Parish in which the ambush occurred, disclaimed any knowledge of the whereabouts of this bullet-ridden and blood-stained vehicle. At the Grand Forks Fair, the disappearance was explained. This relic of death was rolled out of one of the big carnival wagons into the Crime Show tent, as its central attraction.

In 1935, Mrs. Castle contracted the mothers of the two slain outlaws, and the two old ladies posed beside the automobile in which their children had met their death. They were joined later in the season by the father of John Dillinger, who posed along with them at every performance.

In 1934 the United Shows of America had the smallest staff ever carried by a really big carnival. William R. Hirsch was office manager assisted by one man, a man who had never been in outdoor show business before. Robert Lohmar was general agent and John R. Castle general manager. Jack Rhoades was superintendent, Oscar Halverson ride superintendent and Grant Chandler handled the train.

Only other member of the staff was Joe McKennon who assisted Castle in laying out the lot on Sunday afternoons after show train arrived in town. This job, usually done three days ahead of the show was done by these two men "Circus Style." McKennon then helped Rhoades put the show on the lot using rented Caterpillar tractors and inexperienced drivers. During the week he was auditor and handled the entire ticket department with its thirty-five ticket sellers and like number of ticket collectors. Saturday night, he again assisted "Chew of Tobacco" in getting the show off the lot.

The United Shows was a success all three years of its existence. It started a trend with its new fronts and lighting system, that all the other shows tried to outdo in the next few years. No chrome metal and neon were used by the United Shows of America, but its outstanding fronts were the spurs that goaded the boys on the Royal American into using those new materials and ideas that same year; ideas and materials that all of the major midways would be copying before the depression decade was ended.

The Castle Show, the name given to the United Shows of America by most outdoor showmen, was "sold" to Hennies Brothers at the end of the 1936 season. It's doubtful that these Kansas City Boys, who had been operating the largest truck transported carnival in the United States for three years now, ever paid one dollar to anyone to get the big railroad show as their own.

THIS WAS NOT A LOOP-O-PLANE. A West Coast showman had two of these rides made up in a Southern California machine shop, and brought them to the East Coast in spring of 1934 before Eyerly Aircraft brought their ride East for the first time in late fall of that year. These rides were not used after 1934 because of patent infringements. Courtesy Earl Purtle.

OUTLAWS' MOTHERS. United Shows of America, 1935. Mothers of Clyde Barrow and Bonnie Parker and the father of John Dillinger appeared in Mrs. John R. Castle's Crime Does Not Pay Show. They posed along with the "Parker-Barrow death car." This car was not the original, as that one had been seized in Topeka, Kansas by the person from whom the outlaws had stolen it. No time was lost at this 1934 Topeka Fair, as Kansas City friends of the Castles delivered a fake that was as good as the original. These K C Boys did a professional job with their machine guns. Author's collection.

The First National Bank of Shreveport held a big mortgage on all the equipment. Bill Hirsch, who was secretary-manager of the State Fair of Louisiana, was part owner of the carnival primarily to protect the bank's interest in its paraphernalia. The bank advanced money every winter and spring for the necessary renovation of equipment, and Castle always managed to make payments on the principal during the season. The hard-bitten little Irishman was extremely careful in regulating the amount of those payments. Towards the end of a season, he would do whatever he thought necessary to cut down the gross of the big show so that there would be no possibility of paying that mortgage off in full. He shuddered at the thought of ever again being on his own without the resources of that big bank in back of his show.

Those last weeks of a season, Mr. Hirsch was in Shreveport managing the big fair. Consequently, he never knew of the Little Irishman's maneuvers. Lohmar, the "glad hander" of the trio, was one of the best general agents in the business; but at that time, he knew very little about the management end of a midway. Castle would probably have continued those manipulations until the forties, if he had been able to stay sober.

Spring of 1936, Hirsch and Lohmar had given him an ultimatum. Castle vowed that he would remain sober all season. The penalty for breaking that vow would be the disposal of the carnival to other interests in the fall. Castle remained sober all summer. Bill Hirsch left the show on Saturday afternoon after Labor Day, and the gruff little Irishman had a drinking party on the Detroit Fairgrounds that same night. On the long railroad move from Detroit to the Amarillo, Texas, Fair, he had a big party in the "Pie car" for the girls from the Scandals of 1936 Show on the midway. The "Big Blonde" would come up and take him back to the private car, but in a few hours he would be back in the dining car for more "party."

He was sober all week in the "Capital of the Texas Panhandle" and Lohmar kept him "off the bottle" for three days in Wichita Falls. He went into Houston three days ahead of the show to lay out the lot there. No doubt that three days was one big party for it would have been impossible to put the show on the lot, if his location stakes had remained as he had placed them. Boss canvasman McKennon remonstrated with his half-sober boss man. The quick-tempered little show owner pulled up a location stake and threw it at his employee. "Put the God Damned thing on the lot anyway you want to!" he yelled as he stalked off the showgrounds in search of more refreshments. His loyal canvasmen, ride foreman and independent show owners did just what he had ordered. They moved stakes, consulted and moved them again. They fit that great show in its entirety onto that tight showgrounds. Fred Beckman visited the show in Houston that week. The now sober and contrite little Castle escorted Mr. Beckman around the mammoth midway, and proudly boasted, "I have men on this show that can do anything; they put it on the lot all by themselves."

The final date for the season, and for the show, was at the Louisiana State Fair in Shreveport. The three-day layoff before the fair opened was needed as it rained every day, and it took three days to get the show all set up and ready. The now-sober Irishman stayed away from the fairgrounds as long as he could, because he dreaded the showdown that he knew he would have to face when he talked to his Jewish partner in the Fair's main office.

This showdown was inevitable and Hirsch,

backed by Lohmar, was inexorable. Hennies Brothers, who had announced that they intended to build a new thirty-car railroad show for the 1937 season, were called in and they assumed the remaining obligations to the bank. Their truck show was closing that first week of the fair at Shreveport, and on Sunday afternoon all of their trucks pulled onto the fairgrounds and parked back of "Castle Show" midway.

Two hours before closing time, that last night of this great show, Hennies' truck show hands stationed themselves at the still operating shows and rides. It has never been ascertained by whose order this was done, but this evident lack of trust further infuriated the loyal railroad showmen. Many of them had been with Johnny since he started his first big show, and were not happy about his losing it. No other carnival showman had ever opened the office wagon on the flatcar, as he had done the year before in Kansas City, and paid everyone in full when the lot was so muddy that the show could not be unloaded.

The last episode in the history of this great show took place about an hour after its final closing, when all eight hundred of its former employees met in the big girl show tent on the back end of the midway. John R. Castle, the hardboiled little Irishman from the streets of Kansas City, almost cried as he bid

farewell to his friends and employees of so many years. He almost eulogized long-time bosses and staff members. In a final statement, he said, "we have a young man here that has only been with us a couple of years, a man who can do any job that needs to be done with a carnival, a man who brings show equipment back into quarters in the fall in as good or better condition than it left there in the spring, a man who will run off incompetent help and do it all himself, if need by." Do you need to wonder why Joe McKennon and John R. Castle's other employees were fond of the hard-boiled, tender-hearted little "so and so."

As the first work was starting on the "Castle" Show's new midway back in 1934, Rubin Gruberg was filing voluntary bankruptcy proceedings in Montgomery, Alabama. He listed liabilities of $276,169.00 and assets of $450.00. Two hundred fifty dollars of these assets were listed as his clothing. Everyone who knew this little showman (many of the early carnival owners were small in stature), was amused by this listing of clothing. This vain little showman had trunks full of wardrobe, every change of attire complete with spats and piped vests. Why, his gold-headed canes were worth more than $250.00.

Only a few weeks before he had displayed all this rich raiment in Chicago's Sherman Hotel at the

UNITED SHOWS OF AMERICA TRAIN CROSSING THE ROCKIES.
A photographer from Butte, Montana was "set up" waiting for the show train to come into focus. Train was halted for this "shot" to be taken. From the collection of Fred D. Pfening, Jr.

STAFF OF JOHNNY J. JONES EXPOSITION. Starting front center left and going clockwise around the table. Starr DeBelle, publicity director; Tommy Allen, manager; E. Lawrence Phillips, owner; Walter White, general manager; Arthur Atherton, treasurer; Tommy Thomas, general agent; and Johnny J. Jones, Jr. Courtesy Joe Pearl.

Outdoor Showmen's Convention. He leaned back on that goldheaded cane as a bellman moved twice around the lobby paging, "Mr. Gruberg... Mr. Gruberg." At the end of the second circuit, Rubin called him over and gave him a dollar. This ritual was repeated every hour as long as Rubin was in the lobby. He and "Miss Annie" had attended the banquet and ball along with five hundred other show people who had all paid the three dollars per plate charged that year.

In March, Annie Gruberg settled all claims against them for $7,171.00 in cash and a promise to repay Max Shapiro twenty thousand dollars that he advanced to buy a sixty thousand dollar note from a Montgomery bank.

E. Lawrence Phillips' New Johnny J. Jones Exposition opened in Washington, D.C. in 1934, and D. D. Murphy had a few shows and rides playing lots in St. Louis County. On May 5 the front axle snapped on Marjorie Kemp's automobile as she was riding the straight wall in Paducah, Kentucky. Her left leg was injured in the fall to the floor of the motor drome. Her passenger, Sultan the lion, was uninjured. In June promoter Ben H. Vooheis proposed to and married a local girl on the midway, when the couple that were supposed to be married in the public wedding backed out. In July, John Lazia of Kansas City, former owner of the Mighty Doris Shows and partner with the Velare Brothers in the Great Alpine Shows, was shot and killed in front of his hotel.

All midways reported business much improved from the previous year. Rubin changed the title of his Model Shows of America to America's Model Shows. Doc Waddell was with Roy Gray's Big State Shows in Texas, and K. G. Barkoot had three rides and six concessions playing lots in Michigan. Old-time carnival owner, H. (Tubby) Snyder was almost totally blind and was on relief in Chicago. L. Harvey Cann with Travers Chautauqua Shows for the last six years moved to World of Mirth Shows as general agent. In December, J. W. Patty Conklin was elected President of Showmen's League of America.

Practically unnoticed was the advent of a new ride in 1934. Everly Aircraft Co. of Salem, Oregon introduced the new Loop-O-Plane ride. The introduction of this ride was to mark a complete change of concept in riding device ideas for midways. Heretofore, the ferris wheel, sea planes and dangler were the aerial rides. All the others were "flat" rides that hugged the ground. These flat rides had been designed more complex and heavier as new devices were invented. This new Loop-O-Plane gave the rider a thrilling ride way up in the air, and better still it loaded on one wagon or truck where the others required several vehicles. Two men could set it up in a few hours. With the unlimited low-paid labor

available in the thirties, the labor-saving factor didn't become effective until the war years; but the townspeople took to this new ride like flies take to honey. It had a low capacity, but tickets readily sold for two or three times the regular price and long lines of eager riders awaited their turn in the imitation plane attached to the long arm. It did have the "joggle" also.

In 1935, E. E. Farrow changed the name of his Famous Dixie Shows to Wallace Brothers Shows; John T. Tinsley was partnered with Morris Miller in the Miller Brothers Exposition Shows. L, J. Heth now had a new show out on trucks while Walter Savidge's Ride Unit was transported the same way. F. J. Murphy died, and J. C. Simpson was the general agent for Johnny J. Jones Exposition. Otto Ehring, Jr. still operating rides, as his father had done since 1886. His father bought a carousel propelled by manpower in that year. The Ehrings had operated merry-go-rounds driven by manpower, horsepower, steam, gasoline, and electricity.

James Wesley Conklin said he didn't care whether he was called Paddy, Patty or Pattie. It was decided to call him Patty in all future stories concerning this human dynamo. Morris Miller reported that his show had been terrorized by armed

CARNIVAL ELEPHANT. Bill Hames' Shows. Courtesy Albert Conover.

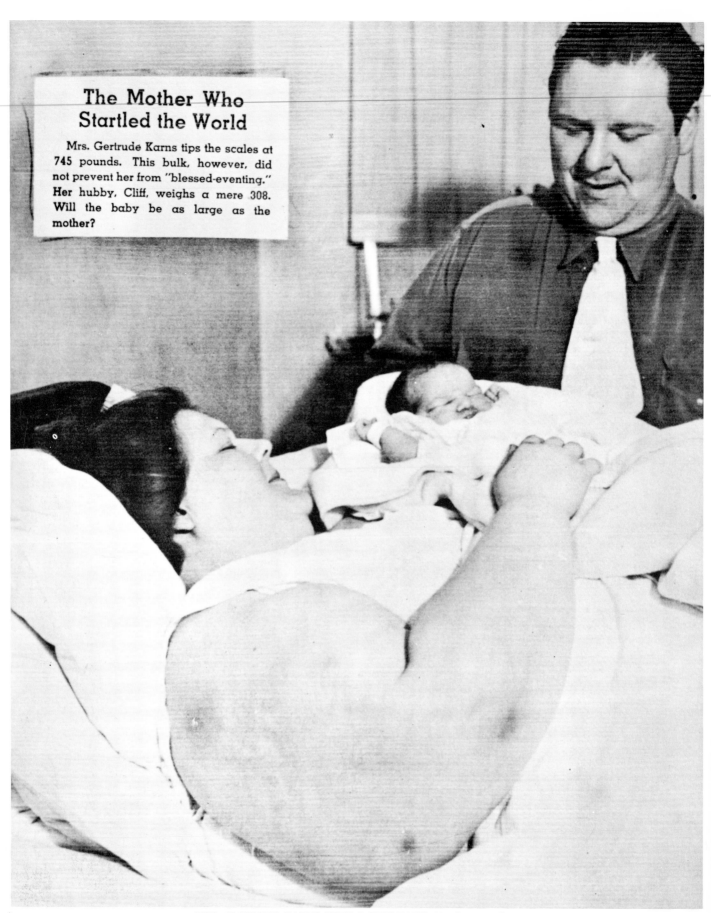

The Mother Who Startled the World

Mrs. Gertrude Karns tips the scales at 745 pounds. This bulk, however, did not prevent her from "blessed-eventing." Her hubby, Cliff, weighs a mere 308. Will the baby be as large as the mother?

MRS. CLIFFORD KARNS WITH A NEW BABY. Her first daughter was born in Shreveport, Louisiana in spring of 1934. United Shows of America had already built a special show for this attraction before the baby came. Mrs. Karns later gave birth to another child. Clifford Karns of "Jack and Jill" fame, was a "lightweight" of less than 500 pounds. His brother, Eddie, weighed close to seven hundred pounds. Photograph from a Beckman & Gerety yearbook in the collection of Fred D. Pfening, Jr.

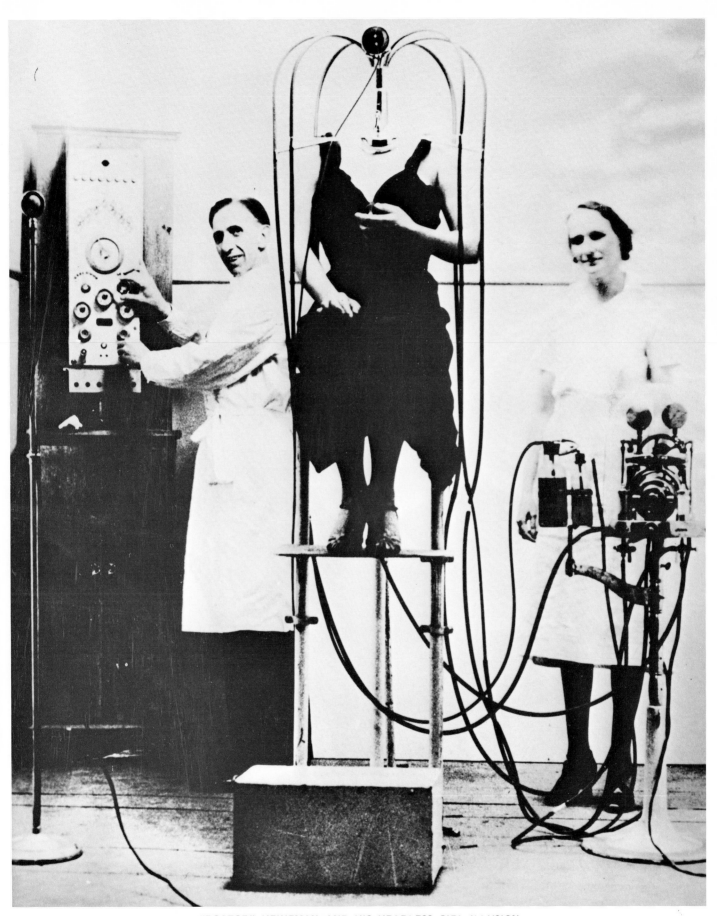

"DOCTOR" HEINEMAN AND HIS HEADLESS GIRL ILLUSION.
Heineman had exhibited this illusion in Blackpool, England, before
coming to America in 1937. This refugee from Hitler came to the
Goodman Wonder Shows with his "Gimmick" from his Hamburg,
Germany home. Goodman superintendent, Joe McKennon, framed the
first American show for Heineman. Courtesy L. Harvey Doc Cann.

Courtesy L. Harvey Doc Cann

LIFE SHOW. At Chicago's Century of Progress, 1933. Courtesy Lou Dufour.

"deputy sheriffs" in Pike County, Kentucky, across the river from Williamson, West Virginia. Pike County sheriff told him not to pay them off, so they "patrolled" the midway all week making arrests on all sorts of charges. Miller should have known not to take his carnival onto the show grounds in that Hatfield-McCoy Feud country. A show grounds where the mountain men sat in the blue seats (bleachers) with their squirrel rifles between their knees as they watched the Great Hagenbeck Wallace Circus performance in 1931. The writer was there.

Frank La Barr, eighty-two years old, started his seventieth year in show business in 1936. The United Shows of America loaded out of Peoria, Illinois, as the Royal American was unloading on the same crossing; Rubin and Cherry shared the town with both of them. Latter show came in middle of week and played opposition to the "Castle" Shows for two or three days, and stayed over in opposition to the Royal American. On Sunday, equipment of the three biggest ones was in the one town.

The United Shows played Davenport, Iowa, the week ending May 30th, and the Rubin & Cherry Shows were across the River in East Moline, Illinois. Much visiting was done between the shows that week. On afternoon of May 29th, the Godino Boys came from the Rubin Show to visit with the Gibbs Sisters on the United Show. They had dinner together in

Eddie Madigan's cookhouse on the latter midway. Only instance on record of two pairs of Siamese-like twins, or joined-together twins, having a meal together. The Godino Boys died later that season. One of them had pneumonia. They were cut apart but both died. Rubin complained, "I told them to be careful and not catch colds."

The Jones Show and Dodson Show day and dated in Both Washington, D.C., and Pittsburgh, Pennsylvania. The Al C. Hansen shows changed to railroad equipment, but the trend was in the other direction. Charles Goss of Standard Chevrolet Company in East St. Louis reported that he had sold thirty-three cars and trucks to outdoor show people in just thirty days. Charlie had a special sales contract that fitted the needs of the outdoor people.

Bill Roberts, sword swallower with Bill Chalkias' Circus Side Show on the Snapp Greater Shows' midway had an impressive funeral in Jacksonville, Illinois. He had used too big a charge in the army rifle he fired while it was attached to the implement he had swallowed. Meanwhile, "La Goldie" was firing her rifle many times daily in the big side show with the United Shows of America. Her rifle was attached to a long lighted neon tube which she ingested as part of her act. On July 11, at the Anderson, Indiana Fair "Prince Neon" broke his tube while it was still inside. This attraction of Carl J. Lauther's with the Jones Show had to have quick surgery. He was expected to recover. Only one high diver was reported injured that season.

Season of 1936 was one of the best in the history of carnival business. Had the usual number of blowdowns, and first one of the season badly damaged Krause Greater Shows in Miami. Both Ringling Brothers and Barnum and Bailey Circus and Royal American Shows sent equipment to Benny Krause to help him reopen. Some of the hottest weather on record was encountered that year. United Shows of America had several days of higher than one hundred degree heat (reached 113 degrees on opening day) at the Fargo, North Dakota Fair. G. Ward Moody was band director on Jack Ruback's Western States Shows. Moody was destined to become the adjutant for the American Legion, Department of Texas.

Mrs. Mary Gaskill, widow of Frank, died on October 22nd and press agent William J. Hilliar died November 15th. Marjorie Kemp was badly clawed by one of her lions at the Regina, Canada, Fair. Starr DeBelle joined Johnny J. Jones Exposition as press agent, and Milton Morris was manager of the William Glick Shows. In December, Max Goodman, concession operator with the "Castle" Shows announced that he had bought the entire Glick Show and would frame a midway of his own for 1937.

On January 5, 1937, Bennie Krause was found dead in the Savannah River. He had gotten off a northbound train which was carrying him to a sanitarium after he had suffered a nervous breakdown. Bennie was one of the first concessionaires in carnival business as he started with Gaskill. Greatest number of carnivals in history were on road, as over three hundred toured the country. Rubin Gruberg celebrated his twenty-fifth year in carnival business with only one show. Royal American was now the biggest of them all, traveling on sixty railroad cars. Goodman Wonder Shows opened in rain at Raleigh, and had eight wet weeks. Show saw its first sunshine in Ft. Wayne, Indiana. Same week Joe McKennon, who had been with the Ringling Brothers and Barnum & Bailey Circus, joined the Goodman Shows as superintendent.

Doc Waddell changed midways middle of season. Hennies Brothers took four days to get on the muddy lot at Waukegan, Illinois; while Max Linderman moved the empty World of Mirth Shows train seventy miles in Ogdensburg, New York. Train was about

FRONT GATE. Johnny J. Jones Exposition, 1940. Designed and built by superintendent Joe McKennon in spring of 1939. The train hands who erected this main entrance called it "Ole Booger Bear." Courtesy Albert Conover.

TRACTOR DEPARTMENT JOHNNY J. JONES EXPOSITION, 1939.
The white-painted "bull-dog Mack" tractor was purchased at the sale of the equipment of ill-fated Tim McCoy Wild West Show in 1938. The driver of the center rubber-tired tractor (called "mules" by the show hands) was Johnny J. Jones, Jr. Courtesy Joe Pearl.

three miles from the lot on the New York Central when the teamsters went on strike. It took a seventy mile move and a railroad transfer to get the train spotted alongside the showgrounds on the Rutland line were Linderman could use his own equipment. K. G. Barkoot had the Barkoot Brothers Shows on the road again. He had an old Ocean Wave Ride which was well received by a new generation of amusement seekers.

Insects made two of the biggest carnival stories of the season. At the Pennington County Fair at Thief River Falls, Minnesota, mosquitoes, swarms of them, almost forced the closing of the fair. In October, at Drumright, Oklahoma, Miller Brothers Shows did have to turn off the lights and quit when swarms of small insects invaded the midway. Attracted by the strong lights, the insects were over two inches deep on the showgrounds.

Patty Conklin was manager of the Canadian National Exhibition midway in 1937. Mr. Conklin was to be manager and producer of that greatest of all annual exposition's midway for over thirty years. In 1937, Harry J. Pollie was killed in an automobile accident, as was Roy Bard, the Ossified Boy.

In 1938, Tom Hasson booked his circus Side Show with the O. C. Buck Shows; and Walter White who as general manager had built the Jones Show back into a major carnival, joined the Beckman & Gerety Shows as an executive. Slim Kelly had his Circus Side Show with the World of Mirth Shows,

Dick Best had his with the Royal American, and Pete Kortez was with the Beckman & Gerety with his big freak show. This 1938 season saw more wagons built, more tented theatres, more equipment of all kinds purchased and more flesh talent employed than any like period in carnival history.

Circus historians claim a thirty-year period (1880-1910) as the Golden Age of the Circus. The fifteen-year period starting in nineteen thirty-four may very well be termed the Golden Age of the American Carnival. The growing industry had remained static for over ten years after the death of C. A. Wortham. Only in isolated instances, such as the Velare Brothers' twin Ferris wheels, had any carnival showman introduced anything new on his midway. True, some new rides were being added to the ride line-ups, but they were either more "look alike" flat rides or another variation of the airplane swings. The shows, which were still the major attractions for a carnival midway, were unimaginative and dull. Only one or two new ideas for midway shows had evolved since the early twenties. Lou Dufour's "Pickled Punk" shows were making a little money, but most showmen were literally starved for lack of money-making ideas that could be used in framing new midway shows.

This writer, discounting for the ebullient enthusiasm of extreme youth, believes that the midways of either of the C. A. Wortham Shows of 1921 were far superior to those of their successors,

Beckman & Gerety and Morris & Castle Shows of ten years later. There were more rides, but the hackneyed ideas of the tired and discouraged showmen were no longer exciting. The lines of shows on most midways gave an appearance of being exactly what they had become, poverty rows.

The renaissance of carnival shows that began in 1934 reached its peak in 1939, but continued for another ten years. Increased costs of producing live shows coupled with the multiplicity of thrilling new riding devices brought about the decline of the big midway shows. A decline that was as rapid as the rise was slow. It is doubtful that any of the few "sit down" type shows still being operated by a few midways are profitable to the carnival office.

Very few producers of "sit down" girl revues have profited from them and fewer midways have ever made a dime from one. These shows have been used as "image builders" by big-time carnival managers ever since they discarded the Cootch Shows and '49 Camps. They put them on their midways so that they would have something besides the rides to show visiting fair managers and committee members. During this fifteen year resuscitation of carnival shows, the "sit down" show was "Queen of the Midway."

"Sit down" shows were just what the name implied. Seats, not comfortable but seats none the less, were installed for the patrons to sit as they watched the performance. Not since the early days of carnivals, when every midway had a circus, horse show or wild animal arena had carnivals carried as much seating as they did in the late thirties. A carnival midway with less than four tented theatres complete with seats could not claim status as a major midway. Girl Revues, Minstrel Shows, Cuban Rhumba Shows, Midget Shows, Illusion Shows, Monkey Shows, Hawaiian Shows, Posing Shows (where the girls 'unadorned and unashamed' posed in various artistic postures) all joined the midway circuses and wild west shows in setting seats in their elaborate new tented theatres.

Each midway designer and builder tried to provide "his" carnival with show fronts and stage settings more elaborate than any of his competitors could produce. Bobby Wick, Nath Nelson, Nat Worman and Vince Book on the Royal American were an almost unbeatable team of designers and builders. Modern design was the rage. Chrome metal, neon, plastics and modern color were splashed from the front gate to the back end of the midways. Every carnival had their own designer, and were constantly trying to steal the other show's builders. New lighting systems were installed and the glare of naked light bulbs was banished from the midways of America.

Courtesy Harry Frost, Minnesota State Fair

141

Ballyhoo Booster

The Story

In the days before electronic sound amplification and canned music, talkers on show fronts and "grinders" in ticket boxes used every conceivable kind of noisemaker to attract the attention of the midway visitor. Sirens, short lengths of railroad iron, bass drums, Scotch Bagpipers, large·steel triangles, six shooters (on Wild West Shows) or any other kind of unusual soundmakers were used to "draw" people to an attraction. A bar of steel drawn rapidly along the row of rivets on an old-type water heater tank made an ear-splitting noise. Each attraction owner attempted to be first on the lot with a new-found noisemaker. This scene depicts an actual occurrence on the Smith Greater Shows. Two showmen had the same idea and tried to "sneak" water heater tanks to their attractions before the others awakened. Original sketch by Marian L. McKennon.

JOHNNY J. JONES EXPOSITION AT SOUTH FLORIDA FAIR
FEBRUARY 12th, 1932

A visit to one or another of these garish "modern midways" probably caused many true artists to have indigestion and nightmares. But the flashy gaudiness that nauseated them was the proper setting for this harlot of the cow pastures and fair grounds. A setting in which she could brazenly kick up her forty year old heels in one last bacchanal display along her sex-laden midways. And sex was the chief commodity exploited on those midways of the late thirties.

One talker on an Illusion Show promised the crowd in front of his bally that the four-legged girl would strip and run up and down the aisles. He turned quite a few from his "tips" with that spiel. Naturally, the two girls in this illusion couldn't leave the apparatus; but the show was good and the "Marks" got their ten cents worth. He used this "opening" for half a season without any "heat" other than occasional "squawk" from some disgruntled seeker of things erotic. Finally, one night in Wichita, Kansas, he made a pitch to a big "tip" and "turned" almost all of them over the bally. After the performance was over, instead of using the regular exit, the crowd of sex seeking Sun Flower Staters came back out "over the bally." The talker took refuge on top of one of the Ferris wheels. In the resultant "Hey Rube" many heads were bruised and possibly a few bones broken. The show's doctor didn't treat the injuries of the townspeople. This was on one of the big railroad shows, and this talker had to find another show for the remainder of that season.

In spring of 1938, after he had gotten the railroad coaches built for the new and ill-fated Col. Tim McCoy Wild West Show, Joe McKennon joined the Johnny J. Jones Exposition as general superintendent. Joining in Washington, D.C., he used the train crew, tractor drivers and helpers as a shop crew, and redesigned the entire midway in just twelve weeks. When the midway was set up on the Indiana State Fairgrounds in Indianapolis, ten railroad cars of equipment had been added to this already great carnival. New modern fronts, stage settings, midway decorations and a new lighting system had all been designed and built as the show moved along on its still date route. "The Mighty Monarch of the Tented World" was back on top of the heap again.

On October 15, 1938 J. C. McCaffery announced that Beckman & Gerety, Rubin & Cherry and the Royal American were pooling all resources as the Amusement Corporation of America. No single show owner could ever successfully combat this corporation with all its material resources and experienced manpower that it controlled. Harry Hennies brought the Hennies Brothers Shows into this combine within a few months after his brother Orville's death midseason 1939. The combine controlled the field, but war would break it up.

As this decade ended, Floyd E. Gooding had purchased land for a permanent winter quarters in Columbus, Ohio. Fred Backman was completing his fiftieth year in outdoor show business, and Specs Groscurth had the girl show on W. G. Wade Show's midway. Eula Whitworth reported that James H. Drew and his brother Harvey had a good season as concessionaires. Ellis Winton was doing very well with his Cumberland Valley Shows, and Dick Best had completed a season with the most elaborate Circus Side Show ever built on the Royal American midway.

Another of the original carnival troupers, Bill Rice, had died, as had William F. Troyk, known as Blooie-Blooie, the Dwarf Clown. Harry L. Wilson, Cary Jones (Snake Oid), J. L. Landes, Bob Hurst, W. C. Huggins, Clyde G. Flanders and T. W. McMahon were among the other old-timers that had answered the call to report to that thousand car carnival that Johnny J. Jones and Clarence A. Wortham planned to open right after the first of the year.

GENE NADREAU. Hawaiian Show producer with Johnny J. Jones Exposition. He was one of the top producers of this type show. In spite of having a speech impediment in normal conversation, he was an excellent talker on the front of a show. Courtesy Joe Pearl.

As the collective amusement industry entered the fifth decade of the twentieth century, it is doubtful if any one of the middle-aged Madam's adherents thought about her age. On May 30, 1940, Patty Conklin up in North Bay, Ontario, the Coleman Family in Hartford, Connecticut, George Loos and Bill Hames down in Texas, Velare Brothers in Milwaukee, Wisconsin, and Guy Dodson in Richmond, Indiana, were all too busy with the daily problems of carnival operation to remember that Gaskill had started the first one just forty-one years before. The midway workers' constant struggle with muddy lots, wind storms, transportation problems, lack of patronage from an often hostile populace and an increasing encroachment of new competitors into the town that had been proven profitable left him little time for anything else.

In January, 1940, Carl J. Lauther announced that he was moving his big circus side show from Johnny J. Jones to the Cetlin & Wilson Shows. J. George Loos played the Washington's Birthday Celebration in Laredo, Texas for the fifteenth time. That spring all carnivals were striving for the "modernistic look," and the usual cold and rainy weather cut down business of the "still date season." K. G. Barkoot had his small Barkoot Brothers Shows in Michigan and Ohio, while Texas Kidd was doing good business in Texas. The latter show featured Jack Hoxie, motion picture cowboy, in its wild west show.

Margie Kemp had another broken axle in her automobile while riding the "straight wall" of the motordrome with Royal American. In the resultant fall, Marjorie was badly hurt, but her five hundred pound passenger, Sultan, was unhurt. Ethel Purtle was giving her lion, King, frequent rides on "the wall" with the World of Mirth, while her husband, Earl, had trained a young lion to ride with him on a motorcycle on the same wall.

Royal American and Beckman & Gerety combined their show trains for a move from Atlanta to St. Louis. Former had played a week in Augusta, Georgia, and then moved to Atlanta to join the Beckman Show as it came out of winter quarters there. In St. Louis the ninety cars in three trains were divided with the Beckman & Gerety going across the river to East St. Louis for a week stand as the Royal American moved onto the Grand and Laclede lot in St. Louis for two weeks.

Walter White, former general manager of Johnny J. Jones Exposition, was manager of the Beckman & Gerety Shows. Many shows and showmen from the Jones Show were now with Beckman. Starting in Dayton, Ohio, the Beckman & Gerety shop crew under the direction of superintendent and builder, Joe McKennon, built a complete colored minstrel show. This equipment consisted of four wagons, a new one hundred ten-foot long neon-lighted front, stage setting, all seating, lighting and props was built in just eighteen days. During this time the midway played the Anderson, Indiana, Free Fair, two "still dates" and made three railroad moves. The new minstrel show was all set up on the Milwaukee Lake Front Lot when Eddie Jamieson brought all of his minstrel show people from Johnny J. Jones to join the Beckman Show.

In Kalamazoo, Michigan, during the week of July 30th, a fire partially destroyed the neon show wagon of the Beckman & Gerety Shows. Owner Gerety and superintendent McKennon decided the wagon was too badly damaged to be repaired. Wheels and undergear were stripped from it, and the half burned derelict was left on a weedy corner of the show grounds, when the loaded wagons were pulled from the lot during the night of August 4th. This wagon from the Great Munday Wild Animal Show of forty years before was now an abandoned wreck. This wagon, the birthplace of Etta Louise Blake Hurd, now Hody Jones, the widow of Johnny J. Jones, had ended its trouping days.

The following week, Beckman & Gerety did not unload the show train in Muskegon, Michigan. Ralph Whitehead, union organizer, had demanded a closed shop agreement for his new Circus, Carnival, Fairs & Rodeo International Union and had pickets at the railroad crossing. Three years before, Mr. Whitehead had arranged a closed shop agreement with the Ringling Brothers and Barnum & Bailey Circus for his American Federation of Actors, and in just one year had called a strike which cost over a thousand people a season's work on that great circus. Many ex-Ringling people were now with the Beckman & Gerety carnival and they did not trust either Mr. Whitehead or his new union. He knew this, but demanded that Barney Gerety take some six or eight hundred union memberships anyway. Many of the show's employees were members of the American Guild of Variety Actors (AGVA), but he wanted them to pay dues to his new organization also.

The carnival lost the week in Muskegon, but it started its fair season the following week at the Ionia Free Fair without pickets. After a few large newspaper ads from both Whitehead and the show, an injunction or two and offers from CIO Locals to move the show if picketing started again, the organizer moved on to other fields more deserving of his attention. Business at Ionia, The Michigan State Fair at Detroit and LaPorte, Indiana, Fair was not adversely affected by this labor strike.

ETHEL PURTLE AND HER PETS. Courtesy Earl Purtle.

EARL PURTLE AND HIS MOTORCYCLE-RIDING LION ON THE
STRAIGHT UP-AND-DOWN WALL. Courtesy Earl Purtle.

Patty Conklin was now Director of the Midway of the Canadian National Exposition at Toronto for the fifth year, and Robert L. Lohmar was manager of the Rubin & Cherry Shows. The Grubergs, Rubin and "Miss Annie," had retired from midway activities that spring. George F. Dorman had died in March, and in October, Beverly White died while working with Max Goodman's Wonder Shows. Beverly was one of the real old-time carnival press agents, and he had invented a full set of cliches to be used in carnival reporting; cliches that many carnival press agents still use.

In September, 1940, Chico, an Apache Indian, left the Texas Exposition Shows in Hot Springs, Arkansas. The management wasn't exactly distressed over his departure, but they were unhappy about losing the twenty-two foot boa constrictor that he carried with him.

During the first week of October, Peter J. Speroni, owner of the P. J. Speroni Shows was shot and killed by the Athletic Show manager with his midway. His wife, Esther, announced that she was keeping the show out on the road. In 1971, Mrs. Speroni was still operating a carnival, the Midway of Mirth Shows. On November 4th, F. H. Bee, Jr., owner of the show bearing his name, died. This ex-school teacher who had become a successful carnival owner had built up a lucrative route in East Tennessee and Kentucky.

Floyd E. Gooding announced that he would have two complete carnivals and five ride units on road in 1941. Noble C. Fairly sold out his interest in the Fairly & Little Shows and went to Max Goodman's show for a few weeks, but he later took an executive position with Dee Lang's Famous Shows.

By mid-October the Billboard was printing almost a full page of names of showmen who had letters from the Selective Service at that publication's mail desks. Billboard had always provided free mail forwarding service for show people, and many outdoor showmen had no other address than The Billboard, 25-27 Opera Place, Cincinnati, Ohio. Thousands gave that address when they registered for the draft, and the Billboard staff forwarded their "draft mail" to them somewhere on some show grounds. Just another service of old "Billy Boy." On March 1st, 1941, two hundred forty-six men had mail from selective service forwarded by Billboard.

Patty Conklin was awarded the Western Canada Class A Circuit of Fairs for the 1941 season. These fairs at Brandon, Calgary, Edmonton, Saskatoon and Regina continued to operate throughout the war; and Patty's shows had the contract for all of the war years. The Canadian Government forced him to transport his midway on only twelve railroad cars, but he carried a big show on those twelve cars. Royal American had this circuit for seven years before the war.

CLYDE AND HARRIET BEATTY. They had a complete three-ring circus as one of the midway shows on Johnny J. Jones Exposition seasons of 1940 and 1941. Courtesy Joe Pearl.

Circus World Museum, Baraboo, Wisconsin.

Floyd Gooding's rides were at the State Fair Grounds in Columbus for the twenty-sixth year, and Clyde Beatty's Circus was one of the shows on the midway of the Johnny J. Jones Exposition. "Doc" Barfield sold his Cosmopolitan Shows and planned to operate a ride unit in the future. Texas Kidd and "Doc" Shugart were operating their little midways in Texas as they had been doing for twenty years. Business was good and getting better all the time in spite of much rain and bad weather in the spring. L. Clifton Kelley, former carnival owner, died in the second week of May.

The Ben Williams Shows closed the second week in June. One hundred ninety-two carnivals and eight circuses were listed as being on lots on July 4th. A windstorm hit the Jones Show midway in North Chicago, near Waukegan, Illinois, early one morning. The Clyde Beatty Circus big top was torn to ribbons. The U.S. Tent & Awning Company had men and material on the grounds within two hours and performances were given that night under an almost all new circus tent.

Marjorie Kemp rode again at the Knoxville, Tennessee, Fair, the first time she had been on the wall in a public performance since her accident over a year before. Joe Fontana had leased and was operating the L. J. Heth Shows, but was planning to lease the Blue Ribbon Shows from Roth for the 1942 season. Guy Dodson offered the Dodson World's Fair Shows for sale at end of 1941 season. The Billboard was now printing several photographs of showmen in armed services uniforms each week.

On September 6th, Dave Stock, ride owner with the Goodman Shows, died in Lincoln, Nebraska. Stock, who had been with Goodman five years, had been with carnivals since 1906. He had been with Barkoot, Boyd & Linderman and Bernardi Greater and with William Glick Shows until Goodman bought the Glick equipment in fall of 1936. He took pride in being a ride owner and kept his equipment well maintained and painted. His employees were all capable ride men and always willing to help anyone on the show grounds who needed additional manpower. These men who handled Dave Stock's rides helped push many wagons off of muddy lots

BILLBOARD READERS. Joe Pearl and friend. Joe has been mail and Billboard agent on major carnivals for almost forty years. Courtesy Joe Pearl.

149

MAX LINDERMAN. The owner of the World of Mirth Shows in Earl Purtle's Motordrome. Max was no animal trainer but Earl was nearby. Courtesy Earl Purtle.

when the light tractors couldn't do the job unaided. During Goodman's first season, Superintendent McKennon had to call on them often. They always responded cheerfully, with Dave being the first to get there.

Another great old timer died on October 17th at Shreveport, Louisiana. Fred Beckman, "Mr. Show Business" to thousands, died while the Beckman & Gerety Shows was playing the Lousiana State Fair. He had made good in all outdoor fields; circus, wild west and carnival. His advice was sought by men who had spent their lives in show business for he had an instinctive knowledge of what could be done with an outdoor show.

In 1942, Alfred Kunz was general agent for L. J. Heth, and Max Goodman called his show the Wonder Shows of America. Mad Cody Fleming now had winter quarters in Hickox, Georgia, and Melvin Dodson was sole manager of Dodson World's Fair Shows. Clyde Beatty's Circus was with the Jones Show another season and Terrell Jacobs Circus was with Patty Conklin in Canada. Goodman also featured a wild animal circus using an Alfred Court act worked by Wilson Storey. Ted Leavitt, son of Victor D. Leavitt, was a special agent for Martin Arthur's Mighty American Shows; and Bob Lohmar

was still manager of the Rubin & Cherry Shows. W. C. Kaus, owner of the W. C. Kaus Shows died on February 15th at Duke Hospital in Durham, North Carolina.

On April 16th, 1942, Rubin Gruberg was "cutting up jackpots" with friends in the lobby of the Mayflower Hotel in Jacksonville, Florida. One of them invited Rubin to have dinner with him and the dapper little man accepted. He asked a couple of the "boys" to come to his room with him while he changed for dinner. They went with him to the room. He unlocked his door, stepped inside and fell to the floor. The hotel doctor said that he had died instantly from a heart attack, but many carnival people said that it was from a broken heart. "Miss Annie" had gone back to the show without him, and these same "Carnies" said that she refused to pay some of his gambling debts.

This vain, illiterate little man who had built a carnival empire was dead. This man who took so much pride in pointing out his possessions with a "Look, I paid $23,000.00 for that front; it's all mine" was gone from the carnival lots on which he had spent thirty-nine years. Rubin Gruberg would never have his picture taken with another dignitary, or pose on the "Magic Carpet" in the Hotel Sherman lobby. Nor would he be embarrassed again by the discovery that he had pointed out Ringling Brothers and Barnum & Bailey Circus advertising paper to a visiting fair manager as Rubin & Cherry show paper. That and not vanity was the reason he had his picture on Rubin Show paper thereafter. Many showmen didn't like Rubin and wouldn't work on his shows, but they all admired his business ability and regretted his death.

Later in the year, John (Dutch) Meyers, snake show owner with the Virginia Greater Shows and his helper, Lewis G. Ringer, were unpacking a shipment of rattlesnakes from a Florida snake farm. These were purchased as "fixed" reptiles with their poison sacs removed. One of them bit Meyers and a moment later Ringer was bitten. Both men died as the huge rattlers had been shipped unfixed.

On August 25th, Earl Purtle closed his motor drome for the duration of the war. The ODT (Office of Defense Transportation) official in a small Maine town ruled that the drome was in violation of regulations. Appeals to Washington failed to get the ruling changed. He had to close, while other drome owners continued to operate as they did not play that particular area in Maine. Earl had seven lions that performed inside his motor drome, so he framed a wild animal circus for the remainder of the war.

In March, 1943, Frank W. Peppers purchased Pryor's All State Shows; and Sam Soloman, owner of Sol's Liberty Shows, bought Rubin & Cherry from Mrs. Annie Gruberg. Later that month Carl J. Sedlmayr bought half interest in The Rubin Show from Soloman, and the equipment was moved to Sol's winter quarters in Caruthersville, Missouri. The Royal American Shows staff all went to the new Rubin & Cherry Shows, as it was announced that the Royal American would not tour again. At the same time, Barney Gerety stated that the Beckman & Gerety Shows would not go out of quarters. The Amusement Corporation of America was dissolved for the time, but J. C. McCaffery would revive it again before the end of the decade. Dee Lang kept his shows off road and operated rides in a park. Most shows reported big business when weather permitted. Mrs. Johnny J. Denton was operating the Denton Shows while Johnny was in the armed services. The Great Sutton Shows were blown down in a storm while Lt. Frank M. Sutton, Jr. was visiting on a fifteen day furlough. Terrell Jacobs Wild Animal Circus was touring with the World of Mirth Shows, and Ralph Clawson was assistant general manager of the Sheesley Shows. Ralph had complete charge of the carnival while "Capt. John" was having his operation.

John R. Castle was in a tuberculosis hospital in Missouri when J. F. Murphy, former show owner, died in Lebanon, Tennessee, early in September. Walter B. Kemp, Marjorie's brother, had been killed in a trainer plane crash near Tampa, Florida, on June 25th, and J. C. Simpson died on October 6th. Jimmy Simpson had been connected with midways since 1902 and could handle any job that came his way on a carnival.

Courtesy Circus World Museum, Baraboo, Wisconsin

RUBIN. Rubin Gruberg (in dark suit). Courtesy Joe Pearl.

THE "RUNS." Rubin & Cherry wagon on the runs. Courtesy Albert Conover.

Beckman

WET AND MUDDY AT THE "CROSSING." Beckman & Gerety, 1940.
Courtesy Albert Conover.

& Gerety

NEW LIGHT PLANTS. Beckman & Gerety, 1940. Courtesy Albert
Conover.

1940

"GETTING IT ON" A MUDDY LOT. Supt. McKennon and Beckman &
Gerety, 1940. Courtesy Albert Conover.

153

RIDEE-O. One of the fastest riding devices built prior to the middle Forties. This ride was featured during the late Twenties and all through the Thirties. Author's collection.

Nat Worman was construction superintendent with the Rubin & Cherry Shows in 1943, and Milt Morris was assistant manager of Johnny J. Jones. The Art Lewis railroad show had poor business that season, and James E. Strates bought all of his wagons and railroad cars on October 23rd. Later in the year, J. C. Weer bought the Lewis properties from Strates to be used in framing a new twenty car Weers Shows. Morris Lipsky, long-time concession operator with the show, bought half interest in the Johnny J. Jones Exposition.

In December, Al Wagner of the Great Lakes Exposition Shows bought all of the Velare Brothers equipment that had been with the Royal American. He planned to use this twenty cars and the equipment loaded thereon as a nucleus for a new thirty-car railroad show for the 1944 season. Robert L. Lohmar was the general agent of this new Cavalcade of America, and Milton Morris had been engaged as manager. Sedlmayr and Soloman announced that they were discarding the Rubin & Cherry title in 1944. Sedlmayr's property from Royal American would be added to the Rubin Show property for a new Royal American Shows.

The division of the former Royal American Show's property took place in the winter quarters at the old street car barns on Chouteau Avenue in St. Louis. Sedlmayr was there to get his equipment moved to the Caruthersville quarters. Velare Brothers were claiming items that had not been sold to Wagner; Wagner was trying to get the equipment that he had bought and Sam Soloman was there supporting the claims of his partner, Sedlmayr. It was an interesting week of dickering and bickering, snatching and grabbing and perhaps just a little bit of larceny. Show hands have a system for solving disputes among owners over show properties. Sometimes the property disappears leaving the litigants with nothing left to argue about.

Max Goodman kept his show off the road in 1944. The midways that were touring encountered the usual amount of rain and cold weather. James E. Strates had two blowdowns in one month; and the last week of June, Royal American pulled off a muddy Davenport, Iowa lot as Army Engineers waited to cut a levee that would flood it. The levee had to be cut to relieve the pressure on a dam downstream.

On May 22nd, C. D. Scott died. For over twenty years C. D. Scott had operated a show using the name Scott. This show of his could not be classed as a "Sunday School Show." Yet, he carried it back into towns where the show had encountered heavy losses in "Hey Rubes" of previous years. His show would do good business in these towns, but would probably have another "Rube" by Saturday night. Mr. Scott was like many other showmen of his day and time. They enjoyed strife. They prized a ten dollar bill gained by outwitting a "town mark" on one of the games more highly than a "C Note" ($100.00) earned

JOHNNY J. JONES
EXPOSITION
WITH
CLYDE BEATTY IN PERSON
AND HIS WILD ANIMAL EXHIBITION

MILWAUKEE LAKE FRONT
MID-SUMMER FESTIVAL
9·DAYS & NIGHTS·9
COMMENCING
SAT. JULY 12

Courtesy Circus World Museum, Baraboo, Wisconsin

legitimately by one of their riding devices. These men were well mannered, likeable fellows, and any one of them could have been highly successful in a more legitimate pursuit in his chosen field of endeavor.

"D-Day" of 1944 brought carnival business almost to a halt for two weeks. The average citizen was in no mood to visit a carnival midway as his sons and brothers fought their way ashore at Normandy and forced a blood-stained corridor across Northern France. It was during this period of anxiety that a sign appeared on the front of the Craft Shows "Grab Joint" which read, "Account of Hitler these hamburgers are littler."

Last of July, Al Wagner found that his truck showmen could not keep his big new railroad show moving. In the ensuing staff changes Grant Chandler joined the show as assistant manager and general superintendent. Slim Kelly was with J. C. Weer's new show and Nat Worman was with the Sheesley Show. Polio cut into business during July and August. Hennies Show set up and opened Saturday night in Paducah, Kentucky, but was forced to tear down and move to Jackson, Tennessee the following day.

In early October, Pete Kortez and Melvin Vaught bought the Sheesley Shows and Ben Davenport bought Frank West's train and wagons. Kortez, a midway side show operator, planned a carnival of his own for the 1945 season, while Davenport planned to put his Dailey Brothers Circus on rails. Wagner's Cavalcade couldn't get on the muddy lot in Pampa, Texas, while J. J. Page Shows closed in Georgia. J. George Loos boasted that he had enjoyed the best season of his forty-two years on carnival midways. Kortez and Vaught bought some of the Beckman & Gerety equipment from Barney Gerety to add to their new North American Exposition.

Max Linderman, owner of the World of Mirth Shows, died November 4th in Augusta, Georgia, as his show exhibited at the Exchange Club Fair there. "Sister Sue" (Mrs. Grant B. Smith) died on November 29th in Crooked Creek, Pennsylvania. This little woman, sister of Johnny J. Jones, was known and loved by thousands of carnival people.

It was announced that Al Kunz would manage Hennies Brothers Shows on its 1945 tour. In January of that year, Carl J. Sedlmayr bought Sam Soloman's interest in the Rubin & Cherry Shows. He was now sole owner of both the Rubin Show and the Royal American title. He shelved the Rubin & Cherry title and put the Royal American name on all his equipment. Johnny J. Bejano booked his circus side show with the World of Today Shows. Max Goodman put his show back on the road again; but Dee Lang sold all of his rides and concessions, after three years in St. Louis parks.

Goodman Show and Royal American "day and dated" in St. Louis while Johnny J. Jones and Strates shared Harrisburg, Pennsylvania the same week. The usual rain, mud and cold was encountered. Floyd Gooding termed it, "worst spring weather in years." O. C. Buck had heavy snow on his shows in New

York State. On July 10th, Prell's Broadway Shows was blown down by a storm in Perth Amboy, New Jersey. Royal American was stuck in the mud on the Oklahoma City fairgrounds for five days after the fair. The show got off the lot too late to play its advertised date in Tulsa, so the trains were routed directly to Jackson, Mississippi Fair, the next date.

In June, Kortez bought Vaught's share of the North American Exposition. Nat Worman was construction superintendent with the Cavalcade of Amusements, and Bob Lohmar had left the Cavalcade and joined Max Goodman's Wonder Shows of America as general agent. Both John R. Ward and Mad Cody Fleming were doing a big business on their routes, and all shows reported big July 4th business. The Animal Oddities Exhibit was featuring a pair of "crap shooting" monkeys as one of its attractions.

Max Cohen, general counsel for the American Carnival Association, in its comments regarding "V-J Day" explained to carnival showmen and ride owners, "V-J means the end of the manpower shortage." Fortunately Max was a better attorney than he was prophet. On August 18th, Sam Lawrence, owner of the Lawrence Greater Shows, was shot and killed by a concession operator on the Kutztown, Pennsylvania fairgrounds. His widow, Shirley, continued to operate the show for several years.

In November Peter Kortez sold his North American Exposition to John Wilson and Izzy Cetlin. The Cetlin & Wilson Shows had operated as the largest "Gilly Show" in the country. Because of labor costs, "Gilly Shows" could no longer operate with a profit, even if labor to move them could be obtained. So Cetlin & Wilson were putting their big show in wagons for flatcar moves. Same month, Frank Bergan bought Mrs. Max Linderman's interest in the World of Mirth Shows, and John R. Ward bought the Dodson World's Fair Shows. Ward, the little "At Show" boxer, after thirty years on carnival midways was putting his successful truck transported carnival "on rails." Johnny Ward was proud of his "At Show" background. He still featured an athletic show on the back end of his truck show midways. He gave first-time visitors to his carnival a personally conducted tour of the show grounds always including a brief visit to the Athletic Arena. As he gazed fondly at the "squared circle" he explained to the stranger that he had gotten his start in a ring just like the one here. With a final loving caress with his hand on the mat inside the ring he would escort his visitors to the cook house for mugs of coffee. John R. Ward was a family man with a clean record. It was distressing that this little man's lifetime ambition to own a railroad transported carnival should turn out as unrewarding for him as it did.

In mid-December, John F. "Blink" Courtney took Curtis Velare as a partner in his John F. Courtney & Company Enterprises. "Blink" had been a concession operator for many years, but was not too successful "behind the counter of a joint," as he spent more time working on plans and models for new and novel riding devices or other carnival

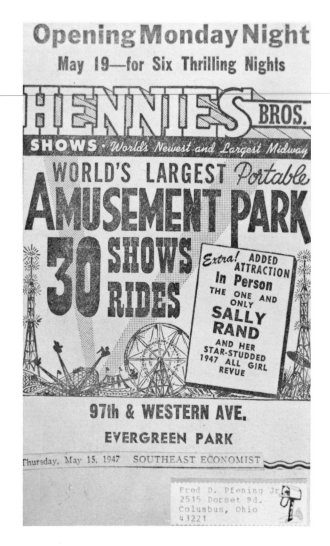

equipment than he did in trying to entice the "town marks" to play his game of chance. Now he had ample financial backing and could spend all his time designing and building the products of his imagination. Although unknown by many carnival people, "Blink" Courtney, in this writer's opinion, deserves to be recognized as one of the "fathers" of today's so-called spectacular riding devices.

Just before Christmas, 1945, James E. Strates Shows were completely destroyed by fire in its Mullins, South Carolina, tobacco warehouse winter quarters. Only the train was saved. Twenty-five years of this Greek immigrant boy's efforts were in the ashes of that warehouse, and there was less than one third insurance coverage on the carnival these ashes represented. It would take a quarter of a million dollars and thousands of manhours of hard labor to replace the equipment lost so that the route contracted for 1946 could be played. This man, whose determination had brought him up from a wrestler in a carnival "At Show" to the ownership of one of the largest railroad transported carnivals, did not hesitate one second.

He bought sixty-five wagons, fronts and other equipment from B. S. Gerety. The Strates flatcars were dispatched to Shreveport fairgrounds and the

156

remnants of the great Beckman & Gerety Shows were loaded on them for the trip back to South Carolina where they would become the nucleus for another great show. Strates contracted with "Blink" Courtney to build new lighting towers and special show fronts. Scores of men were employed in winter quarters as builders and painters. The James E. Strates Shows played their first 1946 spring date on schedule exactly as contracted.

On January 5, 1946, the "Old Dago," as he was fondly referred to by thousands of carnival troupers, died in the Muskogee, Oklahoma, winter quarters of the World of Today Shows. Johnny J. Bejano, circus side show operator for almost fifty years had died at the age of eighty-three. Carnivaldom's only holdout from electrically amplified speech had packed his big megaphone and reported to the Wortham and Jones lot where a "100 in 1" with solid gold pilasters between the spun silk banners waited for him.

"Specs" Groscurth who had been with Goodman Show in 1945 started his own Blue Grass Shows for 1946 season. Dick Coleman bought his brother Tom's interest in their Coleman Brothers Shows. Dick was now sole owner of this twenty-six year old collective amusement enterprise. Dave Endy reported that he had bought Jimmy Strates' interest in the Endy Brothers Shows and was now sole owner

of this twenty-five car show. J. J. Page, owner for past eighteen years of J. J. Page Exposition Shows, died in Johnson City, Tennessee, on March 5th.

Royal American Shows contracted the Western Canada Class A Fair Circuit for the 1946 season. A contract that Royal American was destined to renew for the entire circuit for twenty years. Bob Lohmar was general agent for Goodman, and Grant Chandler was general superintendent on the same show. J. C. McCarter was general agent for Cetlin & Wilson's new flatcar show, as the usual rain and mud hampered the spring dates of most all shows.

On June 2nd, Mrs. C. W. Parker came to Detroit from her Leavenworth, Kansas home to make a presentation. The Automotive Golden Jubilee was being observed in Detroit, as this widow of carnival pioneer Parker made the presentation. The automotive industry had obtained a merry-go-round horse made in the Parker Factory forty years before. This wooden horse had been restored and refinished with gold leaf as a golden charger. Mrs. Parker presented this golden steed to the honored guest of the City of Detroit that day. General of the Armies, Ike Eisenhower, received from his old boss man's widow one of the wooden horses he had sandpapered to shape as a boy.

ALBERT FLEET (with hat). Chimpanzee trainer with Clyde Beatty on the Jones Show. Courtesy Joe Pearl.

BILLPOSTING "STAND." Johnny J. Jones Exposition. This carnival always "billed like a circus." Courtesy Albert Conover.

Early in 1947 it was reported that Buddy North and Jack Tavelin were entering the collective amusement field and were putting three hundred fifty thousand dollars in the Pacific Eastern Amusement Company. North was listed as President and the executive vice-president was Al Wagner. The industry watched mainly for signs of activity from this new combine as Wagner's Cavalcade of Amusements shared the apex of the carnival business with only one show, the Royal American, and those circus men's money might bring about revolutionary changes in the industry. After a few weeks, nothing more was heard from or about this peculiar partnership.

Usual bad weather at spring dates added to midway owners' problems, but they themselves continued to add to those problems by crowding into towns together in the same week. John R. Ward and Wonder Shows of America "day and dated" in Peoria, but no less than four carnival midways set up in Richmond, Virginia, week of April 26th. The World of Mirth was playing the Atlantic Fat Stock Show there; and John R. Marks, Lawrence Greater and Harrison Greater Shows were all on city lots. Polack Brothers Circus was also at the Fat Stock Show.

Sally Rand, whose girl show was the feature attraction on the Hennies Show midway, reported a net gross of over nine thousand dollars after taxes in one day at the Iowa State Fair in Des Moines. The week's take was forty thousand dollars, for just this one midway show, a sum which only a few years

before, an entire carnival midway was lucky to gross. Royal American reported the fantastic net after tax gross of $283,686.00 at the ten-day Minnesota State Fair in St. Paul. The Fair dates were all very good that 1947 season, but the "still dates" grosses were declining.

Forty-seven year old Delard Lampkin, known by all carnival people as "Whitey Dell," died on May 20th in Johnstown, Pennsylvania. A capable ride superintendent and all-around generally useful carnival man, "Whitey" was superintendent of the Johnny J. Jones Exposition when he died. In June, Mrs. Lillian Sheppard was burned to death in her trailer on the lot with Long's United Shows in Sacramento, California. In September it was reported that John R. Castle was having to spend ninety percent of his time in bed.

Robert L. Lohmar was president of Showmen's League of America in 1948. Dick O'Brian was back with Strates for twelfth season as manager, and Earl Purtle had booked his motor drome on the Cetlin & Wilson Shows. J. C. McCaffery revived the Amusement Corporation of America and bought Max Goodman's carnival. The Goodman Show was retitled the Imperial Shows. Royal American had Sally Rand for a feature show this season. Strates had Georgia Southern, Turner Brothers Shows had Evelyn West and John R. Ward was building a new show for Faith Bacon. "Name" performers were the midway fad of the late forties.

In January one hundred fifty-six charter members of the newly organized Greater Tampa Showman's Club elected Eddie LeMay its first president. In February, Bill Hames Shows were hard hit by snow and ice at the Southwestern Fat Stock Show in Fort Worth.

On February 17th, John R. Castle died in Southern California. It is difficult to visualize the soft-hearted, hard-boiled little Irishman, "Coal Oil" Johnny, on any job with The Wortham and Jones Great Celestial Carnival Co. Perhaps he is now working just off their midway with a little tripod set up under the flickering light of a kerosene pan torch, several of St. Peter's lesser minions crowding close around as he demonstrates a feat of magic using three walnut half shells and one little pea.

Morris Lipsky and Harold "Buddy" Paddock were sole owners of the Johnny J. Exposition in 1948; and K. G. Barkoot, now in his eighties, leased all his equipment to others. J. C. McCarter was general agent for Cetlin & Wilson and had a contract for two more years. Sally Rand liked carnival life and carnival people, while the Carnies all liked Sally. In one case the star was not liked very well. Johnny Ward and Faith Bacon were fighting and feuding.

In early June, Faith sued John R. Ward and his show for $5,044.00 which she claimed he already owed her. It seemed that there was a personality conflict here. Ward alleged that she had broken her contract by not working the times she was required to under that contract. Faith retorted that he wouldn't let her work, that Ward, or some of his trusted employees, had thrown handfuls of big-headed tacks on the stage in front of her as she was doing her dance of the veils, barefooted. Miss Bacon left the show, probably without the five thousand. Faith Bacon jumped to her death from a 3rd floor hotel room in Chicago on September 26, 1956. Since she was destitute, the American Guild of Variety Artists provided the burial.

Floyd Gooding played ninety-three fairs and celebrations with his units in 1948. Many fairs reported there were more gate admissions than in previous years, but the per capita spending of those attending was down. However, the Royal American broke several records for grosses on its route. Frank Bergan closed the season with twelve of the best fairs on his route already contracted for his World of Mirth's 1949 tour. Grant Chandler was superintendent of construction on Hennies Show, and Bob Lohmar was on his last show. He was general agent for the Royal America, where he would stay until his death.

W. C. (Bill) Fleming and Mel Vaught had both died the last week in June. John R. Ward got his show into quarters in the fall, but announced that he wouldn't try to carry out a big show again. Mel Dodson was contracted to manage the Imperial Shows in 1949.

STRING GAME.

159

On January 1, 1949, Alonso H. Barkley, one of the founders of Showmen's League, died. Another recent death had been that of Harry J. Six, a carnival trouper since 1906. Originally a pioneer high diver, he lost his sight in 1917. He operated his own show for several years after 1925 with the assistance of his wife. His leg had been amputated in 1943, his twentieth operation. On January 29th, Chris Smith died. He, his brother Ed, and his father "Pop" had operated the Smith's Greater Shows. Theirs was the first organized carnival to play the North Carolina State Fair at Raleigh.

On March 5th Fire Chief Wilfred Vaillancoart of Van Buren, Maine, resigned when the city council refused to issue a permit for the Granite State Shows to show there July 4th week. Bill and Tilly Rice had their Bingo on the World of Pleasure Shows; and Vivona Brothers had eight rides, a fun house and a glass house. Terrell Jacobs Circus was with Royal American and Life magazine photographers visited Mills Brother Circus to do a story on early carnival press agent, Doc Waddell, who was now with the circus. Business was off on most shows, even with good weather.

In early spring the exhibitor of the first "pickled punk," a two-headed baby, died. Walter K. Sibley, who also originated the 10-in-1 type of carnival exhibition, died on March 9th. Other deaths that 1949 season were Harold Barlow, for twenty years owner of Barlow's Big City Shows; ride builder, Oscar Buck, Sr.; and well-known Fat Show operator, Eddie Karns.

Sam Prell operated two units that season as he had thirty-two Eastern fairs booked. In June, Terrell Jacobs had his right eye removed. While working his wild animal act, Jacobs injured the eye with the cracker of his whip. In five days Terrell was back in the big cage with his cats with a patch over the affected area. On December 6 the Penn Premier Shows was completely destroyed by fire in its storage place in a Carthage, North Carolina, tobacco warehouse. Owner, Lloyd Serfass promised his sponsors that the show would be completely restored in time to play the early spring dates. It was.

The decade ended with very few of the pioneer carnival troupers still active. J. George Loos and half a dozen or so others were all that were left. Only three of the founders of Showmen's League were left: Walter Driver, Tom W. Allen and Vernon Seaver. The Collective Amusement Industry was rapidly being taken over by youngsters in the business. Rides and more rides were being added to midways as high labor cost shows were being eliminated. Grosses that would have sounded fantastic at the beginning of the decade were now commonplace. Labor was the problem. Capable manpower was becoming more difficult to find even when prohibitive wages were offered. Many of the big railroad shows had now disappeared forever and the trend of shifting to trucks was accelerating. The next decade would be great for the business, but not along the lines that old-time carnival devotees had learned to love.

Madam Carnival was fifty-one in 1950 and she was beginning to suffer the aches and pains attendant with reaching the maturity of two score and ten. Her entire mode of existence was changing and her foot-dragging older adherents were unable to slow her inexorable progress towards respectability. The spirit of joyous adventure that had prompted so many of her pioneer freebooters had long since disappeared from her midways. The eager anticipation with which each of her earlier followers had greeted the unexpected events of each new day was lacking now among her newer votaries.

A new breed of midway owners and operators had begun to appear in the collective amusement industry, who were applying modern business methods to midway operations. These "War Babies," as they had been contemptuously referred to by the old timers when their newer operations succeeded during the war years, were gaining more voice in the overall direction of the industry. The older carnies had sent their sons to the best schools and colleges to gain the education and polish that their fathers lacked. These educated young second-generation showmen were using their college acquired knowledge to introduce modern methods into carnival operations.

This change in the type of carnival troupers had begun in the lowest ranks of midway employees during the days of the Great Depression of the thirties. Show owners were literally besieged by men seeking employment. High school and even college graduates were eager to take the jobs that had been filled in the past by the rubbing alcohol drinking, canned heat squeezing denizens of the hobo jungles. Naturally, the showmen preferred sober and reliable manpower and many of these men, who had enjoyed the advantages of good homes and school, were employed for menial jobs on the midways. Hundreds of these men were attacked by the virus of "Carnival Fever" long before jobs opened up for them in other industries and most of them chose to stay and worship at the feet of Queen Carnival. The ones who did stay soon worked their way up in the industry and their influence was felt on midways even before the war years of the forties.

In 1950, the hundredth anniversary years of P. T. Barnum's collective amusement organization, Floyd Gooding had eight midway units playing fairs and celebrations in Ohio, Indiana, and Michigan and he had begun to book a few dates outside this chosen territory of his. Sally Rand was with Al Wagner's Calvacade of Amusements; and Bonnie (Oh Johnny) Baker was featured in the Royal American girl revue. Strates and the newly rebuilt Penn Premier Shows day and dated in a snow storm at Chester, Pennsylvania. Al Kunz was secretary of the Hennies show which was sold that fall to a combine headed by J. C. McCaffery. All shows complained about the weather; and the Johnny J. Jones Exposition had torn down on eight muddy lots in nine weeks. Bad weather continued all through the summer and fall. Dave Endy reported in late October that he had endured "6 days of rain and lawsuits" in Savannah, Georgia.

Bad weather is the worst enemy that an outdoor showman has to face because it can bankrupt him within a few weeks. However, the weather has been blamed by these showmen for much of their own mismanagement. As many show owners are egotists, they do not want to admit mistakes made in booking dates that produce little revenue, or in framing shows that wouldn't "draw flies." When the business at a fair or a still date is down they blame the weather. "It was muddy." "It was too cold." "It was rainy all week." "It was too hot." When the weather is good and business is still unsatisfactory, very few of them report it at all.

Dodson's Imperial Shows title was changed to ACA Imperial Exposition in 1950 and Mel Dodson was not with it. Velare Brothers brought their first Sky Wheel to the East to play Illinois State Fair, Canadian National Exhibition, Tennessee State Fair and the Texas State Fair at Dallas. This double ferris wheel mounted on a revolving arm was first conceived by "Blink" Courtney and was built in Velare Brothers own shops in Long Beach, California. This ninety-two foot high sky wheel could ride over six-hundred patrons an hour. The day of the spectacular ride had dawned and many Carnival Midway owners had bought them by the end of the decade.

Joe Pontico, with the Royal American, completed his fiftieth year in outdoor show business and the Gooding name had been used with rides for fifty-two years. Railroad show equipment was not wanted by any showman and Ben Davenport had to sell his Daily Brothers Circus train to the scrap dealers. Mr. Floyd E. Gooding told this writer in 1969 that he had considered transporting some of his ride units by flatcar but had found that his transportation costs would be doubled by so doing. Only three circuses were on rails in 1950 and you could count the railroad-moving carnivals on your ten fingers.

Morris and John Vivona, who had annexed their midway to Prells to play the latter's fair dates in 1950, announced that they were booking a route of their own for 1951. Gooding had played one hundred fifteen fairs and celebrations in 1950 and had one hundred twenty-five booked for the next season.

Dave Endy booked the Bloomsburg, Pennsylvania, Fair, but didn't get his show on the road. King Reid Shows had to come into Bloomsburg on short notice. James H. (Georgia Boy) Drew booked a route of eighteen fairs for 1951; and Doc Waddell had been chaplain of Mills Brothers Circus for several years.

Biggest laugh of the year, for showmen, was provided by Al Wagner in January when he sued Sally Rand and NBC for two million dollars. He asserted that Sally's statement in a broadcast from Chicago's Chez Paree that he owed her $23,000.00 "hurt his reputation." A Dallas court settlement with Sally later on that year cost Al $10,514.00.

Specs Groscurth moved his Blue Grass Shows into Southern Illinois, still dates for the first time, in Spring of 1951. Billie Clark, former operator of the Broadway Shows, died in Tyler, Texas, on May 19th; and Al Wagner had the middle finger on his right hand chewed off by a chimpanzee in Terre Haute, Indiana, on May 31st. Robert K. (Bob) Parker and Sam Soloman had bought the Johnny J. Jones equipment at a forced sale in Bainbridge, Georgia. They didn't put the show on the road again. A great title, oldest of all, had died. Specs Groscurth cancelled the remainder of the Illinois dates in late May and moved back into his old Indiana territory.

Evelyn West, "the Girl with the $50,000.00 Bosom," headed Hennies Brothers' girl revue for the 1951 fair dates; and the title of that midway was changed to Amusement Corporation of America Shows. Another title was gone. Fat woman, Mrs. Clifford Karn, was with this show. This 632 pound woman died on July 16th in Kenosha, Wisconsin, leaving her husband and two daughters.

Ninety-six year old Frank Menches died in Akron, Ohio, in October. He had operated concessions at Ohio fairs for eighty years. One day at the Summit County, Ohio, Fair in 1892 he ran out of link sausages. He instructed his helpers to form ground sausage meat into patties and sell them as sandwiches. They sold very well; so he continued to sell them. He gave them a name two years later at the Elyria, Ohio, Fair and his new sandwich which he called a "hamburger" became a fairgrounds staple. He sold the first ice cream cones in Ohio at the Barberton, Ohio, Fair in 1904. This novel way of serving ice cream was tried for the first time that spring at the St. Louis World's Fair.

Slim Kelly, who had the Circus Side Show on John Mark's Shows, quit the road and moved to Sarasota, Florida, as manager of Selhorn's Trailer Sales there. Dolly Young bought Eddie Young's interest in the Royal Crown Shows. Terrell Jacob's Wild Animal Circus had been with Strates all season and would be with that midway again in 1952. By the last of October, Cetlin & Wilson had booked their route for all of the next year and general agent, R. C. McCarter, resigned as he didn't want to be inactive all winter. A ride man on the Magic Empire Shows had an argument with a native at Troy, Alabama, on October 27th. Show owner, Andrew (Curley) Spheer came to his man's aid and was shot to death by the "towner."

On March 15, 1952, the Cole Brothers Circus train was sold to the scrap dealers. Strates was framing a number two show, the Strates Model Shows. This show was framed with equipment from both Endy Brothers and Johnny J. Jones and Dave Endy was the manager. Patty Conklin was awarded the midway of the Canadian National Exhibition for another five years and Barnes Brothers Circus was the feature show on the World of Mirth. On June 26th Samuel W. Gumpertz, aged 84, died in Sarasota, Florida; and on July 16th Doc Waddell died in Columbus, Ohio.

SYMBOLIC OF THE FUTURE. Now most all collective amusement enterprises move by truck. Courtesy Art Doc Miller.

NEW FACES. Big-time carnival operators, the five Vivona Brothers, sign a contract. Courtesy Amusement Business Photograph.

William Shackleford Andres, known as Doc Waddell, was eighty-eight years old when he died. He had spent over seventy years in outdoor show business and had been an evangelist for forty-five years of this. His widow, Effie Andres, gave him a conventional funeral at Springfield, Ohio. She said that he had given up his idea of having a "showman's funeral" and had agreed to a regular service a day or so before his death. Doc had now joined Wortham and Jones as their full-time chaplain.

On August 21, 1952, a tornado leveled the Cetlin & Wilson shows on the Missouri State Fairgrounds at Sedalia. The entire show was wrecked with damages amounting to a quarter of a million dollars. One person was killed and many hurt. Hundreds of offers of help were phoned and wired to the owners of the wrecked show. Some were accepted and show opened at the Indiana State Fair at Indianapolis as big as ever. On October 20th a fire wiped out the independent midway at the South Carolina State Fair at Columbia. Fifty-seven concession joints were burned, but the World of Mirth midway itself wasn't damaged.

In November J. C. McCarter, who had left the Strates Model Shows in August, announced that he was in a partnership with Shirley Lawrence to build a new railroad show to be called the Metropolitan Shows. Lawrence Greater truck show rides and equipment would be used. Dailey Circus and Johnny J. Jones flatcars were purchased from the East St.

Louis junk dealer. The show was built that winter and opened in Asheville, North Carolina, on May 11, 1953. It was on thirty cars and carried twenty-one rides and fourteen shows. Legion Commander, Joe McKennon, took the first ticket sold on this new show when the front gate opened at six P.M. Weather was bad and the sponsoring Legion Post barely made their expenses. McCarter had already left the show when it played Asheville. He was manager for the new Tri-State Fair at Bristol, Virginia-Tennessee.

Art Lewis bought and operated the John Marks Shows in 1953 for seventeen weeks of wet still dates. He turned the show back to Marks. Jack Ruback's Alamo Exposition Shows shared the San Jacinta Fiesta and Battle of Flowers in San Antonio with five other shows. Ruback had a total of forty-two rides, seventeen shows and one hundred sixty concessions on the plazas that week. King Kong, six and one-half year old gorilla, with the midway at the Charro Days Celebration in Brownsville, Texas, found almost a full quart of rum. Stomach pump couldn't save him, but he died happy.

Floyd Gooding had ten units playing his fair dates; and Pete Kortez had both Jess Willard and Joe Louis with his Circus Side Show on the Dallas Fair midway. Joseph G. Ferari, one of the first midway kings, died in New York on May 9th. He was eighty-five. The fair board at Metropolis, Illinois, attached the Cavalcade equipment after their fair, but had to release the property as it was owned by a

VELARE'S DOUBLE SPACE WHEEL. The first of the American-built "Spectacular Rides." Courtesy Al Kunz.

holding company, not Al Wagner himself. On November 18th sixty-nine year old Mad Cody Fleming died in Georgia. Cody T. Fleming had been with carnivals for forty-nine years, starting as an "At Show" wrestler and having a ten-car rail show when the depression hit. He salvaged three rides and moved to Georgia with them. The following from the Atlanta Constitution indicates the reputation he enjoyed in his adopted state:

"'Always do right,' Mark Twain advised. 'This will gratify some and startle the rest.'"

"A man who lived by that code died Friday in Georgia. He was Mad Cody Fleming, wrestler, carnival owner, politico and friend to man.... Mr. Fleming had lived in Brantley County since 1923. That is, Brantley was his home. He lived all over the state as the Mad Cody Shows made its annual tour from town to town. During those weeks you'd find the colorful grizzled owner in an easy chair near the ticket office, philosophizing, talking politics and making friends with the children who come to try the rides.... They'll miss Cody Fleming down in Brantley County where his show had earned for itself an enviably reputation for cleanliness and honesty.... Other carnivals would do well to imitate the Cody mode of operation."

James H. Drew booked twenty-two fairs and festivals for his 1954 season. McCarter, whose fair at Bristol had been ruined by a polio epidemic, was now general agent for Marks; and Floyd Gooding was to have rides at the Ohio State Fair for the thirty-second year. In March J. Ed Johnson, national-known authority on reptiles, was bitten by a huge rattlesnake while on a snake catching expedition in the "brakes of the Brazos" river, below Waco, Texas. He died.

Federal tax men held Wagner's train in winter quarters for three days before allowing it to move out of Mobile on April 8th. They claimed that the show owed $263,374.00 in back taxes. Wagner might have kept the show out, if he had lived. On April 11th William O. Burke, show painter, went to the office wagon and asked for a payment on his salary. Wagner became abusive. Burke shot and killed him on that Pensacola, Florida, showgrounds. The show train was moved back to Mobile by the receivers for public sale and Burke was cleared of blame by a jury later in the year.

Al Wagner, who with his wife, Hattie, had owned the largest collective amusement enterprise for a brief period, was now dead and his holdings were all gone. This man and wife team, who had spent many years on carnival midways, probably contributed less to the industry than any other major show owner. Their only legacy to the business is a series of fantastic stories not fit be published in this volume.

In 1954 Frank Cucksey was with Nate Eagles' Hollywood Midgets on the World of Mirth midway and Bobbie Hasson was manager of the circus side show with Royal American. Lloyd Serfass had to buy a two-acre patch of spinach to make enough space to set up his Penn Premier Shows on the lot contracted in Levittown, Pennsylvania. Tippy, Earl Chamber's two hundred fifty pound gorilla, bent back the bars in her cage and took a three-hour stroll through the Cetlin & Wilson winter quarters in Petersburg, Virginia. Her handler followed her with her drink bottle as she happily investigated the quarters. All work stopped until Tippy got thirsty. She took her bottle from her friend and drank it dry. When she wakened she was safely locked in a much stronger den.

Spring weather in 1954 was better than usual but some midways lost a few days because they still opened too early. In the fall Hurricane Hazel hit several shows along the Atlantic Coast. Shows suffering the most damage were the Marks and the Gold Medal. Latter show was in Wilson, North Carolina. All electricity was off in the town and the Wilson Daily Times was ready to go to press. It had not missed an issue since its founding in 1896, but presses could not turn without power. Johnny Denton, Gold Medal owner, pulled his light plants to the newspaper building, electrical connections were made and the newspaper came out on time.

This was one example of show people's helping townspeople in an emergency. In 1937 when the Ohio River flooded the adjoining lowlands for a long period, Cole Brothers Circus sent a special train to Southern Indiana from its Rochester, Indiana, winter quarters. Owners, Jess Adkins and Zack Terrell, sent all of their light plants, cook house and dining facilities, tentage and sleeping cars. The trained circus personnel that accompanied this equipment set up a refugee camp that supplied the needs of several thousand displaced persons.

On June 25th Frank M. Sutton, Sr., was playing Denham Springs, Louisana, with his Gulf Coast Shows. He had framed this show from the equipment of the Groves Greater, after he gave the Great Sutton title to his son, Frank M., Jr. Mr. Sutton who had spent forty-nine years on carnival midways died of self-inflicted gunshot wounds on the midway in Denham Springs. A few days before, on June 18th, Mrs. Lyle Hale was killed and Mr. Hale wounded by gunshots in their trailer on the midway of the Hale's Shows of Tomorrow at Kansas City, Kansas. Mr. Hale died on June 20th.

In July, Dolly Young, former owner of Royal Crown Shows, joined Buff Hottle Shows as business manager and legal adjuster. Starr DeBelle was with Gooding Million Dollar Midway and J. C. McCarter was assistant manager of the Hickey's Gem City Shows. The Wagner show property was sold for $64,600.00; the Royal American got the train. Canadian National Exhibition got big publicity from the forty-five mile swim of sixteen year old Marilyn Bell. Miss Bell, a Toronto High School student, swam across Lake Ontario from Youngstown, Ohio, to the CNE. She missed the fairgrounds by less than one mile.

On September 28th J. C. McCaffery died in a Chicago hospital. His biggest contribution to the

SOMETOWN, U.S.A., A FEW YEARS AGO. Author's collection.

industry had been the formation of the Amusement Corporation of America in the late thirties and his continuing efforts to form carnival combines. Wortham and Jones had no need of these talents of "Macs" and he probably has the exclusive rights to the "Celestial Delight" (frozen custard) concession on their midway. Here on earth, he owned quite a few custard machines.

A few days later, William R. Hirsch died in Shreveport, Louisiana, at the age of seventy-four. Manager of the Louisiana State Fair for many years, he had been a friend to many carnival owners and carnival people. He had extended aid to hundreds of persons when they needed help, without any thought of personal benefit. His benevolences in Northwestern Louisiana were legion and he was confident of teenager and bank president alike. Everyone went to Bill Hirsch with their problems. Although he was directly connected with carnivals only five years as a co-owner, he was accepted by all carnies as one of their own. This gentle man who loved flowers and collected miniature elephant models would be missed with fond remembrance by thousands of friends, both in the carnival field and in his hometown.

By February 1, 1955, Floyd E. Gooding already had one hundred two fairs contracted for the new season and the Metropolitan Shows was tied up by litigations in Montgomery, Alabama, winter quarters. Bobbie Hasson was contracted to manage the Ringling Brothers and Barnum & Bailey Side Show, while Strates was signing a ten-year contract to furnish the midway at the Central Florida Fair in Orlando, Florida.

R. C. McCarter and Robert K. Parker promoted a new fair at Ft. Wayne, Indiana, in 1955. Frank Cucksey was back with Nate Eagles' Hollywood Midgets on the World of Mirth for another season; and Starr DeBelle returned to Strates as public relations director. Vivona Brothers renamed their show the Amusements of America. Weather was bad, but help shortage was worse all season. Jimmy Strates had the doors all welded tight after all tools and supplies were loaded in the supply car left in Orlando Quarters; and the Royal American spent several days trying to get onto a muddy Paducah, Kentucky, lot before going on to Evansville, Indiana.

Tommy Tidwell's elephant, Queenie, was killed in a truck accident, north of Dallas, Texas. Norman Joseph, a passenger in the truck cab, jumped out, but Queenie landed on top of him. He was killed too. Shirley Lawrence Levy got the Metropolitan Shows out of quarters but was tied up again on a Rome, Georgia, railroad siding. Show got to Anniston, Alabama in early June and the Levys disclaimed having any problems. It did "make the season."

On December 3rd, Joe Scholibo, long-time carnival executive, married Gladys McDuffie, Louisiana State Fair's "Girl Friday." Gladys has a "first name calling acquaintance" with more fairgrounds' concessions people and showmen than any other fair executive with the possible exception of Harry Frost who has been with the Minnesota State Fair for over forty years. The Scholibos are still with the Louisiana State Fair in 1971 helping secretary-manager, Joe Monsour, maintain that great fair as "the Friendliest Fair in America."

In January 1956 Judge Jim Hughes of the Orangeburg, South Carolina, Fair booked the Marks Shows to play that annual event. This was the first non-railroad transported show ever booked to play that fair. The Reithoffers, who had been operating small midways for generations, moved into larger carnival operations and booked some good fairs. J. George Loos played the Laredo, Texas, Washington's Birthday Celebration for the thirty-ninth year; and John R. Ward's small Pan-American Shows opened in Baton Rouge, Louisiana. Floyd Gooding now owned twelve merry-go-rounds, seven tilt-a-whirls and one hundred fifty other rides.

L. J. Heth, eighty year old pioneer carnival showman died with a heart attack at Birmingham, Alabama. He had been active the day before his death. His nephew, Floyd Heth, was the new owner and Joe J. Fontana continued as general agent. A few days later, Curtis L. Bockus died. He had been active as a promotor and owner of midways since 1902. In March Noble C. Fairly died after more than fifty years as owner, manager and executive of carnivals. On June 4th Ralph Clawson, long-time circus and carnival executive with the Cristiani Circus, died in Fitchburg, Massachusetts. C. Guy Dodson, who had retired from carnival business in 1939, died in Savannah, Georgia, on September 22nd.

1956 season was the most disastrous season, with possible exception of 1938, that circus business had ever encountered. The Great Ringling Brothers and Barnum & Bailey Circus folded its huge tents for the last time. No longer would the rumble of its heavy wagons be heard long before daylight as its "flying squadron" disgorged the first elements of the "magic city" that would blossom for "one day only" on the fairgrounds or out on Joe Doakes' meadow. No longer would young "He-Men Americans" be allowed to engage in that one great adventure of a lifetime, the setting up of the "Greatest Show on Earth."

That adventure of which countless thousands of their predecessors would brag to their grandchildren. Most of them prefacing this boast with, "I carried water for the elephants........" which they never did. This myth of town boys being given a pass for carrying water was press agent's fiction. Sometimes the boys did carry water for the dressing rooms, band or some department but never for the elephants. The

SOMETOWN, CANADA, SEVERAL YEARS AGO. Courtesy J. W. Patty Conklin.

TERRELL JACOBS WILD ANIMAL CIRCUS. Last big circus to tour with a major carnival as one of the midway shows. Courtesy Starr DeBelle.

six hundred horses with the Ringling Barnum Circus consumed more water than the thirty to fifty elephants ever did and nobody has bragged that he carried water for the horses. They were all given water in the same type of portable tank or tub filled from water wagons or at a fire plug. "The water-carrying" myth did sound much better to anxious parents, who worried about the hard work their boys were doing, than the brutal fact that those boys were carrying quarter poles, seat stringers and "bible backs."

Clyde Beatty Circus went bankrupt early that year, but was reopened with new management in the fall. Arnold Maley's and Floyd King's two units of King Brothers Circus both folded quick and other circuses had poor seasons. Carnivals had fairly good business in 1956, and all the bigger ones completed their bookings. Weather did provide some good headlines in Billboard all season.

"Groggy Eastern Units Hoping for Good Biz at Fairs." "Rain Cuts Olson Biz at Illinois State Fair." "Rain Slows Record WOM Pace at Ottawa." "Rain Cuts Reading Turnout Over 20%." "Michigan Gate Skids, Midway Battles Trend." Most of the shows playing these dates reported their grosses satisfactory; and W. G. Wade at Michigan State Fair did break all existing records in spite of the rain.

During this season of bad weather and circus disaster, William R. Dyer renamed his Dyer's Greater Shows. He called it the Lotta Hooey Shows and used

that title for some time in his Billboard ads. After Ringling Barnum Circus closed, Bob Hasson went to the Strates Shows as assistant manager. Strates bought all of the animals from the defunct King Brothers Circus units and added them to their already sizable menagerie. A new type of midway operation was beginning to appear. Special units of rides and small shows were being framed to play on shopping center parking lots and many of them were getting good grosses.

In spite of having a $400,000.00 profit in 1956, the Canadian National Exhibition raised their gate admission from fifty cents to seventy-five cents for 1957. The Conklins were given another long-term contract for the CNE midway; and Specs Groscurth was given a ten year contract by the Plant City, Florida, Strawberry Festival for his Blue Grass Shows. The Reithoffers booked twenty-four fairs for their route. Bobby Cohn was general agent for the West Coast Shows; and Sally Rand was with Raynell Golden's girl revue on the Cetlin & Wilson midway. Usual amount of bad weather hurt business at some spots, but James H. Drew reported the best season he had ever had with his carnival. Late in the fall, Al Kunz bought the L. J. Heth Shows from Floyd Heth. Gooding had trouped ten units again in 1957, and H. William Jones had operated ten big bingo games during the season.

In March Art Eldridge conducted grave-side rites

everybody was wet, broke and hungry. The sun came out and several dozen University of Texas students came on the lot. All of them headed for the merry-go-round which could not turn without power. After a hasty consultation, all ride men from the other devices got around the "Jenney," took a grip on platform rods and took off. They gave those students a fast, long ride on the "swing" that day. J. George said, "the hamburgers we bought with the money from that ride were the best I ever ate in my life." Loos played Laredo for the fortieth year in 1958.

Tom W. Allen, C. A. Wortham's first partner, C. W. Parker's son-in-law and long-time carnival operator, died in Waynesville, Missouri, on January 14th. He was the last charter member of the Showmen's League of America. On February 11th, W. F. Mangels died in New York. Ninety-one year old Mangels was best known as the inventor of the Whip ride, but he had patented and manufactured many other amusement devices. He patented his first device in 1891. J. C. Weer, former show owner and ride operator died on July 31st in Miami.

In 1959 business for all midways was satisfactory. Floyd Gooding had eleven units on road and was building a $750,000.00 winter quarters in Columbus, Ohio. No other show, circus or carnival, has ever had a winter quarters that will equal this one of Mr. Gooding's. Hurricane "Gracie" clobbered several shows in the Carolinas and Virginia in late September, but no great damage was done to anything other than the gross business.

This 1959 season was again highlighted by the deaths of well-known carnival showmen. John F. "Blink" Courtney, designer of the sky wheel, died in Chicago the last day of 1968. J. Allen Darnaby, pioneer carnival manager and pageant producer, died in Evanston, Illinois, on May 3rd. Joe Prell, fifty-four year old general agent of the Prell Shows, died after surgery in Goldboro, North Carolina. Then during the Danville, Virginia, Fair, news was sent out that James E. Strates was dead.

This sixty-five year old Greek immigrant, who had literally fought his way to the top in the Collective Amusement Industry, had a stroke in his private office wagon while talking to his daughter, Elizabeth Alexander. She, at her telephone in Syracuse, New York, sensed quickly that something serious had happened to her father. She broke the connection and placed an emergency call to Mr. Curtis Finch in the Fair Secretary's office. Mr. Finch hurried over to Strates' office, saw the situation, got an ambulance and rushed the carnival owner to a hospital. Jimmy Strates went into a coma in the ambulance and never regained consciousness. This man who had wrestled in a carnival "At Show" to

NEW FACES. Carnival owner Johnny Portemont, Jr. "laying out the lot." Johnny's equipment is the cleanest and best maintained of any show visited in last three years. Courtesy Amusement Business Photograph.

make enough to start his first little Southern Tier Shows, and had built it into greatest show on the Eastern seaboard was now dead.

The Strates Shows was to continue as James E. had trained his son, E. James, to be ready to take over; and this capable young second generation showman is building the Strates Shows even bigger and better each season.

As the decade ended, old carnival patterns and methods had almost disappeared from the collective industry field. Very few of the old-time carnival owners were left now, and those survivors had kept ahead of the others by being the leaders. Second, and even third, generation carnival showmen were taking over the business. The old timers were reporting fantastic grosses with their operations. Carl J. Sedlmayr's Royal American Shows grossed $346,019.00 at the 1958 Minnesota State Fair, and the same year, Patty Conklin reported a gross of $707,515.70 at the Canadian National Exposition. The huge grosses were overshadowed by shortage of labor and high cost of operations.

WALL TO WALL PEOPLE. Carnivals are showing to more and more people each year and their grosses are getting bigger and bigger. Unfortunately, expenses are going up faster than income on most shows. Courtesy Amusement Business Photograph.

As Madam Carnival celebrated her sixty-first birthday alone and unattended, she probably shed a few tears for those riotous, rollicking midways of her past. For most of her over four hundred noisy progeny were now becoming respectable and some of them had long ago attained that honorable station. Many of her midways were getting contracts for next season before this season's commitment had been fulfilled. A few were signing compacts with fairs for three, five and even ten years; and some of her more decorous offspring had played the same fairs and celebrations for thirty years or more. One or two had been furnishing entertainment for some of their committees for over fifty years.

In 1960 a man could bring his wife and children to most midways and get them back to the rides without having to "run the gauntlet" between rows of sharp-eyed gentlemen all determined to fleece him of the cash with which he had planned to pay for his family's hour or two of pleasure. As the children rode on the scooter, the merry-go-round or the bubble bounce, this man and his wife could stand by a "grab joint" and eat a "corn dog" without having to listen to a babel of electically amplified promises of sexual sights and things erotic that could be viewed in the shows around the midway.

This change towards a "Sunday-School" type of operation probably was forced on most midway operators by economic necessity. More and more riding devices were demanded by the carnival-going segment of the public, and fair committees began to specify larger number of devices in their contracts. Midway shows with live performers cost more to operate and very few of them could "make the nut." Most midways were now lined with single pit attractions similar to those that surrounded the very first carnival streets, except that now there were no dancing girls, circuses, plantation shows or wild west exhibitions. The cost of operating those shows would be prohibitive to most managers. There were a few midway operators like Floyd E. Gooding, who had always managed "Sunday School" shows and had never tolerated anything shady or off-color on their showgrounds.

The success of these "clean" operations was bound to influence others to clean up their shows. The example of Mr. Gooding's requirement of ten or eleven complete midways to play the fairs and celebrations for which loyal committees gave him contracts, caused other show owners to see that clean midways were profitable. Contracts that could not be lured away from him by offers of bigger percentages and larger guarantees showed clearly that the fair-going public wanted his type of midway. The

lucrative fair dates with their high grosses which Carl J. Sedlmayr, Jimmy Strates, John Marks and others retained year after year were not kept by them solely because of the brilliance and magnitude of their enterprises. There had been a collective amusement enterprise larger than any of them in the middle forties. It had a superb route for a couple of years and then was in difficulty. This was another warning to those who were lax in enforcing certain standards of business morality.

In January 1960 C. S. Peck sold his Key City Shows to the Thumberg Family. Allen Herschall bought the Velare Brothers patents on the big rides. Al Kunz bought the big Sky Ride from the Brothers and every show owner who could raise the down payment ordered a sky wheel from Allen Herschal. Johnny Portemont of Johnny's United Shows reported that he had booked twenty-four fairs, and on April 21st Ken Garman opened his thirty-first season with his Sunset Amusement Company. Lloyd Serfass reported that he had thirty-one weeks booked for his Penn Premier Shows and twenty-one weeks already signed for his Keystone State midway.

John R. Ward, ex-jockey, ex-professional boxer and ex-railroad carnival owner, died on February 24th in Baton Rouge, Louisiana. Johnny Ward had been in the collective amusement business forty-seven years, when he died. Roland Champagne, owner of the Continental Shows for twenty-eight years, died in Dracut, Massachusetts, on March 23rd; and James Edward Buck, died on May 6th in Los Angeles. Seventy-two year old Buck, better known as J. Ed Brown, had been in outdoor show business since 1900. He started with the Cole Younger & Frank James Wild West Show after the two ex-outlaws went into show business.

Edward (Ted) Leavitt was general agent for the Royal West Shows in California; and Deggeller Brothers started their fourth year as carnival owners with two units. Strates was featuring a free menagerie just inside the front gate at all still dates; and Al Kunz opened the 1960 season with twenty-nine rides and ten shows on his Heth midway. Floyd Gooding said it was "Rainiest May ever," and many shows encountered rain all season. Joe Fredrick, who had started his Motor State Shows in 1945 with two rides, now had forty-two on his midway at some spots.

"Georgia Boy" Drew and Al Kunz combined their midways to play the Exchange Club Fair in Augusta, Georgia. They put fifty-seven rides and twenty-two shows on this fairgrounds which had been played by railroad transported midways for many years. Vivona Brothers had forty-three rides at the fair in Charleston, South Carolina. Only fifty years

BIG CROWDS!! High grosses at Minnesota State Fair. Courtesy Harry Frost, Minnesota State Fair.

before only the largest midways could boast of having more than two rides and none of them carried more than five until after the end of World War One.

On June 24th, seventy-four year old Bill Hames died in Ft. Worth. Bill had bought his first Merry-Go-Round in 1918 and had been playing fairs and celebrations ever since. He owned the only railroad transported carnival in the Southwest; and had provided the midway amusements for some fairs and picnics in the Lone Star State for over forty years. His word was his bond. No other person, with the possible exception of that great West Texas tent repertoire owner, Harley Sadler, could count as many Texans as his personal friends as Bill Hames could.

In 1961 the usual number of small shows opened for the first time, the usual number of them failed to complete the season and the usual amount of bad weather was encountered by all. The World of Mirth was opening late to escape the spring rains, but its business at fairs wasn't as good as it had been in past seasons. The show, itself, was beginning to look a little tired and "worn out," as very little repair work had been done to the equipment in several years. The "front end" had carried the show along during the fifties, and more care was given to the concessions than to the rides and shows on the "back end."

On April 17th the entire carnival world was stunned by the news that Doc Dorton was dead. Doctor J. S. Dorton, fair manager since 1924, had died at his home in Shelby, North Carolina. Sixty-six years old, Doc graduated from a veterinary school, but show business was his chosen profession. He organized the fair in Shelby in 1924 and another one in Charlotte a few years later. He had been manager of the North Carolina State Fair at Raleigh for many years. He was respected and liked by every one who knew him, but his gruff manner of addressing people caused some carnival showmen to be just a little bit afraid of Doc.

This writer met Doc for the first time in 1938 as he put the great Johnny J. Jones Exposition on the Cleveland County Fairgrounds near Shelby. A dapper human dynamo was rushing here, there and everywhere around the fairgrounds and would pause occasionally to observe the movement of the wagons onto the midway area.

Although it was never one of the superintendent's duties to settle percentage matters with the fair office, McKennon was not surprised when he was asked on Wednesday morning to carry the carnival's settlement money, from the Tuesday receipts, to the fair secretary. Doc was seated in his

backroom office. Doc yelled cheerfully "what in the
——————— ——————— ———————
——————— do you want?" To which the
younger man replied just as vigorously, "I have
brought you your ———————
——————— money, if you don't want the
——————— stuff, I'll take it back to our
——————— ——————— office wagon." Doc
jumped up and exclaimed "come in here, boy, let's
talk awhile." A twenty-two year friendship resulted.

In January 1962 three men with over fifty years
in outdoor show business died. Henry Meyerhoff died
in Penticton, British Columbia, after sixty-four years
with midway attraction. Ralph W. Smith, who had
handled untold millions of dollars as treasurer of the
World of Mirth and other carnivals died in Ft.
Lauderdale, Florida, on January 9th. He was reputed
to be the financial backer of several midway ventures,
always remaining unidentified as such. Bernard
(Bernie) Smuckler died in December at Mobile,
Alabama, although his death wasn't reported to the
industry until late in January. Bernie, who had been
in show business fifty-six years, was best known by
the mid-century carnival troupers as the organizer of
the Royal Palm Shows.

On August 19th, seventy-five year old Barney
Tassell, owner of the show carrying his name, died in
Miami, Florida. He had been in show business for
over sixty years, but many of them were with stage

CLYDE PROBST, JR. Progressive manager of the Cabarrus County Fair
at Concord, North Carolina. Courtesy Amusement Business
Photographs.

shows. He was purported to be the originator of
"Tabloid Shows," and eighteen of his units toured
theatres in the Southern States during the late
"teens." On October 27th, J. George Loos died in
Laredo, Texas. Active operator of carnivals since
1902, eighty-two year old George Loos was
undoubtedly the oldest such operator in the business.

The big amusement news of 1962 was from
Seattle, Washington. A group of men, not realizing
that it would be impossible for them to create and
open a World's Fair in the time, with the finances and
on the space they had allocated, opened on time and
operated successfully such a fair. The Seattle Century
21 Exposition was probably the most successful
world's exposition put together in this century. The
promoters of this world's fair did not hesitate to call
in outdoor showmen for advice and help. They even
went so far as to turn the amusement Gayway over to
park man, Batt, and showman, Patty Conklin. Batt
and Conklin produced and operated the Gayway, the
most successful fun zone at any World's Exposition.

Patty Conklin and Harry Batt were not ashamed
to call in experienced outdoor showmen to help them
on the Gayway. When the Velare Brothers, who had
two other big attractions on this midway were unable
to get their Giant World's Fair Wheel (portable) ready
for the opening, Patty called Al Kunz, who now
owned the big Double Double Wheel, or Space Wheel.
In just five days, Al and his crew transported the huge
trucks non-stop thirty-two hundred miles and set the

NEIL BOLTON. Capable manager of the Dixie Classic Fair in
Winston-Salem, North Carolina. Courtesy Amusement Business
Photograph.

LOBBY ACTIVITIES. North Carolina Association of County Fairs Meeting in January each year. These meetings are held in most all states during the winter months. Courtesy Amusement Business Photograph.

Winter Activities 1962

"BUSMAN'S HOLIDAY." Showmen visiting Florida State Fair in Tampa in early February. Courtesy Amusement Business Photograph.

L. I. THOMAS. Friendly owner of the Thomas Joyland Shows, Courtesy Amusement Business Photograph.

AL KUNZ. Owner Century 21 Shows. His is a multi-unit operation. He probably owns more spectacular rides than any other showman. Courtesy Al Kunz.

The World of Mirth Shows ended its 1963 season abruptly at the end of its engagement at the Winston-Salem, North Carolina, Fair. Fair manager Neil Bolton had an uninvited and unwanted guest on his fairgrounds in that North Carolina city. The lonely wagons, still loaded with the components of a once-magic midway, huddled in forlorn clusters in one corner of the grounds. There they remained like abandoned derelicts until they were all sold at public sale to partially satisfy the many claims against this once-great amusement enterprise.

1964 was another average year for carnivals. Some made it, some didn't; some had lots of bad weather, others had perfect weather; some bought more rides, others sold some of theirs; a normal season. Royal American had the big Velare World's Fair Wheel at their fairs, and Gooding still required ten units to play his fairs and celebrations. The Ringling Brothers and Barnum & Bailey Circus was back on railroad cars, as it had been for a couple of years, and was making long jumps between towns to indoor arenas large enough to house its great performance.

In June Lloyd Hilligoss, owner of the Fun Fair Shows purchased the Foley & Burk Combined Shows. Foley & Burk was, and is, the longest continuous carnival title in operation, it having been used for over fifty years. Mr. Hilligoss got the complete show including its railroad train of twenty-two cars. The Royal American reported a gross of $492,000.00 at the Minnesota State Fair, and the World of Mirth equipment brought a total of $47,278.00 at the sale in Winston-Salem on September 2.

Space Wheels up in time for the opening of the fair on Saturday, May 27. When Velare Brothers got their new type wheel ready, Al moved his ride back to the midwest to fill the dates he had booked for it. Bobby Cohn, general agent of the West Coast Shows had two rides of his own on the Gayway; and Morgan Hughes, importer of European riding devices had several of those imports in the ride lineup.

In 1963, the owners of the Marks Shows put their names on it. The Dell & Travers Shows continued to book and play the Marks route of fairs. Al Kunz changed the name of his Heth Shows. It became the Century 21 Shows, but the Heth show title was still used in advertising for some towns. Bobby Cohn was made assistant general manager of the West Coast Shows by that show's president, Mike Krekos. Harry Myers was general manager of this show. Grant Chandler joined the Century 21 midway as manager of the new Century 21 Fun House that Kunz had bought from Velare Brothers after the Seattle Fair closed.

Louie Berger, who had started as co-owner of the Morris and Berger Shows in 1903, died on March 21, 1963, in Chicago. Lee Ulrich Eyerly, founder of the Eyerly Aircraft Company and builder of the Loop-O-Plane and other rides, died in Salem, Oregon, on March 23rd. Orville N. Crafts died on June 18th in Las Vegas, Nevada. He had owned and managed the Crafts Shows (sometimes as many as three complete carnivals) since 1933. Old-time operator of Bantley's All American Shows, seventy-two year old Herman Bantley, died at his home in Reynoldsville, Pennsylvania in May; and L. G. Chapman, owner-manager of the Foley & Burk Shows, died August 18th in Turlick, California. He had been with carnivals since they started back in 1899.

LAVOY WINTON. In 1964, Winton had the lot all laid out ready to spot in his show on the Murphresboro, Tennessee showgrounds when he found a meadow lark's nest (in circle). He pulled all stakes and laid out again so that the entire show would be away from the nest. He also put guard ropes around the nest. Courtesy Amusement Business Photograph.

HEAD PORTER AND HIS CREW. A 1962 photograph of head porter, Willis Tolliver, and his crew on the Royal American Shows train. Courtesy Amusement Business Photograph.

First death of a showman in 1964 was Max Goodman, former concessionaire and show owner, on January 1st in Miami. Eighty-two year old C. R. Leggette, long-time operator of the shows carrying his name, died on January 27th in New Iberia, Louisiana. C. F. (Doc) Zeiger, former owner of Zeiger United Shows, died in Glendale, California, on February 20th; and William R. (Bob) Hammontree died in Chattanooga, Tennessee on July 23rd. Both had been with outdoor shows for over sixty years.

On February 26, 1965, Mrs. Catherine (Mom) Vivona, mother of the five Vivona Brothers was killed in a railroad crossing accident at Coral Gables, Florida. Mom Vivona had finished raising her sons after their father died, supporting them with proceeds from food concessions at church bazaars. As soon as a son was old enough to operate a concession, he was given one of his own. Mrs. Vivona had continued to work in the office of their Amusements of America until her death.

A new corporation took over the operation of the West Coast Shows early in 1965. This corporation headed by Bobby Cohn had Forest Tucker as vice-president. By season's end, Cohn had completely revitalized the show and was planning to use as many as four units to play the dates he hoped to book. He and Lloyd Hilligoss together spent over six hundred thousand dollars for new equipment for their midways before the year was over.

At the Pensacola, Florida, Fair the first portable Sky Driver was set up. Chance's new ride had now been put on a semi-trailer, and the ride folded down onto the truck for moving over the highways. It took five men eight hours to set up first couple of times it was erected, but the time was cut to five or six hours after a few moves. This brightly lighted device gave the carnivals another spectacular ride to spot at the opposite end of the midway from their sky wheels.

Clyde Beatty, one of the greatest of all the wild animal trainers, died on July 19th in Ventura, California. He had cancer. On November 4th, Carl J. Sedlmayr did not come to dinner with the C. J. Sedlmayr, Jr.'s. When the younger Sedlmayrs checked, they found Carl J. dead in bed. He was alone in his home at the time as Mrs. Sedlmayr was in a Tampa hospital. Carl J. Sedlmayr had stayed with it until he got the huge Royal American back into Tampa winter quarters, and then he answered the call from Wortham and Jones, stating that they needed a partner with modern ideas.

As the 1966 Florida State Fair opened in Tampa, the Attorney General of Florida announced that he would not allow any game to operate that gave a prize to the winner. No games worked in Tampa. Strates did get a modified order at his two Florida Fairs. On February 5th, Hilligoss and Cohn bought the Crafts Shows equipment consisting of three complete units. With the fifty-eight rides they acquired from Craft, the two men controlled one hundred eighty riding devices.

William T. Collins, president of Outdoor Amusement Business Association was actively soliciting new members for the organization. O.A.B.A. hired an executive-secretary, Bill McKay, to handle the big volume of business it was generating. On June 7th, Floyd Gooding sold some of the stock in Gooding's Million Dollar Midway, and a new corporation was set up. This new Gooding Million Dollar Midway, Inc. would have no further connection with the other Gooding enterprises. Gooding had twelve other units playing fairs and celebrations on Labor Day week.

Buff Hottle, Sr. died in the Marion, Illinois, Veterans Hospital on March 6th. He had started his own Buff Hottle Shows in 1938, and had operated as many as three or four units. Walter DeVoyne, long-time secretary-treasurer of the Royal American Shows died in a Shreveport, Louisiana, hospital on October 27th. He had been on Royal American since 1932. At one time, he was owner of the L. J. Heth railroad show.

Patty Conklin's midway at the Canadian National Exposition grossed $1,090,715.00, the second year that he had topped the million dollar mark. The W. G. Wade Shows took over seven hundred thousand dollars at the Detroit Fair, while Royal American grossed five hundred twenty-nine thousand dollars at the shorter Wisconsin State Fair at West Allis.

Early in 1967, Patty Conklin became seriously ill while visiting the Velare Brothers in Long Beach, California. He had recovered long before the Canadian National Exposition started and personally supervised the erection of the massive Wild Cat coaster ride for the exposition. This ride, an import from Germany, was delayed in New York by a strike. When loaded on trucks at the docks only a few days remained before the exposition was to open. The trucks were given a special escort of State Police to expedite their rapid movement across the state of New York, and were met at the International Border Station by Canadian Forces who rushed them on to the CNE grounds. In spite of this aid, the device was too massive to be erected in time for the opening day. First two days of the fair were lost by the device as the German factory expert and a large crew of men worked long hours unloading and assembling it. On Sunday, the fair was not open to the public.

Patty Conklin was there with the men until everything was set up and tested, ready for the big Children's Day crowd which would start swarming onto the grounds within a few hours. The Wild Cat helped the midway to establish another record gross that season.

Charles Lampkin, son of the late "Whitey Dell" Lampkin, operated the Lampkin Shows in 1967. He acquired much of the equipment for this midway from Johnny Portemont, who was disposing of his number two show. Earl Purtle was off the road for the first time in fifty-two years. He and Ethel were

TOPSEY AND IRWIN. Topsey, one of Mae and Bob Noell's gorillas, sat for this intimate pose with carnival owner, Irwin Deggeller in 1962.
Courtesy Amusement Business Photograph.

CARNIVAL KING, CARL J. SEDLMAYR. He is now dead but the show goes on under the capable magement of his son, C. J. and his grandson, C. J. III. Neither will use the name Carl J., as they say there was only one Carl J. Sedlmayr. Courtesy Royal American Shows.

"taking things easy" as they worried about what all their trouper friends were doing. No real trouper ever quits, so the Purtles soon had a string of rides working on Richmond, Virginia, Shopping Center lots. At this writing, February 22, 1970, they are enroute from Gibsonton, Florida, to Richmond to get those rides ready for another season, which will be Earl's fifty-sixth in Outdoor Amusement Business.

Royal American took a record number of persons into Western Canada in 1967. The manifests listed over eight hundred people along with the live stock and equipment. As the Royal American trains were entering Canada, Al Kunz reported that the truck on which the front for the "Fiesta in Paradise" Show was built, had been found in a Terre Haute, Indiana, junk yard. This truck had been missing for several weeks, and extensive search had been made for it. Al's son, Wayne, had flown the company airplane over a three-state area in a vain attempt to locate it. All contents were found intact when truck was recovered. Thousands of dollars worth of musical instruments, sound equipment and show property had not been damaged. All carnivaldom was relieved to learn that Tony "Suits" Paradise's trunks had not been permanently lost. "Suits" could again select another change of clothing after each "bally" as he had done for many years. He had over one hundred suits in those trunks.

Deaths in 1967 included another veteran of the midways, Melvin E. Dodson, Sr. who had started with his brother, Guy, around 1900. Mel Dodson died in North Miami on April 8th. A few days later, on April 25th, eighty-five year old Sam Soloman died in Miami. On October 31, Issy Cetlin died in his sleep at the William Byrd Hotel in Richmond, Virginia. Isadore Cetlin, another immigrant boy, had made a name for himself in his chosen profession. His Cetlin & Wilson Shows had been a leading midway on the East Coast for thirty years. Leon Claxton, producer of the colored minstrel revue on the Royal American midway for thirty-four years died in a Tampa hospital on November 14th. Outdoor show business lost a man who had worked his way up from circus roustabout to a position in the top ranks of the Collective Amusement Industry. A position which no one else could ever hope to fill.

In early April 1968, wild animal trainer Harriet Beatty, filed suit for divorce from her husband, Eddie Say, in Dade County. She asked for custody of their three children and her seven lions. A few days later, Ron Hoffman announced that he had a full season's booking for his show on independent midways at fairs. He died before the season was over and left several dates unplayed. His entire troupe of performers was left stranded and without food, as there was no one capable of taking over the show. His

Coyote Gulch Flea Circus was the last of its kind in America. Ludwig Neudorfer, sixty-five year old flea circus operator in Germany, could find no one interested in learning the profession. Possibly this lack of interest coupled with DDT and the bathtub influence of most sources of performer recruits will mean the end of this type of entertainment.

On January 27, 1968, (King) Reid Lefevre, owner of the King Reid Shows for some thirty year, died in Portland, Maine. On March 22nd, John H. Marks, carnival operator for over forty years, died in Richmond, Virginia; and Joseph J. Fredrick, owner of the Motor State Shows, died on September 7th in Highland Park, Michigan. Eighty year old Frank West, former owner of West's World's Wonder Shows died in Norfolk, Virginia, on October 2nd. Morris Hannum, owner of his own carnival for thirty years died on September 16th in York, Pennsylvania. Hannum had been with carnival midways for over forty-five years.

Patty Conklin's midway operations at CNE grossed over one million six hundred thousand dollars; and the Degellers through their agent, R. C. McCarter, were offering the State Fair of Kentucky at Louisville a guarantee for the 1969 fair equivalent to fifty-two and one-half percent of the 1968 gross.

In New York City, the E. Z. Amusements were moving from 102nd Street to 108th Street. J. R. Howard had hired six men to pick up his concessions and carry them intact the six blocks. They were walking along slowly carrying a joint, when one of New York's traffic policemen gave them a ticket. A ticket for going the wrong way down a one-way street. It cost Howard a five dollar fine. The usual number of Carnies were taking time off from their busy schedules to walk their dogs.

Most all carnival people love children and animals. Childless couples on carnivals bestow the same love and affection on their dogs as they would on the child they do not have. Dogs with modern truck show midways do not pose the problems they did on the railroad shows. Now, the dog's owner travels in his own trailer and the pet can be left at that trailer while the family works on the midway. On the older shows, the masters had to live on the show train and the pets were transported on that train. It was a common occurrence for the train hands to have to unload dogs from the flatcars for owners who had overslept.

It has been said that the Castle-Erlich-Hirsch Shows season of 1933 carried more dogs than it did people. Facetious persons have said that every wagon on the flatcars came into town with at least four dogs tied to it, and that the animals were tied to all the rides and show bally platforms. It was told that Carl Wagner, merry-go-round foreman, had to untie dogs from the "jenny" platforms every day before starting the ride; and that while Carl was away from the lot for a dental appointment, his assistant forgot them and started the ride dragging some ten or twelve of the howling pets around as the riders of the wooden horses with the real horse hair tails screamed their disapproval, as did the dogs' owners. Anyway, spring of 1934, there was a "no-dog" edict on the United

WALL TO WALL CROWDS. Canadian National Exhibition, 1968.
Courtesy Amusement Business Photograph.

Shows of America. Only two pets were allowed that season; Johnny Castle's big police dog, "Old Knox" and "Chew of Tobacco" Jack's lap dog, "Mickey."

"Old Knox" gloried in being the midway's only big dog and he quickly learned who his friends were around the midway. He slept most of the day under the office wagon, but made his trip around the half-mile semi-circular show grounds every two hours. He made ten or twelve stops on those rounds for special treatment from the indulgent carnies. If the person at one of the stops ignored him for any reason, Old Knox would make himself known by rubbing against his friend's leg until the required back scratching was done. After each of his well-wishers had done his duty, the comfortable, well-scratched police dog would leisurely return to his bed under the office wagon for another nap.

Jack Ruback's Alamo Exposition Shows opened 1969 season in Del Rio, Texas, on April 15th. Ruback's show was in Del Rio for the 42nd year. The Vivona Brothers toured as many as five units of their Amusements of America, but combined them for the larger fairs and dates. Al Kunz stated in July that he had encountered the worst weather in thirteen years during the spring dates. Some of his bigger fairs were off from preceding years. Patty Conklin's CNE midway had a show and ride gross of $1,708,791.55.

The Velare Brothers, who had just celebrated their seventy-fifth year in outdoor show business, announced that they were introducing a new ride for 1970. They already had one of their new 'Surfer' rides set up at Queen's Park in Long Beach, California. Elmer Velare was busy greeting friends at the Outdoor Meetings at Chicago's Hotel Sherman first week in December.

A woman in London, England, failed on her motorcycle operator's license test sixteen times. Mrs. Doris Smith, 53, was flunked for incorrect hand signals, improper steering, not acting properly at road junctions and other incorrect procedures. Mrs. Smith had been a featured rider in motor dromes, but didn't seem to be able to learn how to get around safely on a motorcycle in traffic.

As the decade ended, more money was invested in midway equipment than ever before. Over six hundred carnival and midway units of various types were touring — employing more people, grossing more money and charging higher prices than any showman had thought possible ten years before. Yet a general feeling of frustrated pessimism was expressed by most owners and operators of carnival midways. This was more evident among the older owners, who were the "War Babies" of the forties. These men had operated midways for over twenty-five years by the end of 1969 and few of them had ever employed all the labor that they needed or wanted; but they are complaining about shortage of reliable manpower more than ever before. The fantastic midway grosses that they report only depresses them more as their operating expenses have increased more than the income. With larger and more impressive midways demanded and expected by the carnival-going public, unbelievable sums must be spent for capital improvements.

Some of the younger operators are more optimistic, but the older heads just shrug and say, "They have never seen a recession. Just wait and see how long they will last." The seventy-one year old Madam has done herself proud with her lavish displays of garishly lighted mechanized "pig-iron," but maybe she has "done 'er self in."

COLORED MINSTREL SHOW. Now feature more girls and fewer comics than the old Plantation Shows did. Courtesy L. Harvey Doc Cann.

As old Madam Carnival approached her seventy-first birthday on Decoration Day 1970, her over one hundred thousand camp followers from "forty milers" to forty year troupers were too busily occupied with the problems of their own survival to give any thought to the antecedents of her over six hundred midways. So, another milestone in the development of the Collective Amusement Industry passed as unobserved by its workers as have the other seventy. The industry does face problems, probably more serious than any it has encountered in its seventy-one years of existence.

In this chapter, we will list and discuss a few of the problems that are the most worrisome to the carnival operator of the Seventies. I have contacted hundreds of carnival people — owners, managers, independent operators and workers promising all of them that I would not ascribe their names to any quotes that I might use in this volume. Many of them have evaded reference to their own problems or the possible solution of them, but have not been so reticent in discussing the other fellow's predicament. Many have listed the difficulties of the industry as a whole, but some frank individuals have freely discussed the plight of their own midway. In my files I have quite a few questionnaires which have been answered and returned to me by showmen, most of whom have unreservedly given me the right to use their names, if need be, in discussing the crises faced by the entire outdoor amusement industry.

Basically, most all the problems faced by a modern midway have been engendered by the complexities of our highly mechanized, regimented civilization. Imagine for a moment, C. A. Wortham has been resurrected and is now in San Antonio winter quarters with his C. A. Wortham's World's Greatest Shows exactly as it was before he died in 1922. His general agent, his showmen and all of his workers as unversed in the accepted ways of living and the laws of 1970 as he. Health and Zoning officers would be harrassing him in winter quarters demanding things that he had never heard of; and his general agent would be telegraphing him that no lots were available for still dates, and that the fairs were all demanding spectacular rides in prohibitive numbers and percentages of the gross that no man with good common sense could ever agree to. As he reads these telegrams, his trainmaster tells him that none of the railroads will move his show trains until all wooden flatcars and sleeping cars have been replaced by all-steel equipment; and all couplers, air brakes and wheels on the steel cars that he does have must be replaced by modern appliances.

He spends a million and a quarter dollars for the spectacular rides, another million for the other rides that he must have to book the best fairs, half a million for the train and another half million for getting the show out of quarters. His help hasn't learned yet that they must have a one thousand percent raise in pay to be in line with other shows. He gets his show on a lot for a still date in some town, U.S.A. As it is being erected, he is arrested by the police for tearing up the streets with his steel-tired wagons, and informed that the wagons can't be moved again until they are equipped with pneumatic tires. After he makes bond at the city hall, a state policeman arrests him for not having license tags on those wagons that he can't move again. He adjusts this by buying state license tags and hurries back to the lot. All is at a standstill as the inspectors have arrived.

A fire inspector is saying that none of that non-fireproofed tentage can be erected, a safety inspector is demanding that the seats in the wild west show be tied down and that all rides must have eight hundred pound "sand bag tests," an electrical inspector orders that all wiring be changed to meet requirements, the health officer has stopped all food preparation for the eight hundred hungry troupers and the dog catchers are chasing, catching and dragging away all the carnival dogs for lack of rabies vaccination and license tags.

Clarence A. looks sadly at the chaos of his beloved midway as he steps up into the office wagon to find a federal employee badgering the show's secretary because there are no social security records for the employees. The bewildered "Little Giant" pleads, "Dear God, please take me back, Johnny J. needs me."; and all the 1922 portion of the carnival fades away leaving four full-suited, button-down collared, brief case-equipped city, county, state and federal tax collectors standing in consternation as their wage and hour associate plops down to the ground from the vanished office wagon. The two and one-half million dollars worth of modern equipment remaining may be taken over by some Harvard School of Business graduate, who is conversant with all modern regulation, and operated successfully provided he has learned how to live with and use such regulations to his own advantage.

The overall picture isn't quite as bad for the old-time operator as the fanciful phantasm described above might lead one to believe. Actually, operators like Floyd Gooding, who has a picnic and a fair both played by Gooding-operated devices for seventy-five years, or Jack Ruback with his forty-two years at Del Rio, Texas, are not bewildered by the multiplicity of rules, laws and regulations. They, like the Colemans,

Courtesy Royal American Shows

Courtesy Royal American Shows

184

Iron

Courtesy Royal American Shows

Courtesy Royal American Shows

NOTHING STOPPED THEM FROM RIDING THE RIDES AS THE DECADE ENDED. Courtesy Amusement Business Photograph.

the Reithoffers, the Wades, the Sedlmayrs and the Strates families have evolved midways that can meet all the requirements of the changing times. Most all of them play routes that vary little from year to year. They are all known and respected by most everybody in the towns they play, and everything is made a little bit smoother for them than it would be for some first-time stranger. The changes have been gradual for all of the old-time operators and their midways, and it is doubtful that many of them would like to bring back the "good old days."

Most carnival owners bemoan, as a fact, the lack of good towns for spring "still dates," and the lack of lots with plenty of parking space for a "no-walk-anywhere" oriented midway visitors' vehicle. The rule that a good showgrounds must be located alongside a street car or bus route no longer applies, as those public conveyances pass rapidly by such grounds today without disgorging a single pleasure-seeker. The average amusement-seeker will pass up any entertainment facility which does not provide a place for him to park that "automotive second home of his."

Most carnival owners do have men working for them as general agents and promoters who have been capable of finding lots, booking and promoting a good route of "still dates." It would probably be good for these agents, as many of them have become fat and lazy from doing virtually nothing on a "cut and dried route," if their employees demanded good old-time "spring dates." In spite of the moans, very few midway operators actually want those "stills" that they shed nostalgic tears over. The really profitable "still date" towns can probably be counted

DOUBLE DOUBLE OR SPACE WHEELS. Courtesy Al Kunz.

on your fingers today. The heavy expenses of operating cannot be recouped in the three or four hours of spending of a normal night-time carnival crowd. Then, bad weather will cut the number of nights that a spending group will come to a midway. From references made in previous chapters, you can see that a carnival was fortunate if they had decent weather on spring dates. Most all of them started their "Fair Dates" in the red on the season. Don't let the Boys kid you; very few of them want "still dates." Carnivals today need Swarms of People, not Crowds.

Perhaps the reader has felt that an excessive amount of space has been devoted to equipment in this narrative. No history of the carnival can be accurate unless equipment is featured, for it is the basic constituent of any midway. Even in the early days of few rides and many shows, the equipment was the most important thing on the lot. A manager could train one of the regular musicians to play a flagolet. This musician, properly attired, could provide the "theme music" for the "cootch dances" of two recent recruits from the Snow White steam laundry of some town on the route. The tent, the stage and the front were much more important than the easily-replaced featured performers. Replacements for "Little Egypt" could be picked up in almost any town, but the equipment stayed with the show.

One or two featured human freaks of nature were all that many of the large 10-in-1 or 20-in-1 type Circus Side Shows carried on carnival midways. The other eight or eighteen performers were so-called

"working acts" which most anyone could do, if they were properly instructed, and had the "gaff" required for the act. The circus type performers who worked in the free acts on the midway were high caliber acts; but few of the midway shows had more than one or two competent performers. This changed somewhat in the thirties when all the big carnivals were fighting to stay in business. Some of them did have "sit down" shows with performances equal to anything presented in a theatre. Good singers, dancers and comedians were working for as little as sixteen or eighteen dollars per week then.

Of course, equipment still had "top billing" in the thirties as the "battle of chrome metal and neon tubing" was waged between midway owners. By the end of the twenties many carnivals carried as many rides as they did shows, and each new ride was given featured space in advertising. Carnival press agents featured live entertainers in most of their news stories as city editors wanted newsworthy stories about people, not a pile of "pig iron." The press agent also got a little extra pay from independent showmen, if he could place a story about their attraction. In the midway office, the owner valued the equipment above all else as he could replace a show at any time at no cost to that office.

Now, carnivals that can be classed as small shows carry as high as twenty-five or thirty riding devices. The few shows that they do have are mostly "Singl-O" attractions with no live performers inside. Fun Houses, Glass Houses and the like are classed as shows in these midways, and a "string" of twelve "shows" may have no more than twenty-five people to man them. The larger midways still carry large girl

CONCESSION BOYS "CUT UP JACKPOTS."
Courtesy Amusement Business.

BOSS MAN WORKS. Assistant manager Wayne Kunz puts gravel on muddy Century 21 Shows midway. Courtesy Amusement Business.

CAN ANY CARNIVAL TODAY AFFORD TO CARRY A SHOW LIKE THIS? Courtesy Royal American Shows.

revues, on which some of them expect to lose money during the season. They still need the elaborate show on their midway to satisfy "Fair Committees" and to give some midway-goers the "gals" that they have been accustomed to seeing on a carnival show. The emphasis is more on equipment now than ever before.

"Twenty-eight rides, three of them spectaculars." "Gooding now owns twelve merry-go-rounds." "Bobby Cohn controls over one hundred fifty rides." "Royal American carried eighty railroad cars on the Canada tour." "Strates adds ten cars to the train." "Al Kunz has eleven light plants." "The Drews travel on fifty-nine trucks of their own plus booked units." These are the type headings that you will see on carnival stories today. Equipment is really king of the collective amusement industry.

A survey of the ride manufacturers and importers reveals that the devices to equip a twenty-eight ride midway would cost one million, four hundred forty-five thousand ($1,445,000.00) for the new rides alone. This would be for twenty-one major rides, three kiddie rides and four spectaculars. Good trucks, trailers and light plants would cost

another half million. To buy the best equipment and pay cash for it would require two million dollars today, and it would be only a medium-sized show. One spectacular ride costs more today than Harry Hennies received for his entire big railroad carnival when he sold it less than twenty years ago. All carnivals that aspire for top rank in the industry must have at least two of the spectaculars.

True, these huge "piles of brightly lighted pig iron" with their large capacities, do bring in big grosses, but how much do they cut the older ride grosses? Many ride owners evade, when asked that question, but as many more are frank in answering. "My gross from all rides is no more," says one. "My gross is up a little, but total number of riders is down," adds another. In both cases, the other rides have grossed considerably less. My personal opinion is that the small operator with his ten to twenty year old rides playing his established route of small fairs is better off financially than the big boys with their over-extended credit.

This small operator has his problems trying to keep his committees satisfied with one new major ride booked in by an independent each year. His problems are compounded when one or more of his fair boards gets "delusions of grandeur," usually brought on by the agent of a competitor, and demands that he bring in a riding device that sells for twice as much as they have invested in their entire fair. A fair that probably pulls in fifteen thousand people for the entire week wanting a ride that has the capacity to handle every one of those patrons in one ten-hour day, if all of them wanted to ride. No riding device ever entices more than half of the patrons of any event, even a teen-age festival where they are looking for that joggle.

The boards of these small fairs can't be blamed for thinking that their event deserves more than its attendance warrants. They have been served drinks, fed, complimented and flattered by agents and owners of rival carnivals that would like to add this annual festival to their own route. It is this foolish practice, engaged in by men who should be too smart for such things, that has brought the collective amusement industry to the point that it has reached today. A point where something will have to give way, or the industry cannot survive this decade. That is the conclusion of many of the leaders in the business today.

Another question, often asked in a low breath, is how many fairs as they are constituted today can survive another ten years? As the carnival industry is definitely "fairgrounds oriented," where would the carnivals go without fairs? The larger fairs are working desperately to solve the problem of getting more usage from all of the high-priced real estate, especially parking lots, needed for a really big annual event. It is considered an economic waste for a hundred or more acres of ten thousand dollar per acre land to have a utilization of less than two weeks per year. Even when used for longer terms, does the return justify the usage?

In the rural areas, where the citizens are becoming less agriculturally oriented each year, where are the agricultural fairs headed? They have the same problem of under-utilization of land, with a much smaller income from it, when it is used. Can they continue to exist, and do they have a right to exist, in a largely urban population center? These questions are being asked more frequently now, and answers are being sought lest they do cease to exist. Most of these fairs are operated by groups of dedicated citizens who are trying to keep alive a historic and time-honored meeting place for the citizenry of their community. Carnivals must keep them alive to live themselves, and all such events would have to close up without a midway. The survival of both depends on the management of both working together for their common good.

More and more independent ride operators and small units are playing shopping center parking lots in the spring and then booking into small fairs and celebrations nearby during the summer and fall.

HOW MANY 1972 GIRL SHOWS WILL HAVE THIS MANY PEOPLE?
Brown & Dyer Shows, 1924. Courtesy L. Harvey Doc Cann.

Family Dynasties

SEDLMAYR FAMILY. Owners Royal American Shows. Courtesy John Colville, The Calgary Herald.

On Carnival Midways

KUNZ FAMILY. Owners Century 21 Shows. Courtesy Al Kunz.

These "forty milers" of which there have been too many, do the collective amusement industry no good. Their rides, their help and they themselves, are all too well-known in the community. Their presence on a midway takes away that air of mysterious professionalism that is the main source of a carnival's attraction. If the riders have paid fifteen cents to ride his device down at Five Points all spring, are they going to pay a quarter to get on it at the fair? If they begin to distrust the price of their local man's attraction, how are they going to feel about the outsiders? It is bad enough for ride operators to have to buck the prices charged by permanent operators in the parks without bringing them in on the lots as competition.

JOHNNY PORTEMONT, Jr. Owner Johnny's United Shows. Courtesy Amusement Business.

PAT REITHOFFER. Owner of the Reithoffer Shows. Courtesy Amusement Business.

The carnival industry has a unique advantage over all other branches of show business. It is the only branch of the business that has firmly established family dynasties as owners and managers of many of its major segments. True, circus performer families often boast five, six, even seven generations skilled in their particular field; and many of the European Circuses have been ably managed by the same family of performers for several generations. But this has rarely happened with the American Circus. When a circus founder died, another fragment of the circus died as no heir had been reared and trained to take over the show. No young circus showmen, trained in the profession by experts, has ever been standing by ready to take over a faltering enterprise when the owner became ill or infirm.

LOU DUFOUR . Courtesy Lou Dufour.

Earlier in this volume, you have read of scores of early carnivals that went to the junk yards because the owners had no eager sons to assist him in times of distress.

Fully half of the carnivals in this country today are being operated and managed by second or third generation midway showmen, or by owners who have that second and third generation working with them on the lot ready to take over. These young showmen are the greatest asset the business has, because they will work out ways and means to keep the midways open. They know no other way to make a living, and they love what they are doing. They are a product of

SEATTLE WORLD'S FAIR SPACE WHEEL. Built and operated by Velare Brothers. Now on Royal American Shows. Courtesy Royal American Shows.

a way of life where Mama and the children all work together with Papa in his chosen profession. A profession that has been more receptive to the needs of family life than any other outdoor enterprise in or out of the amusement business.

The collective amusement industry has always been conducive to family life. The liberal outlook of midway people towards all things, including sex, made marriage an easily attained accomplishment. True, so-called "Carnival Marriages" were condoned but many of these "Carny Weddings" have endured much longer than the single season expectancy of a mating without ceremony. Legally married couples have always been the main peg to which the industry has been "guyed out," and the offspring of those couples have more firmly anchored carnival business to its solid foundations.

The Drews, the Strateses, the Hameses, the Sedlmayrs, the Kunzes, the Steeles, the Hilligosses, the Thumbergs — I can fill several pages of names of carnival families active in the management of midways. Many of them with the first, second and third generations all working together for the good of the show, and the family. Go down any of their midways and count the family people who are operating cook houses, concessions, shows and rides. There is one fun house operator whose daughter represents four generations of carnival troupers on her mother's side, and three from her father. When this child played back of the fun house, she had the same playgrounds that both her mother and her maternal grandfather had. Many of these second and third generation carnies have college and university degrees, but they are back home continuing the work that their fathers and their grandfathers started.

There are still a few midways that do not always adhere to "Sunday School Show" principles. I have mentioned one or two briefly in this volume, and neglected the others, as the overwhelming majority of carnivals and carnival people are now operating on sound, honest and upright business principles. Actually, it is an economic necessity for them to so conduct themselves. In the "good old days of freebootery" the shady operations on the "front end," concession row, often turned in more cash to the office than all the other attractions. In a time of need, the "Lucky Boys" from the front end would supply the cash needed for the train move, or for unexpected emergencies. All of the show-owned equipment could be replaced for a few thousand dollars, if it should be destroyed by "Hey Rube", brought on by a disgruntled loser on one of the joints. Paint was cheap and new titles could be put on a show quickly, if the territory had been "burned up" by joint-engendered "Heat."

A TICKET SELLER AND TALKER. On Carl J. Lauther's Coney Island
Side Show. These men were, and are, called talkers and "grinders."
They have never been referred to as barkers by outdoor show
people. Courtesy Joe Pearl.

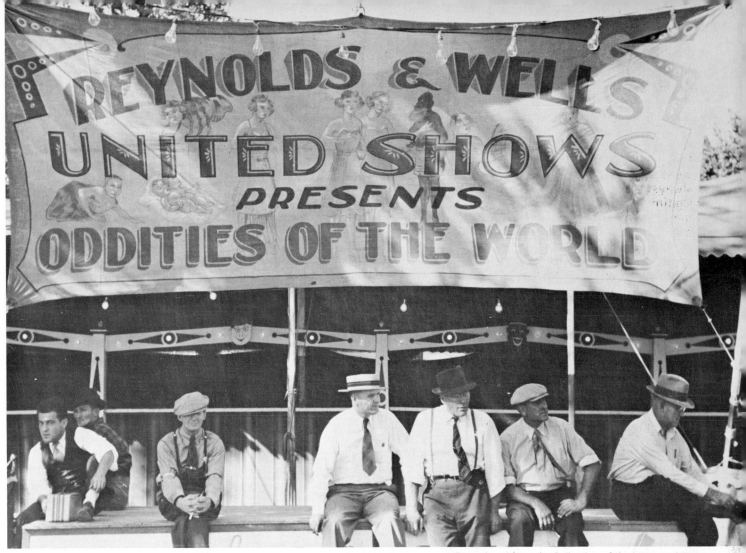

CONEY ISLAND SIDE SHOW. Owned and operated by Carl J. Lauther, long-time operator of such attractions. Courtesy Joe Pearl.

Things have changed now. With millions of dollars worth of equipment standing vulnerable on the midway, owners would be fools, indeed, if they allowed practices to be followed on that midway which could endanger that valuable property. Again, the touch of the family is evident. The "lucky boys" for the most part were unmarried, and if married, childless. Their peccadillos on the "front end" were always damaging to the family people who owned the legitimate concessions, shows and rides. As these family people became more numerous, they gained more voice in midway operations, and they demanded more protection for their own investments. The owners themselves, no matter how wild they had been fifty years ago, became more conservative with age; and with wives and children on the midway, they naturally cleaned up their carnivals. As their sons came home to the midway from college, they brought with them different concepts of good business practice, which gradually became accepted carnival methods.

To some of us, the old Madam's midways have mellowed a little too much. We remember with nostalgic yearning the midways of yesteryear with their long lines of rag banners flapping in the breeze, backed by mysterious tents and interspersed with an occasional riding device. The people all gypsy-like and strange, peering with suspicious eyes at the eager stranger who wanted so much to be friendly with them. The people, who in those days, you could always identify as Carnies when you met them on the streets have changed. Today, tourists and carnival people all dress, talk and look alike. If you follow a strangely dressed couple down the street today, you are not likely to find a carnival midway at the end of the journey. They will probably lead you to a tourist motel.

The old Madam still has her allure, and each of her six hundred or more offspring provides this lure in its own way. Even the little dejected six-ride midway perched on the hillside grounds of a "ten-minute-fair" (one which takes ten minutes or less to view all that it has to offer) gives promise of an hour's relaxation to the tired farmer and his wife as their TV-educated young ones cavort from ride to ride. Midways of all sizes still provide "poor man's entertainment" at a reasonable price, and are the meeting place for amusement seekers of all ages and stations in life. On these midways, the young men of America, from sixteen to sixty-six, can carry their favorite girl friend on a thrilling riding device enjoying that "Joggle" of Mr. Mangels' which has been incorporated into so many of them since 1914.

The old Harlot is ultra-respectable now. Everybody meets on her midways and everyone rides her wooden horses from little Owen and young Angie Pie to the president's wife herself. Yes, one of her midways has been set up on the White House lawn.

Truly, Frank Gaskill knew not what he wrought.

FIRST LADY RIDES THE RIDES. On the White House lawn, 1967. Courtesy Amusement Business Photograph.

END VOLUME ONE

INDEX VOLUME I

AFTER A HEATED DISCUSSION. An organization of carnival owners was formed in Chicago, 1964. Twenty-five show owners joined at the outdoor meetings in December. Courtesy Amusement Business Photograph.

DISASTER — WRECKS. D. D. Murphy Shows. Courtesy Nat Worman.

DISASTER — BLOWDOWNS. Courtesy Earl Purtle.

DISASTER — WRECKS. Truck shows have them too. Courtesy Amusement Business Photograph.

M. E. POLHILL'S
BEACON SHOWS

ONE OF THE CLEANEST AGGREGATIONS OF
AMUSEMENTS IN AMERICA.

ABSOLUTELY NO GIRL SHOWS OR GAMBLING DEVICES.

PERMANENT ADDRESS BEACON, N. Y.

**SKY DIVER RIDE ERECTED AND OPERATING. Courtesy Royal
American Shows.**

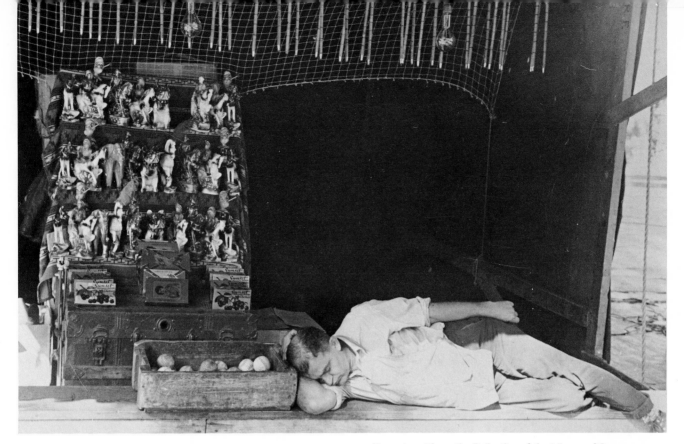

A Pictorial History of the American Carnival

Courtesy Royal American Shows

A PICTORIAL HISTORY OF THE

AMERICAN CARNIVAL

By Joe McKennon

Volume II

Courtesy Albert Conover

CARNIVAL PUBLISHERS
of Sarasota
Sarasota, Florida

Dedicated to my wife,
MARIAN,
whose forbearance has
made it possible.

CARNIVAL AT ROSWELL, NEW MEXICO, 1936. Courtesy Library of
Congress.

CONTENTS

VOLUME II

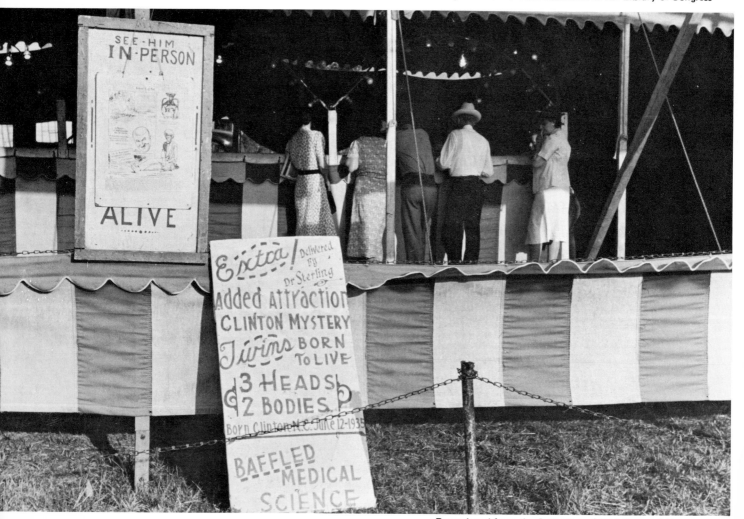

Carnival Greats

BIOGRAPHICAL SKETCHES

FRED BECKMAN

Fred Beckman, a man destined to be a leader in the outdoor amusement field, ran away from home and joined a circus when he was fourteen. This man, who was affectionately referred to by thousands as "the Grand Old Man" of the outdoor show world, was born in Oskaloosa, Iowa, in 1854. He was reticent about his early life, but the facts known about this great showman would make volumes of interesting reading.

Like most showmen of the old school, Fred Beckman was inclined to be taciturn about most things. A large man with the heavy responsibilities of co-ownership of one of the really great collective amusement enterprises, he regulated all his movements with the dignity befitting an old time circus "Governor." Calm, collected, dignified, his dimmed eyes missing no detail as he peered out of his office wagon window, this man in his middle eighties demonstrated he still had a firm grip on the reins of authority.

Although he had probably been "rough and tough" in his younger days, as most outdoor showmen of the period were, he would give a young showman much of his time explaining kindly and patiently how some problem of management or logistics should be handled. He had a certain amount of pride in the young men he trained in the carnival field, and many leaders of the industry were not ashamed to ask "Uncle Fred" for advice.

In 1873, young Fred Beckman already had a responsible position with the W. W. Cole Circus. He

FRED BECKMAN. From the 1937 Beckman & Gerety Yearbook. Courtesy Fred D. Pfening, Jr.

FRED BECKMAN. Before he entered carnival business. Courtesy Circus World Museum, Baraboo, Wisconsin.

learned much from the tutorship of "Chilly Billy" Cole, but was to learn much more from that master of them all, James A. Bailey. He worked for Mr. Bailey for several years as an agent on the Barnum and Bailey Circus, "the Greatest Show on Earth." It was on the Barnum show that he met Eddie Arlington. Eddie's father was a long-time trusted employee of Mr. Bailey, but young Eddie wanted a wider scope for his activities than that afforded by any position open to him on the circus. The forty year old Beckman was an ideal partner for one with the promotion ideas and skills of Arlington.

For eighteen years Beckman and Arlington promoted and managed Wild West Shows. The 101 Ranch Real Wild West Show was one of their first efforts. They finally had a large show out under their own name, the Arlington and Beckman Wild West Show. Some years during this association, they worked for other individual show owners. (For instance, in 1901, Beckman was special agent for the Buffalo Bill Wild West Show, and in 1906 he was treasurer on the Frank A. Robbins Circus.) The partnership was dissolved in 1914. In 1915, Beckman, now in his fifties, moved into the carnival field. He and Ed Heinz operated their Heinz & Beckman Shows that season. Fred managed the World at Home Shows for Mr. Clyde, seasons of 1916 and 1917.

In 1918, Beckman joined Clarence A. Wortham as manager of the number two show, Clarence A. Wortham's Worlds Best Shows. He continued as manager of this show until Mr. Wortham's death. Then he, in partnership with Barney S. Gerety and George E. Robinson bought the show from Mrs. Wortham. Robinson died within a year and Beckman and Gerety became sole owners. They continued to use the Wortham title until the end of the 1930 season. It became the Beckman & Gerety Shows in 1931, and that title was used until Barney Gerety took the show off the road in the early years of World War Two.

This writer will always remember Fred Beckman best from an incident that happened midseason of 1940. I was in Barney Gerety's office wagon discussing the final plans for the new minstrel show we were to start building the following week, when the eighty-six year old co-partner slowly climbed the steps into the wagon. Fumbling for a seat as he was almost totally blind now, he stated quietly, "Boys, Jess is dead." A dear friend of ours, Jess Adkins, co-owner of Cole Brothers Circus had died that day on the circus he so dearly loved.

All eight hundred employees of the Beckman & Gerety Shows were worried about the old man's health and welfare. He would not admit that the infirmities of age had impaired his physical abilities in any way, and he took his daily strolls around the entire twenty-six hundred foot inner circumference of the midway. As he moved out of the office, any employee that saw him would join him and ask some question that could be answered as they walked along slowly. If the employee stayed with him too long, the old man would peer at him closely and say curtly, "Is that you 'Mississippi'? You better get back to that ride." And, 'Sip' Baker would return to his regular duties, as some other foreman had cut short the revolutions of his ride to fall in behind the slow

FRED BECKMAN. From the 1937 Beckman & Gerety Yearbook. Courtesy Fred D. Pfening, Jr.

moving old carnival owner. They would stay behind him close enough to catch him if he fell, but out of reach of his cane. This ride man would pace him until the boss man would stop, look around blindly, swing his cane and expostulate, "Is that you back there, Felix? Get back to that Hey Dey." His loyal employees worked in relays until they had safely escorted the aged carnival owner back to a chair under the office wagon canopy tent. Then the office help would look after his safety and well being.

In his later years, Fred Beckman attended the Outdoor Meetings in Chicago as usual. He would sit on the third step of a stairway leading up from the lobby of the Sherman Hotel. (This stairway has been closed off now). There he could hear the babble of voices from the lobby in front of him, and remember the many active days that he had spent out there standing on the floor "visiting" with other showmen as the "wheeling and dealing" went on around them. Now as he sat, show owners, agents, suppliers of carnival properties, working men and hangers-on all stopped with a handshake and a greeting for this sage of the midways.

On October 13, 1941, the Beckman & Gerety show train was enroute from Lubbock, Texas, to Shreveport, Louisiana. Fred Beckman fell in his private car on that train. When Mrs. Beckman found him, he was barely conscious. When the train reached Shreveport, the badly injured showman was removed to the North Louisiana State Hospital. There he died on October 17th. He had broken a vertebra.

His funeral in Shreveport was attended by over five hundred show folks, over one hundred sent flowers, and another five hundred sent telegrams. Train Master, "Arky" Bradford; boss electrician, Dan Fast; ride foremen, Fred Baker, Felix Charneski and John Logan; and midway thrill show operator, Zeke Shumway, were the pallbearers. The list of honorary pallbearers was a "Who's Who" of carnivaldom. His body, accompanied by Mrs. Marie Beckman, Mrs. Peter Kortez and J. C. McCaffery was carried to Chicago, where it was interred in Showmen's Rest with impressive rites. A builder of the collective amusement industry had left his beloved midways forever. A late comer to the carnival field, but a builder nonetheless.

JAMES WESLEY CONKLIN

When the great Columbian Exposition opened in Chicago on May 1, 1893, four day old James Wesley Conklin was interested only in regular nourishment and clean dry clothing. Had he been born twenty years sooner, there is no doubt that James Wesley would have been on that exposition grounds — probably in sole and complete charge of all midway activities. He was born on April 27th in Brooklyn, New York and stayed over on that side of East River for eight or nine years before he started commuting across to Manhattan.

Young Conklin wasn't exactly a school dropout, but he never let school interfere with his getting ahead in his pursuit of the material things in life. He peddled peanuts on the street across from Old Madison Square Garden long before there was any thought of building a new one up on Eighth Avenue. He was a good salesman, even then; but he needed a sideline that could be worked along with his "goober pea" business. He and three other peanut sellers purchased some umbrellas and escorted the "Ladies and Gentlemen" across the street on rainy days. Regular patrons of the Garden were intrigued by the resourcefulness of these well-mannered and cleanly-dressed young boys and the boys profited thereby.

J. W. Conklin's father, Jim, was an independent concessionaire at fairs and with carnivals, so the youngster was operating his own concession when he was fourteen. He worked as an independent operator for some seventeen years, before he owned his own midway, but he had accumulated much paraphernalia and many friends in his climb to carnival ownership. The former was helped by an invention of his, special buckets, for the bucket game. These buckets, patented by the young concessionaire, had controllable bottoms and were sought by all operators of such games. His friends were made by his genial, efficient love for his fellowman. No one, showman or town "mark," was ever turned down for aid by this husky little showman, if they really needed or deserved such aid.

The friendship of Patty Conklin, as he was affectionately known to uncounted thousands of Americans in the United States and Canada, was their most valued possession. This friendship was bestowed on the recipient without regard to rank, status, religion, color, creed or material holdings. He greeted a "down on his luck" carnival working man with the same quiet smile of welcome, the same sincere handshake and the same feeling of comradeship with which he welcomed prime ministers and state fair dignitaries. It was not an act with Patty, he loved his fellowman and demonstrated this love in his daily relationship with people. He was sought after for chairmanships of boards and fund-raising drives. For,

J. W. Patty Conklin.

if Patty Conklin took it, the objectives were reached or the quotas exceeded.

Patty's avocation was the same as his vocation — midways, midway people and midway operations. His working hours were as long, and ofttimes longer, as any of the younger show owners; yet he always was ready to help out in some new worthy project. He could do manual labor on a behind schedule project or on any recalcitrant piece of equipment that needed the hand of the midway master.

Patty Conklin first booked his concessions in Canada in 1912, but came back to the United States to tour with his father's carnival, the Clark & Conklin Shows, for five years. After this midway partnership was dissolved, Patty went back to Western Canada in 1921 and never returned to the United States to live. In 1924 he and "Speed" Garrett opened their Conklin & Garrett Shows in the provinces of Western Canada. This two car "gilly" show had a hard struggle to exist for a few years. But, it did continue to exist and to grow. In 1929 Patty's brother, Frank, bought Garrett's interest in the show, and the brothers began moving into larger towns and more profitable business. His greatest advancement in the midway field came in 1937 when Patty was asked to take over the active production and management of the midway at Toronto's annual Canadian National Exhibition, a contract his son still holds.

A few years back an enterprising young reporter on one of Toronto's newspapers attempted to upset the affairs at the CNE by running an "expose" of Conklin's long term "sweetheart-contract" with the fair. The reporter admitted that he had left Conklin's office rather hurriedly after "a very noisy interview." The "expose" stirred no one other than the reporter's own confreres. It was suggested by angry newsmen that he be denied admittance to the Tornonto Men's Press Club for even bothering their old friend, Patty. Citizens of Toronto were not bothered by this exclusive contract at all. Sure he had made big sums of money for himself from this arrangement; but Patty Conklin had spent most all of it for improvements on the grounds, and he turned more percentage money over to the CNE office than anyone ever dreamed possible. Who was capable of taking the contract and doing as well as Patty? No one could.

Now, Patty's son, Jim, handles the entire operations, but never will it be run with that indescribable flair of one to whom each minute of each hour was looked forward to as heralding another adventure. For, Patty Conklin was an adventurer of the old school. A man to whom each little adversity or big calamity was just as necessary for his full enjoyment of life, and living it, as the pleasure of having a wonderful family and thousands of loyal friends or the anticipation of that two million dollar gross from the Canadian National Exhibition midway this year — or next year. Such a man never grows old nor quits striving for something just a little better.

The midway in Toronto does not have the high admission prices for rides and shows some midways do. Prices are kept low to encourage patrons to spend more time on the amusement zone of the fair. Patty liked to keep prices down so that a midway visitor could enjoy every show and device on the grounds for an expenditure of no more than the price of a good seat at a New York musical show. The long lines of potential riders in front of ticket boxes attests to the popularity of this concept among the midway visitors of the CNE.

Patty Conklin built a fortune for himself and his family from his midway operations. He stopped moving a big traveling carnival across Canada as he did for many years, and devoted his time to a few fairs and the Canadian National. His long-time home and winter quarters is at Brantford, Ontario, but no one who knew him expected to find him home for long. His true home was every city, town and village across North America in which he had ever spent a day. He met few people in his life time that did not become his friends, if he wanted them as friends. His friends, regardless of their own financial condition, never begrudged Patty's affluence. "He deserved it, he earned it," they will all point out to an inquiring stranger.

MRS. JIM CONKLIN. Courtesy J. W. Patty Conklin.

JIM CONKLIN. Courtesy J. W. Patty Conklin.

his brother, who was getting top prices for his young animals. Patty replied quickly, "I am no damned fool. I don't want to own anything that eats during the winter." Another time he was escorting Lord and Lady Mountbatten around the midway of the Canadian National. He halted the party and picked up a five-cent piece some patron had dropped on the shavings-covered ground. He wiped the nickel carefully and stuck it in his pocket before proceeding with the tour. Before the year was out, he probably donated thousands of dollars to charitable causes and needy individuals without any hesitation, but he never believed in needless waste.

This writer, who knew Patty Conklin for nearly forty years, cannot describe the magnetic personality of this veteran of the carnival midways. This man, who in his sixty year carnival career, did so much to lift the industry from the disreputable state it was in, to the highly respectable position it now holds all across North America. As James E. Coleman, columnist for the Southern Newspapers in Toronto wrote for an edition of Amusement Business honoring Patty, "That's Patty! He has some friends who can get into Buckingham Palace and he has some other friends who can't get out of Leavenworth."

While final preparations for the 1970 Canadian National Exhibition were being completed, Patty became ill and was persuaded by his aides to check into a hospital. His veteran assistant, Malcolm M. (Neil) Webb, who was working on a six hour per day schedule because of recent heart attacks, personally reported all of the day's happenings to the bed-ridden showman. After the fair was over, Patty had a chance to turn over all the details of management to his son and partner, James F. On November 8, 1970 Patty Conklin died in a Hamilton, Ontario, hospital. He was buried in Showmen's Rest in Toronto on November 12.

People who did not know him might conclude that Patty was parsimonious from some things he said and did; but he was liberal with anything that he owned and wanted to share with his friends. One time a friend inquired why he didn't raise race horses like

FERARI BROTHERS

The Ferari Brothers, although they did go their separate ways after the 1905 season, must be considered as a team — a team that contributed much to the development of the collective amusement industry. Sons of an Italian showman who had toured England for many years, the brothers were third generation traveling amusement purveyors. Francis A. Ferari was born in Hull, Yorkshire, England, on September 15, 1862; and his brother, Joseph G., was born in Leeds, England, on January 4, 1868. In spite of their Italian father, they were proud of being "Cockney" Englishmen.

When they arrived in New York with Frank Bostock during the summer of 1894, their "cockney" dialect amused everyone at Coney Island. A dialect that neither of them ever completely lost. Colonel Francis and Captain Joseph, military titles acquired by frequent encounters with wild animals, were both big men — big men, picturesque men. Colonel Francis, who early in the nineteen hundreds billed himself "The Carnival King," took the limelight for himself, so that Captain Joseph was not as well known in the early days of the young carnival industry. Joseph had stayed with their father's wild

THE BILLBOARD

Vol. XIII, No. 12.　　　CINCINNATI, SATURDAY, MARCH 23, 1901.　　　Price 10 Cents
Per Year $4.00

COL. F. FERARI,
The Well-Known Street Fair Promoter.

STREET FAIRS   FAIRS   CIRCUS   PARKS   BILLPOSTERS   DRAMATIC

THE BILLBOARD

Volume XV. No. 12.   CINCINNATI, MARCH 21, 1903.   Price, 10 Cents.
Per Year, $4.00.

JOSEPH G. FERARI,
Vice-President Ferari Brothers' Great London Carnival Co.

14

animal show in England when the hot tempered Francis left them in the 1870's to start his own show.

Joseph Ferari had never worked a trained wild animal act until one of his relatives died unexpectedly, leaving an act without a trainer. Young Ferari donned that trainer's colorful wardrobe, went into the arena and worked the lions without any trouble from them. His future as a trainer of wild beasts was now assured. A few years later, his father's show caravans were passing the summer residence of the Queen, when a courier stopped the first caravan with the order, "Halt in the name of the Queen." They stopped and gave a performance for Queen Victoria's palace children. They were rewarded with a purse containing five pounds, which was quite a lot of money in those days. This incident reminds us of the time George Sanger, British circus owner gave a command performance for Queen Victoria. After the performance, the Queen praised George and told him that he was probably without a peer in his field. He replied gravely, "It is as you wish, Your Majesty." Thereafter, George Sanger advertised his circus as "Lord George Sanger's Circus."

When Francis Ferari left his father's show, he started a novelty show and exhibited such things as giants, midgets, and freaks. In 1881 he secured a group of Zulus and toured the United Kingdom with them. In 1892 he married Miss Emma Warwick, daughter of another British showman. The same year, he bought an established wild animal show and changed its name to Noah's Ark. He met Frank Bostock, another third generation animal showman, and formed a partnership with him. In 1894 the two Ferari Brothers and Frank Bostock brought their equipment and animals to the United States. Ferari opened his show on a Flatbush Avenue lot in Brooklyn and later moved it to Coney Island.

Feature of the Ferari Show at Coney Island was Big Frank, the "Hoochie-Coochie" bear. In 1896, the Englishmen put out a small show which toured the New England states for a few weeks. Had this organization stayed out a full season, it would have been the first collective amusement organization. For, "Ye Olde English Faire" carried all the elements of a carnival. Among its attractions were: "Colonel" Francis Ferari's trained wild animals, Captain Joseph Ferari's trained dogs, ponies and monkeys, Kemp's Royal Midgets, Cottrel's Deep Sea Divers, George Kemp's talking fish, Billy Russell's gondolas (a riding device), an elaborate Carousel imported from England and concessions. One of the concessions of the gaming variety was a coconut throwing game. Before the season ended, Francis Ferari carried this aggregation to the Toronto Exposition. He booked some of his shows and rides at Toronto for ten years.

In 1899, the Bostock-Ferari Midway Carnival Company was formed and toured through the 1902 season. In 1903 the show became Ferari Brothers Great London Carnival Company, "successor to the Bostock-Ferari Carnival Company." Ferari Brothers Shows United was the last title they used before splitting up in 1905. Season of 1906, Francis Ferari was on his own as was his brother, Joseph. Once a year or two before Francis' death, the two brothers announced that they were combining their shows; but the combination broke up before the end of the season. Francis Ferari sold all his show property and returned to England in 1909, but was back with another carnival bearing his name in 1911. In a 1912 ad in Billboard, he pictures himself as a king and heads the ad, "Royal Proclamation from King of All Carnival Kings." He got his show back into winter quarters in fall of 1914 and died on November 12th. He was buried in Calvary Cemetery in New York on November 14th.

This picturesque individual with his flashy dress and striking manner was dead, but his show was to live on for some time without its founder. His widow, Emma, continued to operate the Colonel Francis Ferari Shows through the 1920 season. The title was then changed to the Doris-Ferari Shows with several partners in the deal. Mrs. Ferari retired that year. In 1922, Mrs. Felice Bernardi bought the Doris-Ferari Shows for cash and used the equipment to frame a new Bernardi Greater Shows.

Mrs. Francis Ferari, who was born in Burton, England, in 1869 retired at the end of the 1920 season and went to Pottstown, Pennsylvania to live. She died in Pottstown on September 4, 1934. She was buried there on September 6th.

"Captain" Joseph G. Ferari went out on his own in 1906 and continued to tour until the end of the 1918 season when he retired as a trainer. Never as colorful as his brother, Francis, Joseph was an engaging personality on his own. By 1912 he had promoted himself to a rank equal to his brother's. All of his advertising matter now touted "Colonel" Joseph G. Farari Shows. He sold all of his equipment in 1919 to Williams Standard Shows and opened a carousel factory on Staten Island. He retired from all work in a few years as his health began to get worse. On his frequent trips to the showmen's "hangouts" in downtown New York, he would regale visiting troupers with stories of old-time outdoor show business. His anecdotes narrated in a broad "cockney" English dialect were always amusing.

Eighty-five year old "Colonel" Joseph Ferari died in St. Vincent Hospital on Staten Island, New York, on May 9, 1953, after a long illness. He was buried in Moravian Cemetery at New Dorp, Staten Island, on May 12th. The Ferari Brothers were now gone, but stories of their exploits and their carnivals are a heritage of the amusement business.

THEATRICAL CIRCUS BILLPOSTERS FAIRS

THE BILLBOARD

Volume XVI. No. 12   CINCINNATI, MARCH 19, 1904.   Price, 10 Cents. Per Year, $4.00

FRANK W. GASKILL,

Proprietor of the Gaskill Carnival Company and one of the
Reconized Heads of the Street Fair Business.

16

FRANK W. GASKILL

Frank W. Gaskill, the organizer of the first collective amusement organization to tour an entire season, was born in Alliance, Ohio in 1857. He operated a grocery business in Alliance from 1875 to 1897. In 1897, he moved to Canton, Ohio where he managed a hotel. He joined the Elks in Canton. Labor Day Week, 1898, the Canton Elks Lodge sponsored a street fair in their city. Gaskill was chosen as chairman of the midway committee. He made trips to Chicago, St. Louis and New York selecting shows and show people for this midway. The promoters, and many of the show people, stayed at his hotel while they were in town. The Canton Street Fair was a success and Gaskill was impressed by the possibilities of financial gain in the amusement field.

In late fall of 1898, Frank Gaskill went to his old home town of Alliance and promoted a street fair. It was a small, amateurish affair and it rained all week. In spite of this, Gaskill made some money from the celebration. This was proof that a good show with decent weather could be highly profitable. He hired Harold Bushea and sent him out to book a route for 1899. Meanwhile he was building the new midway in Canton. This new concept in the outdoor amusement industry loaded out of Canton in one baggage car.

The first successful collective amusement organization, the Canton Carnival Company, opened in Chillicothe, Ohio, on Decoration Day, 1899. It played a season of twenty-two consecutive weeks and grew in size as it moved along its route. It came back to Canton that fall on a special train. The 1900 season was as disastrous as the first season had been successful. Gaskill closed his show in New York State and established residence there so he could take advantage of that state's bankruptcy laws. Before his death, he did repay everyone who had lost by this bankruptcy action.

He reorganized and reopened in 1901 with good business. His carnival was a money-maker from then on. Early in the season, his midway was called the Frank W. Gaskill-Canton Carnival Company, but he changed this title to Gaskill's Midway Shows before the season ended. In 1902 he formed a partnership with Percy J. Munday, animal show operator, and they toured the Gaskill-Munday Carnival Company and enjoyed good business all season. The animal school and winter quarters for this new combination was established in Jacksonville, Florida, but the new equipment needed for the enlarged show was built in Baltimore, Maryland. Gaskill continued to operate his Canton Carnival Company in 1902 also, as E. H. Lewis advertised for twenty-five women for a "Gipsy Camp" for the Nashua, New Hampshire, date of this unit.

In 1903, another partner was taken in. Victor D. Leavitt, long-time associate of the Ferari Brothers joined in the Gaskill-Munday-Leavitt Carnival Company. Eastern Unit managed by Gaskill wintered in Cleveland, Ohio, and the Western Unit managed by Munday wintered in Dallas, Texas. Both units had successful seasons but the partnership broke up. Vic Leavitt wanted to take his equipment back to the Feraris and Munday wasn't happy because his picture was not featured on the advertising paper. Property was divided in Texas and Gaskill put his Gaskill Carnival Company in winter quarters in San Antonio, where he opened a zoo.

Although Munday booked the San Jacinta Celebration which Gaskill had first proposed, for his own show, he had to let Gaskill share it with him as neither had enough equipment for this big date, which was actually San Antonio's first Battle of Flowers. They both enjoyed profitable business, and Gaskill bragged that the 1904 season would break all records. It did, but Frank did not live to profit by it.

Frank W. Gaskill died in Pittsburg, Kansas, on May 4, 1904, with pneumonia. After an impressive funeral in Pittsburg, his body was carried back to Alliance, Ohio, for burial. His show continued the 1904 season under the direction of Mrs. Gaskill and Harold A. Bushea. They established another first in the collective amusement field that season when the entire show played the Minnesota State Fair. The Gaskill Carnival Company was the first organized midway to play an agricultural fair in the United States.

FLOYD E. GOODING. Being presented an award as Ohio's outstanding showman April 12, 1964. Left to right are Harry Dearwester, President of Ohio Showmen's Association; Governor James A. Rhodes of Ohio; and Floyd E. Gooding. Courtesy Gooding Amusement Company.

FLOYD E. GOODING

In any discussion regarding the acceptance of the collective amusement industry as a respected branch of the business world, one name in that industry stands out above all others. The name Gooding has meant clean entertainment for the public and honest dealings with everyone on picnic and fair grounds for over seventy-five years. When Harry B. Kelley retired as manager of the Hillsdale County Fair in Michigan at the end of the 1969 fair, after forty years in that position, only one segment of the entertainment department of the fair remained unchanged during his long tenure. Units of the Gooding Amusement Company occupied the midway at Hillsdale in 1969 as such Gooding Units had been doing for seventy-five years.

John Gooding was an Ashtabula County, Ohio, farmer until the early eighteen nineties when he fell in love with a beautiful steam-powered merry-go-round on the Ashtabula County Fairgrounds. He spent the whole day watching this noisy ride and was fascinated by the big bag of nickels that the ride operator lugged away at the end of the day. John Gooding, the very next day, hurried to the general store and convinced the store-keeper that he wanted to buy one of those new steam-driven riding devices. It was ordered and arrived in time for him to set it up at three Ohio Fairs the next fall. He soon expanded his operations all over the state and into neighboring Michigan and Indiana. He added a Ferris Wheel, and then acquired another set of rides which he persuaded his brother, Louis, to manage for him.

When John Gooding formed a third unit, none of his other brothers were interested in managing it for him; but his nephews, sons of his brother, James, were eager to work for Uncle John. Young Floyd had sold tickets with the other hawkers around the merry-go-round when he was only ten years old, but his brother Roy was the one who left the farm to manage Uncle John's third ride unit. Roy soon started a unit of his own though, then his brother Arby came fr the farm to manage the unit for Uncle John.

When Floyd E. Gooding graduated from high school he joined his Uncle John for two years, then he decided to start his own unit of riding devices. His brother Arby joined him in this venture and with borrowed capital, they became the third group of Goodings in amusement device business. Floyd and Arby didn't do as well as they had hoped for, but they still made enough to pay off their indebtedness and acquire other equipment. Around 1918, Floyd, Arby and Roy pooled their holdings and bought out their Uncle John. They operated the five units they now owned until Floyd withdrew from the partnership in 1920. There was no disagreement of any kind. Floyd just wanted to organize his business a little differently. He lined up several fairs for his two units forming regular circuits which Gooding units are still playing fifty years later.

The success of Floyd's booking maneuvers were so effective that in 1948 he had no less than eight separate units playing his booked dates. Two of these were now full-fledged carnival midways with booked-on independent shows and concessions. All such shows and concessions were required to accept and work by the Gooding standards of cleanliness and honesty. In the late fifties, Floyd E. Gooding operated no less than twelve units, one of which was a major carnival playing the bigger state fairs. This larger unit has been disposed of to other ownership now.

Uncle John Gooding died December 10, 1937. He hadn't been idle since selling his rides to his nephews. Uncle John had developed one of the largest and most modern farms in Northeaster, Ohio. He had also built the Puritas Springs Park in Cleveland. His brother Louis had died in 1934.

Roy Gooding died February 12, 1942, and Arby had retired because of ill health. After World War II service, Blaine never returned to the midways. Floyd E. Gooding remained to carry on the amusement traditions founded by his Uncle John. Proof that he has done this well is demonstrated by the scores of long-time contracts still held by his amusement organizations. Ohio State Fair at Columbus fifty-two years and nine other Ohio Fairs for sixty-two or more, this is a record of longevity that no other traveling amusement organization can claim. Many of these "contracted dates" were played for years without a formal written contract. A handshake from

a Gooding was all that was needed to make a commitment as "good as gold."

A life-time crusader for clean outdoor amusement — for midways where everyone could obtain release from the worries of everyday existence at reasonable prices — Floyd Gooding has been an industry leader in other phases as well. This man who owns so many riding devices and trucks that he cannot number them, established his first permanent winter quarters in 1939. These quarters in Columbus, Ohio, were ample for his needs at that time, but he now owns a greatly expanded plant. Very few carnivals had ever owned their own winter quarters, until these last two decades when many of the older established midways have been installed in permanent quarters by owners who were convinced the carnival was here to stay. Floyd Gooding's first permanent quarters in 1939 was a pioneering effort on his part.

The present winter quarters, repair shops and factory are the most complete any amusement organization has ever had. Elaborate, well-equipped offices, backed by a shop building which includes ample space for every conceivable renovation required by any type of amusement property are supervised by highly experienced and capable department heads all under the direction of Master Showman, Floyd E. Gooding. Here, over two hundred tired trucks are restored for another season, one hundred fifty riding devices are repaired and repainted and all the countless tasks of preparing for the coming season are performed. Department heads and unit managers are all veterans of ten, twenty, thirty and even forty years of service with Gooding. There is a pride among these Gooding employees seldom found with any other outdoor amusement organization. In spite of their long years with Gooding, these employees do make a newcomer "feel at home" as they know that new men must be attracted to the industry, if it is to continue to operate as efficiently as Gooding Units must operate.

Floyd E. Gooding is one of the most unassuming midway purveyors in the business. Some traces of his Ohio farm background are still discernable in this man who has spent a long life-time on fairgrounds, picnic grounds and street celebrations. Yes, some Gooding units will play annual events this year held on the streets of Indiana and Ohio towns. Mr. Gooding will tell his visitors about the old days, but he had much rather tell them about the plans for next season, or the next. He is not as active as he once was, but with the many loyal and capable people he has surrounding him, he only needs to supervise, and he is a master supervisor.

Floyd E. Gooding, ex-farm boy, business and civic leader, family man and midway owner, has built a legacy for the carnival industry. A legacy that will serve as a model for all future midways in their relations with their patrons and their sponsoring committees. Floyd E. Gooding kept one beacon light aflame in a faltering industry. A light that has led the industry to the pinnacle it occupies today.

BILL HAMES. Courtesy Buster L. Brown.

No doubt Bill Hames' parents named him William H. when he was born back in South Carolina in 1880; but it is doubtful that any one of his million or so friends in the great Lone Star State of Texas ever called him anything but Bill. Those friends whose fathers and grandfathers Bill first started to entertain with his old horse-drawn merry-go-round back in 1910. A merry-go-round he knocked down, packed and shipped in box cars between the country pcinics he played. He drove his team of horses over sandy land or black mud roads to reach those picnic towns in time to unload that "flying jenny" and get it set up for the opening of the picnic.

Some of those picnics, like the Old Settlers' Reunion at Alvarado have been served by a Bill Hames merry-go-round for over fifty years. Of course, Bill added a full-fledged carnival to that "jenny" many years before Texas celebrated its first centennial. Fact is, he didn't keep for long that original horse-drawn device which had been abandoned by its former operator at Bill's stirrup factory in Pilot Point, Texas. When Hames saw his first steam-powered jumping horse carry-us-all from the C. W. Parker factory, he bought it for twenty-five hundred dollars. That was his first improvement — replacing old equipment with something better for his yet unborn midway. As long as Bill Hames lived, as his midway grew bigger and bigger, he continued to improve that midway by replacing old equipment and devices with newer, more modern paraphernalia.

Bill's parents brought him from South Carolina when he was a young boy, and both died before he was ten. He went to live with grandparents at Denton, Texas. They sent him to school there, but not for long as young Hames was ambitious and anxious to get started on his life's work, whatever that might be. He worked as a farm laborer and as a railroad hand. All either of those jobs offered was long hours of hard work under the hot Texas sun, or the biting cold of a late fall "Blue Norther." By 1910, he and his wife were operating a stirrup factory in Pilot Point. After the horse-drawn merry-go-round had lain in his factory shed for several months, he took it out and set it up for local children to ride.

The next step was to take the device on the road and play a picnic or two. Those picnics, which lasted for days, attracted ranchers from miles around who came in their covered wagons and camped on the grounds. They rode that "Jenny" of Bill's several times a day, as it cost only five cents a ride, and there wasn't anything else to ride except horses and they did all of that they wanted on the ranches. Those picnics grossed more money than Bill thought possible, and he was "hooked" by amusement business.

He added other equipment to his new jumping horse carry-us-all and soon had a full-fledged carnival. He never forgot his old friends at those first picnics and reunions, but continued to take them more and better entertainment each year. Fifty years ago, this writer saw Bill Hames Shows at the Alvarado Reunion and hopes to be able to get out there this next August to relive some of those thrills of half a century ago. Hames made it a rule not to book any date that he could not get his equipment in and all set up for the opening morning. He boasted all his life, that he had "never failed to get there yet and don't aim to."

Along with that other great midway showman in Ohio, Floyd E. Gooding, Bill Hames shared the reputation of bringing the patrons the cleanest entertainment it would be possible for them to find anywhere. Those two showmen's honest dealings have made it possible for them to book many dates by telephone or by a handshake without any formal written contract. Neither of them ever allowed any questionable game or show on their midways. Some of Bill's competitors in Texas chided him frequently because he allowed nothing on his midway that could offend any patron. His reply to all of their reproofs was, "Look at what I have. Now look at yours."

When Bill started expanding he joined his rides with the small wild west shows which the Texans of fifty years ago loved to attend. His first connection was with Booger Red's Wild West Show, and later he booked Texas Bud's Wild West. Most all carnivals carried wild west shows in those days, but none of them were as good and entertaining as the ones touring with the small carnivals in Texas. They had to be good as most of the spectators were capable of coming into the arena and doing a little riding, bull-dogging or calf-roping themselves. Those wild west shows on the Texas carnivals were more like small town Rodeos than they were a regular wild west show. With the drawing power of those shows, Bill was soon able to book a continuous route, by filling in still dates between his picnics, fairs and

HAMES SHOWS STAFF. Left, Buster L. Brown, manager. Right, Gene Hames, president and Mary Helen Hames Brown, secretary-treasurer. Courtesy Buster L. Brown.

celebrations.

By the early twenties the Bill H. Hames Shows was traveling on its own train of flatcars with the equipment all loaded into its own wagons each week. The Hames Show was the only railroad show in the state of Texas for many years. Its route has always been mostly inside the boundaries of the big Lone Star State. A few dates were played in Kansas, Oklahoma, and New Mexico, but there were plenty good towns in Texas for Texas' own show, so why bother about the others?

Bill Hames was the friend and confidant of some of the wealthiest and most influential men in the state of Texas, yet he never failed to greet mechanics, working men, hotel porters and children with that same reserved kindness which had gained him the admiration of the influential few. He probably could have been governor of Texas, had he desired. His friends could have almost insured his election, but Bill could never spare that much time from his midway. Of course as he grew older, his material holdings increased. He owned scores of riding devices, not only on his midway, but in amusement parks. He had a ten thousand acre ranch stocked with blooded cattle, and other real estate holdings all over Central Texas.

Bill Hames had wintered his shows in Ft. Worth for many years when he entered the hospital in that city in spring of 1960. Like many eighty year olds he was suffering from complications of diseases. On June 14, 1960, he had a heart attack and died. He was buried on June 17th. He had no worries about his beloved show as he died, as his son and daughters had been trained from early childhood in the Bill Hames system of fair play and honesty. His show is being capably managed by his grandson, Buster Brown. Buster is assisted by his uncle, Gene Hames, president of the corporation, and his mother, Mary Helen Hames Brown, secretary-treasurer. Bill Hames not only built a strong carnival, but he provided for its continuity.

JOHNNY JENKINS JONES

Johnny Jenkins Jones was born in Arnot, Pennsylvania in 1874. His family later moved to Du Bois, Pennsylvania. Young Johnny got little formal education, as he was working in the coal mines when he was ten years old. As soon as he could get away from them, he quit the mines and started selling newspapers on the streets. He went from newsboy to "news butcher" on railroad passenger trains. A "butcher" if he was given good "runs," could make quite a lot selling newspapers, magazines, cigars, candies, fruit and sandwiches. The little fellow evidently did make money from his "train butching" as he had his own concession playing fairs in 1895.

The first concession of Johnny J. Jones was a cane rack, however, within four years he had bought a miniature railroad and had built himself a Ferris wheel. In 1903, he and Bert Hoss incorporated the Columbus Carnival Company in the spring. Ad also said Jones and Zimmerman were the owners of the new outfit, but a September advertisement listed Johnny J. as sole owner. He opened as Johnny J. Jones Carnival Company in spring of 1904, but formed a partnership in the Jones-Adams Shows before the season ended. The next two years Jones-Adams Shows toured the Carolinas and the Southeast.

Partnership broke up and the little man put out his Johnny J. Jones Exposition Shows & Trained Wild Animal Exhibition in 1907. He now had the big drooping mustaches of which he was evidently proud, as he sent in frequent photographs of himself to the Billboard. He continued to use the Jones title in conjunction with Exposition as long as he lived, and the Johnny J. Jones title was used for over fifty years.

In the early days, his favorite territory was the Carolinas and the states bordering them on the North and South. As his midway grew in size, he expanded the territory in which he exhibited. By 1912, he was touring a twenty-five car railroad show, and playing a profitable route of dates and fairs in Florida each winter. He established winter quarters in Orlando, Florida in 1914. He had never needed quarters as he never closed, and he was one of the few carnival showmen who could book profitable dates for a winter tour. It was said that Johnny J. Jones knew every inch of the Florida East Coast Railroad's right of way, as he routed up and down its tracks every winter.

As his show continued to grow, he moved farther away from his established route, as many of "his towns" were too small to support the larger show. Washington, D.C. and Pittsburgh, Pennsylvania were played as "still dates" each season; and in 1916 he carried his midway west of the Mississippi River for the first time. That year, the Jones Show played

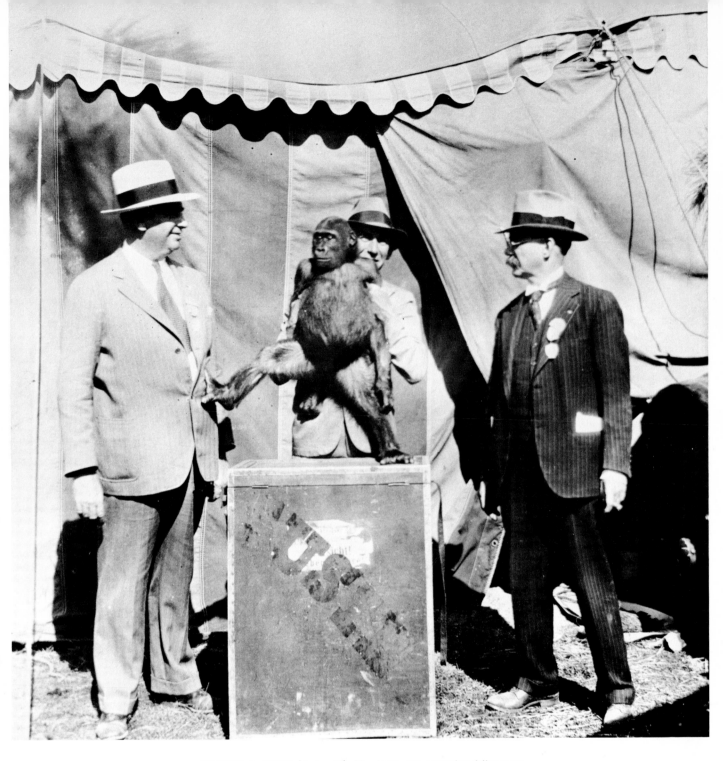

JOHNNY J. JONES (dark suit). Mr. Jones was accepting delivery on Susie, the chimpanzee, who had just arrived in the United States on the GRAF ZEPPELIN. Other man was the mayor of Orlando, Florida. Author's collection.

Davenport, Iowa; Oklahoma City; Lincoln, Nebraska; Jackson, Mississippi; Shreveport; and Beaumont, Texas. Season of 1920, he played the Canadian National Exhibition for the second time and the Class A. Circuit of Western Canada for the third year. C. A. Wortham got some of those dates in 1921 and 1922, but the little Welchman from Pennsylvania had everything on the East Coast tied up. He could have his "pick of the fairs" in that area.

After Wortham's death in 1922, Mr. Jones played the dates that he chose, as no other midway could compare with his in size or quality. With the massive Maynes Riding Devices, he continued to have them all outclassed. He had so many fairs in the middle twenties, he was forced to organize another carnival to play them. He combined this Southern Exposition Shows with his number one show to play the larger fairs. He combined them permanently in 1928 as one fifty-car show. With his long, all steel car train, this fifty cars was easily the equivalent of any two of the other thirty-car shows.

He had gotten married for the second time in

1920 to Etta Louise (Hody) Hurd. His first wife had died on December 31, 1909. On August 5, 1921, Johnny Jenkins Jones, Jr. was born in Crooked Creek, Pennsylvania. Birth took place at the home of Mr. Jones' "Sister Sue." The little showman had an heir. An heir to whom he was to leave very little except an honored name. The greatest name in the collective amusement industry.

Johnny J. Jones was the genius of the carnival industry. No other midway operator could match his ability or his show. When his carnival once "played a date," the committee for that "spot" became Johnny J. Jones' fans, and it was difficult for any show to take one of his "established dates" for their route. His great midway with its long lines of entertaining shows, its extraordinary riding devices and its rows of "clean" concessions could not be matched by any of his competitors. A full generation of District of Columbia citizens thrilled at the simple announcement, "JOHNNY IS COMING," when it appeared in the newspapers and was blazoned on the billboards in the city of Washington.

Johnny J. Jones had drunk in moderation ever since his teenage days as a railroad "news butcher." He had increased his consumption of alcohol as he spent long hours on wet, muddy, and sometimes freezing midways. As his carnival grew in size, more and more "social drinking" became necessary as he entertained fair boards and committees at state and regional meetings and conventions. Also, entertainment of visiting committees and dignitaries on the showgrounds was a daily occurrence. In the middle twenties after a particularly distressing hospitalization with the D.T.'s in a Knoxville,

Tennessee, hospital, the little man realized that he had become a drunkard.

His renunciation of alcoholic drink and his conversion to Christianity, he announced himself; and for a time his thousands of friends rejoiced with him, as Johnny J. Jones was "on the wagon." His wife Hody was happy with this change in her gentle little husband, but those muddy showgrounds were still wet and cold, a showman's hours were still long and arduous, the thirst of friends and committee members still had to be assuaged, and human appetites were still stronger than human will power.

Johnny Jenkins Jones died in his private car at DeLand, Florida, on Christmas Day, December 25, 1930. He had been bedridden only two days with this attack, which hadn't seemed to be as serious as ones he had suffered previously. The attending physician attributed his death to uremia. His funeral services at the Elks Club auditorium in DeLand resulted in a "turn-away house," something Mr. Jones had been adept at achieving in life. Two trucks were required to haul the floral pieces to the cemetery in Orlando, forty miles away, where graveside rites were performed.

Sixty automobiles were used to transport the mourners from DeLand to Orlando. The pallbearers were Chet Dunn, W. C. Martin, Vernon Korhn, Harry Illions, Eddie Madigan and Jack Murray, all of them long-time employees or associates of the dead carnival owner. Honorary pallbearers were mayors, bank presidents, fair managers, and fair board members. Western Canada Class A Circuit flew a personal representative of those fairs to Florida for the funeral.

CHARLES W. PARKER

Charles W. Parker was born in Griggsville, Illinois in 1864, but was moved by his parents to Dickinson County, Kansas in 1869. His father, a farmer, and his mother, a niece of Mr. William M. Thackery, moved their children and their possessions to the new frontiers of Kansas in a covered wagon. They moved to Clay County, Kansas in 1878. Young Parker worked on the Clay County farm for only two years, for in 1880 he went to Abilene, Kansas to work at any "odd jobs" that could be found.

In 1881, he saw a man operating a "high striker" on the streets of Abilene. Seventeen year old Parker liked it, borrowed $14.50 from friends and bought half interest in the device. Within a week, he had repaid his friends and bought the other half interest. The next year he built a shooting gallery which he set

up in Abilene. The cowboys, after their long cattle drives from the Southwest, had plenty of cash to spend in Abilene before they rode back down the dusty trails to their home ranges. Eighteen year old Parker's shooting gallery got its share of "traildrive money." After a short time he sold this shooting gallery and engaged in other amusement activities until 1892. Then he bought a Merry-Go-Round. He had now found his chosen field of activity.

This Merry-Go-Round was a rather crude device, and even though it was profitable, as it was, he redesigned it. In 1895, he began building his redesigned Merry-Go-Rounds in a small factory in Abilene. His new Parker Jumping Horse Carry-Us-Alls were first built in this factory in 1902, the year he began operating his own midway, The C. W. Parker

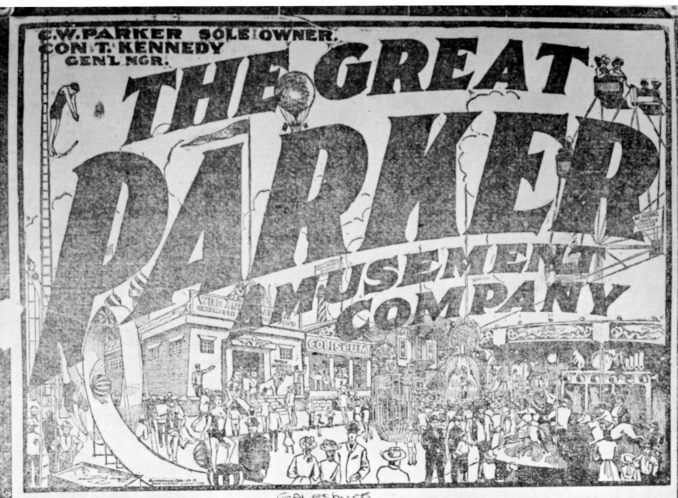

STARTS LABOR DAY

BENEFIT OF

Trades and Labor Assembly

A FEW OF THE MANY GREAT ATTRACTIONS

PARKER'S JUNGLE ACTORS
SUNFLOWER BELLES
"SUPERBA," THE SHOW-BEAUTIFUL
MERRY-WIDOW'S HOME
ALPS, OR BEAUTIFUL SWITZERLAND
GEORGIA MINSTRELS
$10,000.00 CARRY-US-ALL
HALE'S TOURS-OF-THE-WORLD
LEMON "23"
GORILLA-MAN
JUMBO, BIG BOA-CONSTRICTOR
FERRIS WHEEL

Jack Valere in the Limit Act

MLLE. LISETTE, LEAPING THE VOLCANIC CHASM
$5,000.00 STEAM CALIOPE
PARKER'S MILITARY BAND OF 32 EXPERT SOLOISTS.
$20,000.00 ELECTRIC LIGHT PLANTS.
SPECIAL TRAIN, "SUNFLOWER SPECIAL" 33 DOUBLE LENGTH CARS.

Don't Miss the Grand Parade—9:30 a.m. Labor Day

Amusement Company. The name for this jumping horse machine, a motion which Parker originated in merry-go-rounds, was suggested by the French name for them, carousel.

His first sign for the new machine, one which he carried on his first midway, read, "CARRY-US-ALL 5¢". He changed this sign later that season down in Oklahoma. A farmer with a large family bought one five-cent ticket and demanded a ride for every member of his family for the single admission. He argued that the sign promised a ride for all for a nickel. Parker let them all ride, and immediately changed his sign. Parker managed his new midway himself, seasons of 1902 and 1903. Winter of 1903—04, he built another complete midway and leased both of his shows to competent operators for the 1904 season.

His Abilene factory now kept him busy all year. In addition to merry-go-rounds, he built shooting galleries, high strikers and any other amusement device a customer might order. He built complete carnivals including the wagons and railroad cars in that little factory. In 1905, he built two more new carnivals complete in his plant for 1906 operations. This first multi-show owner had all four "Parker" shows operating for several seasons, but they were all leased to other showmen, who managed them. Parker demanded that all his carnivals be operated as "Sunday School Shows," and he headed one almost singlehanded drive to clean up midways. He was president of a Showmen's Association started in Chicago which aimed for clean midways. Like many drives of the kind, this one failed for lack of compliance from members.

In 1910, Parker moved his manufacturing business to Leavenworth, Kansas, where he had built a large plant. Then he began building shows as well as rides and devices for other showmen. Almost every big midway in the country carried one of his "Night in Chinatown" shows one season. His factory designed and built shows, rides, fun houses, wagons, concession equipment and free act rigging.

The Velare Brothers did some of their first carnival trouping on a C. W. Parker midway as a free act. Some of their first concessions were booked on a Parker Show. When the Velare's Acrobatic Act disbanded, their understander, Jack Velare, did a sensational free high act for Parker. Jack was no relation to Elmer and Curtis, but adopted the name of Velare when he joined the act. Many other successful carnival showmen did their first midway trouping with Parker midways.

C. W. brought a man from Paris, France, in 1907 to design an airplane for possible manufacture in the Abilene plant. He bought a new plane in Los Angeles in 1910, planning to use it as a free act on one of his midways. It didn't work out as well as he had hoped, and the idea died after a few trials. Tom W. Allen, C. A. Wortham's first partner, was a son-in-law of Mr. Parker, being married to the former Gertrude Parker.

Charles W. Parker died at his home in Leavenworth, Kansas, on October 28, 1932 after an illness of eighteen months. He was buried on October 31st in Abilene, Kansas. His factory was still active when he died, and it continued to operate for several years after his death, but there was never as much activity in the plant after 1916 as there had been in that frenzied period of growth of the young carnival industry prior to the start of World War I in Europe.

CARL J. SEDLMAYR

CARL J. SEDLMAYR, SR. Courtesy Royal American Shows.

Although Francis Ferari advertised himself as "King of the Carnival World" early in the twentieth century, the man who was destined to become that "King" hadn't entered the collective amusement field yet — and wouldn't for another ten years. The undisputed "King" of the carnival industry was born in Falls City, Nebraska, on October 20, 1886. Eleven year old Carl J. Sedlmayr was brought to Kansas City, Missouri, to live after his father's death in 1897. Young Sedlmayr did not run away from home to join a circus as many of his contemporaries did. He worked in a drug store and thought that he might become a pharmacist. When he was fourteen he tried unsuccessfully to get employment as such in Omaha, Nebraska, and in Council Bluffs, Iowa.

Carl J. Sedlmayr's failure to get a job working in his "chosen" profession was fortunate for him. His was not the temperament to long endure the "closed in by four walls' atmosphere of a drug store. Perhaps it was lucky chance that caused young Sedlmayr to read an advertisement wanting salesmen for fountain pens. Anyway, he answered that ad and began to sell the new writing devices. On his selling trips he met several outdoor showmen and became interested in that business. He took his first summer job in the outdoor field in 1907, but continued to sell the fountain pens in the winter months.

He was talker on a side show at Chicago's Riverview Park, and he spent several years as a ticket seller and superintendent of tickets on Campbell Brothers' and Cole Brothers' Circuses. He had the Side Show on Coop & Lent's Circus season of 1918, and booked a side show with Jim Patterson's Great Patterson Shows for the 1919 and 1920 seasons. His next connection was with another carnival with circus ties. The Siegrist & Silbon Shows was owned by the well-known Siegrist-Silbon families, who had to go to Australia that 1921 season.

Sedlmayr purchased the equipment in the fall of 1921 and toured the show under its original title in 1922. In 1923, he coined a name for his new show, taking Royal for Canada and American for the United

States — the Royal American Shows was born. With the exception of the war years, Royal American Shows has toured ever since. In 1925, Carl J. took Elmer and Curtis Velare as partners in his new enterprise. The three men, pooling their own talents and engaging capable men as department heads began building their show into a top rank organization. This was a slow process, as carnival business wasn't too good in the last half of the twenties. In fact, Carl J. Sedlmayr wrote in 1937 that the show grossed more in two weeks of that depression year than it did in an entire season ten years before.

The three showmen were dedicated to the principle of carrying clean, high-class entertainment to the public. The carnival had always been the "poor man's entertainment," but now the motion picture theatres were catering to that same market, and a new source of competition, radio, was free. Carnivals had the advantage over these competitors but few of them realized it. The partners in the Royal American did know that they possessed the superior selling point of personal contact. Neither of the other media could let their patrons really feel the product they sold. Carnival midway patrons could feel, smell and even enter into all the amusements offered on that midway. They could participate in every activity on a carnival midway as they breathed the crushed grass, wet sawdust and frying hamburger-laden aroma of its sexy atmosphere. They could personally enjoy the thrill of being jostled against each other in one of a score of the noisy riding devices. And if they applauded long enough, and yelled loud enough, the girls on the "Gal Shows" might possibly lower the fans a little longer, or take off a little more.

The Royal American owners evaluated all factors. All carnivals had the same riding devices, concessions and shows. To stand out, a midway must be made more inviting to its patrons, and they must be treated as patrons, not as "marks" or suckers. With this in mind, a midway was planned to fit the requirements of its patrons and all efforts were applied towards creating it. It was a slow process, but it was accelerated by the acquisition of the Minnesota State Fair to its route in the late twenties and the adding of the Western Canada Class A Circuit of fairs in 1934. With those proven money-makers on its route, cash could be expended to build the midway that would be pleasing to all amusement lovers.

With the Velares as partners, Sedlmayr could devote more time to creating good will with the fair committees and other important people who might visit their midway. No hired general agent can ever do as good a job on public relations as the show owner himself. No doubt he was the best general agent his show ever had, because he worked with the authority of ownership behind him, and he was building relationships for his midway, himself and his family that would last much longer than from year to year. As a consequence, the Royal American Shows can point to forty-one years at the Florida State Fair and Memphis Cotton Carnival, thirty-seven years at the

"STEPPING OFF THE LOT." Carl J. Sedlmayr, Sr., teaching his grandson, C. J. III, how to lay out the lot. Courtesy John Colville, Calgary Herald.

Minnesota State Fair and Davenport, Iowa, Shrine Festival, and thirty-five years on the Canadian Class A Circuit and state fairs in Mississippi and Louisiana.

By 1935 the Royal American was accepted as the leader in the industry and continued in that position until it closed in the early war years. When the title was again used, Carl J. Sedlmayr emerged as the sole owner and continued as such for twenty years. He hired Robert L. Lohmar as his general agent, but the show's route was so firmly set that Bob's principal duties were to help the "Carnival King" entertain visiting dignitaries. A capable staff kept the show moving with such punctual precision that late openings and lost days were eliminated except through train wrecks or "Acts of God." As Sedlmayr grew older, his one big problem was the fitting of his monster midway onto the fairgrounds lots. This he continued to do himself.

Carl J. Sedlmayr prided himself on having a step that was exactly three feet, no more, no less. He disdained the use of a tape measure in laying out his midway. He went into town three days ahead of the show, leaving the management to his capable employees. He carefully stepped off the grounds and placed location stakes for all the shows, rides and concessions. When the show trains arrived, the equipment was located exactly between those stakes. One sure way of arousing the wrath of the boss was to tamper with one of the location stakes. No one in authority has ever admitted that in his last year or two, Carl J.'s steps were just a little shorter than they had been. His long-time employees — ride foremen, canvasmen and concessionaires — made allowances for this, lapped a little here, pulled in a little there, pushed out somewhere and quietly changed a stake here and there as their boss man went into the office to be briefed on the business for the last three days in last week's town.

In regard to using a tape line, there is a story on the Royal American lot about the new superintendent who had been hired from another show. He, not knowing how Mr. Sedlmayr laid out the lot, bought his new boss a fancy long tape line, thinking that it was a gift that would be appreciated here as it would be on other shows. He almost got fired. This writer was fortunate in 1962, as he was able to spend the time on the fairgrounds in Regina, Saskatchewan, and watch Carl J. Sedlmayr step off and lay out the grounds for his huge show; and on Sunday afternoon see the show move onto the lot directly from the flatcars and fit between the location stakes. Having laid out many show grounds himself, the writer must bow in reverence to the master of them all.

Royal American ended its 1965 season in Shreveport, Louisiana, as it had for twenty-nine years, and the show trains had brought the show back to its Tampa, Florida, winter quarters. Everything was unloaded and stowed away under the direction of the C. J. Sedlmayrs, Senior and Junior. The next night the family was to have dinner at the home of C. J., Jr., as Mrs. Carl J. was in the hospital. C. J. and his family waited, but Carl J. did not come for dinner. When C. J. went to his father's home, he found him dead in bed where he had gone to take a little rest. He was gone, but he left his midway in the highly capable hands of C. J. Sedlmayr, Jr., and C. J. III is being carefully groomed to follow his father and grandfather on their beloved carnival.

Over twelve hundred showmen and friends crowded in and around the Greater Tampa Showmen's Club rooms as funeral services were held for Carl J. Sedlmayr, Sr. on November 9, 1965. A showman, a Protestant minister, and a Rabbi shared in the services as music from the great German pipe organ carried by the show was heard from the nearby winter quarters. The Rabbi, David L. Zielonka of Schaarai Zedek Temple, summed up his concluding words the creed of Carl J. Sedlmayr and of most outdoor showmen. He said, "... In Mr. Sedlmayr's world there are no Catholics, Jews or Protestants — just men and women of faith." His body was placed in a mausoleum at Showmen's Rest in Tampa, with full Masonic burial rites.

ROYAL AMERICAN SHOWS. Office wagon, Minnesota State Fair, 1933. Courtesy Harry Frost, Minnesota State Fair.

JAMES E. STRATES. Author's collection.

Many of the early collective amusement organizations were started and operated by men who had immigrated to America. None of them achieved the high position in the business that James E. Strates did in his forty year carnival career.

Jimmie Strates, as he was known to thousands of friends along the Eastern Seaboard, came to America from Greece in 1909. Those were not easy times for immigrants, and young Strates had to work at many menial tasks before he joined his first carnival ten years later. He worked in cotton mills, a Child's Restaurant, a hotel and he shined shoes. He had a job in the Endicott-Johnson shoe factory and worked in the ship yards during World War I. At Endicott-Johnson he became interested in wrestling and "worked out" at the local YMCA.

Jimmie Strates was a proficient wrestler and in 1919 he joined Lee Schaefer's Athletic Show to wrestle all comers on a carnival midway. He saved his money, and in 1923 he organized a carnival of his own. This show, the Southern Tier Shows, was built in Bath, New York and opened for the first time at Wayland, New York. The move to Wayland was only twenty-two miles; but it took twenty-four hours to get the old hard-tired trucks loaded with a merry-go-round, a Ferris wheel, an athletic show, and a small pit show to the first show grounds. This Southern Tier Shows was not too successful, and several seasons James E. Strates closed still in debt for improvements he had made the past spring. Some sources say that he still wrestled in the "At" show on the midway, but there is no proof of this available to this writer. It is a fact, though, that the Athletic show did move the midway many weeks when rides and other shows didn't lure enough patrons to the little show grounds. Nick Bozinis, an old friend of Jimmie's, managed the At Show and continued to wrestle in it.

Strates always paid his debts as soon as he could get the money to do so, and his credit was good so he continued to improve his little show. He had been married in 1923 and he had a family to support when the depression of the thirties curtailed business for all outdoor amusements. Jimmie Strates didn't curtail his show though. He expanded it.

When many former railroad transported carnivals were turning to truck and highway operations, James E. Strates reversed the process and put his midway on railroad cars. In the middle thirties the Southern Tier Shows was put on flat cars and renamed the James E. Strates Shows. He loaded seventeen of his truck show trailers onto steel double-length flatcars for that first season on rails. Each year he added five more cars to his show train until he had a train of forty cars. He explained this by saying that when he had fifteen cars, his press agent advertised twenty; when he added the five, the press agent would go up another five. When he had reached forty cars with his train, Strates said, "I am through pacifying press agents, I am not going to buy any more rolling stock."

In 1943, Strates bought the Art Lewis Shows for a partnership with J. C. Weer with a number two show. He let Dave Endy have this equipment in 1945 for Dave's Endy Brothers' Shows. On December 22nd of that year he needed all the equipment that he could find. The entire forty-car James E. Strates Shows was destroyed by fire in a Mullins, South Carolina tobacco warehouse where it had been stored for the winter. With nothing except a show train and a quarter of a million dollars from the insurance company, Strates had to decide whether he was quitting show business or not.

If he stayed in the business, he would have to build a complete new show in less than four months to play dates already booked for April 1946. Equipment was scarce and prices were high. With the quarter of a million and the cash the show train could be sold for, the Strates family could go into some other line of endeavor where they could all stay home every night. Jimmie Strates' show was often referred to as a one-man operation, but after the fire he found that he had fifteen people who had been with him ever since he started twenty-three years before. He reasoned that he had to reopen his show, as these loyal employees had no other show that could offer them comparable positions.

He did rebuild and the show played its first spring dates as contracted. This was probably one of the most expensive midways that had ever been put together up until that time. Top prices had to be paid for makeshift equipment, but Strates paid whatever was necessary and the show rolled out of quarters on time.

James E. Strates learned early in his career as a carnival owner not to be too hasty in making changes. He decided in 1926 to take his little show south for late fall dates. He had only four shows and three rides then, and he carried it all into a town in Virginia. When he went to the City Hall he was told that the fee for his show would be one thousand dollars. The show was carried back to New York State for the winter.

In his later years, when the stresses of big-time carnival management became too rough, James E. Strates would go off quietly and take a nap. Some crisis that would have other midway owners almost hysterical would be met by Strates as he slept quietly on a cot in his hide-out. He had four of the biggest fairs on the East Coast in his route, but he never let many of the problems of midway management bother him. Neither did he intend for any carnival to ever bother his family unnecessarily. They helped him on his show but by choice. He did not train his two daughters or his son to follow him on a midway. It was their choice when they came on the show for their summer vacations.

At the Danville, Virginia, Fair in 1959, James E. Strates had a stroke while sitting in his office wagon talking by telephone with one of his daughters in upstate New York. He was rushed to the hospital and died there. His funeral at the Greek Orthodox Church in Raleigh, North Carolina, was estimated to be the biggest ever held in that city.

His body was carried to Endicott, New York and interred there October 15, 1959. The show he founded is being managed successfully by his son, E. James Strates.

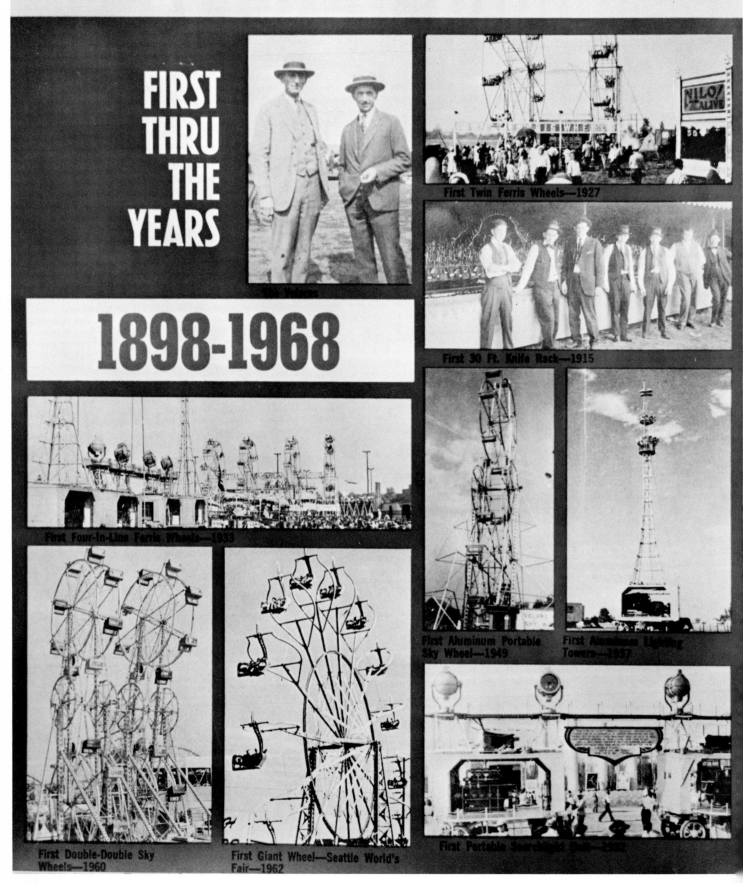

VELARE BROS.

FIRST THRU THE YEARS

1898-1968

First Twin Ferris Wheels—1927

First 30 Ft. Knife Rack—1915

First Four-In-Line Ferris Wheels—1933

First Aluminum Portable Sky Wheel—1949

First Aluminum Lighting Towers—1957

First Double-Double Sky Wheels—1960

First Giant Wheel—Seattle World's Fair—1962

First Portable Searchlight

VELARE BROTHERS

Much has been written in this volume about the younger generation of showmen, second and third generations carrying on for their fathers and younger showmen having to solve the problems faced by the collective amusement industry, but the most revolutionary change in that industry was pioneered by two men already in their seventies, and who now, at eighty-five and eighty-eight, are planning and building still more innovations for American midways. An insight into the philosophy of these two men can be illustrated by this story. A few years ago, the men were approached by a real estate agent, who wanted to acquire and develop some acreage they owned near Long Beach, California. They were both past eighty, and the realtor was sure they would be happy to dispose of the unused property. The older of the two, then nearly eighty-five, disillusioned him with, "That property will be worth a lot of money in about twenty-five years. No, we will hold onto it."

Curtis and Elmer Velare celebrated their seventy-fifth year in outdoor show business in 1969 by introducing a new riding device to the public in their Queen's Park in Long Beach and by planning possible nationwide distribution of the same. The City Council of Long Beach proclaimed "Elmer and Curtis Velare Day in Long Beach" and honored them as "two of the greatest names in American show business." Asked about the possibility of their retirement, Elmer replied, "Not if we feel like we do now. We just don't do any more acrobatic stunts," he added with a grin, "but at 85 I can still do a handstand." Curtis, the taller of the two, at 88 has quit the handstands now, but he has always been the quieter, more conservative brother.

The Velare brothers started in outdoor show business in their home town of Seattle, Washington, doing acrobatic stunts for their friends. They were soon giving exhibitions of their skill all up and down the Rogue River Valley area. They took on a partner as an "understander" in their act and began to give professional performances. This partner adopted the name "Jack Velare" and used that name until his death in the early twenties. The acrobatic act worked on circuses for several years until early in the new century they joined C. W. Parker as a free act on his number one show. They stayed with Parker for several years, but broke up the act and went into concession business.

They were already veteran outdoor showmen in 1913, when they helped form the new Showmen's League of America and elect Buffalo Bill Cody as its first president. They were not charter members of the organization though. By the late teens they owned rides, concessions, wagons and flatcars and furnished a large portion of the Nat Reiss Shows. They leased that show from the Melvilles and operated it themselves the 1921 season. In 1922, they had all their equipment with the Mighty Doris Shows operated by John Lazia out of Kansas City. The last week in December of that year, all equipment of the Mighty Doris Show was destroyed by fire in its Belleville, Illinois winter quarters.

In 1925, they became partners with Carl J. Sedlmayr in the new Royal American Shows. This was probably one of the ten most important events in the history of collective amusement business. The three partners collectively possessed talents that no other combination in carnival management has ever had, and they had the daring of young men. With this daring and their separate abilities, they built the Royal American into the Greatest Collective Amusement Organization On Earth. This position, attained by the end of the 1935 season, has never been relinquished by that great show. This writer believes that it required this team of carnival greats to build the show, and that it probably would never have reached that supreme position had any one of them been lacking during the formative period.

During the early years of World War II, the partnership was dissolved and the Velare Brothers "retired" to operating a few rides in a park. Before long, they had discovered the beauties of Long Beach, California and the desirability of living in that community. They booked their rides on the Nu-Pike Amusement Pier in that city. About the same time, they formed a partnership with the late "Blink" Courtney to build riding devices and carnival equipment. In summer of 1950, they moved their first big Space Wheel out of Long Beach for a circuit of big fairs. This ninety foot high double wheel began the new era on carnival midways. The so-called spectacular ride had now been introduced to a few choice fairs.

The brothers then joined two of the double sky wheels to form the double-double space wheel. Al Kunz bought this wheel and the double sky wheel from them and released the double sky wheel manufacturing rights to Allen Herschell Company. In 1962, they built the huge portable wheel, later known as the Seattle World Fair Wheel. One of them seventy-seven, the other eighty-one, they not only designed and supervised building this towering device, they also carried it to Seattle, supervised setting it up and personally operated it. Eighty-one year old Curtis operated the device many hours at that great exposition. Like George Ferris, they did not get their wheel ready for the opening of the fair. (Al Kunz brought the double-double wheel from Birmingham,

Alabama, to fill their space until they were ready.) Also like Ferris' wheel, the Velare Brothers' Giant Wheel was the hit of the Seattle Fair. Though it didn't get to Seattle until July, the ride carried 662,000 persons before the exposition closed in the fall.

The boys operated this ride in Seattle the following summer, then toured their circuit of choice fairs with it. Then they sold it. "Now, the Velare Brothers will quit the road," everyone thought — except the Velare Brothers themselves. They reworked an imported heavy device, the Rotor, and made it more portable than before. Each summer the Velare Brothers Rotor has been booked on their fair and exhibition route of the choicest "spots" in North America.

"Why do these two brothers with plenty of resources, still travel over a circuit of fairs at their age?", a bewildered "town mark" might ask.

"Because it is their life," the midway trouper would answer with positive assurance. The answer is probably only half right as there is more than the ordinary carnival trouper's love for the life on fairgrounds and midways to motivate these extraordinary individuals, the Velare Brothers. Could it be that these two men without sons, are carrying on themselves the work that might have been passed on? Since the death of Curtis, Elmer is still carrying on their work. Slowed down a little by the death of his beloved wife a few months ago, but still working.

At the Toronto Exhibition, it is a common occurrence to see five men together on that great midway looking admiringly at some new device. Between them, Patty Conklin, Lou Dufour, Neil Webb and the Velares represent several years over three hundred years of midway trouping and experience.

Since this was written in early 1970, two of five have died. Patty Conklin and Curtis Velare have gone on to lay out the lot and scout good "locations" for all their friends.

CLARENCE A. WORTHAM SHOWS WRECK. Courtesy Harry Shell.

(Great Wortham Shows bought the cars of the Mighty Haag Circus at end of 1914 season, which was Haag's last year on rails.)

CLARENCE A. WORTHAM

MARCH 28 1914   **The Billboard**   VOLUME XXVI, NO.13

72 PAGES   10 CENTS

Clarence A. Wortham was born in Paris, Texas, on October 14, 1882. As young boys do everywhere in this country, young Wortham sold newspapers in his home town. He was owner of a cigar stand in his middle teens, and had worked at several things including a short period as a hotel bellhop before he was eighteen. A job he took and stayed with for some time was manager of the baseball team at Danville, Illinois. He liked Danville, made many friends there and always thereafter considered it his home.

While Gaskill, the Feraris, Dan Robinson, Brundage, Bill Rice and the other carnival owners and promoters were rampaging across country with that new collective amusement toy of theirs, young Wortham was managing baseball teams, theatres and amusement parks in or around Danville. He had met a nice young lady, and on June 29, 1904, he married Miss Belle Snapp. Sometime in 1907 or 1908 he met C. W. Parker's son-in-law, Tom W. Allen. After considerable planning they built and opened the Wortham & Allen Shows, a two-car carnival. Literate Barney S. Gerety, a native of Danville, had been a fifth grade drop-out, Wortham's secretary and "man Friday" for some time in Danville. Twenty-two year old Gerety was the new carnival's secretary when it opened in 1910.

The Wortham and Allen Shows was a success and had grown from two to twenty-eight cars when they dissolved partnership in fall of 1913. C. A. went into Danville and built the new C. A. Wortham Shows for the 1914 season. From then on, he never had less than one big railroad show under his personal ownership. One season, as is stated in the narrative, he had five midways of his own on tour. He never had enough midways to play all of the fair and celebration dates that were offered him. Dates that other shows schemed and pled for were his for the asking. Many of those dates were played for years without formal written contracts. A verbal agreement and a hand shake was all that was required from this master carnival showman.

By Labor Day, 1922, he owned outright two huge carnivals and had financial interest in five others. In addition he owned interests in numerous riding devices on fairgrounds and in amusement parks. He owned all the rides at the Dallas Fair Park, and had a ten year exclusive contract for their operation there. J. C. Simpson was in Dallas as manager of this operation. In both 1921 and 1922 his Clarence A. Wortham's World's Greatest Shows was playing the Canadian National Exhibition in Toronto while his Clarence A. Wortham's World's Best Shows under the management of Fred Beckman was playing the high-grossing Minnesota State Fair at St. Paul. The latter show also held the contracts for the Western Canada Class A Circuit of Fairs. Never before, or since, had one man held and controlled as many high-class profitable fair dates as Clarence Wortham did in 1922.

When the number one show pulled into Cincinnati for a date the third week in September, the Little Giant wasn't feeling as well as he should, and he didn't leave the private car. After a few days he entered Deaconess Hospital for a checkup and rest. He got worse, and the show train left for Knoxville without the bossman. Bob Lohmar's telegram reached the train as it went through Lexington, Kentucky. Wortham was dead. His overworked and abused stomach had given out. He died at 11:25 A.M. on September 24th. Lohmar sent telegrams across the nation that the carnival king was dead. He and Mrs. Wortham accompanied the body to Danville for burial.

Wortham was buried in the Springfield Cemetery in Danville with one of the most impressive services ever witnessed there. His twelve and fifteen year old sons were brought from a Chicago military school by a member of Showmen's League. The Showmen's League Chaplain conducted the service assisted by local minister. The eight pallbearers had been friends of C. A. before he entered carnival business. The seventy-two honorary pallbearers were the top men from the outdoor amusement world.

All seven shows that Wortham owned an interest in closed for the afternoon and held memorial services on the grounds. Most all other midways across the country ceased activities for a few moments of silence. Perhaps the most impressive service of all was held on the Abilene, Texas, Fairgrounds where Clarence A's brother's John T. Wortham Shows were playing.

The wooden grandstand of the Taylor County Fair was packed with some five thousand people waiting for the afternoon show to start, when a small man, later identified as a local minister, rose among them and asked that all rise and all heads be bowed for a moment of silence. As they stood in silence the grandstand announcer led them in the Lord's Prayer and then gave a brief eulogy for the departed showman. As he closed, the grandstand band started playing "Nearer My God to Thee." This refrain was echoed from the back end of the long, black crepe-draped midway, as Mr. Johnson picked it up on the water show una—fon. Not a person was visible on this long mourning midway, when the music started down at the water show. As the first strains of the sacred number played on that raucous instrument answered the band at the grandstand, carnival troupers began to appear from their tightly closed tents and gaming joints, from their living wagons and sleeping tents and from back of the cook house. All of them dressed in their Sunday best, they filed slowly down the midway toward the sound of music. The water show arena was quietly filled by mourning carnies who then held a memorial service for the brother of their own boss man.

The "Little Giant" was gone, but he left behind him hundreds of "Wortham-trained" carnival people who would be the mainstays of most midways for over a decade.

More Carnies

KHALIE GEORGE BARKOOT

Khalie George Barkoot was born in Beyrouth, Syria, on March 12, 1878. He came to the United States the first time to work at the Columbian Exposition in 1893, where he operated a concession booth selling oriental goods. He was one of the youngest concessionaires at the fair. He returned to Syria for three years but was back in Chicago operating an importing business for Oriental goods in 1896.

Friends persuaded him to enroll in Dixon College at Dixon, Illinois in 1897. He made Dixon his home for many years after that. Seasons of 1898 to 1900 he sold oriental goods at fairs and expositions. In 1901, he framed an Oriental Show which he booked for four weeks on Frank Gaskill's midway. He then joined the Ferari Brothers until the end of that season. The next season he booked his show with the Morris & Berger Carnival Company until it closed. Then he framed and opened his own little carnival. Business was bad, but the Syrian kept the midway open, and by 1906 he had accumulated a good "bankroll."

He invested everything he had at the Jamestown Exposition of 1907, and was bankrupt at the end of the season. He started another small show and built it up. In 1912, he had a twenty-car railroad show on tour, and owned quite a lot of real estate. He operated the big show for ten or fifteen years, but had to close and reorganize, changing the title from K. G. Barkoot Shows to Barkoot Brothers. He also changed his residence to Toledo, Ohio. He operated the Barkoot Brothers Shows until summer of 1948, when he sold the show after having a stroke. He died in a Toledo, Ohio, hospital December 14, 1948. He was a thirty-second degree Mason.

F. H. Bee, Jr. was born in Liverpool, West Virginia on May 13, 1896. He was educated as a teacher and taught in the public schools for twelve years with time out for two years of army service in 1917 and 1918. He was partially disabled during that war-time service.

He started in carnival business with Dodson's World's Fair Shows in 1923, operating his own 5 cent candy wheel concession. Next three seasons he was secretary for C. D. Scott on one or another of the Scott operations. He also had his candy wheel concessions on the Scott midways. In 1927, Bee framed his first carnival, the Bee Amusement Company, and in 1929, he changed the title of his show to the F. H. Bee Shows. This show, although never a major carnival, was successful in his chosen territory of Kentucky and Tennessee.

He and his wife, Hattie, continued to operate the show until a few weeks before his death when they sold all of the equipment to David J. Huis and Leonard McLemore. At that time, the Bees incorporated the title, Bees Old Reliable Shows, Inc. In the late thirties, Mr. Bee spent most of his time handling his real estate and oil interests.

F. H. Bee, Jr. died in the Good Samaritan Hospital at Lexington, Kentucky, on November 4, 1940 of a blood infection after an eighteen week illness.

FELICE BERNARDI

Felice Bernardi probably would have been nothing more than a concession operator with carnivals if he had not met and married "the Queen of Concessionaires" in 1906. Mrs. Bernardi was born in Liverpool, England, on March 20, 1880 and came to the United States in 1896. In a short time, she was acknowledged to be one of the smartest concession operators in the country. After their marriage, she and Felice continued to operate a string of concessions.

In 1917, they organized their Bernardi Greater Shows and operated it until Honest John Brunen was killed in March, 1922. They bought the remainder of the Doris-Ferari Shows from Brunen's estate, and Felice managed that show while Mrs. Bernardi managed the Bernardi Greater. Mrs. Bernardi died on October 17, 1922, at Richmond, Virginia. She was buried in the Oakwood cemetery in Richmond on October 21st.

Felice sold one show and the Bernardi Greater Title. In 1923 he operated the Bernardi Exposition Shows and continued to operate this show until the end of the 1932 season. He had been in ill health for some time, when he died in a Tampa, Florida hospital on April 9, 1932. His body was buried at the Showmen's League Showmen's Rest at Chicago on April 14, 1934.

JOHN THEODORE BRUNEN

JOHN BRUNEN. Courtesy Billboard Publishing Co.

"Honest John" Brunen as he was known to all of his friends and associates, was born in Dusseldorf, Germany, on May 10, 1874. He came to the United States when he was fourteen and began working at Coney Island, New York. He operated his own concessions at Coney Island until 1898, when be bought the Idle Hour Motion Picture House at Rockaway Beach. in 1899 he built a motion picture theater at Union Street and Fifth Avenue in Brooklyn, which he operated for three years. In 1902, he had charge of concessions at a park in Bridgeport, Connecticut.

In 1903 he bought the opera house in Nyack, New York, and spent thirty thousand dollars, his entire savings, to remodel the building. After operating it just three months, the theater burned, and "Honest John" was broke. He went down into West Tennessee where he had friends. His friends in Paris, Tennessee helped him to open a theater there. He operated this theater for several years, then disposed of it in order to go back into the concession business.

In 1916, Brunen organized and operated the Mighty Doris Shows, but changed the title to the Mighty Doris Exposition Shows which he operated for next four years. In 1921, he combined it with the Ferari Shows for the Doris-Ferari Shows. Plans were already made to use this title in 1922 when "Honest John" Brunen was shot and killed with a shotgun. He was murdered in his home at Riverside, New Jersey on March 10, 1922. His wife had just gone upstairs when she heard a shot. When she hurried back downstairs, she found her husband dead. He was interred on March 14th in Monumental Cemetery at Beverly, New Jersey.

Late in the following year, on evidence supplied by the man who actually pulled the trigger, Mrs. Brunen and her brother were tried on charges of murdering Brunen. Mrs. Brunen was acquitted, but her brother was convicted and received a ninety-nine year sentence for his part in the murder plot.

JOHN R. CASTLE

Johnny Castle, as he was known to thousands of carnival people, was born in Jackson County, Missouri, on May 19, 1879. He claimed downtown Kansas City as his home town, but his home was actually near former President Harry Truman's. They were boyhood friends. John R. Castle started in show business as a "pony punk" (pony boy) with Ben Wallace's Great Wallace Circus. Then he worked as a candy butcher and on the games in the side show tent. His contemporaries on the Great Wallace show were Jerry Mugivan and Bert Bowers, who later owned the American Circus Corporation.

He moved to the carnival industry in the teens with concessions, and in 1916, he and his first wife,

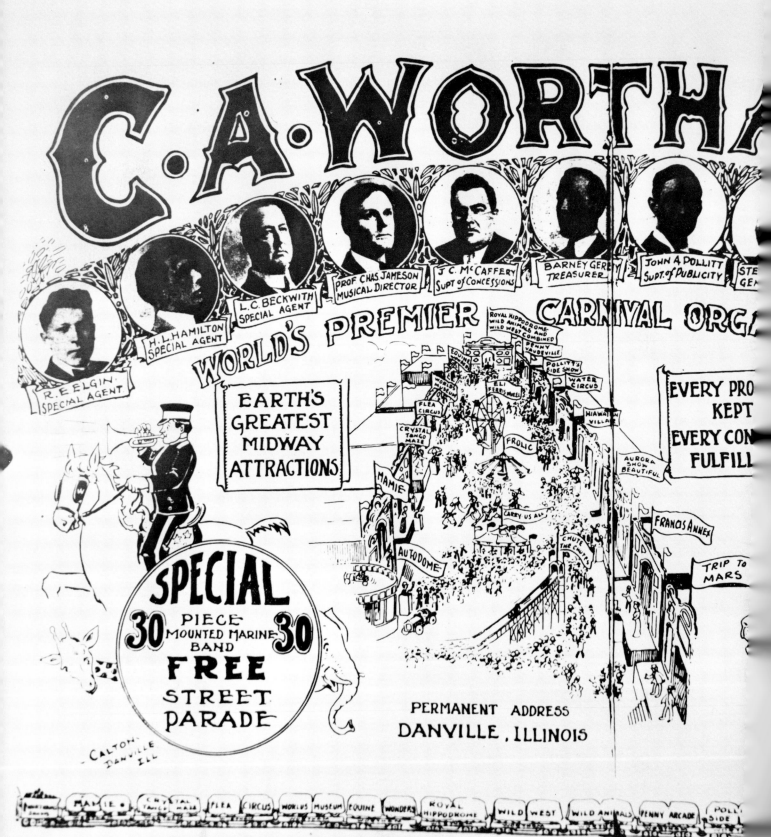

SHOWS

M SHOWS

NED STOUGHTON GENL. MGR

C. A. WORTHAM SOLE OWNER AND GEN'L DIRECTOR

ALL NEW
TTRACTIONS
CARS
SPECIAL TRAIN 35
HANDSOME
EW CARVED
WAGON
FRONTS

"RECKLESS" RUSSELL
ONE-LEGGED
BICYCLE RIDER

HAWAIIAN VILLAGE   AURORA SNOW SENTINA   FRANCIS ANNEX   TRIP TO MARS

Courtesy Billboard Publishing Co.

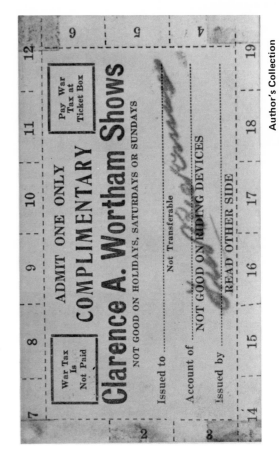

ADMIT ONE ONLY
COMPLIMENTARY
Clarence A. Wortham Shows
NOT GOOD ON HOLIDAYS, SATURDAYS OR SUNDAYS

Pay War Tax at Ticket Box

War Tax Is Not Paid

Issued to

Account of   Not Transferable

Issued by   NOT GOOD ON RIDING DEVICES

READ OTHER SIDE

Iva, were with the Great Wortham Shows which had winter quarters in El Paso. Altogether he was with C. A. Wortham's Shows for five years. In 1919 he was legal adjuster with the Rice & Dorman Shows, with which he also had five concessions and the cafe car. In October, 1920, he and Milton Morris bought the Rice & Dorman Shows at El Reno, Oklahoma, and brought it out in 1921 as the Morris & Castle Shows. In January, 1923 they took over all the equipment and shows from C. A. Wortham's World's Greatest Shows.

The Castle Show, with Bob Lohmar as general agent, traveled on forty railroad cars through most of the twenties. After Morris left the partnership, the show was sold to a Shreveport bank at a forced sale in fall of 1931. After three reorganizations, show finally became the property of Hennies Brothers at end of 1936 season. Castle was connected with several midways after 1936, but none of his latter carnival affiliations lasted long.

John R. Castle was a smart carnival operator, but he could not stay sober in his later years. He was one of the best legal adjusters or show "fixers" in the industry. If Johnny couldn't "patch" a "beef", it couldn't be "fixed." He, a small Irishman, and Lohmar, a hearty German, were a perfect team around a carnival office. One time at the Shreveport Fair, the Whip ride threw one of its tubs ninety feet across the midway into a bally platform. Walter Beckman, the foreman on the Whip, brought the injured occupants of the tub to the office. The two Negro girls were more frightened than injured, but their dresses were badly ripped and torn. The show's doctor, who also managed the "pickled punk" show was sent for. Castle began "sweet talking" the girls while Lohmar found a needle and thread and began to repair the damage to their dresses.

As Bob sewed, always being a ladies' man, he fondly patted the fanny of the recipient of his crude dress repair. The other girl being close, Bob, the gentleman, gave her a pat or two to keep her from thinking he was playing favorites. The girls were nice girls, but they were frightened, and Lohmar's pats and Castle's soft words soothed them. As the sewing was being completed, Castle suggested kindly that three dollars each should get them other dresses. Lohmar put in softly, "Don't be cheap, Johnny. These are nice girls, give them five dollars." The girls giggled, signed the release forms Castle handed them and accepted their five dollar bills. Doc, who had been tied up making a sex book "pitch" in the back of the "pickle punk" show tent, came rushing in as the girls left the office. "Where are they?" he asked. "That's them. They're O.K.", Lohmar replied as he put away the sewing kit.

One "beef" came to the show office that Castle couldn't fix, though.

Show was playing the Muskogee, Oklahoma Free Fair, and one of Mike Rosen's joint men worked a little stronger than he was supposed to. A "fleeced" Oklahoma individual came to the office and demanded his money back. He had one refrain, "I am a Christian man and I don't gamble. I want my eighteen dollars back." Castle vainly tried to reason with him, but this citizen of the Sooner State just repeated his two sentences. Finally, John R. disgustedly gave the man eighteen dollars, and said pleadingly, "Please go home now."

Johnny Castle was ill for several years before his death, but he planned a "come-back" in the outdoor amusement field long after he was bedridden. The last letter this writer received from Johnny described in glowing terms the big promotion he was going to work on as soon as he could get out of that ————— ———— bed. He never got out of that bed again. He died at Pottinger's Sanitarium in Monrovia, California, on February 17, 1948. He was buried in Showman's Rest in the Evergreen Cemetery at Los Angeles on February 21st.

ISADORE CETLIN

Isadore Cetlin came from Russia as an immigrant boy, and almost immediately became involved in carnival concession business. Born in 1896, he was working with East Coast midways by the time he reached his majority. In 1928, he and John Wilson organized and opened their Cetlin & Wilson Shows. This show soon grew into the largest "gilly show" in the United States. They put it on wagons and flatcars and it continued to grow until it shared top rank on the East Coast with the World of Mirth and James E. Strates.

After the World of Mirth broke up, the Cetlin & Wilson Shows was second only to the Strates Shows in this Eastern territory. After John Wilson's retirement and death in 1961, Is Cetlin managed the show single-handed for a couple of years. He turned over management to others in the middle sixties but still traveled with the show. The end of the season of 1967 ended the show's fortieth year on the road, making it one of the oldest carnival titles, active or inactive.

Isadore Cetlin died in his sleep at a Richmond, Virginia hotel on October 31, 1967. He was buried in Philadelphia, Pennsylvania, on November 3rd.

WILBUR SCARBORO CHERRY

WILBUR S. CHERRY. Courtesy Billboard Publishing Co.

Wilbur Scarboro Cherry was born in Macon, Georgia, June 9, 1871. He was educated in Macon and started work with daily newspapers when he finished his schooling. He held jobs such as reporter, printer and editor with newspapers until 1905. In 1896 he married Miss Sara Sanford in Savannah, Georgia. She died in 1909 leaving a son and two daughters.

Wilbur Cherry started in outdoor show business as general agent for the Smith Greater Shows and stayed with this carnival eleven years. In a January 1916 ad, he is listed as general agent of the DeVaux & Cherry Shows, but no more information was released on this proposed midway. Sol & Rubin's United Shows is mentioned in March 1917 as being owned by Rubin Gruberg with W. S. Cherry as general agent. However, that title had been used in 1916 and wasn't used in 1917. Sol's United Shows toured in 1917 as did the Rubin & Cherry Show. Cherry stayed with the latter show until his death every year except 1922.

In 1922, he joined Guy Dodson's World's Fair Shows and they changed the title to Dodson and Cherry Shows. Cherry went back to Rubin in 1923, and this same year made the Sherman Hotel in Chicago his permanent home. It was here, on December 5, 1928 that he had a paralytic stroke while having breakfast with the Grubergs. Rubin rushed him to the American Hospital where he died on December 16th. His funeral was held in the Showmen's League Quarters on December 18th and he was buried in the League's Showmen's Rest.

This man who had started in the business as a general agent, and had done nothing else for twenty-three years was recognized as one of the top agents. Rubin owned the show and there is no record that Cherry ever received remuneration for the use of his name.

COLEMAN BROTHERS

The first Coleman Brothers, men's clothing store [sale]sman Dick, and weaver Tom, opened their little [tw]o-ride show in 1917. They were on the road only [se]ven weeks when they ran out of cash and had to [m]ove back home to Middletown, Connecticut. They [fo]und a vacant lot there, set up again and started [fif]ty-three years of continuous successful carnival [op]erations. Tom has long since retired from the [ca]rnival field, but brother Dick is still with it [rig]htfully using the Coleman Brothers title as his two sons are now active in the management of the show.

Francis (Tody) Coleman was born November 25, 1919 and his brother Bobby was born October 29, 1925. Tody is interested in the mechanical operations, while Bob works with his father, Dick, on the front end handling management and booking duties. The show plays a compact twenty-six week route each season repeating in towns that it has played for many of its fifty-three years on tour. It plays Connecticut and New England territory and

DICK COLEMAN. Courtesy Amusement Business.

has dates on his show route that no one else can get as long as he wants to play them. His two sons have continued this relationship and the Coleman Brothers route should be safe for another generation anyway.

Actually this route will be Coleman Brothers' territory for several generations as there is already another set of Coleman Brothers, some of them grown now, who have learned all details of carnival operations with their fathers and grandfather on the family's midway.

DICK COLEMAN AND GRANDSONS.
Courtesy Amusement Business.

never gets very far away from Middletown. It isn't exactly a "forty-miler" organization, as it does have fairs on its route nearly four hundred miles from winter quarters. Like Floyd Gooding, Dick Coleman

WILLIAM T. COLLINS

William T. Collins was born in Greece on February 24, 1905. Son of a farm family, he immigrated to the United States while still young. With very little formal education but plenty of ambition and determination, Mr. Collins owns one of the largest motorized carnivals in the United States, and has many diverse interests in and around Minneapolis, Minnesota. He is one of the leaders in the collective amusement industry and was the president of the Outdoor Amusement Business Association which he helped to found. Presently, in 1970, he is the president of Showmen's League of America.

He started in carnival business as a ride hand on the Ferris wheel with the Blue Ribbon Shows in 1926. In 1928, he was on the Tilt-a-Whirl ride with the Macey Barnhart Show, and the following two seasons was manager of Claude Bremer's concessions on the Frank Lang Shows. Next twelve years, he owned and operated concessions on independent midways. He started his own carnival in 1943, with a Ferris wheel, a chairplane and one kiddie ride. His wife, Mildred, helped him in the office that first year, a position she still fills with their great show.

During that first tour of the William T. Collins Shows, a tornado demolished all of the show's equipment, none of which was covered by insurance. It was a discouraging time for Mr. Collins, but adversity was only a goad for him to work even harder. He replaced the wrecked equipment and played out his route. Show grew and grew fast, as this man gave his patrons and committees exactly what he

WILLIAM T. COLLINS. Courtesy Amusement Business.

county and state fairs extending from North Dakota and Minnesota to Oklahoma and Arkansas. It was the first show to install eight foot long fluorescent lighting tubes on its riding devices.

Success in the carnival field has been a stepping stone for Mr. Collins in other lines of endeavor. He is president of Arcadia Development Co., and privately owns several large industrial buildings in the Minneapolis area. He has substantial interest in a bank and owns a large mobile home park. He has served on committees both to and from Washington, D.C.; and is the first carnival owner to respond when help is needed to enlighten a legislative body in regards to proposed legislation that could be harmful to the collective amusement industry. His speeches, sometimes interspersed with salty rhetoric, are inspired by his own sincerity and belief in fair treatment for everyone.

William T. Collins went into carnival business because he liked the outdoor freedom it afforded him. He grew to love the business, and has no thought of retiring from it even though he is successful in other fields. He is not quite satisfied with many practices commonly used by the carnivals and fairs in regards to percentages paid for the privilege of playing such fair, a practice that is of growing concern to most reputable carnival owners; and he is trying to find a solution to it. If anyone can solve this problem, the solution of which may determine the survival of both carnivals and fairs, Bill Collins will. He is that kind of man. In 1971, he combined his equipment with that of the Murphy Family. The Murphys now manage the Murphy-Collins Shows.

promised them; so many units of clean entertainment operated on a high plane of honest and fair dealings. The shows now consist of twenty-five rides with at least ten booked independent midway shows and sixty-five concessions. It has an established route of

ANDRE K. DEKREKO

Andre K. DeKreko, one of carnivaldom's pioneers, was born in Karpoot, Armenia, on September 26, 1861. He came to America in 1880 and was soon engaged in importing foreign novelties. In 1883, he imported the first Oriental rugs sold in the United States and continued in this business for five years. He became interested in Armenian relief work and politics. He and his four brothers, Charles, Jean, George and Gabriel built a big "Streets of Cairo" Oriental Show in Chicago in 1894 and took it on tour. Andre managed this first touring Oriental Village until it burned in the old Chicago Colliseum fire of Christmas Eve, 1897.

The brothers rebuilt their "Streets of Cairo" and carried it to the Omaha Exposition in 1898. There they met Baba Delgarian, who had another Oriental Village. They combined with him and later took P. J. Munday with his animal show as partners. They toured their DeKreko and Munday Oriental American

Midway Company in 1899, but Munday left them when they started a Mexican tour. After the Mexican tour, they routed back to St. Louis where they set up on a semi-permanent location.

In the winter of 1902, Andre built his "Roman Carnival" which carried several American and Oriental acts performing in a Roman arena featuring chariots pulled by lions. The big feature was the "Burning of Rome." Andre and Charles took the Roman Carnival on tour while Jean, George and Gabriel toured with the "Streets of Cairo." Baba Delgarian remained in St. Louis as manager of their third show. Andre traveled with the show for five years. After a second tour of Cuba, he returned to St. Louis and went into commercial business.

Andre died of a paralytic stroke in St. Louis on January 12, 1931. Brothers Jean, Charles and Gabriel survived him.

C. Guy Dodson was born in Ohio, October 7, 1884. (Some accounts show him born in Defiance, others in Delphos. Unable to verify which town before deadline.) Young Dodson started in show business with his father's dog and pony show in 1899. His father, S. R. Dodson was active in the outdoor field until his death, but Guy didn't continue with him. In 1907, C. G. Dodson was secretary of C. Coley's Wonderland Shows and then trouped with medicine shows, dramatic shows and his own concessions before he finally entered he carnival business to stay.

In 1911, he started his own carnival, and the show grew rapidly until it was one of the major shows of the twenties and thirties. It travelled on forty railroad cars during the several years of its existence. Although Guy's brother Mel was long-time general agent of the show, he did not become a full partner in the Dodson's World's Fair Shows until 1929. Guy retired from active management in 1939, and Mel sold the show in 1946. The brothers built and operated a tourist court in Savannah, Georgia, after quitting show business.

This show had some of the best midway shows, and some of the most "haywire" equipment of any of the major carnivals. It was a "permissive midway," as the owners never believed in being too strict regarding living and moral patterns followed by their employees and co-workers. It is said that Doc Waddell had a fertile field to work, when he joined the Dodsons as mail man and show chaplain. Some say that as Doc preached his daily noon-time sermon from the Jig-Show stage to a congregation of regular attending converts, other denizens of the midway were engaging in illicit and immoral practices under that stage. (This I cannot verify.)

C. Guy Dodson died at his home in Savannah, Georgia, on September 22, 1956, after an illness of several weeks.

GEORGE FRANCIS DORMAN

A new carnival aggregation in the field this season, and one that promises to be first-class in every respect, is Solomon and Dorman's Liberty Shows, of which Mr. Dorman is part owner and manager. Mr. Dorman was formerly secretary and treasurer of the Krause Greater Shows, and is a thoro showman and an indefatigable worker.

GEORGE F. DORMAN, 1915. Courtesy Billboard Publishing Co.

George F. Dorman was born at Alliance, Ohio, on August 5, 1879. He became a circus performer as a young boy and had trouped for several seasons when Frank Gaskill asked him to help on the 1898 street fair in Alliance. After the street fair, Gaskill engaged him to come to Canton and assist Joe Conley in building the Canton Carnival Companies properties for that first 1899 season. When the show began its tour, Dorman was given the front gate ticket box and sold the first ticket ever sold for a successful organized collective amusement company. In 1900, George was one of Bill Rice's partners in that short season "mail order" street fair company.

His last partnership with Rice was in the Rice & Dorman Shows of the late teens. This was the show Morris & Castle bought for the nucleus of their Morris & Castle Shows. At one time Dorman was partners with Sam Soloman in the Soloman & Dorman Shows. Later, he was secretary-treasurer of the Krause Greater Shows, and in 1939 he was with the Wolfe Amusement Company.

In March, 1940, George F. Dorman was enroute from his home in Taft, Texas, to Royston, Georgia to pick up his riding devices, and take them to the Down East Attractions in South Carolina. He had to enter a hospital in Mobile, Alabama, with an attack of cardiac asthma with which he had suffered for years. He died there on March 21, 1940.

JAMES H. DREW

JAMES H. DREW. Courtesy James H. Drew Shows.

James H. Drew, known as "Georgia Boy" to thousands of carnival troupers, is one of the most successful of the younger carnival operators. Ably assisted by his wife, Eula, he has built his show into one of the foremost motorized carnivals in the United States. His reputation for providing clean entertainment and dealing honestly with all persons gained him more contracts than he could play with one carnival, so he put out a second unit for several seasons. This reputation was built in less than ten years as the first James H. Drew Shows was launched on March 27, 1949, in North Georgia.

This little show was successful as it played its way into Ohio, Indiana and Illinois and back to South Georgia and Florida. Still playing the same territory with thirty-one riding devices and six shows, it now has the choice fairs and celebrations in those states. In its big, modern winter quarters eight miles south of Augusta, Georgia, the James H. Drew Shows is completely renewed each winter. All riding devices are put into "direct from the factory condition," as the Drews have found this pays good dividends in safe, trouble-free operation during the summer season.

James H. Drew was born in Alston, Georgia, on October 1, 1913. He joined the Rubin & Cherry Shows in April, 1933 as a concessionaire. He later worked with concessions on the Johnny J. Jones, Dodson, Barkoot Brothers, Frank West and Floyd E. Gooding shows. From the latter, the Drews have adopted the system of having nothing on the midway that can possibly offend or harm anyone. The Drews are referred to in plural for the midway is a family operation. Ever since they started, Eula has been at "Georgia Boy's" side on booking trips and in the show office. Now, James H. Drew III, better known as Jimmy, and his sister Malinda, have assumed duties with the show. Jimmy is manager and Malinda has learned all the office details from her mother. Mother and Dad can now take off for a mid-season vacation and the show moves along efficiently. While in his middle teens, Jimmy was given a second unit to manage; and when his father was ill in 1969, the big consolidated show moved along guided by the hands of a young but veteran carnival manager.

The James H. Drew Shows is a friendly show operated by friendly people. A visitor is made to feel that he or she is welcome, and the big midway is shown with well-deserved pride. The big German-made band organ is shown to all visitors as such instruments are a hobby of the Drews. In their Augusta winter quarters, they have one large building devoted to these melodious music machines. If you should be fortunate enough to be given a tour by one of the family, each machine will be turned on to play its own particular type of tune. Had "Georgia Boy" been born twenty years earlier, there is no doubt that he would have followed the first steam caliope he heard into a circus career. It is well that he didn't as the carnival industry has profited from having the Drews as its devotees.

CODY T. FLEMING

One of the most picturesque of all carnival owners was born in Aid, Ohio, on August 6, 1884. Cody T. Fleming owned his own carnival longer than any other person, prior to his death. He was wrestling in Fostoria, Ohio, when the broken-down Maxwell-Jessup Shows played there in 1906. He liked the show, bought it, changed its name to the Big Four Shows and began his forty-seven years of carnival ownership.

Mad Cody Fleming, as he was known to three generations of midway pleasure-seekers, was a son of poor farm workers near Toledo, Ohio. He quit school and ran away from home to be a boxer. He didn't like boxing and changed to marathon running. The ten-mile races, popular at that time, were easy to win by the big country boy from Aid. In three years he returned home with enough money to buy his father the best farm in the county. He then became a wrestler. It was as a wrestler that he gained the cognomen, "Mad." It was said that Fleming could not be beaten in a match, if he got mad; and he was mad in most of his matches.

His ownership of a carnival did not stop his wrestling. Indeed, he had to wrestle more often than before for without his "At Show" on the back end of his midway, the little show would have closed many times. When the carnival office was completely broke, Fleming would line up some local champion to wrestle on the show grounds. The town sports would all come out and pay to see their man wrestle the carnival men. Many of them would spend more money at the other carnival shows, and at the games. Enough would be made by the carnival to move to its next town.

Even after Fleming's midway became a medium-sized show, he still booked his "At Show"

MAD CODY FLEMING, 1929.

Spring of 1931, he took his three rides and new wife and headed South and never went back North again. In 1932 he played his first date in Georgia and never carried his show outside that state again. He liked Georgia and the "Crackers" liked him. He became so firmly entrenched in Georgia and its politics that he was a confidant of both of the Talmadges, father and son, when they were governor. As his show crossed the big state from side to side, corner to corner, his "neighbors" came to visit him at his office trailer. Sometimes they just came to "Howdy with Cody," but often they needed advice on business matters or politics. Cody Fleming obliged all of them and often threw in a few anecdotes for free.

His wife Grace helped him with the operation of his show, which was and had always been one hundred percent "Sunday School." Cody said that he had nothing against "Joints and Strong Gal Shows" just so they stayed off his own midway. He had used a few of them himself back prior to the 1930 breakup. He decided to operate a clean show, when he brought the remnants of his once-big carnival down south in 1931. This clean operation had paid off in friendship and respect of the people of Georgia, and in a few years Cody Fleming again had a big show, big enough to please everyone in his adopted state. He decided to retire in 1950, but he hadn't announced his decision when another Georgia carnival operation, a newcomer of six years standing publicly boasted that he was going to run that Fleming out of the state of Georgia. Mad Cody got mad again, booked his old route, and stayed in the business until his death.

He died of a heart attack on November 18, 1953. Funeral services were held in Jesup, Georgia on November 22nd. This showman, Mason, politician and friend of Georgia's people was gone. The Atlanta Constitution in its eulogy to him, concluded with the statement, "....Cody Fleming will be missed by the people of Georgia."

with other carnivals for their winter tours. For instance, in March of 1919, he had completed three winter tours with the Northwestern Shows, and in October of the same year his Congress of Athletes was a recent arrival on the Ed A. Evans Shows. This show, which featured two lady wrestlers and boxers, as well as three male athletes, had moved to the Peace Exposition Shows in November.

His own midway never played farther south than Kentucky prior to 1931. His territory consisted of Ohio, Michigan, Indiana, Illinois and Missouri from 1906 to 1930. He had built his midway up to ten railroad cars and a fleet of Model T Ford trucks, when the Great Depression started in fall of 1929; Mad Cody was one of early casualties. In 1930 his whole world crashed. Not only was his show broke, but his marriage of seventeen years ended in a divorce. He sold all equipment except a merry-go-round, a chairplane and a kiddie ride and paid all of his debts. That winter he met and married Grace Mack, a musical comedy performer.

49

Edward M. Foley was native son of California, as he was born there in 1870. He started in outdoor show business at the California Midwinter Fair of 1894, and was active in the outdoor field until his death over forty-nine years later. He was with several little overland "Mud Shows" before 1900, working at various odd jobs. When Nat Reiss brought the Dixie Carnival Company to the West Coast about 1903, Ed Foley joined the show. He worked as an executive with Reiss for several years and had his Crystal Palace, glass house on the midway. He was agent for the Hall Shows for a short time and then became an independent promoter.

In 1912, in partnership with a great promoter, E. M. Burk, he started the Foley & Burk Shows. He remained active with this big railroad show which never left the West Coast, as long as his health would permit. His wife Catherine, who was not active with the show, died in January, 1943.

Edward M. Foley died in San Francisco on June 5, 1943, and was buried in that city on June 8th. The show that he founded is still active on the West Coast; this 1970 season will be its fifty-ninth year of operation. Since the Johnny J. Jones show left the road in the fifties, the Foley & Burk Shows has been the oldest railroad transported carnival in the world.

JOHN T. FRANCIS

John T. Francis was born in 1877, and as his trader father acquired a horse-drawn merry-go-round, young John was soon getting midway training. Later, his father, A. B. Francis, operated a dog & pony circus, but the older Francis was always a trader first and showman last. At one time, A. B. had twenty horse and wagon rigs carring sewing machine salesmen around the countryside.

In 1899, John was married and he booked a tin type camera with the Bostock-Ferari Carnival Company. He figured a process for speeding the drying of the tin type photos and bought a Cadillac Automobile for the customers to pose beside. From 1901 to 1908 he and his wife played fairs with their photo machine and platform shows. In 1908 they joined the Nat Reiss Shows for two seasons. After that they were with Cosmopolitan, C. A. Wortham,

Heinz & Beckman, L. J. Heth and Tom W. Allen. With the latter as partner, they framed the John T. Francis Shows on twenty railroad cars for the 1920 season.

In 1921 Francis became sole owner of the show. Depression caused him to cut the show to fifteen cars in 1930. He put the midway on trucks in 1933, and two years later moved his winter quarters from Houston, Texas to St. Louis, Missouri. He did most of his general agent work himself, and kept the show out under his own name until 1953, when his son Crawford's name was substituted for the John T.

Eighty-three year old John T. Francis died the last week in September, 1960, on the Bob Hammond Show's grounds at Houston, Texas. He was buried in Dallas, Texas, on September 26th.

Joe Scholibo, long-time carnival worker and press agent, recently wrote the following: "B. S. Gerety, a scholar of Wortham's, the Little Giant, will always remain the 'gentleman' of the carnival world." That sentence sums up Barney Gerety's midway behavior through all the years in which he was active in the collective amusement field. Retired for many years with, "I have owned the biggest of them all. Why should I break my neck with no-count or none-at-all labor trying to move this thing around the country when I have all I will ever need to live on?" Bernard S. Gerety lived at his home in San Antonio, Texas. Still the gentleman and a perfect host to any outdoor show friend of former years who came to visit with him.

Bernard S. Gerety was born in Danville, Illinois on Christmas Day 1887. He attended school in Danville and acquired a good education. He met the Little Giant, Wortham, right after the latter came to

BERNARD S. GERETY. From Beckman & Gerety 1937 yearbook. Courtesy Fred D. Pfening Collection.

Danville as manager of the baseball club. They liked each other, and Wortham, who had little formal education, persuaded the younger man to start working for him. Soon Gerety was handling all of the young promoter's bookkeeping. When Wortham and Tom W. Allen put the little two-car gilly show on the road, Barney, as he was known to all his friends, started trouping. He was show treasurer as well as being Wortham's own secretary. As the Wortham enterprises expanded, Barney Gerety's duties increased.

A fateful decision was made by the Little Giant in the late teens when he decided to send Barney out to San Bernardino, California, to assist Fred Beckman of the Wortham's World's Best Shows. Four-time loser Beckman; he had failed with his own circus, carnival, wild West show, and Days of Forty-Nine Shows, was having a difficult job keeping the huge midway moving and operating. The equipment was badly run down and shop crews were not doing too much to improve the appearance of the midway. Barney went out there to represent Mr. Wortham (he still referred to him as Mr. Wortham forty-eight years after the little showman's death), and he did just that. In order to properly represent his boss man, he had to assume some of the duties of management. In a few weeks he had the show back in good mechanical condition and moving on time. He and Beckman were to be co-managers of big midways for twenty-five years.

After Wortham's death in 1922, Beckman and Gerety took over the World's Best Shows and finally in 1930 they put their own names on the equipment. Barney remained very much in the background managing the little details that kept the show open and operating, while his colorful partner got all the publicity for himself. This situation prevailed until Beckman's death in the early forties. Barney managed the big midway for one season after his widely heralded partner's death, and put the huge midway "in the barn for good" at the end of that season.

He stayed in Shreveport for several years until all equipment was disposed of. He operated a small amusement ride unit on the Shreveport Fairgrounds for a few years, then retired to his home in San Antonio. Beckman & Gerety equipment was sold to various individuals, with James E. Strates getting most of the wagons after his winter quarters burned and all his wagons were destroyed.

Barney Gerety was a quiet man and slow to become involved with anything or anyone not connected with his own interests, but he was never a cold man. To the men who worked for and with Barney, he was the perfect "Boss Man." He died in San Antonio on July 3, 1971.

RUBIN GRUBERG

Rubin Gruberg was born in Austria on July 17, 1885. He came to America an illiterate immigrant boy, and worked his way to the top in the collective amusement industry. For several years he owned and operated two of the largest carnival midways in the United States. He and his wife, "Miss Annie," had a staff of loyal employees, all of them top men in their profession, who stayed with the Grubergs as long as there was a "Rubin Show."

Rubin started in show business with Bostock in 1898. This thirteen year old boy liked carnivals and midway life, and he moved up rapidly. He was with Gaskill, Jin Sturgis, Danny Robinson, Nat Reiss and several other shows with concessions. His first venture as a midway owner was in 1916, when he and Sam Soloman operated their Sol & Rubin Shows. The following year Rubin engaged W. S. Cherry as general agent and organized the Rubin & Cherry Shows which continued to tour until after both of their deaths. Cherry never owned any part of the show.

As Rubin could not read or write, "Miss Annie" was always the office manager of their enterprises.

The vain little man would mutter imprecations as he opened and pretended to read telegrams handed to him on the showgrounds or in hotel lobbies. Then he would hand the wire to the person to whom he had been talking. "Read it," he would invite. If this person was a stranger, he would glance at the message and say nothing. The impatient Rubin would then command, "Read it, read it aloud!" It has been said that he had his own picture put on his advertising paper after he had bragged to a visiting fairman about how well he advertised, pointing to a stand of Ringling Brothers and Barnum & Bailey paper as an example.

Rubin was vain, both in his personal appearance and in his appreciation of his material holdings. Unlike most midway owners of his period, he loved to have his photograph taken, usually with some strange or important person. Of course Rubin's midway operations were such that he didn't worry about having such photographs available to possible hostile law enforcement officers. For a few years in the late twenties, he allowed no gaming concession of any kind to operate on his two midways. This propensity of his for being photographed resulted in some unusual pictures, several of which are reproduced in this volume.

Rubin Gruberg died unexpectedly in his room at the Mayflower Hotel in Jacksonville, Florida, on April 16, 1942. He was in the midst of friends when he died, but he would have been much happier if he could have died on his beloved midway with "Miss Annie" at his side. Both were in Arizona and the show was being managed by others. His body was escorted to Chicago by Mrs. Gruberg, C. J. Sedlmayr, Sr., and J. C. McCaffery and he was interred in Showmen's Rest there. Like most other show owners, Rubin was a joiner. He was a Mason, a Shriner and a life member of the Showmen's League of America.

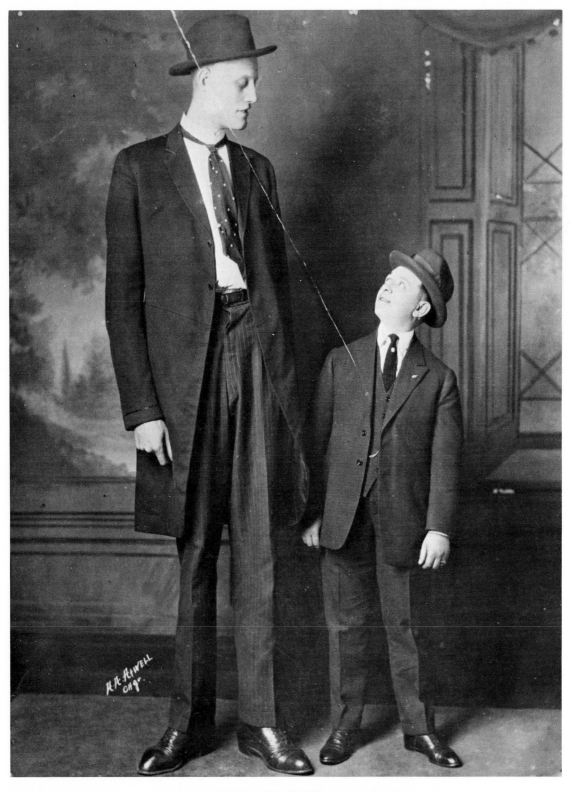

RUBIN GRUBERG AND FRIEND. Courtesy Joe Pearl.

L. J. Heth was born in Wisconsin in 1876. His parents were German-Americans. In 1893, he visited the Columbian Exposition in Chicago and got the idea of starting a cigar factory. He was successful with the cigar-making, but the shop was too confining for young Heth. He framed a ball game concession, loaded it in a one-horse wagon and booked it at fairs. In 1902, he joined the Gaskill-Munday Shows for a season. Then he added more concessions and trouped with other midways.

In 1909 he quit show business and started another cigar factory in Clinton, Iowa. He owned a retail cigar store in conjunction with this factory and planned to expand this into a chain of retail cigar stores, but again the lure of the carnival midways was stronger than that of commercial business endeavors. In 1912 L. J. carried a string of concessions to the Mark Wescott Shows. Show was doing bad business, and Westcott put Heth in charge as manager and went ahead to book towns. As there was no cash in the office for expenses of a booking agent, Westcott rode freight trains on his booking trips.

Heth got the carnival back into winter quarters in East St. Louis. In 1914, he had acquired the equipment and the twenty-car show left quarters as the L. J. Heth's United Shows. He had incorporated his holdings in the twenties, but business was down so much in 1929 the corporation's credit rating was zero. To keep the twenty-five car show he now had on the road, L. J. was forced to borrow money on his own signature. In the resultant crash, the big show was forced to close. He framed a ten-car show for 1930 and was hounded by his creditors all season. He was forced to file personal bankruptcy before the year ended.

L. J. HETH TRAIN WRECK. Chippewa Falls, Wisconsin, 1917. Courtesy Earl Purtle.

L. J. acquired a set of "diggers," loaded them in a 1926 truck, and booked with other shows and at fairs. He made enough in 1931 and 1932 to start another carnival. A man named Cecil Rice had a broken-down little show. Heth bought it for two thousand dollars and spent two thousand more for a Ferris wheel, acquired some trucks and started another L. J. Heth Shows. This show was successful as a truck operation and grew back into a big show. With the aid of carnival troupers such as Joe Fontano, Kelly, and other old-timers, he kept the show out through the 1955 season.

On February 1, 1956, J. Heth worked in the Birmingham, Alabama winter quarters preparing for the spring opening of his show. The following morning he dropped dead from a coronary thrombosis. He was buried in Elmwood Cemetery at Birmingham on February 5th. One of his nephews, Floyd, continued to operate the Heth Shows until the carnival was sold to Al Kunz. Kunz operated it as his number two show in 1969. L. J. Heth had been married three times, but none of the marriages was successful.

LLOYD J. HILLIGOSS

LLOYD HILLIGOSS (white shirt). On the Foley & Burk "wrong way" Merry-Go-Round. This machine was brought around the Horn from England almost one hundred years ago. <u>It was built for the horses to go in opposite direction from those on American-built machines.</u> The machines in this country that travel in the wrong direction were not factory built for that direction of travel. Courtesy Amusement Business Photograph.

Lloyd J. Hilligoss is one of the youngest major midway owners in the business. His enthusiasm for his chosen profession, his spectacular accomplishments in that profession and his helpful family make it imperative that this man be included when any mention is made about the builders of the collective amusement industry. Lloyd J. Hilligoss's parents were game concessionaires so it was natural that he became interested in that field. He was born in Eldorado, Kansas, October 12, 1927, but it was nearly twenty years before he operated games of his own.

He first ran games on the Nu Pike, the Long Beach, California amusement area. He then booked X-Ray Poker machines at the Pomona Fair with the Crafts Shows midway. In 1961 he purchased a small show from William H. Mayer and added his own rides and concessions to it. This new show, the Fun Fair Shows was successful and in 1964 Hilligoss purchased the Foley & Burk Shows from the estate of L. G.

Chapman, second owner of that great old railroad carnival. This purchase gave Hilligoss possession of the oldest continual carnival title in America.

He also acquired in this sale the famous Foley and Burk Carousel brought from England by ship around the Horn to California. The horses on this almost one hundred year old machine travel clockwise, not counter-clockwise as all American-built merry-go-rounds do. The wagons from the Foley & Burk Shows have all been rebuilt and repainted by the new owner. He has moved the show by rail past few seasons, but now the rides have all been loaded onto semi-trailers and the wagons may become museum items. The title is still very much alive though with an energetic owner and his family all working to keep it active. After purchasing the show, Hilligoss bought nine more flatcars and added twenty-five rides. The forty riding devices can now be transported by highway or by train.

The 1961 Fun Fair Shows played three fairs and

CHRISTMAS, 1916. Courtesy Albert Conover.

STEAM TRACTORS. Con T. Kennedy Shows in Mid-teens. Courtesy Albert Conover.

RUBIN & CHERRY SHOWS, 1907. Gilly cars. Courtesy Albert Conover.

many shopping centers with only ten rides and two shows. Now they operate three twelve-ride units each spring playing shopping centers, celebrations and small fairs in Northern California. For the regular season, all equipment from both shows can be used if need be; and a midway of forty-six riding devices, one thousand kilowatts of electrical lighting plants, and innumerable concessions can be furnished from the one ownership. This equipment will all be in factory condition as their winter quarters in Redwood City is the best and most modern in the country.

This operation is a family endeavor. Mrs. Mary Lou Hilligoss works in the private office, entertains fair officials and visitors, handles the office-owned concessions and the show's publicity. Sixteen year old Robert and fourteen year old Tom work on the family concessions; twenty year old, recently married, Stephanie has worked on all money-handling midway jobs, and twenty three year old Gregory now owns his own concessions. Lloyd Hilligoss has much to be thankful for and the industry needs to thank him for revitalizing the collective amusement business on the West Coast. He has his problems and his worries — labor shortages, spectacular rides, high operating costs and inequitable fair contracts — but if these problems can be solved, Lloyd Hilligoss and his family can solve them.

PHIL ISSER

Phil Isser started in show business at Revere Beach, Massachusetts, in 1909 as a partner of Eddie Bremer. The following year he promoted fifteen hundred dollars and opened a knife rack concession in Wonderland Park with his brother as a partner. After two years in New York, he and Max Linderman formed a partnership in a string of gaming concessions at Eastern Fairs. After Linderman went into the management end of midway operations, Isser took on still another partner in the Isser-Karres Shows. This midway played fairs with rides and concessions.

In 1927 Isser started a midway company for the purpose of playing lots and on the streets in New York City and nearby towns. This show, known as the I.T. Shows, probably became the largest "40-miler" outfit in the country. Two units of the I.T. Shows operated. One played the New York City streets, while the other showed on lots in far-away Long Island. This operation continued successfully until Isser's death.

Phil Isser died June 7, 1958, in Maimonedes Hospital of Brooklyn, N.Y. He was buried in Acacia Cemetery in Queens on June 9th, with a couple of hundred of his friends standing in a heavy rain for the graveside ceremony. Phil had spent over forty-nine years in outdoor amusement business, most of it within forty miles of downtown New York.

CON T. KENNEDY

Con T. Kennedy was born in Union City, Ohio, on May 5, 1870. In 1899 he started in show business with C. W. Parker. That year he married Miss Christina Westrupp, sister of Mrs. Parker. The Westrupps were natives of Dickinson County, Kansas. Kennedy worked at various jobs for Parker until the winter of 1903-04, when he took over as active manager, or "Lessee" of the number one Parker midway. He continued as manager and lessee of this unit until 1912. As early as December 1904, the lessees of the Parker Shows were listed as owners.

In January 1913, Con T. announced that he wasn't leasing the Parker Number One Show again. For 1913, he would have his own show under his own name. No doubt, he used Parker equipment for this new show which did tour under the Con T. Kennedy title in 1913 and 1914. His wife died in Leavenworth, Kansas, on March 8, 1914, and Kennedy never again enjoyed the family relationship that had existed in Kansas. On August 2, 1916, he married

SEPTEMBER 4, 1915

The Billboard

PRICE 10 CENTS
80 PAGES

CON. T. KENNEDY
GENERAL MANAGER
CON. T. KENNEDY SHOWS

CON T. KENNEDY, 1915. Courtesy Billboard Publishing Co.

again. His second wife was Miss Mary Snyder of Massillon, Ohio. They were married in Cleveland, and the new Mrs. Kennedy immediately began helping her new husband anywhere she was needed on the carnival grounds.

On November 22, 1915, the Con T. Kennedy Shows train was met head-on by a Central of Georgia Railroad passenger train near Columbus, Georgia. The show train enroute from Atlanta to Columbus was a total loss. All shows and rides were destroyed. All cars and equipment was jammed into an area not over two hundred feet across. Nine flatcars were thrust on top of one another, and all burned. Only eight were killed, but many were badly injured. More would have died had it not been for the heroic example set by Con T. Kennedy that night in Georgia. Half dressed, his nightshirt tucked in his trousers and shoeless, he rushed to the burning wreckage and began to pull broken equipment away from injured men who were pinned under it. He rallied uninjured working men, talkers and attraction owners and they literally lifted wagons off of and away from badly injured men.

These injured men themselves demonstrated the close comradeship that exists among outdoor showmen. That night as men with crushed and broken limbs were carried out to places of safety, their plea was not for themselves but for the boys still in the burning wreckage. "Don't worry about me," was heard many times that night. "Get Slim, he's under nineteen wagon," or "Jim and Blacky are under the 'hot wagon,' I'm alright now, get them before the fire gets to them."

The show owner (he now had his shoes brought to him by Mrs. Kennedy), was everywhere, pulling, pushing, directing, until the flames got so hot that it was impossible to approach the wreckage of a great show.

The force of the impact may be judged by the fact that the Ferris Wheel, which was loaded on the fourth flatcar from the engine was literally twisted around the wreckage of that engine. No other show train wreck, other than the Hagenbeck Wallace Circus wreck of 1918 near Hammond, Indiana, ever approached the force of impact of the Kennedy wreck of 1915. The greater loss of life in the circus train was caused by the empty troop train crashing through the circus sleeping cars in which hundreds of men, women and children were sleeping. There probably would have been as many dead in the carnival wreck, if the speeding passenger train had hit the sleeping cars on the rear end of that show train, instead of head on.

The Kennedy Shows lost one week after the wreck. Con T. and his men had pushed several cars away from the burning wreckage in their rescue efforts. C. W. Parker rushed surplus equipment from Leavenworth and Irving J. Polack sent over five shows from his Rutherford Greater Shows. The carnival played out its route of booked dates before closing to rebuild.

Season of 1924 was disastrous for the Kennedy Shows. Federal men seized it in Detroit for unpaid taxes. It was allowed to move only on promises to make payments on the arrears each week. A wreck in the Frisco yards in Ft. Worth destroyed some equipment and caused the show to lose the opening day at the Abilene, Texas, Fair. Business wasn't good in the fall, but Con T. booked a route of winter dates hoping that by some miracle some of them would help pay off. Regular season had closed several weeks before in Waco, Texas, when Kennedy became ill in Greenville, Mississippi, and he had to go to the hospital with pneumonia. He and Mrs. Kennedy had planned to go to Chicago for the Outdoor Meetings the next week.

The next week, on December 2, 1924, Con T. Kennedy died. Body was carried to Miami, Florida, by Mrs. Kennedy where it was met by Miami Shriner and Elks bodies. He lay in state at Villa Macon, the Kennedy's home, under a miniature big top, and on December 5th was entombed with Masonic and Elks' honors at Woodlawn Cemetery. The carnival was sold at auction to Lackman & Carson.

ALFRED H. KUNZ

There has been much written about the young boys who dreamed of traveling with circuses, and of the young fellows who realized their ambitions of owning a "one-nighter"; but no one has ever seriously suggested that any boy not already connected with a carnival midway could have dreams of someday owning one. Young farmer boys historically ran away with circuses, not carnival midways. Undoubtedly the number of "carnival struck" youngsters will equal that of the "circus worshipping" boys. There has been no literature whereby the young "run-away" with a carnival could be glorified as has been done for his circus counterpart. The largest motorized midway in America is owned by a man who "day dreamed" of having his own carnival as he did the chores around his father's farm in Wisconsin.

ALFRED KUNZ. Showmen's League of America president with Miss America, Chicago, December 1967. Courtesy Al Kunz.

Al Kunz never actually ran away with a traveling show, but he did plan to own one, after his first visit to a carnival at the age of twelve. Below is Al's own anecdote regarding this ambition:

"When I was 19 and my wife-to-be was 17, we were courting and I carried her to the Northern Wisconsin State Fair at Eau Claire. I was going around drawing sketches of the various attractions; I told my girl friend, who is my wife now, that some day I was going to own a carnival like this. At that time, the Beckman & Gerety Shows was playing the fair. Of course, my girl friend thought I had lost my marbles and told me so. That day has come to pass, and every season I make her eat her words because now we not only have one of the largest shows in the nation, we also play the Northern Wisconsin State Fair."

Alfred H. Kunz was born March 17, 1916, in Eau Claire, Wisconsin. As a young farm boy in Northern Wisconsin, Al had to do his share of the chores before and after school. He worked many cold mornings before daylight and many evenings after dark "forking down" hay to hungry farm animals or doing other necessary tasks. He didn't need an elaborate gymnasium at his school as he exercised enough on his three-mile walk each morning to reach that school. The walk back to the farm each afternoon conditioned him for the arduous chores yet to be done. As there was no "idiot box" or "boob tube" in those unenlightened days, young Kunz had nothing to do except prepare his school homework

under kerosene oil lamps. He did quite well in school and graduated from Eau Claire Senior High School in 1935.

Al got a part-time job working in a clothing store, but he wanted to be a carnival showman. He knew nothing about the business and didn't know where to find a show to join. Accidentally he saw a copy of the Billboard that belonged to a neighborhood popcorn vendor. From the routes listed in Billboard, he found the show nearest to Eau Claire was at the fair over in Jamestown, Minnesota. He joined that show, the Harry Zimdar Shows, as a talker on the girl show. His first few weeks were lucrative, but ten weeks after joining his first carnival he found himself in New Orleans, broke. A brother, Ted, provided bus fare back to Eau Claire, but Al was a showman now and nothing else would replace his love for the business. He knew about the Billboard and he sent letters out to show owners asking for employment. He got a reply from one old-time show owner, who was trying to build back the carnival that he had lost in the early depression years. L. J. Heth wrote Kunz saying that if the young man had anything between the ears and could make himself generally useful, he could come on at $25.00 per week.

Alfred Kunz kissed his wife, Esther, goodbye, promised to send for her, and took off for L. J. Heth's little truck show down in Birmingham, Alabama. That spring, Mr. Heth gave the young man a job in the office and taught him the details of the business. Al stayed with Heth as office manager until he was drafted into the army in 1942. In the meantime Mrs. Kunz had joined the show and had operated a string of concessions for several years. Kunz was discharged from the army after a few month's service as he was the father of three children, and season of 1943 was engaged by Harry Hennies as assistant manager of the Hennies Brothers Shows. Al stayed with Hennies through the 1950 season. Last few years with Hennies, he was office manager and Mrs. Kunz operated their concessions.

In 1956, Floyd Heth, the new owner of the L. J. Heth Shows engaged Al as manager of the show. The following year Kunz bought the Heth Show and startled the entire carnival world by booking six major fairs for this little truck show. He added enough rides and equipment so that all fair committees were satisfied, and he has played all except one of those fairs ever since. He startled carnival owners even more when he bought outright the Double-Double Space Wheels from Velare Brothers. The quarter of a million dollars paid for them was more than many major carnivals were valued at. Al sold the patent rights to manufacture the Single Sky Wheel to Allen Herschall Co. so that other midways could have these first spectacular rides. At one time Kunz owned more spectacular wheels than anyone else in the world. He owned the Double Double Space Wheels, Giant Wheel from Seattle World's Fair and two Sky Wheels; three quarter of a million dollars invested in spectacular sky wheels.

Al keeps some of his spectacular rides on his own midways, now named the Century 21 Shows; he books the others as independents at big fair dates. He claims that his show is now second only to Royal American, and a visit to that midway at the Iowa State Fair in Des Moines bears out that claim.

The Kunz collective amusement operations are a family affair. Mrs. Esther L. Kunz is secretary-treasurer of the organization, and their son Wayne A. Kunz is assistant manager. When the show splits into two units for smaller fairs, Wayne is manager of one of the units. When the show is playing its season of big fairs, over one hundred semi-trailer loads of carnival equipment moves between the towns on the routes. They have to be broken down into small units on the highways to cut down on congestion. This huge show sometimes makes jumps of over six hundred miles on the highways between fair dates.

Al isn't as optimistic as some owners appear to be regarding the future of the business. He cites the fact that labor costs alone have doubled in the last five years, and that it is impossible to raise the price of tickets on the standard rides enough to offset this increase. Also, the contracts with major fairs are making it impossible for the large shows necessary to play them to have any net profits from such dates. Profits which all major midways have depended on to carry them through rainy weeks, epidemics and other profit-eating misfortunes.

Then insurance coverage for carnival operations have gone way up. Some shows with good safety records now have to pay as much as seven percent of their ride gross receipts for proper coverage. Al states, "This business has become plagued with so many problems with an operation as large as Century 21 Shows that it has taken the romance and joy out of it that I used to know 30 years ago."

A visit with the Kunz family on their show is a pleasant interlude for any real carnival fan. For us, who remember the L. J. Heth Shows, there is much with the Century 21 Shows to remind us that this man got his early training from the old master. In spite of the spectacular rides, this midway could have been framed by L. J. himself. It has that same happy, friendly, gracious atmosphere that you felt when you walked on the front end of L. J. Heth's midway. All carnival fans join with Al Kunz in hoping that the problems besetting the industry can be solved soon. We all hope, as he does, that the second and third generation carnival showmen now taking over can work out the problems. Al states it plainly with these words, "The reason I say this is because I have a son who has ants in his pants the same as I did when I was a young man, and I solved many of the problems of those days." Yes, and there is a grandson coming along too.

CON T. KENNEDY SHOWS. About 1915. Courtesy Albert Conover.

J. GEORGE LOOS

J. GEORGE LOOS, 1912. Courtesy Billboard Publishing Co.

J. George Loos was born in 1880. At sixteen he got his first show business job selling tickets in a Baltimore, Maryland theater. Later he got a job as manager of a traveling burlesque company. He moved to Chicago and was manager of a theater there for three years. J. George organized a girl revue with ten girls and booked it on the Morris & Berger Carnival Company. Later, he and Dave Lackman organized the Lackman & Loos Shows, which they toured for two years. The following season, Loos took his own five-car "gilly" show on tour.

The Loos show grew as J. George added more equipment. His route was extended to take in Texas and Louisiana as well as Illinois, Indiana, Missouri, Kansas and Oklahoma. He got equipment from C. A. Wortham to make his show a wagon and flatcar show. He used the Loos title until the early thirties, when he started using the Greater United Shows in his advertising. He took the show off the road in 1951 after developing a blood clot. He still organized the midway for the George Washington's Birthday Celebration at Laredo, Texas until his death. He furnished a midway there for thirty-eight years, and at the Beeville, Texas, Fair for over forty years.

His show was noted as a training ground for future carnival owners. Twenty-two owners of big carnivals received early training on his midway. Such men as Max Goodman, Rubin Gruberg, Orville N. Crafts, Frank Sutton, J. C. McCaffery, the Hennies Brothers and George Dorman were associated with Loos in their early days with carnivals.

Loos was married in 1928. After his 1951 retirement, he continued to operate his Kiddieland Park in Laredo. He died in Laredo on October 27, 1962, with funeral services and burial in that Texas border town.

HARRY G. MELVILLE

Harry G. Melville was born in New York City, June 2, 1883. He served in the Cavalry during the Spanish-American War in the Philippines. He had done nothing of importance in carnival business until Nat Reiss died. Mrs. Bertha Reiss selected Melville as general manager of the Nat Reiss Shows.

Harry G. Melville and Mrs. Reiss were married on December 3, 1919. They continued to operate the show under the Nat Reiss title until end of 1928 season when the title was changed to the Melville-Reiss Shows for the 1929 and 1930 seasons. Due to Melville's illness, the show stayed in winter quarters in Charlotte, North Carolina, during the 1931 season. His wife and friends tried to prevent him from learning that his illness was a terminal case of cancer, but he had known for several months before his death.

Melville died in a Charlotte hospital on December 11, 1931. His body was taken to Chicago for burial in Showmen's Rest. All of his Masonic and other fraternal memberships were in Streator, Illinois, Lodges. The show was sold at auction one week after his death.

PERCY JAMES MUNDAY

PERCY J. MUNDAY, 1902. Courtesy Billboard Publishing Co.

Percy James Munday was born in Exeter, Devonshire, England, February 24, 1865. He came to the United States in 1885 and settled in Rochester, New York. He had an attraction in Chicago in 1893 during the Columbian Exposition. After the big fair in Chicago was over he booked his attraction at fairs and celebrations. In 1899, he formed a partnership with DeKreko Brothers whereby he joined with them in forming a carnival company.

When DeKrekos carried this company to Mexico, P. J. Munday pulled his wild animal show away from the combine and went back to the central states. In 1902 he was partner in the Gaskill-Munday Carnival Company and in 1903 was partner in the Gaskill-Munday-Leavitt Shows. After the partnership broke up, he renamed his midway the Great Munday Shows. In 1904 he played the Winnipeg, Canada, Fair, which had been played in 1903 by Jabour (the first organized carnival at any fair in North America). His show is not listed after 1907.

P. J. Munday had been away from carnivals for many years, when he died in a Jacksonville, Florida, hospital on December 11, 1943. He was buried in Oaklawn Cemetery on December 13th.

DAVID D. MURPHY

David D. Murphy was born and raised in St. Louis, Missouri. Thirteen year old Murphy got his first experience at the St. Louis World's Fair in 1904 as a concessionaire. He didn't rise very high in the carnival business until 1923, when he organized his own midway, the D. D. Murphy Shows. This show jumped to a top place in the industry in just two years. By the late twenties, the D. D. Murphy Shows

was getting some of the top fairs in the Central States for its route.

The depression hurt many of the old established shows, but most of them survived. The D. D. Murphy Shows was completely bankrupt at the end of the 1931 season. There wasn't enough cash on the Atlanta, Georgia, closing night to get the show train out of the Atlanta railroad yards, and there was no possibility of its getting back to St. Louis or opening again in Atlanta. David D's midway had gone down as fast as it had risen. Former D. D. Murphy Shows employees still extoll the wonders of that show. Two of them at the 1970 Tampa Fair said it was "the best show ever."

David D. Murphy died in St. Mary's Hospital in St. Louis, March 19, 1943, of diabetes. On March 22 he was buried in the Calvary Cemetery there.

JAMES PATTERSON

JAMES PATTERSON WINTER QUARTERS. Elephant barn and office building. Raymond E. Elder standing by office. Courtesy Fred D. Pfening, Jr.

James Patterson was born in 1860, and was operating a merry-go-round in Southwestern Missouri in the early 1880's. He added concessions and still later added a little circus to his ride. (If he carried another show or two, he would have had the first organized carnival. As it was constituted, he operated a circus with a merry-go-round on the circus lot, as one or two other circuses tried to do.) He started his first full-fledged midway with "Pop" Brainard as a partner. This show, the Patterson & Brainard Carnival Company, was opened in 1902 and continued for about five years. Jim Patterson married Brainard's daughter during the partnership.

Patterson operated carnivals under various titles for over twenty years, and his father-in-law, Brainard, trouped with these midways. Such titles as Patterson Carnival Company, Patterson Greater Shows, Greater Patterson and Great Patterson were used. In 1917 he bought and operated the Gollmar Brothers Circus. He toured big circuses for ten years, but still kept his carnival on the road. He booked his rides in a Corpus Christi, Texas, park for several years before his retirement in 1941.

James Patterson died at his long-time home in Paola, Kansas, May 25, 1948. He was buried in Paola on May 28th. The eighty-eight year old showman was survived by his widow, two sons and two daughters.

DAN R. ROBINSON

"Winchester, Kentucky
May 12, 1906

"On and after Monday, May 14, 1906, all members and employees of above company will be prohibited from visiting any attractions other than the one on which they are employed unless furnished with complimentary tickets by their respective managers. This rule is imperative. There will be no breakfast served in the dining car after 8:30 A.M.; no lunch after 1:30 P.M.; nor supper after 6:30 P.M.

"All members and employees must, at all times, conduct themselves as ladies and gentlemen:

"Business affairs of the company positively must not be discussed in hotels, boarding houses, on railroad trains or public places.

"Band and free act managers shall report each night at the office, in the Penny Arcade, where they will receive instructions for the following day. On and after Monday, May 14th, no railroad tickets will be sold later than close of the day preceding the date for which the tickets are issued. It is absolutely necessary that railroad tickets be purchased by time named, so that we can stipulate to the various railroad ticket agents the exact number of poeple carried. All persons connected with the above company are kindly requested not to point out to anyone, managers or owners of various attractions,

Concession property, etc., or to give any information concerning them.

"Each and every employee is expected to attend strictly to business and not to interfere with matters concerning other persons. Concession people will, under no circumstances, be permitted to visit shows unless furnished with complimentary ticket by Superintendent of privileges, Mr. T. D. Forde.

"After locating concessions, there can be no change, either in location or character of privilege granted. No privilege will be sold for less than one week. No concession will be permitted to locate in front of any pay attraction.

"There will positively be no "kidding," drunkenness nor misconduct on the midway, and employees entertaining ladies will be dismissed without notice. Members and employees shall not dictate to or pass remarks concerning members of the band and performers. The management is ready and willing, at all times, to fight the battles, and all complaints should be registered with the management of this company, or of the various attractions.

"Members and employees will under no circumstances, be permitted to ride the Ferris Wheel or the Merry-Go-Round.

(signed) Dan R. Robinson
General Manager"

The above notice posted by the Dan R. Robinson Amusement Company in 1906 was not as strict as some other managers posted, and enforced.

THE BILLBOARD

Volume XIV., No. 30.   CINCINNATI, SATURDAY, JULY 26, 1902.

DAN R. ROBINSON.
Manager of The Robinson Carnival Company.

This writer has known personally several men who had worked for "Danny" Robinson, and every one of them said he was the best carnival owner they ever worked for. Every Sunday afternoon, after show got into town, his band in full uniform played a concert for the townspeople. Program consisted of all sacred numbers.

The Robinson Carnival Company in 1902 was owned by E. M. Robinson of Cincinnati, Ohio and was managed by Dan R. Robinson. They played Ohio and Michigan that season. In March 1903, the Robinsons announced that they would spend fifty thousand dollars and add fourteen new shows. On April 20th, Dan R. Robinson married Miss Bessie Hern of Cincinnati. The name of the show was changed to the Famous Robinson Amusement Company for the 1904 season.

In 1907, the title was shortened to the Robinson Amusement Company, and Dan R. Robinson was in complete charge of show. In 1909, Dan R. bought the Great Munday shows for twenty thousand dollars; included was the right to use the Munday title. Things began to go bad for the show, and in the fall of 1911 it was attached for debt and sold by court order. Danny was in a "retreat" in Cincinnati with a nervous breakdown in January 1912. Show was put out in 1912 as the Robinson Shows United and was attached by two bandsmen for back salaries. It broke up after that and never went on road again. In September 1915, Dan R. Robinson was committed to the insane asylum. Had he been sane, he would have been sent to prison for writing bad checks.

JACK RUBACK

JACK RUBACK AND FRIENDS, 1962. Courtesy Amusement Business Photograph.

Jack Ruback starts his fifty-third year in carnival business when he opens his Alama Exposition at the San Antonio Fiesta and Battle of Flowers in April 1970. He started as a concessionaire in 1918. He was connected with the Alamo carnival title, but not as owner nearly fifty years ago. The Alamo title is the oldest carnival title in use today, but it has not been in continuous use since it was first introduced by W. H. (Bill) Rice for his Alamo Carnival Company back in 1904.

Jack Ruback, who was born on December 22, 1900, would never have been happy in any business except his chosen profession, carnival and midway operations. He has had partners in his enterprises, but he operates best as sole owner of his own midway. He has played the same route of fairs and celebrations through West Texas, New Mexico, Colorado, Kansas and Oklahoma for over forty years, which demonstrates the esteem with which he is regarded by the officials and committee members along this route. Jack, like many old-time showmen, is not prone to discuss business matters with anyone except his lawyers or his bankers; but most outdoor showmen think that he could leave his equipment on his trucks and live very nicely on the income from his savings.

The Alamo Exposition carries twenty office rides on its route, but Jack Ruback will book in more if needed for certain dates. His show has many people with it who have been with Jack for twenty or thirty years. If an old-time carnival trouper needs a place to do what he is still able to do around a midway, Jack Ruback will make a place for him on the Alamo show. Mrs. Ruback works in the show's office.

HOMER H. SCOTT

HOMER SCOTT'S CHAIROPLANE. This is the ride with which he started in business for himself. Courtesy Homer Scott's Georgia Amusement Co.

"Honest" Homer, as he is called by his many friends and neighbors in northeastern Georgia, does not own the biggest carnival on the road, nor does he aspire to that honor with its attendant problems. Homer H. Scott does claim that his Georgia Amusement Company is the cleanest show on the road, both in its character and its appearance. He never allows anything on his midway that would offend any one of the thousands of church-going people who visit with Homer and his wife each year on their route. He keeps his fifteen rides and his trucks clean and well painted, and his show never leaves a dirty lot behind it when it moves to the next town. Homer and Mrs. Scott and their show are perfect examples of the small collective amusement operations that are the backbone of the carnival industry. Small shows unknown outside of a limited area, they bring amusement to the rural communities all across North America.

Homer H. Scott was born near Toccoa, Georgia, on March 24, 1905. This Stephens County boy joined his first carnival when he was sixteen. In the fall of 1921 he took a job as a "stick" for a ten-cent "pc" wheel concession on the Rubin & Chery Shows. He stayed with Rubin two seasons and then joined J. V. Rogers' Sunshine Exposition Shows for three seasons. In 1926 he joined Dad Hildreth's Dixie Land Shows and the following year he began a three-year sojourn with David A. Wise. Then he worked with Rogers Greater Shows, Lee Amusement Company, Browney Smith and Cumberland Valley Shows. Then on July 19, 1947, after twenty-six years with other men's shows, Mr. and Mrs. Homer Scott opened their Georgia Amusement Company.

The first Georgia Amusement Company wasn't pretentious by any standards. All it consisted of was one second-hand chairoplane and six small concessions. The Scotts, who had been married on August 8, 1927, worked hard that first season with their own little midway, and have continued to devote all their time to their show. That first old chairoplane, which was the nucleus on which they built, still has an honored location on their showgrounds. Rebuilt and well decorated, it is like a friend to them. They have never ventured far from Stephens County with their midway, as they get all the business they require from their friends and neighbors close at hand. The show does go into Western North Carolina for a few dates each season, but their total mileage on the year is only sixteen hundred.

A first-time visitor to the Georgia Amusement Company will find a friendly rural atmosphere on the showgrounds or fairgrounds much like that of fifty years ago. A slender, short-sleeved, weather-beaten but spry man will be seen here, there and everywhere, greeting friends and leisurely discussing weather, family and crops with them. If the visitor has never met Homer Scott, no need to ask an employee of the show to point him out — ask any one of the older patrons on the showgrounds — they will point out Homer to you and probably add an accolade to him and his show before you leave them. Homer Scott will greet you like an old friend, for that is what you will become as he proudly escorts you around the midway to meet Mrs. Scott.

He plays the same fairs and celebrations every year, because he doesn't promise the committees things that he can't give them. When his first ad for help appears each spring in Amusement Business it ends with, "Winter quarters is now open. Plenty hot biscuits and feather beds;" old troupers like this writer feel the urge to get down to Toccoa and visit Homer's winter quarters.

ADOLPH SEEMAN
"A son and grandson of Showmen"

Adolph Seeman was born in Stockholm, Sweden, on July 21, 1852. A son and a grandson of noted magicians he was sent to school in Sweden, Berlin and Saxony. He acquired a degree in Civil Engineering. He then served his allotted time in the Swedish Navy and was discharged in 1874. Baron Seeman, his father, asked him to join the magic show as assistant. In 1876, he helped transport a circus overland into Siberia and back with good financial returns.

In 1881 Baron Seeman's magic show was brought to Coney Island for the summer season. After the Coney Island season closed they toured the larger cities of the United States with Adolph as manager of the troupe. Baron Seeman died in Texas in 1886, and Adolph took over the duties of magician. He billed himself as Adolph the Magician until 1893. He built the first Crystal Maze ever built in America at 38th and Broadway in New York. It was a huge success. He and Victor Leavitt built a portable maze to tour fairs in the late nineties. In spring of 1898, he was approached by the Elks Club of Zanesville, Ohio, asking for information about street fairs. He produced a street fair for them, which was copied by other Elks Lodges in Ohio. Frank Gaskill was a visitor and took notes. Seeman always claimed that this was the first Elks' Lodge Street Fair anywhere.

He then went into the carnival business exclusively. He was partnered with many showmen including Bostock, Jarvis, Millican, and Leavitt in midway operations. He was manager of the Dan Robinson Show and always managed the shows in which he was a partner. He joined the new Rubin & Cherry Shows as builder and designer. His designing and building of show fronts, shows and wagons have been given credit for the success of that show. He was a genius as a designer and builder.

He was with the T. A. Wolfe Shows in 1923, but his recurring throat trouble took him back to Chicago for medical treatment. He died of throat cancer in Chicago's American Hospital on August 21, 1924. Showmen's League of America took charge of the services which were held in a local funeral home on August 21. He was interred in Showmen's Rest by his brother showmen.

"ALTHOUGH NOT DESTINED TO ACHIEVE CONSPICUOUS EMINENCE IN THE SHOW WORLD, IT WOULD BE A GREAT MISTAKE TO SAY THAT ADOLPH SEEMAN WAS NOT A SUCCESS."

CHRIS (POP) SMITH

Chris Smith was born in Manheim, Baden, Germany, January 12, 1853. Came to the United States when he was sixteen. As a confectioner and baker, he became interested in candy and other concessions at fairs. In 1890 he bought a second-hand merry-go-round, and for the next twelve summers he operated rides, concessions and a motion picture show at Conneaut Lake, Pennsylvania. In winters, he worked with minstrels, Tom Shows (Uncle Tom's Cabin), and church movies. In 1898 he organized a two-car Palace Amusement Company for the winter months. Took it south in fall of 1902 and each fall and winter thereafter.

He financed the Hoss-Smith Shows in 1904 and booked his Palace Amusement Company on the midway. Partnership ended that fall, and he named the show the Smith Greater Shows. This show grew to be a twenty-car railroad show at one time. Pop Smith was the first carnival to use gasoline engines for ride power. He also was one of the first to carry an elaborate Carousel. Litigation broke up his show in South Georgia fall of 1926. His long-time winter quarters was in Augusta, Georgia.

From 1926 to 1931 Pop was active as general agent, concessioner, etc. until ill health forced him to quit the road. He had kept all of his Lodge affiliations in Ohio, so he entered the Masonic Hospital in Springfield, Ohio. He was bedridden from July 12, 1932, until his death on July 30, 1933. Mom Smith was in constant attendance. Mom Smith and two sons, Chris and Ed survived him.

C. SMITH

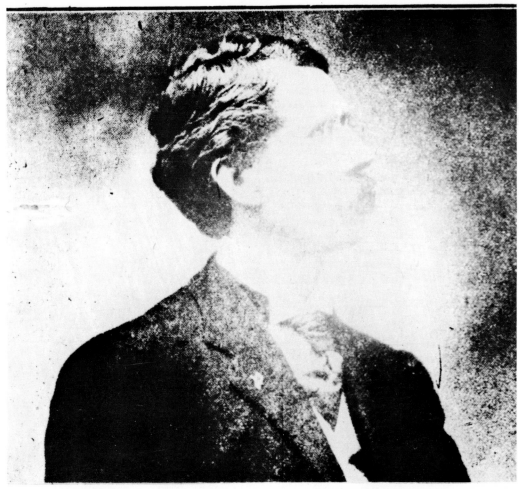

Courtesy Billboard Publishing Co.

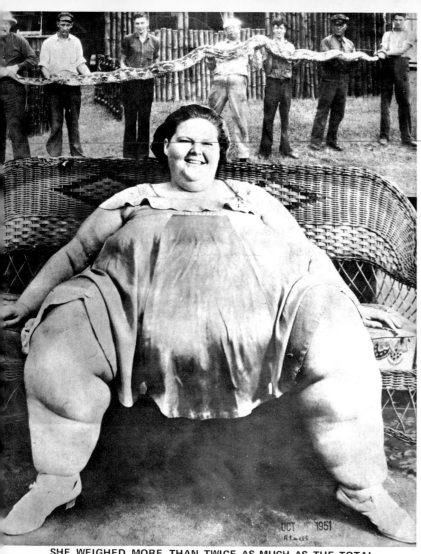

Courtesy Harry Fros[t]

SHE WEIGHED MORE THAN TWICE AS MUCH AS THE TOTAL
WEIGHT OF THE NINE PERSONS PICTURED BELOW. Courtesy
Fred D. Pfening Collection.

MIDGETS. With Royal American Shows in the Thirties. Courtesy Harry
Frost, Minnesota State Fair.

HARD WORKING   MIDGETS

PAUL DEL RIO. Royal American Shows, 1939. Courtesy Harry Frost, Minnesota State Fair.

FRANK CUCKSEY.
A hard-working midget on the Royal American Shows, 1942.

Courtesy Frank Cucksey.

SAM SOLOMAN

Eighty-five year old Sam Soloman died in Miami, Florida, April 25, 1967, after open-heart surgery. He was interred in Miami on April 27th.

His carnival career started in 1902 when he opened his Sol's Golden West Amusement Company. He used such titles as Sol's United and Sol's & Dorman's Shows for the next twelve or thirteen years. In 1916 he organized a new show with a concessionaire as a partner. The Sol's & Rubin's United Shows was Rubin Gruberg's first season as an owner. He began using the Sol's Liberty Shows title in 1928 or 1929 and continued its use through the 1942 season. In March, 1943, Soloman bought the Rubin & Cherry Shows from Mrs. Annie Gruberg, and moved the equipment from Aurora, Illinois, to his own quarters in Caruthersville, Missouri. It was on this occasion that "Miss Annie" made the statement, "Sol, you put the Grubergs into carnival business, now you are taking us out of it."

In December 1943, C. J. Sedlmayr and Soloman announced that they were changing the title of the Show from Rubin and Cherry to Royal American. The following year, Sedlmayr bought Sol's half interest in the Rubin & Cherry property and Sam Soloman was out of carnival business for the first time in over forty years. He never organized or trouped another collective amusement organization.

BERNARD P. THOMAS

The wheat-belt area of the Northwest which extends from the northern boundries of Nebraska and Western Iowa to central Saskatchewan and Alberta has always been lucrative territory for collective amusement organizations. Back in the depression ridden mid-thirties the Dakota fairs were always profitable for the carnivals playing them, even though the territory was experiencing something much worse than the depression, a prolonged drought. This writer has looked from the show train windows at hundreds of miles of dustbowl desolation all across North Dakota from Fargo to Miles City, Montana. The fence posts along the railroad right of way were completely covered by drifting dust with only wind swept eddies in the drifts marking their locations. Abandoned farm houses and barns were obscured by drifts of blown top soil up to their second story windows.

Bernard P. Thomas was only ten years old when those drought induced dust storms ravaged so much of his parents chosen territory. They were show people accustomed to taking the things as they were and they survived along with their friends and neighbors. The Art B. Thomas Shows would have been classed as a "forty-miler" outfit along the East Coast, but picnics, small fairs and celebrations are not that close together out in Western country so that forty-miler would have to be classed as a four hundred-miler. Even though it was a small show, it ranged over quite a large area before Bernard Thomas took over its management in 1947.

Bernard P. Thomas was born in Hurley, South Dakota, November 28, 1923. His parents were show folks so he has never been engaged in any other business. When he took over the Art B. Thomas Shows it carried only ten rides. He immediately began to upgrade the show and it now carries thirty riding devices over its route which extends over the entire upper Midwest (wheat belt) and into Canada. He was the first showman to carry spectacular rides into his territory and they have helped his growth.

The Thomas show equipment is handled quickly and efficiently by ride men who have been accustomed to playing two dates a week at the many three-day events in that territory. This means that they tore down the show, moved it, and set it back up in time to open the following afternoon. Many small carnivals continue playing circuits of several weeks made up of such dates through those wheat belt states. Bernard Thomas doesn't play many such split week dates now as his show is too heavy to move so rapidly and with his larger show, he books fairs that play longer periods.

Bernard Thomas is optimistic about the future of the business and foresees a period of growth that will require expenditures of large sums for new equipment. This can be done, he thinks, providing committees for the fairs and sponsors will work out equitable contracts that will allow the midway manager to expend the cash needed for such expansion. Being born into the business, Bernard Thomas hopes to work out the problems now besetting it so that his carnival can continue the growth it has experienced in the last two decades.

W. G. WADE, JR.

W. G. Wade, Jr. is a third generation midway operator, and he has the fourth generation employed in his offices watching after the family business. His great-grandparents came to the United States from Ireland, and his grandfather was a successful farmer in Michigan. In the eighteen nineties, an owner of a merry-go-round, Andrew Miller, left his machine as security for a three hundred fifty dollar loan with grandfather Wade. Miller didn't come back and farmer Wade rented a front yard on Main Street and set the ride up. Did very well with it and started booking it at fairs and celebrations.

Grandfather Wade's three sons, Lee, W. G. and Roscoe T. all entered ride and midway business as young men, and there was a multiplicity of ride and midway units bearing the Wade title. To further complicate the title situation, their sister, Leila Wade married Clay May with the resulting new midway, the Wade and May Shows. W. G. Wade, Jr. was born in the business on December 5, 1918. He worked with his father in summers until 1938, when they started a second unit, Wade & Son Congress of Rides. This unit consisted of a merry-go-round, a Ferris wheel and a chairplane. After four-year naval service ended in 1945, young Wade went back to work for his father.

In 1948, the younger Wade started the Glen Wade Amusement Rides with a merry-go-round and a Ferris wheel. He built this new unit up into a medium-sized midway before his father's death in 1956. He now had control of the W. G. Wade shows that had been started by his father and his uncles back in 1912, when they bought a new merry-go-round from Allen-Herschell Company. This show had been a major midway for many years and had played the Michigan State Fair at Detroit since 1952. That fair has been played by the W. G. Wade Shows seventeen times now.

Although the show is now part of a large carnival syndicate, W. G. Wade, Jr. actively manages the shows bearing his name. He is assisted by his daughter, Linda who handles the office work in the main office at Mason, Michigan and daughter, Debbie who handles the show office on the road. These two charming young ladies add much towards brightening up the usual drabness of a carnival office. There doesn't seem to be another W. G. Wade to carry on the title, but Glen Wade is a comparatively young man yet so this problem shouldn't bother anyone for some time.

HARRY BERNSTEIN (AL WAGNER)

Harry Bernstein, known in the carnival field as Al Wagner was a native of Providence, Rhode Island. He started as a concessionaire after World War One, and operated various concessions until 1938 when he, with the aid of his wife Hattie, began operating a motorized carnival. They bought the Velare Brothers' equipment from the Royal American Shows in 1943, and launched a railroad show in 1944. This Cavalcade of Amusements was the biggest show on the road in 1946. Traveling on fifty railroad cars, it had the best route of fairs and still dates in the country.

This show, which Hattie took pride in telling visitors had been financed from her earnings, dropped back into minor rank almost as fast as it had gained the pinnacle. The Wagners could not adapt themselves or their huge show to the requirements of the large fair's committees. When season of 1954 opened the show did not have one major fair for its route and the United States Internal Revenue Department had claims of over a quarter million dollars against it, when the show moved out of winter quarters and to Pensacola, Florida.

On Sunday afternoon the show painter William O. Burke went to the show office and asked for some of his back pay. In the ensuing argument quite a few shots were fired and Al Wagner was killed. Wagner died on the lot April 11, 1954 and was buried in Showmen's Rest in Chicago on April 16. Show folded. Burke was acquitted of all charges a few months later.

Side Show Owners!!

Past and Present

FRANCIS LENTINI. Side show owner and three-legged man. Courtesy Harry Frost, Minnesota State Fair.

CARL NORWOOD. Side show owner and frog boy. Courtesy Amusement Business Photograph.

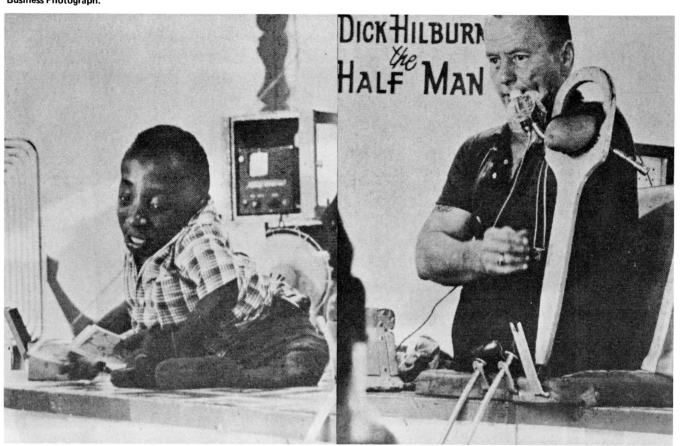

DICK HILBURN. Side show owner and half man. Courtesy Amusement Business Photograph.

And More Carnies

RICHARD EUGENE (DICK) BEST

After Walter K. Sibley combined several of his single pit attractions into one long "string show" back in 1904, most all single attraction show operators copied his 10-in-1 shows. By 1910 all carnival midways featured a show of this type, if an operator with the necessary attractions could be obtained. These shows required at least one or two human freaks of nature who could be featured, plus the required number of working acts. Before long, these side shows with living human freaks were adding the name "Circus" Side Show, to distinguish them from other "pit" shows using long lines of canvas banners in the "string show" format. Several hundred individuals have framed and operated these circus side shows, but no more than a dozen of them have presented outstanding shows for more than a few years. Johnny J. Bejano, Samuel W. Gumpertz, Peter Kortez, T. W. (Slim) Kelly, Carl J. Lauther and Meyer Meyer have been the leaders in the field, as has been Dick Best.

Richard Eugene Best was born in Greenfield, Indiana on November 7, 1897. In 1910 he secured his first job in amusement business as a candy butcher in a Detroit theater. In 1914 young Best went to sea as an able-bodied seaman on a cattle boat. He made two trips to Europe with this boat. He was in the Army during the war and was discharged in 1919. He had received some injuries in a truck accident and the Army doctors wanted to keep Best in a hospital until he died, as they didn't think he could live very long. He wanted to get away from the Army and Army doctors so took his release. Later that year he secured his first job in outdoor amusement business.

"Dick" Best, as he was to be known on carnival and circus midways, was employed by "High Grass" Bill Campbell as a candy butcher with the Campbell, Bailey, and Hutchinson Circus. The following year he toured with the same show as boss candy butcher, or superintendent of candy stands. In 1921 Dick joined his first carnival, the Ziedman & Pollie Shows with

KNIFE THROWER. Royal American Shows, 1934. This type act in a side show is known as a "working act." Courtesy Harry Frost, Minnesota State Fair.

two fun houses. He stayed with Ziedman & Pollie until 1928 when he joined the Royal American Shows with a snake show. Within a few years he was operating the big circus side show on the Royal American midway.

In 1939 when all the carnivals were striving for the "modernistic look" on their midways, and more and more "sit-down" shows were being framed, Dick Best built the most elaborate circus side show ever put on the road. He spent over sixty thousand dollars in a depression year to build this huge show with its elaborate neon-lighted "modernistic" front and its big tent theater with 2000 seats for the patrons. A "sit-down" show for a freak exhibition!! Many old-timers were skeptical regarding this new show but others were sure that it would make lots of money for its owner. Rubin Gruberg offered Dick thirty-five thousand dollars for half interest before the show opened. Best should have sold that half interest as the show was "twenty years ahead of the patrons." They could understand a string show with its long line of canvas banners and its open front, but freak show goers were afraid to go into a tent theater to see freaks. Dick lost every dime he had keeping the show open to the end of the season and gave the front to the Royal American management when the show got back to quarters.

It was in 1943, while still with Royal American, operating a "string" type circus side show, that another doctor told Dick to get his business in order as he didn't have much longer to live. Best had his teeth all extracted and has done pretty well ever since.

In 1943 he sold his Royal American side show to Curtis Lorow and leased Chadwick Beach at Englewood, Florida for two years. In 1946, he and T. W. (Slim) Kelly went into partnership and framed five shows for the midway of Al Wagner's Cavalcade of Amusements. Kelly sold his interest to Best the following year.

This teller of "tall tales," excelled only by Slim Kelly in this art, had side shows on both the Johnny J. Jones Exposition and the Cole Brothers Circus in 1948. Mrs. Best stayed with the carnival midway, while Dick trouped with the show on the circus midway. Early in the fifties the Bests went back to the Royal American with a big circus side show and stayed there through the 1970 season. In 1969 Dick took another partnership with a younger man, Stuart Miller, who had been managing side shows with circuses. In addition to the Royal American side

show, they had another one in Houston, Texas at the Astro-Hall for the ninety-three-day engagement of the Ringling Brothers and Barnum & Bailey Circus there.

Dick Best has developed a philosophical viewpoint regarding the world and life. He doesn't let much disturb him now. If things get "rough," just quit and go fishing; problems have a way of solving themselves if people will let them. He can and will entertain his friends with stories of past midways. One of his best stories is of the time he was jailed in the backwoods down in Georgia. He had heard that there was a girl with one head, two bodies, three arms and four legs living down in that area. Dick went to the village and inquired. "Nobody knew nothing" about such a girl. Dick persisted and finally a man told him that he had someone coming who could help him. The person who came to help was the local sheriff who locked up this crazy man who thought there were people with four legs in Georgia.

After eight hours in the Richland, Georgia jail, he convinced the law officer that he was sane and was released. After more fruitless inquiry he became disgusted and was ready to give up and return to the show but he asked one more person, a school boy, if he knew where this freak of nature could be found. He offered this boy a brand new dollar bill if he could point out where she could be found. The boy calmly led Best to a house within a few hundred yards of the area he had been searching; there little Betty Lou Williams was found. This little colored girl, before her death, had earned enough to educate herself and put eight of her fourteen brothers and sisters through college. This gentle little girl doomed to early death in poverty, was given many extra years of pleasant living because she had been found by a benevolent showman.

Well-intentioned, but misguided "do-gooders" and some plain meddlers are making it more difficult every year for human freaks of nature to make a living for themselves. True, life in a circus side show may not be exactly what those arrangers of other people's destinies might want for themselves, but it is much better than an isolated existence on the public dole. Many of these human oddities have much better incomes than do the busybodies who worry about them — several of them own and operate their own shows. Dick Best has helped many of them get a start as a self-reliant earner of his or her own living. Dick and his fellow side show operators are always happy that another one of their "children" has "made good."

HAROLD A. BUSHEA

Harold A. Bushea, the General Agent for the first carnival, was born in Providence, Rhode Island on February 19, 1860. He was a well-known promoter and agent when Gaskill engaged him to lay out and book a route for what was to be the first successful collective amusement organization. Bushea continued with Gaskill until the latter's death in 1904 and managed the Gaskill midway for Mrs. Gaskill for the remainder of that season. He has the distinction of not only booking the first fair date for an organized midway in the United States, but also managing the show that played the fair.

Bushea went back to circuses after the Gaskill Show closed and worked for such shows as Al G. Barnes, Sells Floto, Gollmar Brothers and 101 Ranch Wild West. He handled every job on the advance such as press, contracting and general agent, and promoter. He was also a competent manager. He worked on every kind of amusement enterprise. Circus, carnival, dramatic show, minstrel show, museums, showboats and promotions — he had worked with all of them.

Harold Bushea spent several years with the Con T. Kennedy shows and went with Lackman & Carson when they bought the Kennedy show property. He retired from Lackman & Carson because of illness in 1927. He had been in Chicago for three years of treatment when he died at the American Hospital on May 4, 1930.

L. HARVEY CANN

L. HARVEY DOC CANN. His "Hawaiian Show" on M. J. Lapp Shows, 1920. Courtesy L. Harvey Doc Cann.

L. Harvey Cann, Doc as he is known to all midway troupers, will not tell anyone what the "L." represents. He was born in Lynn, Massachusetts, August 16, 1897. His father was engaged in the drayage business and young Cann was raised among horses. The elder Cann used four and six-horse teams to pull wagon loads of shoes from the Lynn shoe factories to the Boston docks for export. He brought leather, shoe findings and supplies back to Lynn from Boston. Because of his familiarity with horses, L. Harvey was able to brag to Johnny Baker, Buffalo Bill's arena director, "I can ride anything that has hair on it." Baker hired him as a rider with the "Bill Show" at $30.00 per month and board.

Young Cann put his one good suit of clothes in a pasteboard suitcase and started his forty-year trouping career. He, being a "First of May," didn't know about the "tip" system around all circuses and wild west shows and thought all of that thirty dollars per month was "take-home pay." He didn't tip the waiter in the cookhouse, so his food was always cold. He didn't tip the coffee boy, so he got no cream and worst of all he didn't tip the property men. One afternoon during a performance, a property man "accidentally" dropped quite a lot of heavy props on that pasteboard suitcase. It and its contents were ruined. Consequently, Buffalo Bill's youngest cowboy wore his cowpuncher clothes everywhere he went all season.

Along about 1915 L. Harvey Cann found that you didn't have to eat in show cookhouses on carnivals, and switched to the collective amusement industry. A man named Greene had set up a structure resembling a large farm silo on a vacant lot in Buffalo, New York. In this structure men were supposed to ride motorcycles around on its straight up and down walls. L. Harvey started practicing and after a few days he could go halfway around on the straight portion of the wall. Within a month he was able to go two laps around the wall. Greene had already started selling tickets there in Buffalo for spectators to watch the practice rides and they booked this new silodrome with the Joseph G. Ferari Shows that season. This was one of the first straight wall dromes with any carnival and such structures meant the end of the older slant wall dromes. Cann used the name Capt. Hal Clayton for several years in his early silodrome riding career. In 1920 "Snapper" Lane, another rider, rode a fully equipped 4-cylinder Henderson on a straight wall in Haverhill, Massachusetts.

Although he owned dromes over thirty years later, this pioneer straight wall rider soon was working on other jobs around carnival midways. In 1920 he was a talker and escape artist on the M. J. Lapp Shows. Like most carnival troupers of that period, Cann moved around and worked with such shows as Frank West's Worlds Wonder and the Brown & Dyer Shows. He was engaged by George W. Traver as general agent for the Traver's Chautauqua Shows. Doc, as he was being called now, was able to book the show into towns that had been closed to carnivals as Chautauquas were highly respectable in those days. When the midway got to town and started setting up, committeemen and city officials would all protest, "this is nothing but a carnival, and they are barred in this town." Doc then would prove by the dictionary that it was not a carnival, as the only definition given by Webster in those days for the word defined them as religious festivals. Mr. Traver's little three car gilly show could never have been mistaken for a religious festival, though it wasn't a chautauqua either.

After a general agent got the season's route booked for a midway, he came back to the show in a "generally useful" capacity. On Traver's show, Doc Cann framed a "Hawaiian" show. He says he called it a Hawaiian show because the only banners not in use were for such a show. He promoted a Salvation Army bass drum, had Jimmy Collins build a front, found the Hawaiian banners and picked up a couple of girls to dance in it. The young ladies were later very well known carnival people. Doc made money with this show as he spent very little to frame it and the "nut" was low.

A few years later Doc framed the first Headless girl show to appear in this country. This illusion show paid off very well for him, and he continued to operate motordromes, shows and concessions as well as acting as general agent for the carnival itself. He joined Max Linderman on the World of Mirth Shows, and stayed with that show for many years. In 1948, he owned two dromes, a "big horse" show, a "little horse" show, a Looper ride and a string of popcorn, caramel corn and catering concessions. With the concessions, he played many fair contracts not held by the World of Mirth Shows; contracts where he held the exclusive for his specialty on the entire fairgrounds.

For several years now, L. Harvey Cann has lived in one town all year. He lives in Sarasota, Florida, and operates a charter boat for deep-sea fishermen. Like all good carnies, Doc has figured all the angles and can now engage in the one sport that he really loves, while someone else helps pay the expenses. He misses the carnival midway, as all retired troupers do; but there are plenty other retired showmen around Sarasota to "cut up jackpots" with; and Doc is happier than he would be in some town where no one who can talk about outdoor show business ever comes by. Captain L. Harvey Cann, skipper of a deep-sea fishing charter boat, is another outdoor showman whose life story would fill a volume with interesting anecdotes and delineations.

Unfortunately many of these stories will never be told as Doc died last year.

LEON CLAXTON

LEON CAXTON. Producer of colored revues. Courtesy Harry Frost, Minnesota State Fair.

Leon Claxton died on November 14, 1967 in Tampa, Florida. This best-liked member of his race in all of carnival history had produced and operated the Harlem in Havana revue on the Royal American Shows for thirty-four years. This "Jig Show," as colored shows were, and still are, called by all outdoor show people, was the greatest and most elaborate show of its kind produced anywhere. The Royal American has discontinued using this type show since the death of the master producer, Claxton.

Colored performer type shows were not called minstrel shows until several years of the twentieth century had elapsed. Minstrel was reserved for the all-white shows using black-faced comedians as "end-men." The colored shows on carnivals were all called "plantation" shows, when the business was first started. Sometime around 1910, the word minstrel was applied to some of them; but most of the old-time lot layout men still labeled the colored show location stakes as "Plant" or "Plant Show." The word "Jig" began to be used in the twenties, and the writer has a location stake from a large Eastern railroad show dated 1963 with the words "Jig Show" thereon. It is his belief that the word "Jig" so used referred more to the performance in the show than to the color of the performer's skin. For those performers, regardless of the location of the showgrounds, whether on the Brockton, Massachusetts fairgrounds or Montgomery, Alabama, lot — were carnival troupers; and as such, the same loyalty was extended to and exacted from them as was to all other troupers, regardless of race, color or creed. This writer has been in a few nasty incidents, "protecting our show jigs."

Leon Claxton, who had worked his way up in show business from a Ringling-Barnum Circus roustabout at the age of sixteen, to producer of the great Showboat Revue at the Chicago Century of Progress in 1933, contributed much to the "Golden Age of the Carnival." His new concept of colored entertainment and his outstanding productions not only lifted that type carnival show to new heights but also compelled producers of other type midway shows to upgrade their productions. Much credit can be given Leon Claxton for the really great midway "sit-down" shows presented on the big railroad shows of the late thirties and all of the forties.

Leon Claxton was not only a great showman and show producer, but he was also a good citizen of his new hometown of Tampa. Not only a good citizen of Tampa, but of the entire United States over which he had traveled so many miles. He and his wife, Gwendolyn, built and operated a thirty-four unit Motor Motel, Claxton Manor. Leon was survived by his wife, two daughters and a son. He was interred in Shady Grove Cemetery, Tampa, on November 18, 1967.

LOU DUFOUR
The following was written by Lou Dufour.

"In my teenage years I toured with the Foley & Burk Shows, the 101 Ranch and the Barnum & Bailey Circus.

"At the age of 23 in association with an actor, Lew Tilford, we organized in 1919 the Robinson's United Shows, retitled it Dufuor & Tilford Shows in 1920; it was a three-car gilly show.

"Buying out Tilford in 1920, I went on rails in 1921 — as the Dufour Exposition Shows. In 1923 I secured the Veal Brothers Show, which enlarged my show to 25 railroad cars. Some of my concessionaires became carnival owners; namely, Patty Conklin, John Marks, Heath Brothers, Bobby Gloth, Max Gruber, Sammy Laurence, Art Lewis and Bill Stone; the late Frank Miller operated the cook house and the privilege car.

"The show was hit by a cyclone at Fitchburg, Massachusetts in 1924, and practically demolished. I decided that while the carnival owner got the glory, it was the concessionaires with the show who got the money.

"After retiring from this field of endeavor, I originated "THE UNBORN" back in 1927 and at one time had twenty (20) units operating at parks, beaches, and all the leading fairs in the United States and Canada.

"In association with Terry Turner (an R.K.O. executive) in 1931 I brought to this country from Africa the UBANGI SAVAGES, opening the troupe in the 5000-seat Massbaum Theatre at Philadelphia, then playing a circuit of theatres, before going on tour with Ringling Brothers Circus.

"We also did the WARDEN LEWIS E. LAWES SHOW "SING SING."

"For several years I had been identified with and financially interested in fairs in the United States and Europe. Remembering my first successful venture as a young man at the Panama Pacific Expo at San Francisco, California, in 1915.

"In association with the late Joe Rogers, we participated at a Century of Progress, Chicago 1933-1934, and have figured conspicuously on midways at Brussels, Belgium, 1935; California Pacific Expo, San Diego, California, 1935; and in 1936 and 1937 participating simultaneously at Texas Centennial, Dallas, Texas; Frontier Centennial, Fort Worth, Texas (with Billy Rose), and the Great Lakes Expo., Cleveland, Ohio; The Golden Gate Expo, San Francisco, California, 1939 and 1940; and New York World's Fair 1939 and 1940.

"Our outstanding presentation at the Chicago Fair was the Hawaiian Village. Lee McCayer had his 25 Hawaiians, musicians and dancers and Selvano's Bands supplied the music for dancing. We had a cast of sixty people; FAITH BACON was the Star of the Show.

Lou Dufour, Carnival Historian

"The HAWAIIAN VILLAGE was an artistic success but made no money; but at least we were able to break even.

"The money makers were THE TROPICAL VILLAGE called DARKEST AFRICA, THE LIFE MUSEUM and the COCOANUT GROVE, and were all smash hits earning $240,000 in profits, a sizeable fortune in those depression years.

"At the New York World's Fair with an investment in excess of three hundred thousand dollars, we presented JOHN HIX "STRANGE AS IT SEEMS," PHILLIPS LORD'S "GANG BUSTERS," SEMINOLE VILLAGE, WE HUMANS, NATURE'S MISTAKES, CRIMSON TOWERS, FAKETORIUM, and the famous RONDERVOO that grossed over a half million dollars. Their combined gross was $2,400,000, a tremendous sum in those prewar, pre-inflation years.

"We believed in diversification of investments; when concessionaires couldn't cut it, we would buy them out. We wound up with 38 attractions with Billy Rose at Forth Worth and at the Dallas Fair, including the STREETS OF PARIS.

"For the next fifteen years, I was identified in the motion picture field and a legitimate show producer.

"Patty Conklin, a close friend for many years, lured me back into outdoor show business. In 1955 I began producing shows at Riverview Park, Chicago; Belmont Park, Montreal; Palisades Park, New Jersey; Velare Brothers at Long Beach, California and Ocean Park, California; also had units on various carnival shows.

"For the past fourteen years I have produced two or three shows each year for the Conklin Midway at Toronto Canadian National Exhibition.

"At the New York World's Fair, 1965, I had a few profitable concessions with Archie Gayer.

"I am a member of the Missouri Athletic Club and the Variety Club of St. Louis, American Legion, Masonic, Past President of the S.L.A., Past President of the International Association of Showmen and President Emeritus of the S.L.A. St. Louis Chapter and a member of 15 Showmen's Clubs."

CLIFFORD CLARENCE (SPECS) GROSCURTH

Clifford Clarence Groscurth was born April 12, 1909. He began to wear eyeglasses when he was seven and acquired the nickname of "Specs." Very few people call him anything else. Specs also fell in love with carnival business while he was in grade school and spent more time reading the Billboard than he did his textbooks. He is one of the few owners of midways who never worked on concessions. He started as a ticket seller and worked his way up in the business until he now owns almost fifty riding devices and transportation for them.

In 1924 the fifteen year old boy hitchhiked from his home town, Owensboro, Kentucky, to Evansville, Indiana, and joined the L. J. Heth Shows. His first job was selling tickets for "Skidoo" Wilson's Jolly Dixie, Fat Girl Show. For over twenty years he traveled with other people's midways as ticket seller, talker, promoter and independent show owner. He got his first midway show, a girl show, on W. G. Wade Shows in 1937 and had several shows with Max Goodman season of 1945. (He bought "Doc" Friedman's Unborn Show, which had been with Goodman since the carnival was formed in 1937.)

In 1946, Specs and his wife Esther, started their own Blue Grass Shows with two second-hand rides. They spent all their cash for those rides and didn't have enough to purchase trucks to haul them. It was midseason before they bought semi-trailers, but still rented tractors to pull the trailers for several more weeks. They got those tractors, more rides, more trailers and more tractors until they built the show into one of the truly great motorized midways. The show plays some of the biggest and best fairs along its ten thousand mile route through thirteen states. It is one of the best-lighted and decorated carnivals in America, as Specs likes to maintain an attractive midway for his patrons. For several years his trucks and trailers were decorated with scrolls and art-work like circus wagons, but circus painters are difficult to find now.

Col. C. C. Groscurth has two winter quarters. He maintains his old, well-fenced quarters in Owensboro and keeps quite a lot of equipment stored there; but in recent years he has built a huge, modern quarters in the Tampa Bay area of Florida. This Tampa Quarters is second only to the Gooding Quarters in Columbus, Ohio, but probably does have to share the second place with the Lloyd Hilligoss quarters in California. The Blue Grass Shows is the only carnival with two well-equipped winter quarters, and they are both used.

The Blue Grass Shows plays several weeks of good county fair dates in Florida each winter month, then some of the heavier equipment is "deadheaded" to the Kentucky quarters as the lighter rides play a route of shopping center dates on the trip North.

C. C. SPECS GROSCURTH. Courtesy Blue Grass Shows.

Latter part of May or early in June the entire show opens for its route of big fairs and celebrations. Specs has some contracts awarded for periods of ten years — that should give some hint of the esteem with which he is regarded by fair committees.

Specs Groscurth will tell the truth regardless of the consequences to himself. He is noted for his honesty on and off his midway, and he tries to live in a way that will be an example to others. He and Mrs. Groscurth attend church services as regularly as it is possible to do when they may have a four hundred mile drive to make before they get to their next date. They are liberal in their support of religious and charitable organizations and drives.

Colonel Groscurth is also proud of having been elected as president of three of the Showmen's Clubs in the United States. He has served terms as president of the Tampa and St. Louis Clubs and Showmen's League of America. He was the fiftieth president of the latter club which had William (Buffalo Bill) Cody

as its first president. Mrs. Groscurth served a year as president of the Ladies Auxiliary of the Greater Tampa Showmen's Association.

Specs is a believer in giving his patrons good, clean entertainment at reasonable prices. He works with local merchants in many towns on his route in promoting special days on the midway with reduced prices. The merchants issue coupons to their customers which can be used on the midway for a reduction of price for the attraction. Where used, a million or more such coupons are distributed on the assumption that a definite percentage of them will be brought to the show grounds and used. They are.

Mr. and Mrs. Clifford Clarence Groscurth and their Blue Grass Shows are a credit to the collective amusement industry. An industry that has moved a long way towards respectability and acceptance which the Groscurths and the Blue Grass Shows have long since attained.

JOHN L. KEEF

John L. Keef was born in Nashville, Tennessee on June 2, 1909. He says that his father was a horse trader who died in 1918. This wasn't an unusual occupation in Middle Tennessee early in this century. Many men made good incomes from horse trading in those days as most horse owners fancied themselves good traders, and would make wild deals with the professional traders. Young Johnny Keef started with carnivals soon after his twelfth birthday working for concessionaire Jimmie Merritt on H. V. Rogers' Sunshine Exposition Shows.

In the next twenty-five years, Keef worked with such shows as L. J. Heth, C. D. Scott, Page & Wilson, Rogers Greater, Reading's United, Playland, Shan Wilcox, Regal Exposition and Max Goodman's Imperial. On March 15, 1946, he opened his own Capital City Shows in Nashville, and toured Tennessee, Kentucky, Alabama and Georgia. This small show soon grew into a medium-sized motorized carnival and now tours with twenty-one rides and six to ten shows and funhouses. Practically the same territory is played each season as Johnny Keef has built a good reputation with the fair committees on his route.

He played his first July 4th spot in Stearns, Kentucky in 1946 with a formal contract. Since then, his show has played the date every year with one handshake as a contract. He also has four fairs on his route that have been played for many years with only

a handshake for the contract. Johnny's slogan is, "The South's Cleanest Midway," and he says every word is true. As a visitor to his midway at some of his fair dates, this writer can vouch for the veracity of this statement. Although his is a carnival catering to the family trade, Keef was one of the first owners of a medium-sized show to carry spectacular rides on his route. He has carried such rides as a Rotor, Trabant, a Tip-Top, a Skydiver, etc. over the route without cutting too deeply into the gross of his standard riding devices.

His is a family show operated by the family for family trade. His wife Evelyn, his wife's parents, Mr. and Mrs. C. C. Wills, and his daughters and their husbands all help in some phase of the midway activities. Johnny Keef wasn't born in the business, but he started young, and says that he could never be happy in other fields. He is more optimistic than some operators regarding the future of collective amusement business. He says as long as we have more children coming along each year, carnival business will continue to be good. Johnny Keef starts his fifty-second year in carnival business this spring and is as enthusiastic about his chosen profession as he was when he joined that first midway back in 1921.

A visit to the Capital City Shows has been much changed last two seasons as Evelyn Keef died two years ago, and Johnny now handles much of the office work himself.

WILLIAM ABRAHAM KING (SNAKE KING)

William Abraham King was a small man in size, but he loomed large over the collective amusement industry for some forty years. For Snake King, as he was known to everyone in the carnival field, was the one dependable supplier of rattlesnakes and reptiles to that industry. Later in his career, he branched out into the import business and supplied wild beasts of every sort for shows. In the thirties, he owned and operated his own circus for a short time featuring his son Manuel, the world's youngest wild animal trainer. Manuel was working an act of full-grown black-maned African lions when he was only eight years old. He was no taller than his big cats, and his act was sensational.

William Abraham King was born in New York in 1875. He moved to Brownsville, Texas in 1904, and started selling snakes he caught himself to street vendors who used the reptiles for "ballyhoo" purposes. He met Manuela Cortez, a direct descendent of the conqueror of Mexico, in Brownsville, and they were married. His reptile business grew as carnival business grew. At one time, Snake boasted that he kept ten thousand rattlers in stock at his "snake ranch" at all times. He had many full-time snake catchers working for him, and his stories of snake-catching expeditions into the bandit-infested regions of Mexico were exciting. He also established a laboratory for extracting venom and built up quite a big business in the sale of this commodity.

Snake King retired from active business and moved to Mexico City, but had to return to Brownsville for medical attention. He died in that Valley City of Texas on November 10, 1952. He was buried there on November 10th. This man who had been bitten by innumerable rattlesnakes died of natural causes. (It was estimated he had been bitten 200 times.)

CAPT. DAVID LATLIP

David Latlip was born in Waterville, Maine, August 14, 1885. He left school at the start of the Spanish American War to enlist in the armed forces. After the war, he started in show business as "the youngest net high diver" with H. H. Linn's Variety Show. He dived into a net outside the theater as a free act. The next season, Latlip started with Herbert Perry's Variety Show, but left them and joined Walter L. Main Circus. He stayed with this circus for two seasons billed as "the Lady with the Auburn Hair." He dived into a net from top of a high pole on the circus grounds after the parade. He then joined Welch Brothers Circus for two seasons as a high diver and ticket seller.

He closed the 1905 season with the J. Frank Hatch Carnival Company, and toured the South with Sam West Amusement Company in winter. Spent next two seasons with C. W. Parker's carnivals, with winter tours on other midways. He was with the J. L. Landes Carnival Company in 1908, and formed his own carnival for 1909 season. Next five years he was with the Hall & Latlip Shows. 1916 he helped organize the Harry Lukens Carnival Company, and the following year put his own show out again. The Latlip Shows toured under family management until 1942.

His wife Marion, a former high diver, mothered five daughters and a son for him. The five daughters were all aerialists, and Capt. Latlip's greatest hobby was his fine free acts for his midway. His daughter Rita also attended to many of the management and office details of the show. After she was killed in a traffic accident, Latlip never seemed to enjoy show business as much as he had in the past. After a long illness, Capt. David Latlip died in Pinecrest Sanitarium in his home town of Charleston, West Virginia, September 5, 1944. Survived by his wife, four daughters and a son, David, Jr.

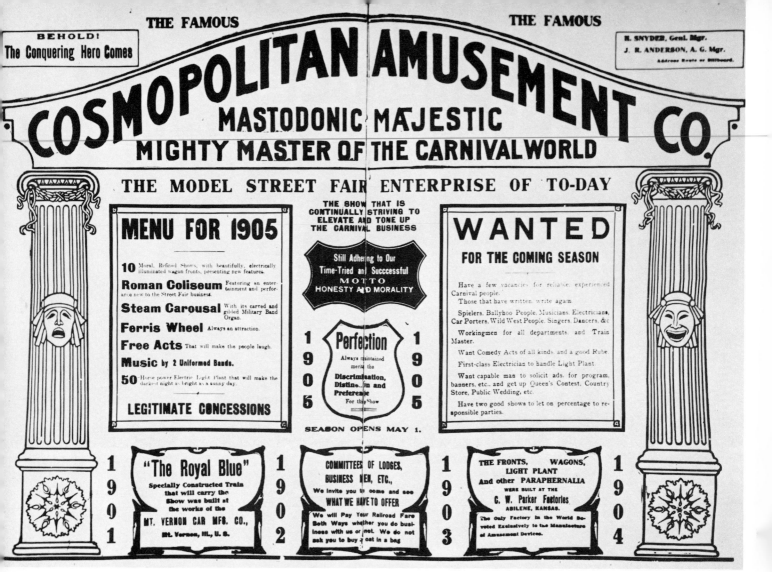

THE FAMOUS   THE FAMOUS

R. SNYDER, Genl. Mgr.
J. R. ANDERSON, A. G. Mgr.
Address Route or Billboard.

COSMOPOLITAN AMUSEMENT CO.

MASTODONIC MAJESTIC

MIGHTY MASTER OF THE CARNIVAL WORLD

THE MODEL STREET FAIR ENTERPRISE OF TO-DAY

THE SHOW THAT IS CONTINUALLY STRIVING TO ELEVATE AND TONE UP THE CARNIVAL BUSINESS

MENU FOR 1905

10 Moral, Refined Shows, with beautifully, electrically illuminated wagon fronts, presenting new features.

Roman Coliseum Featuring an entertainment and performance new to the Street Fair business.

Steam Carousal With its carved and gilded Military Band Organ.

Ferris Wheel Always an attraction.

Free Acts That will make the people laugh.

Music by 2 Uniformed Bands.

50 Horse power Electric Light Plant that will make the darkest night as bright as a sunny day.

LEGITIMATE CONCESSIONS

Still Adhering to Our Time-Tried and Successful
MOTTO
HONESTY AND MORALITY

Perfection
Always maintained merits the **Discrimination, Distinction and Preference** For the Show

1905   1905

SEASON OPENS MAY 1.

WANTED

FOR THE COMING SEASON

Have a few vacancies for reliable, experienced Carnival people.

Those that have written, write again.

Spielers, Ballyhoo People, Musicians, Electricians, Car Porters, Wild West People, Singers, Dancers, &c.

Workingmen for all departments, and Train Master.

Want Comedy Acts of all kinds, and a good Rube.

First-class Electrician to handle Light Plant.

Want capable man to solicit ads. for program, banners, etc., and get up Queen's Contest, Country Store, Public Wedding, etc.

Have two good shows to let on percentage to responsible parties.

1901

"The Royal Blue"
Specially Constructed Train that will carry the Show was built at the works of the
MT. VERNON CAR MFS. CO.,
Mt. Vernon, Ill., U. S.

1902

COMMITTEES OF LODGES, BUSINESS MEN, ETC.,
We invite you to come and see
WHAT WE HAVE TO OFFER
We will Pay Your Railroad Fare Both Ways whether you do business with us or not. We do not ask you to buy a cat in a bag

1903

THE FRONTS, WAGONS, LIGHT PLANT And other PARAPHERNALIA
were built at the
C. W. Parker Factories
ABILENE, KANSAS.
The Only Factory in the World Devoted Exclusively to the Manufacture of Amusement Devices.

1904

C. A. WORTHAM SHOW PERSONNEL, 1921. Edmonton, Canada.

MAX LINDERMAN

Max Linderman was born in Russia in 1886. He came to the United States when he was still a boy. His first show business experience was gained at Coney Island. In 1912 he was in partnership with Phil Isser operating concessions at fairs along the East Coast. He was a co-owner of a show bearing the World of Mirth title for two or three years starting in 1919, and was co-owner of the Boyd & Linderman Shows in 1923.

When Frank Bergan and Julius Griffel bought Willie Glick's interest in the Bernardi Greater Shows early in 1930, they brought Linderman, who was a relative of Griffel, into the partnership as manager of the carnival. They used the Bernardi title through the 1932 season. World of Mirth title was put on the equipment starting in 1933. Linderman was manager of this carnival until his death. He built the show back into a first class carnival by the end of the thirties, and had taken several good fair dates from Johnny J. Jones and other big shows.

Max Linderman died of a heart attack in Augusta, Georgia, on November 4, 1944. His remains were shipped to New York where the National Showmen's Association handled funeral and burial arrangements. Max was past president of the club and had served four years on its board.

ROBERT L. LOHMAR

Robert L. (Bob) Lohmar was born in Donnellson, Iowa, on January 22, 1884. His family moved to Peoria, Illinois, and Lohmar attended public schools there. In 1900 he worked as a roustabout and candy butcher with Harris Nickel Plate Circus. His father wanted Bob to help in the family grocery, which he did part-time for next seven years. He engaged in insurance business three years starting in 1909. Then in 1912, he went back into show business to stay. He joined Wortham & Allen carnival company as promoter and general agent.

When the Wortham & Allen partnership split up in 1914, Lohmar stayed with Tom W. Allen Shows. Bob was already courting C. W. Parker's secretary, Mary Rhodes, and he stayed with Parker's son-in-law, Allen. Lohmar and Mary Rhodes wre married in 1915, a marriage that was to last until his death forty-three years later. He rejoined the Barnum & Bailey Circus in 1916 as contracting agent for three years. The next three years he was with the Velare Brothers on the Nat Reiss Shows.

In 1922 Lohmar joined the Morris & Castle Shows as general agent and stayed with that show through its last season in 1936. He had been part owner of the show, known in its last three seasons as the United States of America. It was on the United Shows that he was able to indulge in one of his best-liked hobbies, woodworking. He designed the new fronts for the 1934 season, and worked with Joe McKennon's tools during the construction period. He stayed with the Castle show equipment when the Hennies Brothers took it over at end of 1936 season. He was Hennies Brothers' general agent for the 1937 and 1938 seasons.

In 1939, Bob became a carnival manager for the first time. The Amusement Corporation of America retired the Grubergs and sent Lohmar over as manager of the Rubin & Cherry Shows. He remained in this position through the 1942 season. He then spent one year working for the United States Chamber of Commerce out of the Washington, D.C. office. Al Wagner engaged him as general agent for the new railroad show which Lohmar named the Cavalcade of America. (He had coined the United Shows of America title for the old Castle show also.) He booked the route for the Cavalcade for both 1944 and 1945, but joined Max Goodman's Wonder Shows of America midseason of the latter year. The Cavalcade routes those two war years were noted for the "Lohmar jumps" as Bob loved to lay out routes with long rail moves between towns.

He stayed with Goodman through the 1946 season and then moved to the Royal American, where he stayed until his death. Rotund, cherub-faced, as he has been described, Bob Lohmar was one of the best-liked men in carnival business. Ride hands and bank presidents, "roughies" and fair managers, "mitt readers" and newspaper editors, "gal" show dancers and railroad presidents all knew Bob and considered him a friend. He was father confessor and advisor to hundreds of carnival people. He could have stepped into any one of dozens of jobs that would have given him more security and salary, but he loved carnivals and carnival people.

Bob was always conservative in his dress with suits of blue or grey. His one affectation was white piped vests, but on Bob they were correct. In his later years, he carried two big trunks of wardrobe, but he was not so fortunate in his youth. One of his first winter jobs in show business was as agent for Paderewski. One of his duties was to stand in the front lobby on concert nights dressed in white tie and tails furnished by the company. Bob, a lady's man, had found favor in the eyes of a young soprano appearing in the show. Unfortunately the young lady was considered by Hans Schroader, Paderewski's manager, as his own girl friend. He accosted Lohmar in the lobby one evening and became violent in his denunciation of the young agent. Bob quit literally on that spot. He removed the company's "soup and fish," flung the dress clothing at the irate manager and stalked out onto the street in his long underwear. He walked two blocks to his hotel in twenty below zero weather. However, this show of temper was an unusual occurrence with this patient man.

Robert L. Lohmar, lifetime showman, family man and amateur cook, died on May 29, 1958 in a Peoria, Illinois, hospital where he had been brought several weeks before, after he suffered a stroke in Tampa. He, a fifty-year Mason, was buried with full Masonic honors in Morton, Illinois, on June 2, 1958. The Sedlmayrs, father and son, and four other friends and brothers from the Royal American Shows were the pallbearers. This veteran of fifty-eight years with outdoor shows, this man who knew how to live and enjoy living, was sadly missed, as no one could fill Bob Lohmar's place on the carnival midways.

D. C. (MAC) McDANIELS

ROCKY ROAD TO DUBLIN. Courtesy Albert Conover.

When D. C. McDaniels died in Spartanburg, South Carolina, on October 29, 1933, he had worked with collective amusement organizations for thirty-three years. Born in 1882, he started with carnivals when he was eighteen years old. He had been a ticket seller and talker with the Gaskill and Gaskill-Munday Shows. Later he worked with the Ferari Shows, Tubby Snyder's Shows, Wortham and Allen and Tom W. Allen. He was special agent under Wilbur S. Cherry on the Sol & Rubin Shows, and was the builder with the different C. W. Parker Carnival Units where he built fun houses. He bought the first fun house, the Joy Ship, Hyla F. Maynes built in 1911, and fall and winter of 1921-22 he built the Rocky Road to Dublin attraction for C. A. Wortham's own show.

In 1916, Wortham had a front, the Pike's Peak, built for the '49 Camp; and in 1917 Joe Conley built a ride called King Solomon's Mine and used this front for it. McDaniel worked the ride for Wortham until the "Little Giant" got his investment back. Then he discarded the ride because it took too long to load and unload from one side of the donkey carts. In 1921, McDaniels with Conley assisting built a new version of this ride and called it the Rocky Road to Dublin. Carts pulled by donkeys were routed around back of the attraction's front along roughly built wooden tracks. The carts on this ride could be loaded from both sides and capacity was increased.

McDaniels played the Toronto Exhibition in fall of 1922 with this ride on Wortham's Worlds Best Shows. He played Toronto again with it in 1924 with the Johnny J. Jones Exposition, and played the Western Canada Class A Circuit of fair that same year with Jones. The McDaniels family booked the ride and "Gyp's" Penny Arcade which they bought in 1925, with Willie Glick and Max Linderman's Bernardi Shows, Brown & Dyer Shows and John M.

Sheesley Shows in the late twenties and early thirties. They were with Rubin and Cherry Shows in 1923, and carried their attractions to Cuba the winter of 1927.

They were back with Rubin & Cherry when McDaniels died in 1933, but had already booked their equipment with the Royal American for the 1934 season. Mrs. McDaniels honored this contract and stayed with Royal American that one season. McDaniels probably didn't leave his widow, Bertha (Gypsy), too much cash back in those depression days; but he did leave her well provided for as the two attractions were readily booked on almost any midway. "Gyp" has never remarried and still operates the penny arcade with the James E. Strates Shows.

JOHN H. MARKS

John H. Marks was born in Greece in 1891. A neighbor of his in Greece was another future American carnival owner; James E. Strates. Marks came to the United States when he was seventeen and immediately found work in a restaurant at ten dollars per month. After a year on this job, he was making top salary of twenty-five dollars per month. He had saved from this salary though, as he opened his own restaurant in Richmond, Virginia in 1911. "Full meals 20 cents," "coffee, roll and doughnut 5 cents" and "dozen oysters on half shell 25 cents" were a few of John's specials in this restaurant. He made money and was looking for a chance to expand when a friend told him about carnival "Cookhouses."

He built himself a good cookhouse and joined Schaffer's midway in Pottsville, Pennsylvania. One of his first customers in this new cookhouse was his old friend, Strates, from Greece. Jimmy Strates was wrestling in the "At" Show on the back end of the midway. By 1923, Marks had bought a merry-go-round and a string of concessions; and in 1927, he framed his own carnival with L. T. Stone as a partner. In 1928 he bought Stone's interest in the midway. His was a "gilly show" operation with three rides and four or five shows. In 1932, he bought three more rides and ten new GMC trucks. Although he did

have some trucks, as the show grew he continued to "Gilly" most of it in baggage cars until the forties.

He married in 1933 and his wife, Elizabeth, helped him on their midway. He established winter quarters in Richmond and wintered there every year except 1942. Had to go elsewhere that year as suitable quarters were not available. He bought land and built his own Richmond quarters afterwards. When he gave up the baggage car gilly-type operations in the forties, he wanted to build wagon-type show fronts on his semi-trailers. Most carnival owners, both railroad and truck operators, scoffed at him. John Marks visited the World of Mirth Shows, a railroad show, and came away with Max Linderman's builder, Charlie Kidder. The fronts were built on semis. Former builder, Joe McKennon, who was now operating his own tented dramatic shows, advised.

John H. Marks died in a Richmond, Virginia hospital on March 22, 1968. Almost blind, he had relinquished control of his show to others along with one of the best truck show routes on the East Coast. When Marks contracted a fair, he kept it. His operations were such that the fair committees kept him at their annual. Dell and Travers Shows are the successors to the Marks Shows. John Marks was buried in Forest Lawn at Richmond.

CARMELO GLORIOSI (TONY PARADISE)

CARMELO GLORIOSI (TONY PARADISE). Courtesy Amusement Business Photograph.

Carmelo Gloriosi is a native of New York, but ran away from home when he was fifteen and hitchhiked to Texas. This was back in the middle thirties and jobs were hard to find. Young Gloriosi changed his name to Tony Paradise and landed a job with the Roy Gray Shows selling tickets. Jess Wrigley

hired him but wouldn't let him take over a job as talker. Doc Waddell was on the Gray show as press agent that season and pulled one of his front page-getting stunts. The show had a "geek" attraction on the midway. One day this imitation wild man ran out onto the midway in his wild man's costume with a huge rattlesnake in each hand and one clasped in his teeth. Probably a good thing this didn't happen the first night the young hitchhiker was on the show; carnival business might have lost one of its best talkers before he started.

When Wrigley wouldn't let "Tony" have a talking job the following spring, Paradise went to the Sheesley Show where he landed a job as Emcee in the Minstrel Show. He had emcee and talking jobs on W. C. Kaus, Johnny J. Jones, Dodson, World of Mirth and John Marks Shows before he went into the Army for two year's overseas wartime service. When he was discharged he worked with Strates, King Reid and Reithoffer Shows before getting a job as talker on the front of Leon Claxton's Harlem to Havana Show, on Royal American Shows. In recent years he has had the front of shows with Strates, Al Kunz and other midways.

Tony is famous among outdoor showmen for his many changes of wardrobe he carries in his trunks in the "front wagon." He will make an opening, step off bally into the wagon or truck and come back out with complete change of wardrobe. He makes the change from his hundred or so suits and sequined jackets while one record is playing.

JOSEPH A. PEARL

"It's a pleasure to do business with you;" this pleasant remark has been uttered over four million times to over thirty thousand carnival troupers by Joe Pearl, carnivaldom's best-liked devotee, during his forty-eight-year tour of duty as mailman and Billboard agent on the larger collective amusement organizations. In this forty-eight years, this big man has walked at least a hundred thousand miles on his midway routes, handled not less than six million pieces of mail and sold more than two hundred thousand Billboards and Amusement Business, the

outdoor amusement business trade journals. Now pickup man, mailman, Amusement Business agent and boss of ticket takers for spring still dates on the Royal American Shows, Joe Pearl's route extends from Tampa, Florida along the show's exhibition route to Calgary, Canada and back to Tampa; a total distance of some twelve thousand miles traveled during the thirty-week season.

No matter how much rain and mud, hot weather and dust or cold weather and illness the show may encounter, Joe Pearl is always on time with his deliveries and his cheery greeting. This writer, who has known Joe for almost forty years, does not know of one instance where the big hearty fellow has ever really lost his temper. Sure, he gets out of sorts and complains sometimes; any carnival trouper would have to be a saint not to "bellyache" a little once in a while. But never does he get so mad that he "blasts" as some individuals connected with the business are prone to do. Now, this man is not a saint, he just likes his job and people and tries to get along with both.

Joseph A. Pearl was born in Montgomery, Alabama on August 15, 1902. His first introduction to amusement business was with a concession stand in a Battle Creek, Michigan Amusement Park in 1917 and 1918. He joined the T. A. Wolfe Superior Shows in 1919 as a side show ticket seller. The next two years was spent selling tickets with the Gentry-Patterson Circus and the Walter L. Main Circus. He spent 1922 and 1923 with the 101 Ranch Wild West Show as ticket seller and side show talker. He joined the Rubin & Cherry Shows in 1924, as mail agent, ticket seller and talker and stayed with the Rubin Show through the 1932 season. The next ten years was spent on the Johnny J. Exposition doing the same work as he had done with the Rubin &

JOE CARRIES THE MAIL. Joe Pearl on Royal American Shows. Courtesy Amusement Business Photograph.

Cherry Shows. From 1943 through 1948, he was with Al Wagner's Cavalcade of Amusements, and then went to Johnny Denton's Gold Medal Shows for three seasons. Next, he worked with Specs Groscurth's Blue Grass Shows for five years and seasons 1957 and 1958 were spent with Oscar Buck's Model Shows while Buck was on rails. Then in 1959 Joe joined the Royal American and for the first time in forty years sold no tickets nor did any talking. Joe likes the Royal American and its people, and if his feet hold out, he hopes to spend another ten years at least with that great show.

You know, back in the "good old days" there were few real "Sunday School" shows. On the others, ticket sellers and such got very little if any salary. They had to "make" it from the show's patrons. Some of the money handlers carried their proclivity for illicit gain with them when they joined the higher class shows. Two of Joe Pearl's favorite stories have to do with this unenlightened period in outdoor amusement business. He tells them as follows.

"When I started selling tickets on the Walter L. Main Circus, I told Mr. James Shopshire (Side Show Manager) I was an 'experienced ticket seller.' He started me on a ticket box and in about an hour he came by and I asked him, 'how much does this job pay?' He stared at me and replied, 'Young man you lied to me, you said you were an experienced ticket seller, I expect you to take care of me.' And, I had to come up with money for him as long as I was over there."

"The Johnny J. Jones Exposition was showing Ft. Myers, Florida. I was selling tickets on the wild animal circus. Three men came up to me and bought three tickets and went in. About five minutes later, William Hilliard (Publicity man) came up and said, 'those three men who just went in, call them back and refund their money, they are Henry Ford, Harvey Firestone and Thomas Edison.' I said, 'call them back, nothing doing. I just shorted them a dollar on their tickets.'"

The Johnny J. Shows was getting to be a "Sunday School" show in those days, but old habits were hard to break among some of the employees. Joe Pearl doesn't sell tickets anymore, he has too much to do with the mail and other jobs on the Royal American. He turned "Sunday School" many years ago. He explains it this way, "I found that the money I made 'shorting the public,' never did me any good. I was always broke at the end of the season and had to "scuff" all winter. When I started being careful how I handled the patron's money, I found that I always had a little of my own laid away for the winter." Joe Pearl, another old-time Carnival Trouper (I use capitals advisedly), has many stories to tell about the old days, but like all of the modern showmen does not long to go back to them. He enjoys life too much as it is.

A CROWDED WALL. Four men riding on a motordrome wall at same time. Courtesy Earl Purtle.

In 1913 a new attraction began to appear on the carnival midways. Joe Conley built a new motordrome for a feature show with Rice and Dore Water Carnival and the Parker factory started building them. Other show owners and builders began to build the new thrill shows and then started recruiting competent motorcycle riders to work in them. These were not the later silo-drome straight wall structures, as the walls were slanted. Bicycle riders had been working in this type drome for some time, but not the higher speed motorcycles. For the latter, much heavier structures had to be built.

In the spring of 1914, a young motorcycle rider from Kansas City, Missouri was persuaded by C. W. Parker to take one of the new attractions on the road with the B. R. Parker Shows. This nineteen-year-old boy was a good rider and loved motorcycles. He had never ridden on a wall before, but soon was doing a creditable performance. That year, young Earl B. Purtle started a forty-eight-year career as performer, owner and operator of motordromes. This season, 1970 will be Purtle's fifty-seventh season in outdoor amusement business.

Earl B. Purtle, who was born on his father's farm

near Kansas City, Missouri carried his brother, Warner Purtle on the road that 1914 season. Their motorcycles were 1914 model 2-cylinder, seven horsepower Excelsiors with 2¼" x 28" tires. They were equipped with special short coupled frames and rigid forks. They also had one 1913 special Hedstron Indian machine. The slant wall drome, which had been built the previous year in the Parker factory, was fifty feet in diameter. Purtle had a very successful season with Parker and stayed with dromes on Jarves & Seeman, W. W. Brundage, Ed L. Heinz and L. J. Heth Shows. He spent five years with Heth before moving on to Morris & Castle, Dodson's World's Fair, George L. Dobyn's, Melville-Reiss, Bernardi and the World of Mirth Shows. He and his wife, Ethel, stayed with World of Mirth until 1942, when a minor federal bureaucrat in Maine refused to allow the drome to work because of wartime restrictions. No other drome operator was closed down. Earl and Ethel had a big group of lions working in the drome, so they framed an animal show for the duration. They

booked at Palisades Park on the Jersey side of the Hudson and stayed for nine years. Their last motordrome operations were on the Cetlin & Wilson Shows where they stayed for ten years. They quit the road in 1962.

In addition to the drome, they had operated rides since the early thirties. So, they kept those rides in Richmond, Virginia, the spring of 1963, and began booking them on shopping center lots in and near Richmond. They now have ten rides so booked. The Purtles, like all ex-troupers, are not too happy off the road; but they realize the shortage of competent labor makes road tours an unpleasant experience instead of the happy carefree circuits of those enjoyed by the troupers of thirty years ago. Ethel and Earl visit with every show that comes close to Richmond and then go to the Tampa Bay Area of Florida where thousands of midway nomads spend their winter months. There in the Showmen's club rooms, they meet all their old friends and relive many incidents of a long and happy midway career.

JACK B. RHODES (RHOADES)

Jack B. Rhodes, "Chew of Tobacco" as he was known by thousands of carnival troupers, was a small man in size but a giant in his accomplishments on a midway. During the Morris & Castle Shows engagements, none of the thousands who bought their popcorn from the little man with a big lump in his clean-shaven jaw, realized they were doing business with the one individual who literally speaking held the movement of the entire midway in the palm of his hand. Few carnival people, that last season of the Castle Show in 1936 when it was called the United Shows of America, as they spoke to "Chew of Tobacco" or stopped to chat with "Ma" Rhodes as she sold tickets for the Whip, knew that this was the indispensable family on that mighty midway. If, in the winter time, they were fortunate enough to be invited to visit the Rhodes family in their small home in Shreveport, they would have been startled to learn the real importance of this gentle little man, with the ever-present big cud of tobacco, to that huge show sleeping out in the State Fairgrounds.

Jack Rhodes performed all of his indispensable duties away from the public sight. In the winters, he was superintendent of construction. This man who had built and repaired more show wagons than any other man who ever lived, stated without boasting, "Give me fifteen good men and I can build and paint

every wagon, front and property needed for a forty-car carnival in five months." Jack meant that he could build all of this property new. As he stated further, "Give me four good men, besides myself, and I can repair and rebuild all wagons and properties used on a forty-car show in three months." This he could do and did every winter. He repaired the wagons so well in winter quarters, that the Castle show carried no regular shop wagon on the road, as the breakdowns were too few to warrant the expense of such a wagon.

"Chew of Tobacco's" other job was one not often viewed by the public. He put the show on the lot and took it off. Many lot superintendents make that claim today, but they have experienced men to do the work. Jack Rhodes had worked with many circuses back in the latter part of the nineteenth century before he started work with Dan R. Robinson on the first Robinson Carnival Company. With that show, K. G. Barkoot Shows, Frisco Exposition and C. A. Wortham Shows, Jack had continued to use horses to pull wagons on the lot and spot them. But, a new motive force replaced those horses in the twenties; track-laying, gasoline-powered tractors were taking the place of the horse on the carnival showgrounds. These local owned "Cats," with their untrained in carnival method drivers, meant that the "lot man's" duties became more arduous.

With them the "lot man" must walk in front of the tractor and guide the driver as each of the one hundred twelve heavy wagons were pulled down the length of the twelve hundred foot midway and "spotted in" on its location. Sometimes, if the driver was competent, the superintendent could ride the back of the tractor back for another wagon without risking a collision with other equipment. Some of the local "Cat Skinners" were not capable of doing this, and had to be guided back to the next wagon. This writer has vivid remembrance of Jack Rhodes, his small body bent forward with age, hurrying down the midway with a firmly held flashlight as he guided the first wagon off of some midwestern fairgrounds about one o'clock Sunday morning. The pace would slow a little, but at daybreak, Jack would still be leading that tractor as it pulled another wagon off the grounds to the waiting lines of trucks which moved them to the train. As dawn broke the tractor could move faster to pick up the scattered wagons remaining on the deserted grounds. There were no impediments lying around now. It was all loaded in the big wagons and the tractor could make "bee line routes" on each trip.

Jack Rhodes disdained riding on back of a tractor, "that's for the kids to do," he often explained to the one-year assistant of his. So as the pace accelerated with the coming of daylight, the little man's chew of tobacco stood out more prominently from his pale face as he hurried down to hook the tractor to the last wagon off the lot. As this wagon, "the hot wagon," rolled down the street behind a truck, Jack was riding in the cab of that truck. At the "crossing," he would remark to Trainmaster, Grant Chandler, "It's all here," as he hurried down the lines of loaded flat cars to his stateroom on the sleeping cars where "Ma" Rhodes had a bucket of hot water waiting for his sponge bath before breakfast.

The Rhodes couple stayed with the Castle equipment on the Hennies Shows for a few years but soon retired to their little home in Shreveport. Both are gone now, but their place could never be filled if by some impossible chance the midway operations of yesteryear should return.

BILL RICE

Courtesy Bill Rice, Jr.

Warren Hoyt Rice was born in 1876 in Kingston, Pennsylvania. Eight years later, the year the young Ringling Brothers opened their first tented circus, this son of sober church-going people saw his first circus, the Walter L. Main Show. Before that circus day in Kingston was ended, Warren Rice had decided that he would be an outdoor showman. He never reconsidered this fateful decision, and thereafter all his games, his plans, his thoughts were directed toward that one objective. He bought his first New York Clipper in 1888 and read it from cover to cover. The outdoor show news that he read that day made him realize how vast this chosen field actually was.

This natural showman, whose life history would require volumes to record, had his "wagon show" playing country school houses when he was fourteen. He had learned some sleight of hand and magic and had acquired two goats and some white rats which he trained. He loaded his goats, rats, magic and Punch & Judy equipment into his father's grocery store wagon on show nights and moved out to the school houses. In two years he had accumulated enough to purchase a tent for his show but the following year the seventeen-year-old left home and joined the Burk Circus doing magic and Punch and Judy in the Side Show.

WATER SHOW. C. A. Wortham Shows, Detroit, 1919. Author's Collection.

The following year when he was eighteen, he organized a small wagon outfit called Rice's Great Olympic Shows and made a little money with the venture. He realized that he needed more education, passed the entrance examinations to the University of Pennsylvania and studied there for two years. He made his expenses while in college by operating a fruit commission business. Becoming bored with college, he joined Sun Brothers Circus in 1896 as side show manager.

In 1897, he owned a profitable printing business in Saginaw, Michigan; but spent more time promoting street fairs than he did with his print shop. In 1899, he was one of the promotors for Gaskill's first organized carnival; and Harry Polack's description of his ''mail-order show'' of 1900 is given in Chapter Five of Volume one. When this outfit closed, he went back to Gaskill for a while; and in two years had been with the Rice & Morely, Ferari Brothers, Rice & Potter and P. J. Munday Shows. He then started the

Great Alamo Carnival Company on three railroad cars. He made quite a lot of money with the Great Alamo show which played for sixty-three continuous weeks. He quit the carnival business in 1905 saying that carnivals were not going to last much longer.

In the next twenty years he tried just about every type of entertainment that could be produced under a tent. He made and lost several fortunes in such diverse enterprises as minstrels, dramatic shows, street fairs, indoor and outdoor circuses, state fairs, public weddings, Noah's Ark shows, midways and water circuses. He was one of the originators of the water circus. In 1915, he was the managing partner of Rice & Dore's Water Carnival, a regular midway featuring a huge water circus, which opened in Portland, Oregon, and closed a highly successful season in Montgomery, Alabama. In the spring of 1916, the largest showboat ever built was launched at Pittsburgh, Pennsylvania. Rice & Dore's Water Carnival was loaded on it for a tour of the river towns. The boat, the show and Bill's fortune was lost in a wreck in Whirlpool Rapids near Davenport, Iowa, the following August.

With the aid of Clarence Wortham, he launched the twenty-five car Wortham & Rice's Carnival. Wortham sold his interest to George F. Dorman at the end of a successful season. The Rice & Dorman Show was a success for quite a while but Bill sold the show to Morris & Castle in middle of 1921 season. It hadn't done so well that year, and Bill just didn't like to stay at one thing too long.

He took a job with Capt. John Sheesley as agent for seventy-three highly successful weeks. In 1923, he organized W. H. Rice's Water Circus and took it to Japan, China and Singapore with big business. Came back to the States and organized the Rice & Emerson's Boat Show. Had one big season and went broke the next. After that "the Amusement Trader" as Bill liked to refer to himself, did nothing but promote.

He promoted police shows, fraternal organization shows, water circuses, marathon races, fairs, milkmaid contests, balloon ascensions, auctions, parachute jumping, churning contests, dog races, theatrical shows, girl popularity contests, horned toad races, industrial expositions, turtle races, fortune teller acts, and dozens of other types of exhibitions, contests and expositions. He even operated a monkey farm at Los Angeles in 1929, but that was too slow for Bill. An occupational hazard of a promoter is that of being either well-fixed financially or broke. Bill was no exception, and he was alternately "living high on the hog" and within a few weeks, broke again.

Whenever he found that he really needed some cash, he would promote a public wedding. Those public weddings were always "surefire" money raisers for him. He never kept a record of how many weddings he had managed. Hundreds of happily married couples from coast to coast were married under Bill Rice's auspices. He was welcomed by them whenever he came through their towns again and was godfather to many of their offspring. He never had any way of estimating how many thousand children had resulted from his promotions. He never faked any of his weddings, if he could get local couples interested. If not, he had a happily married team that would come on for the event. He did use this couple regularly one season as they were "married" in a lion's den each week.

Genial Bill explained to some how he became "Bill." He said that his mother named him Warren Hoyt while his father named him William Henry, and that he always used the name each liked when he wrote either of them. As he said this with a breezy twinkle in his eye, one never was sure whether he was joking or not. This brilliant, happy-go-lucky post-graduate student of human nature had an uncanny ability to anticipate the public's wants in the amusement field. Then he had the ability of producing that entertainment for them. He lacked the patience necessary for running a successful business long. He wanted to get out where the action was and try something new. Had C. A. Wortham lived, he might have kept Bill's restless energies harnessed to a carnival midway; but having known Warren Hoyt Rice, I doubt it.

He died in St. Louis, Missouri on February 7, 1939, and was buried in the Showmen's League of America's "Showmen's Rest" in Chicago, Illinois. Outdoor show business had lost its "Happy Warrior." His son, Warren Hoyt Rice, Jr. has retired from the outdoor show field, and is now owner and operator of Rice's Tropical Fish Farm in Ruskin, Florida.

JOHN MERTON SHEESLEY

John Merton Sheesley, known to all carnival troupers as "Captain John," was born in Dauphin, Pennsylvania, near Harrisburg, on July 25, 1881. He was educated in the public schools and at Dickinson College in nearby Carlisle. He was twenty-seven years old before he joined his first carnival, the Johnny J. Jones Show. He had his own candy wheel concession with the Jones midway all season in 1908, and bought half interest in the Human Laundry attraction last half of the year. In spring of 1909, he gave this half interest in the fun house back to Johnny J. and joined Bennie Krause on the Krause Greater Shows. Before this 1909 season was over, he had worked five weeks with the Ye Olde English Carnival Company midway.

Seasons of 1910 and 1911, he operated concessions with the Beister Carnival Company. Spring of 1912 he opened with the Macy's Olympic Shows, but he soon left Macy and started his own carnival, Sheesley Amusement Company which he opened in Headland, Alabama. He was traveling on fifteen railroad cars in 1915 and added seven more by middle of 1916 season.

He was one of the pioneers in the use of Girl Revue-type of girl show attractions. His "Girl Shows" were copied by many operators of midways, but his midway featured the Tango Girls in 1916 when most all carnivals were building "Days of '49" attractions. The "Tango Girls" attraction was a musical comedy with ten girls in line, two lead vocalists and four comics. William C. Fleming was the general agent for the Greater Sheesley Shows in 1916.

While "Captain John" produced some of the best midway stage shows of any early carnival, he did not have the pride of ownership of equipment that Johnny J. Jones and some other owners displayed. He, like Frank West and the Dodson Brothers, never seemed to care what their equipment looked like as long as it was movable. Actually, much of it wasn't movable, and a Monday morning visitor looking for the showgrounds of the three shows named could find them very easily by following a trail of broken-down wagons along the streets.

Sheesley routed his midway on a transcontinental tour season of 1921 and went into winter quarters at San Diego, California in November of that year. He did not report any great success with that trip to the West Coast and he never tried another one. Very few of the Eastern midways ever really made profitable tours of the West Coast. Some circuses like Sells Floto and the Ringling Barnum Show did good business out there, but carnival operations on the Coast are unlike anything the Eastern showman has been trained to cope with.

"Captain John" sold all of his equipment to Pete Kortez and Mel Vaught on October 11, 1944. Seventeen days later he was dead. He died on October 28, 1944, in a Pensacola, Florida hospital. The cancer that had been eating on him for several years finally killed him. Funeral services were held in the Baker Mortuary in Harrisburg, Pennsylvania on November 1st and the body was interred in the family plot in the Raynor Cemetery at Penbrock, Pennsylvania.

WALTER K. SIBLEY

Walter K. Sibley never gave his birth date to anyone in an interview, but he often said that he made his quarter million and sold his carnival when he was forty-nine. If that was so, he was born in 1874 or 1875. He quit grade school in Boston to enter show business. His first job was as usher for B. F. Keith at four dollars per week. Keith was to be the founder and owner of the Keith Circuit of vaudeville theaters. As Sibley grew older, he worked as a super (extra) in most of the spectacles and plays that appeared at the Boston Theaters. In summers he worked as a super in the big fireworks spectacles of that time. (Some of these pyrotechnical displays like the Burning of Rome, etc., used hundreds of people as living "props.")

Walter K. tried prize fighting, when he was old enough to work in the ring, but he didn't win as often as he wanted and quit. He turned to professional bicycle racing and worked at that for seven years. He married in 1893 and followed more genteel lines of endeavor for a few weeks. In later reminiscences he stated simply, "We both got hungry." He bought a two headed baby and booked it at Coney Island. He named his show Taka-Tama and did very well with it that season. Feeling that he wasn't getting ahead as fast as he should, he became a "book maker" at one of the race tracks. He lost everything he had in just nine days.

In 1894, he found the Karns Brothers, "Jack & Jill" and exhibited them until they were well grown fat boys. He put them in a show as a single "pit" attraction at Revere Beach near Boston. He also had two other "pit shows" at the beach — a Big Snakes Show and a baboon which he called "Zeno the Ape Man." These three shows gave him big grosses, but Mrs. Sibley got them booked on the midway at the Canadian National Exhibition at Toronto. There they netted plenty, and began to book their shows at more fairs.

It was in Toronto in 1904 that Walter K. Sibley created the type show that was later to be called a ten-in-one. Until 1904 all attractions playing the fairground midways everywhere were shown as single exhibits, either in Pit Shows or in "Platform Shows," the latter being a show built upon a platform. As no organized carnivals played fairs (except for Gaskill's first appearance at Minnesota State that same year) all attractions were independently owned. In 1904, the Midway was short of space, so Sibley put two of his little pit show tents side by side and put all four pits under them for the single price of admission. All of his competitors complained about this "four-in-one" of Sibley's, but it grossed more than the four single shows would have. It was another year before Sibley had a special tent made to house several attractions, and I believe it was used at the Waco, Texas, Fair for the first time. The competitors complained, but all of them rushed to get new longer tents for grouping their attractions.

Around 1910 Walter K. wanted to book with the Herbert K. Kline Shows, but Kline already had the same shows on his midway. Sibley built an

STRING SHOW. Ten-in-one type show such as Walter K. Sybley originated. Author's Collection.

elaborate Water Show and booked it with Kline, where he stayed until Kline's Shows went broke in 1914. He had four cars of his own equipment; with this as a nucleus he built his own midway. Sibley's Superb Shows toured successfully for three years starting in 1916. Years before, Walter, half in jest, promised Mrs. Sibley that he would retire from show business when he had a quarter of a million dollars saved. In 1919 she reminded her husband of his promise. He did have the quarter of a million, so he sold his carnival to Frank West. He always said that he was forty-six that year.

Later he bankrolled a man for a midway to play South America. Sibley wasn't getting the "first count" on the proceeds so he went down and managed it for three years, and made plenty. A year or so later, he lost it all in a partnership with Eddie Arlington. Their Wild West Show wasn't wild enough for the South Americans. Walter claimed that he had contracts to display a gorilla named "Buddy" at the Chicago's Century of Progress in 1933, but the big monk wasn't released to him. Sibley said later that Buddy was renamed Gargantua for his circus career. The showman had a whale on exhibition at the Chicago Fair for the first season. The whale did very little business until an octopus was added and more

ballyhoo added to the front.

In 1934 he operated an old Waltzer ride purchased from John R. Castle that spring. It grossed very well all summer. Sibley was persuaded to go to the Brussel's Fair in 1935. There he had several attractions, including a nudist camp show. When he got to the Texas Centennial in the spring of 1936, he found Billy Rose managing the Fort Worth midway. He swapped Rose the Nudist Show idea for space on which to operate a snake show. Season of 1937 Walter managed the big Circus Side Shows on Max Goodman's new carnival. In 1938 he went to San Francisco to be midway coordinator of the Golden Gate Exposition. Was fired but enjoyed a good season's business there with his Headless Girl Show.

In 1942 Sibley accepted the executive secretaryship of the National Showmen's Club in New York. He worked hard on cash-raising drives for the club. While on one of these drives in the spring of 1948, he became ill in Florida. He never fully recovered and was confined to his room in the Belvedere Hotel the first week in March, 1949. He was sent to the Polyclinic Hospital on morning of March 9, and died that afternoon. Funeral services were held on March 13 and he was buried in the National Showmen's plot in the Ferncliffe Cemetery.

JOSEPH S. SCHOLIBO
Written by Joe Scholibo

"I had show business knocked into my head while still a 'youngster'," said Scholibo when questioned at the Louisiana State Fair.

"He (Scholibo) while still attending grade school in Houston, Texas, his former home, until the early fifties, went out to the circus lot where the old Forepaugh-Sells Circus was to set up for showing the following day, along with six or seven other youngsters to watch proceedings of a circus 'set-up,' and like all kids, not satisfied, they slit a sidewall to look into the menagerie. Joe, being the smallest, was last to get a 'look-in,'" and a roustabout took a lick with a 'bullhook' used in herding elephants at the head stuck into the canvas.

"With his head all bandaged, he insisted on an aunt taking him to the circus matinee the next day, after convincing his father not to take action against the circus management.

"Upon graduating from the Houston High School in 1910, he started his show career, handling the box office of the Prince Theatre, the opera house of Houston and one of some scores of theatres of the American Theatrical Circuit of New York City.

"The following year, 1911, he was sent to Oklahoma City to manage the opera house there, named then the Overholzer Theatre, the youngest theatre manager of the entire circuit. This same theatre had the one and only woman stage electrician, Mrs. Alton ('Mother Alton'). His outdoor show experience started when he was called upon to take management of a large amusement park called 'Eden Park' built by some influential businessmen of Houston, who needed a promotional man to take management of same — so Joe got his first taste of outdoor amusements.

"His connection with the Prince Theatre and then Eden Park, put Scholibo in the "lime-light" in this always progressive city, and when the "Red Roosters" were organized, he was made director. He staged not only big night parades, but street carnivals in downtown business districts of Houston.

"As a director of the "Red Roosters" he had much to do with contracting the midway attractions and free acts for this yearly big week of fun, frolic and parades, leading to a solid friendship between him and the "Little Giant," C. A. Wortham. Finally in 1917, Wortham made a deal with Joe to represent him on one of his three different carnival companies, The Wortham, Waugh and Hofer Shows, wintering in Phoenix, Arizona.

"From 1919 until the "Little Giant" or "China" Wortham, as he was called by his millions of friends in both the show and Fair world, died, Joe S. Scholibo was always on Wortham's staff, in some executive capacity.

"The first part of the following year, Scholibo was an agent for Con T. Kennedy Shows, promoting a two-week engagement for this show in St. Louis, Missouri, and finishing this, he went with the Morris & Castle Shows, for the next ten years as Director of Publicity, and given much credit for this show's being recognized as the top carnival for State Fair midways.

"Scholibo had a mind to quit the road, but was talked into returning by Orville and Harry Hennies with their then-motorized show, when their show was wintering in Houston, Texas, the winter of 1934.

"During 1936 with the Hennies Bros. motorized show, Scholibo handled the concession office, and went ahead to lay out the lots prior to the show's arrival, and toward the end of the season, Orville and Harry had nothing else in their mind but trying to "go on rails" the coming season, and after traveling around and looking over railroad equipment of shows about to leave the road, talked same over with Scholibo, who advanced the idea that the United Shows of America (the old Morris & Castle Shows) most likely could be bought and outlined to Orville and Harry Hennies just what steps to take to purchase same, which was accomplished the latter part of the 1936 season, when the show completed its engagement at the Louisiana State Fair, Shreveport.

"During the winter of 1937, Scholibo was general agent of the Hennies Bros. Railroad Show booking the western route for this 30-car railroad show as far West as Seattle, Washington, which was termed an impossiblity for such a large railroad show due to the long jumps between enough large-populated towns for a show this size; the railroad moves would be prohibitive in cost, but after the route was set by Scholibo tentatively, he was successful in contacting the Union Pacific Railroad "higher-up" officials and obtained a consolidated contract price for the seven moves west, they being prorated equally for each of the seven moves, making this route possible for the show.

"It was the largest railroad show ever to play this western route, and up to this date, none has ever attempted same, although this proved profitable for the Hennies Brothers.

"During the winter of 1940-41, McCaffery, who was the general manager of the Amusement Corporation of America, via long distance, arranged a meeting with Barney S. Gerety, of the Beckman and Gerety Shows, at which meeting Scholibo was engaged by Gerety to join the show for the coming season, as of 1941. These services were terminated by the show leaving the road at the close of the 1942 season, and going into winter quarters at Shreveport, Louisiana, Fairgrounds. The following year the show set up rides on the Louisiana State Fairgrounds, and

Scholibo managed those.

"In 1952, Gerety interested Joe in taking over the management of a "Kiddie" Park he had established the year previous on the State Fair Grounds, in Shreveport — they closing same the end of that year. The following spring, Joe handled the sale of those rides and equipment, and that Fall he went with the State Fair, Shreveport, where he was engaged full-time until 1956.

"He married Miss Gladys McDuffie, secretary to Joe T. Monsour, in the winter of 1955.

"Since partially retiring, Scholibo each year is handling the concessions for the State Fair, along with acting business manager of the basketball games of Centenary College of Shreveport."

VIVONA BROTHERS

MORRIS VIVONA. Courtesy Amusement Business Photograph.

Probably the most potent force in the collective amusement industry along the East Coast is a combination of truck show units and the family that operates them. One week there may be as many as five units of this show working hundreds of miles apart, and the next week equipment from three of them has converged to play the big fair in Ottawa, Canada, while the other two have joined to play a big date in Pennsylvania. The amount of equipment and trucks involved with these units make them formidable competition for any show regardless of size; but the real deadliness of this competition is not realized until the owners of the organization are all seen together working as a team for the family welfare.

Anthony (Papa) Vivona immigrated to the United States around 1900. He and his brother closed their tailor shop to join the armed forces in World War I. When Tony came back after the War, he married Catherine Bellantoni, daughter of an ice cream manufacturer. Tony began selling ice cream from the factory at local church bazaars and celebrations. He purchased a truck and traveled farther away from Newark, New Jersey selling the ice cream. Then he bought a frozen custard machine as the profits from the soft product were much greater than from regular hard frozen ice cream. His first son, Morris, was born in Newark on October 31, 1920; and a second son, John, on April 3, 1922. Then other children were born to Mom and Papa Vivona — Babe, Ann, Phil and Dom were all born in Newark before the family moved to Irvington, New Jersey, December 7, 1941.

As soon as Morris was old enough to work for himself, Papa bought a custard machine for him and they booked it with the Sheesley carnival. A couple of years later a machine was bought for John and booked along the East Coast. Family councils were held frequently and even the youngest children sat in as soon as they could understand family finances. As each boy grew old enough to work alone, he was given a custard machine and a route was arranged. On the last day of the New York World's Fair in 1940, the whole Vivona family went to the fair together. John and Morris, who had learned how to erect and handle riding devices with the carnivals they had been with, saw a Ferris Wheel at the fair that could be bought for twenty-two hundred dollars. They persuaded the family to buy it.

In 1941, the first Vivona Brothers Shows opened with a Ferris Wheel, custard machine, popcorn joint and a ball game. Later in the season they bought a chairplane. Each year thereafter a custard machine was sold and a ride bought. Morris and John both went into the armed forces for World War II, but Papa and the family carried on until 1943, when Papa died. Then it was Mom and the family. When the two older boys returned from wartime service, they soon had two good-sized units organized again. They bought Mom a popcorn wagon, but saw that she would require more than that to keep her busy. In 1949 they combined their equipment to play a route of fairs as the number two Prell Shows. They now needed an office wagon. They built one and installed Mom as office manager.

They played the Prell route for two years and learned all they could about fair booking and routing. In 1951 they started on their own with their own route of fairs booked. Morris started as general agent and still handles that part of their activities. John was manager of the first big show and still manages the number one unit. They have never neglected their bazaar, church festival and celebration route in New Jersey and still send units to play spots at which Papa sold ice cream forty years ago.

By 1959 the five Vivona Brothers owned no less than thirty-six riding devices and forty-seven trucks and they have added to that number each year for the last eleven years. Now they have five big units, each managed by a brother and have built up a corps of competent bosses and department heads. They feature spectacular riding devices and have booked some of the biggest and best fair dates along the East Coast. They can play two such dates at one time as they own the equipment necessary to do it.

On February 26, 1965 the family lost Mom Vivona. She was killed in an auto-train collision at Coral Gables, Florida. All three Catholic clergy from her home parish in Irvington, New Jersey served at Requiem High Mass and a sixty-car cortege followed the body to its place of interment in Holy Sepulchre Cemetery in Newark. Mom is gone, and her family still miss her, but they are self-sufficient now. The principles taught by both Papa and Mom are adhered to by the Vivona Brothers.

If I were a young man considering starting a collective amusement organization, I think I would join one of the Vivona Units for at least one season. I know that I would learn much about modern methods of midway operation; and it might be that I would decide not to start for myself at all. It would all depend on just how many second generation Vivona Brothers there are coming along to need more units in that family operation.

3-IN-LINE BIG ELI WHEELS AND A BABY ELI. On midway of
Amusements of America (owned and operated by Vivona Brothers).
Photograph Courtesy Eli Bridge Company.

STREET FAIRS   FAIRS   CIRCUS   BILLPOSTERS   DRAMATIC

THE BILLBOARD

Volume XV. No. 18.   CINCINNATI, MAY 2, 1903.   Price, 10 Cents. Per Year, $4.00

DOC WADDELL,
Specially Engaged as General Agent for the Ted Faust Minstrels.

One of the strangest individuals destined to work in the carnival field was born in Portsmouth, Ohio on August 26, 1863. William Shackleford Andres claimed that two of his grandparents had been circus performers, but his father was an engineer on railroad locomotives. Young Andres quit school just a short time before he was to graduate and took work with a newspaper. He later joined John Robinson's Circus as a candy butcher. In the ensuing years, he worked as canvas man, ticket seller and side show talker. He claimed the world's title as champion all day front talker. He worked on circuses until 1899, when we first meet him as the young press agent with the buggy whip on Gaskill's first carnival.

While with the Robinson Show, he met Kid Waddell and became Doc Waddell in outdoor show business. After putting in a summer at the Pan-American Exposition at Buffalo, New York in 1901, he was with Sell-Floto, Hagenbeck Wallace and Sells and Gray Circuses. He was pretty much of a reckless, happy-go-lucky scamp in his early days, if news reports of the day are to be credited. As a press agent, he used any methods he could devise in order to gain space for the attraction that he represented. His father was killed in 1905; there was a change in Doc's behavior immediately thereafter.

In 1909 he took off for six months of meditation. After that he preached wherever he could get listeners. He visited jails, orphanages and slums on his missions. He continued to work with outdoor shows as he did his evangelistic work. He was ordained as a minister by the Methodist Church of Springfield, Ohio. In 1925 he left Hagenbeck Wallace Circus to go to Herrin, Illinois to preach to the warring gangsters in that town. In 1929 he left Dodson carnival to perform the same services in the gang wars of Camden, New Jersey.

At one time in his preaching career, two well-dressed, hard-faced individuals came to Doc late at night and asked him to preach for the burial service of a friend. Doc agreed and asked them what time the services would be held. "Tonight" was the terse reply. Doc went with them to an isolated farmhouse where the body was lying in wait. Only six mourners were present for this after-midnight funeral. All of them young, smoothly dressed and silent individuals. Doc asked the name of the corpse and got the laconic order, "Preach." Doc preached a funeral for this unknown victim of gang guns and never knew who the man was and where the body was buried.

In the thirties, Doc retired from outdoor show business and entered the Ohio Masonic Home, but not for long. Mills Brothers Circus engaged him as Circus Chaplain and he trouped for several more years with this truck-transported circus. He joined the show in Spring of 1952 as usual, but illness forced him to return to Columbus, Ohio where he entered the county hospital there. He died on July 16, 1952. He had always asked that his coffin be wrapped in a piece of circus tent side walling and that everybody have a good time at the ceremony. His ailing wife said that Doc had recanted from this unusual idea and he was given a conventional funeral in Springfield, Ohio on July 18.

NAT C. WORMAN

Ferari, Levitt-Meyerhoff, Morris Miller, Felice Bernardi, World of Mirth, Morris & Castle, Strates, Hennies Brothers and Cavalcade of Amusements; those were the carnivals Nat C. Worman trouped with during his thirty-six years in the collective amusement business. He started in outdoor show business in 1906, but was with Welch Brothers Circus that season and did not travel with a carnival until 1913. That season he worked with the Ferari show on various jobs. Leon Washburn was part owner of Ferari midway, which used a downtown bandwagon pulled by elephants, Jip and Judy, as a "street bally."

Nat C. Worman was born in Flemington, New Jersey, January 7, 1886. His father was a dealer in horses. Nat not only worked with circuses and carnivals, but he also worked as a performer in both vaudeville and minstrel shows. It was with carnivals that he excelled and built a reputation as one of the top-rank builders and all-around generally useful midway worker. He handled such jobs as trainmaster, shop superintendent, lot man, ride superintendent, or anything else around a carnival that required a man who could do anything necessary to be done. In 1944, for instance, Nat Worman framed a railroad circus for Art Concello and Jack Tavlin at the Shreveport, Louisiana fairgrounds. He converted the carnival equipment they had purchased from Barney Gerety and added their truck show equipment to it making a nice little circus which later became the Clyde Beatty Circus.

In 1913, his first year on road with a carnival, Nat helped Benny Krause frame a merry-go-round

GUN WAGON. Merry-Go-Round center pole mounted on a wagon. Nat Worman and Benny Krause mounted a center pole on a wagon for the first time in the middle Teens, but it was not mounted exactly as the one shown here. Courtesy Nat Worman.

center pole on a wagon. This was the first "jenny" so handled. These "gun" wagons, so-called because the folded-down center poles on later models resembled a piece of heavy artillery, were used by all of the flatcar shows after the middle twenties, but Krause did have the first one and Nat Worman helped him build it.

Worman retired from outdoor show business in 1949 and built a motel which he sold in 1962. He is now in complete retirement in Shreveport, Louisiana. Let a carnival come within driving distance of Shreveport though, and Nat will be on the midway sometime during the week telling the younger carnies stories about the "old days." The following Rubin Gruberg story is an example:

"Several years ago a fellow by the name of Evans put out several pit shows with Gnus in them. He called them horned horses. There was an animal trainer over on the Rubin show named Dan Riley who had one pit show featuring snakes and an ape or two. He asked Rubin if he could frame and book another one featuring the "horned horse." Rubin said yes. Dan told Rubin that he would have to have a little help on it and Rubin said he would come up with the necessary finances. The thing came into winter quarters with six hundred fifty dollars due on it. Dan told Rubin it had arrived at the express office and that he needed the money to "lift it." Rubin asked how much and when Dan told him, Rubin exclaimed, 'Vat six hundred fifty dollars for a Gnu? I can buy a battleship for that.' But, Rubin "lifted" it anyway."

Nat misses the hustle and bustle of daily carnival existence, but he probably was right when he retired in 1949. A man with his capabilities was indispensable during the "golden age of the carnival," with all its huge shows and show fronts. This period ended about 1949, and a true old-time carnival trouper gets little comfort from the riotous sounds arising from the many fluorescent light bedizened piles of "pig iron" "spotted" around a modern midway.

NAT WORMAN. Courtesy Nat Worman.

LEON WELLS WASHBURN (Wells Leon Sawyer)

Wells Leon Sawyer, who later adopted the name Leon Wells Washburn, was born in Rome, New York, in 1852. He was educated in Rome until, at the age of thirteen, he ran away with a circus and was given a job as pony "punk" (handled the ponies). This circus, which belonged to John Robinson's brother, Alex, played Rome the same day that news of Lee's surrender in Virginia reached that New York town. Young Sawyer thought that the big celebration was for the circus. He was dissatisfied with his circus job and returned home before his father's death, late that year.

A variety show using all Indian performers played in Rome a few weeks after the elder Sawyer's death and Wells Leon joined it. The owner, a man named Washburn, liked young Sawyer and adopted him. In the name change, the given names were reversed and the result was Leon Wells Washburn. Leon stayed with Washburn until the latter's death and then started a variety (vaudeville) show of his own. In 1882, he found the type show that eventually made a fortune, the "Tom Show."

The Uncle Tom's Cabin Shows, of which Leon Washburn operated as many as five, criss-crossed the United States above the Mason and Dixon Line for over forty years. They played in tents, in theaters and in town halls. Some actors spent their entire careers doing "Marks," "Uncle Tom," "Simon" or some other part in this play. An entire volume could be devoted to this one branch of the American Stage. There have been many amusing stories told about the "makeshift" scenery, or the dogs used as bloodhounds and the accidents occurring as "Little Eva" ascended to heaven. Washburn's Statson's Uncle Tom's Cabin Shows had plenty of these little incidents, but his "Tom Shows" were high quality productions compared to many others. He always carried competent actors, real bloodhounds and good equipment.

After having engaged in every branch of amusement business; he had even been partners with Eddie Arlington's father, George, in a Wild West Show; Leon W. Washburn entered the collective amusement industry in 1912 as a silent partner of Francis Ferari. Two years later he opened his own Leon W. Washburn's Mighty Midway Shows, which toured until 1919. The Washburn & Weavers Shows title was used that last season. Although his carnival made no impact on midway business, his wide experience in other fields make it necessary to mention him.

Washburn was one of the few individuals who ever ventured to take a "Tom Show" into the South. In 1883 he booked a two weeks' route in Virginia and Carolina theaters. The theater owners hadn't read the

LEON W. WASHBURN
Owner and General Manager
Washburn's Mighty Midway Shows

book and had no idea what they had booked until he opened in Richmond. The next day he received wires cancelling out all his booked theaters. He got his actors, equipment and himself back "North" safely. He was much more fortunate than an operator of a tented "Tom" Show many years later, who booked a stand in a Texas Panhandle town. The tent and equipment were wrecked and burned on the lot. No lives were lost though.

In the twenties, seventy-year-old Washburn closed his outdoor and traveling amusement enterprises and operated the Washburn Theater in Chester, Pennsylvania. He died at his home in Reading the third week in October, 1930. His funeral was held October 25 and he was buried in the Bellvue Cemetery in Lawrence, Massachusetts.

Carnival Women

It is estimated that over one hundred thousand people are now employed in some phase of collective amusement business. If so, not less than thirty thousand of these carnival workers are women. Some of them naturally are working with midway "gal" shows, but the vast majority are employed at other tasks. They sell tickets, work behind counters of sales and gaming concessions, "man" the office wagons and are housewives for their tired husbands. One even goes so far as to actually supervise the setting up and dismantling of the riding device of which her husband is foreman.

Some of the carnival wives have been married to their midway-following husbands, and the carnival, for over fifty years. They are just as anxious for the new season to open as their husbands. They probably have more to do than their menfolk as they do their own midway work as well as provide a home for the family. It is doubtful that many of the present-day carnivals would be open or could continue to operate without the owner's wife in the office. In the old days, many show offices had regular paid secretaries who "got the first count" on all the funds that were turned in to that office. With the high operating costs of the present, a very few carnivals could spare that collection the treasurer made for himself. With "little women" running the office, all the cash is kept in the family.

Without the carnival wife, there would have been no carnival family; and the family dynasties that are operating so many of the older midways would not have been born. These sons and grandsons, and daughters, are carrying on the family midway enterprises without interruption, and the entire industry profits from this perpetuity. The lack of family dynasties in the circus management field is probably the basic cause of the decline of the circus. American circus owners, unlike their European counterparts, have not been very prolific in reproducing their own kind. Mr. Clark did advertise M. L. Clark & Son's Circus, but does any circus historian know much about this son? He surely didn't make any name for himself in circus business.

The drudgery of everyday existence on a carnival midway doesn't wear on the carnival women as much as the same amount of long hard hours does to feminine workers in other lines of endeavor. The carnival "gals" have the advantage of living and working right out on "the good earth." The work may be hard, but existence can never be humdrum, there is too much going on and conditions are constantly changing.

The carnival women selected as worthy of being discussed in this section are representative of uncounted thousands of other just as worthy "carnival cuties," midway "gals" and wives and mothers engaged in the collective amusement industry. Each of the ladies discussed has had fifty years or more on carnival midways and still loves the business. Each of them, as have hundreds of other carnival women, has a live story worthy of a full-volume biography.

THE HURD SISTERS

The lives of the Hurd Sisters, Bootsie and Hody, have been inextricably entangled with collective amusement business since their births. Bootsie Hurd was born about the same time the industry was, and Hody was born in a carnival wagon on one of its first midways. Both of Tom and Pauline Hurd's daughters are retired from the business they love so much, but either or both would welcome a chance to relive just some of their carnival experiences once again.

Bootsie and Hody have other names but they prefer being called either Bootsie and Hody or Mrs. Harold (Buddy) Paddock and Mrs. Johnny J. Jones, the former by their thousands of friends and the latter by acquaintances. Their childhood given names will be used here once and for the record only.

Adeline Hurd was born in Washington, D.C. She

MRS. JIM CONKLIN. Mrs. Conklin and Patty with a display of flowers for a season's opening. Courtesy J. W. Patty Conklin.

was not born on a showgrounds but in a room. Her mother, Pauline, a well-known wild animal trainer cancelled bookings so that her baby could be properly taken care of. When only two years old, the little girl already had her own wild animal act. She presented lion cubs in the arena until they were old enough to be dangerous, then she would be given other cubs to work with. It was during this period that she was presented a diamond ring by the President of the United States, "Teddy" Roosevelt.

On the first carnival midways, the little girl was here, there and everywhere around the grounds. In and out of shows, getting in showmen's ways as they worked, running up and down the midway on sunny days and sloshing through the mud on rainy days. The latter gained her a nickname, as one of the working men gave her a pair of little boots to wear on muddy lots. She wore them on muddy lots all right, but she liked her boots and wore them all the time. She didn't want to take them off when she went to bed in the living wagon back of the wild animal show tent. The show people called her "Bootsie" then, and she is known to thousands of troupers by that name.

Etta Louise Blake (Hody) Hurd was born in that living wagon when it was parked back of Percy Munday's animal show with the Gaskill-Munday Carnival Company. She was born on a young girl show worker, Etta Louise Blake's birthday and was given a name in accordance with the occasion. For many years she and Miss Blake, a successful producer of girl revues for carnivals, celebrated their birthdays together. I have no record that Hody Hurd, worked any wild animal acts, but she was a good horse trainer.

The Hurds moved to the K. G. Barkoot Shows and spent several years with that carnival. Bootsie landed a contract with Selig to work as an animal trainer in some of his early jungle movies. Selig hired quite a few people from the Barkoot show and carried them to Jacksonville, Florida for some of the location work. They then went to the Chicago studio and from there to his new lot in downtown Los Angeles. Bootsie worked in both the "Darkest Africa" and "Lost In the Jungle" movies of that early period.

The family stayed with Barkoot until 1914. Tom Hurd was classed as one of the best front talkers in carnival business and Pauline was a good animal trainer so they could find places on almost any midway of the day. Then the Hurd sisters themselves were becoming an asset as they were working as a dance team with the girl revues featured by most carnivals. Bootsie also got them bookings in vaudeville as a dance team.

The family stayed together until the spring of 1916. They had all moved over to the Con T. Kennedy Shows in 1915 and had enjoyed a pleasant season with this show until the wreck on the move out of Atlanta, Georgia. In this most disastrous of all carnival wrecks none of them were injured physically, but the chaos of the often futile efforts to rescue men from the burning wreckage made an impression on Tom Hurd from which he never recovered. The family was back with Kennedy the following spring, but Hurd became ill soon after the season started. His womenfolk finally had to take him away from the midway. The girls stayed with Tom and Pauline in Atlanta, Georgia until their father had regained some of his strength. They then went back to their own jobs with the show. Tom never trouped again. He died in 1919.

The sisters were not together in 1917, as Bootsie had married F. G. Scott, the treasurer of the Johnny J. Jones Exposition and was with that show. Both girls were on the Jones show season of 1918 and stayed with it for over thirty years. Hody married Johnny J. Jones and bore him one son, Johnny Jenkins Jones, Jr. Bootsie is the mother of a daughter, Frances Scott. The death of Johnny J. Jones on Christmas Day, 1930 not only stunned the carnival world but also staggered Hody Hurd Jones. She now had a huge debt-ridden, over-extended collective amusement organization to operate in the midst of the worst business depression the country had ever experienced.

Many highly experienced carnival owners folded up under the impact of the Great Depression. The Jones Show did have to close, but not before Hody, with the backing of Bootsie, fought a three year battle for survival. This young, feminine, carnival owner assisted by loyal employees was unsuccessful in her efforts to keep the show open, but her fighting spirit drew the admiration of everyone in the business. When E. Lawrence Phillips offered to take the show, she was content to let him have it. He would keep the Jones Show title alive and that mattered more than anything else to the mother of the young son who bore that name.

Mrs. Jones traveled with the show as long as Phillips operated it, handling many details of management with which the one-armed gentleman from Washington was not conversant. Bootsie was now married to Harold (Buddy) Paddock, co-owner of the Lipsky-Paddock concessions with the show. She had the exclusive on Midway "Mitt Camps" and used two of those fortune telling booths at the fairs.

The show was built back up to a top position in the industry and had some very good fair dates; but was never able to regain a full route of such events. The Royal American and the Amusement Corporation of America provided too much competition in bidding for the better dates. Bids that the Jones Show couldn't meet and continue operate. During the war years, Phillips grew weary of carnival ownership, and in the late forties sold the struggling show to Paddock & Lipsky. It had been on the down grade since the start of World War II. The expenditure needed for the new owners to meet the competition from other shows was not possible and the equipment was seized and sold for taxes in the early fifties.

Neither Hody nor Bootsie have been in carnival business since the Jones Show folded. but both yearn for more days and nights of midway life, the only life either knew for fifty years. Buddy Paddock died three years ago, and now the two sisters are both widow women. It is one of the ironies of carnival business that two of the most experienced women in every day carnival operations no longer have a place on some one of its midways.

ETTA LOUISE BLAKE (HODY HURD) JONES. Mrs. Johnny J. Jones (center) in retirement. Courtesy Joe Pearl.

JACKPOT ROW. Sherman Hotel lobby during "outdoor meetings."
Courtesy Amusement Business Photograph.

"Cutting Up Jackpots"

Favorite Carnival Pastime

JACKPOTTERS ON LOT. William T. Collins Shows Office Canopy,
1964. Courtesy Amusement Business Photograph.

SAME CANOPY — OTHER JACKPOTTERS. Courtesy Amusement
Business Photographs.

BERTHA "GYP" BENOITON MCDANIELS

MRS. BERTHA "GYP" McDANIEL AND FRIEND. Courtesy Robert "Bobby" Wick.

Behind almost every successful carnival trouper there is a woman, his faithful wife who keeps the show, the ride or the joint running while he attends to more important things. Go on any carnival midway and you will see groups of men having leisurely cups of coffee in the cookhouse or at the back end grab joint and other groups gleefully "cutting up jackpots" in the shade of the office wagon. You may be assured that their business is not being neglected, the little woman is back there some place supervising the help or serving the patrons herself. This is the story of a little carnival woman who lost her husband over thirty-eight years ago and still carries on the work that he started.

Bertha Benoiton was born in Nantes, France on June 6, 1897. Her parents were owners of farms and orchards in the Loire Inferieux regions of that country. When this little French girl was seventeen she was already with an American carnival. She was dancing in Joe Callis' Fantasie Noveltie Show on the Barney Parker Shows midway, and in 1915, she was with the Harry H. Deveaux attraction on the Patterson midway. She went to the C. A. Wortham midways the next two years and there gained her carnival soubriquet of Gypsy or "Gyp" as she did Gypsy dancing in the Oriental Show for some time. She also worked as a dancing girl in '49 Camps with Wortham, Clifton L. Kelley, H. W. Campbell and the Alamo midways before she began working on concessions for Wortham in 1919.

As a concession wheel operator she was with Wortham, Patterson and Noble C. Fairley Shows through the 1922 season. Her husband, D. C. McDaniels, needed her for his own enterprises after 1922, and they operated the privilege car and booked their Rocky Road to Dublin ride on the Rubin & Cherry Shows seasons of 1924 and 1925. The next season they were with the Johnny J. Jones Exposition with their ride and Gyp's new penny arcade. The next six years they were with the Sheesley, Brundage, Morris Miller, Snapp Brothers, John Francis and Rubin and Cherry Shows. It was on the latter show that D. C. McDaniels died in fall of 1933. They were already booked with Royal American for the 1934 season, and the widow carried their equipment to that show and fulfilled their commitments.

Season of 1935, Gyp McDaniels carried her Rocky Roads to Dublin and Penny Arcade to the Johnny J. Jones Exposition where she stayed for sixteen years. She hired a skilled arcade mechanic to manage the arcade and personally managed the ride herself. No matter how bad the weather might be the little woman was on the lot getting her equipment set up and keeping it operating. When the Jones Show was sold in the early fifties, she moved to the World of Mirth Shows for three seasons, and from that midway to the James E. Strates Shows where she still operates the Arcade. Labor costs, extra care required for the donkeys and high-grossing rides forced her to retire McDaniels' Rocky Road ride after so many years of continuous work on practically every big fairgrounds in North America. Sentiment alone would have kept the ride operating if Gyp could have found any way at all to do it.

Actually, she has been, in her own words, "show hand, boss canvasman and chief mechanic" for her arcade for six years now. After she had several men get drunk during her best "dates," she quit depending on regular hired help and hired local mechanics for the better spots. This little woman is starting her fifty-eighth season on carnival midways this spring, and says she has no intention of quitting anytime soon.

Gyp's brother and his wife have both helped her for a few weeks when she was playing Eastern Canada with the World of Mirth Shows. Ben and Alice Benoiton live in that area. Their two sons joined their Aunt Bertha for the summer seasons while they were in high school in Montreal. They are both grown now and established in their chosen fields. Randy Benoiton is a public accountant with offices in Western Canada and Dr. N. L. Benoiton is Associate Professor of Bio-Chemistry at the University of Ottawa. Bertha Benoiton McDaniels is proud of her family, but she has no intention of joining them anytime soon.

At the 1969 State Fair in Raleigh, North Carolina, lack of space prevented Gyp McDaniels from setting up her penny arcade there. A new girl appeared behind the counter of the duck pond concession that week, yes, for the first time in forty-seven years, little Gypsy McDaniels was back behind a concession counter. Should that arcade become too burdensome for her to handle, there are still plenty of jobs on a carnival midway for a woman with fifty-six years experience. Although her husband has had to leave her much longer than the "Front end loiterers" do their wives, little Gypsy McDaniels has been as faithful as they in carrying on his project for him.

BERTHA "GYP" McDANIELS. Working the counter of a concession at the North Carolina State Fair, 1969. First time that she had been behind a counter in forty-seven years. Courtesy Amusement Business Photograph.

ELSIE CALVERT AND PEGGY FORSTALL. Los Angeles County Fair, 1967. Peggy, with the maul, operated the "high striker" and Elsie ran the jewelry stand. Between them, these two troupers had seen one hundred two years on outdoor show midways. Courtesy Amusement Business Photograph.

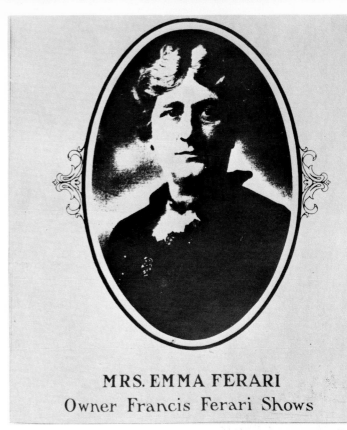

MRS. EMMA FERARI
Owner Francis Ferari Shows

MRS. FRANCIS (EMMA) FERARI, 1915. Courtesy Billboard Publishing Co.

MRS. FAHREDA SPYROPOULOS (LITTLE EGYPT?)

Fahreda Mahzar was born around 1872, and she was dancing at the Columbian Exposition in Chicago in 1893. She later claimed to be the originator of the "muscle dance" in America and as such was entitled to be called the original "Little Egypt." The title was never used on the Exposition grounds during the run of the fair though. She did have documentary proof that she originated "that dance" which helped make that 1893 exposition a success.

Miss Mahzar married Andrew Spyrpoulos, a Chicago restaurant owner in 1905. She made her last public appearance at Chicago's Century of Progress in 1933-34 as Queen of the Midway. She died April 5, 1937 in Chicago and was buried in Elmhurst, Illinois.

STREETS OF CAIRO. Lackman & Loos Shows, Bedford, Indiana, 1907. Courtesy Albert Conover.

ETHEL PURTLE. Courtesy Earl Purtle.

FIVE CARNIVAL WOMEN. From left to right, Hattie Wagner, Virginia Shumway, Ethel Purtle, Grace LeMay, and Betty Hartwick. Courtesy Earl Purtle.

Carnival Families

THREE SEDLMAYRS. Carl J., C.. J. and C.J.III discussing a mechanical problem. Courtesy Royal American Shows.

Much has been said elsewhere in this volume about the carnival dynasties, or family management of collective amusement organizations. Little more needs to be said here other than to reiterate that it is the conviction of almost all of the older Carnies that the final salvation of the industry lies with these carnival born, bred and trained second and third generation midway operators. That unless these young people, both men and women, do solve the many problems facing the industry, they will be forced to go into some other line for which they have neither inclination nor training. And, that facing the prospect of losing the industry which they love, they will desperately work until solutions to the problems are found.

Therefore, this section will deal only with three of the thousands of carnival families now engaged in the business. These families will be dealt with here as being representative of those thousands. Families owning and operating three different carnivals, different in both size and methods of operation, will each be discussed briefly in the following pages.

FOUR DREWS. The Drew Family. Courtesy James H. Drew Shows.

THE DREWS

James H. Drew has been discussed briefly in another section. His show and his family have been selected as the proper representatives for all the larger truck transported carnivals in the United States. Starting with three secondhand rides and a few concessions back in 1949, the James H. Drew Exposition played dates in 1969 where it had over fifty riding devices on its midway. It is a family owned and operated show catering to the family trade all the way from its huge priceless German concert band organ to its spectacular riding devices.

It is difficult to refer to the Drew show in the singular, for any recollection of a pleasant visit to its midway is a remembrance of a happy family working together as a team. James H., Jr., Eula, Jimmy (James H. Drew, III) and Malinda, all of them busy doing their individual job on the family team that keeps the huge midway operating efficiently. James H. Drew, Jr., who has been ill recently, will be found around the office attending to details of over-all management, while Eula, Mrs. Drew, who is office manager attends to the innumerable duties of that job. Twenty-two year old Malinda, who assists her mother in the office as well as attending to liaison between the office and departments on the lot, will be seen briefly as she hurries to or from the office.

If you stand in one place on the midway for a few minutes, you are likely to see a slender "teen-age" appearing young fellow hurrying by as he rushes from one crisis to another around the show grounds. Being manager of a fifty ride show takes plenty of good horse sense and years of midway experience. Twenty-four year old Jimmy Drew has plenty of both.

"Georgia Boy," as everyone called him, Drew and Eula Wentworth met for the first time on Frank West's Worlds Wonder Shows where Drew operated a concession and Miss Wentworth danced in the Girl Revue. Neither had ever trouped with a truck show until after they were married. It was quite an adventure in 1949, when they started that first little show with very little money to finance it. This young couple with two young children hardly made expenses that first season as they picked up the rudiments of midway management by owning and operating one. Starting the next season, they began to grow.

As their show grew in size and reputation, they determined to operate in such manner as to make them welcome back at any spot they played. They had their own young children on this showgrounds, and nothing would be allowed on it that those young ones shouldn't be exposed to. This policy of having a clean family-type show from its very inception has paid the Drews big dividends, as everyone who has contact with them and their carnival respects them as being "Sunday School" showmen from preference not through necessity. When their show grew too big for some of their smaller fairs and celebrations, they did not mark those dates off their routes, as some are prone to do. They split the big show into smaller units for such dates.

Drew and daughter, Malinda, would handle one unit, while Mrs. Drew and Jimmy handled the other one. Jimmy Drew was managing a unit of his own when he was sixteen years old. In spite of all the work he has done with the family midway, Jimmy Drew has graduated from high school near their home town of Augusta, Georgia and has completed three years at Augusta College. Malinda has completed high school also.

The Drews have a big winter quarters at Gracewood, Georgia on U.S. 25 highway south of Augusta. Here, in addition to the priceless collection of antique band organs mentioned elsewhere, Mrs. Drew has accumulated one of the really large collections of circus and carnival historical materials and historic equipment. She is an avid circus fan, having worked with Cole Brothers Circus as well as with the big railroad carnivals. There have been rumors that the Drews might set up a circus and carnival museum there on their winter quarter grounds. To them, as with most outdoor show people, their vocation is their avocation.

Both of the older Drews have served as officers in Showmen's associations and clubs. Mrs. Drew was president of Showmen's League of America Auxiliary in 1964, and James H. Drew, Jr. has been a member of Showmen's League Board of Governors for some time. In 1966, Jimmy Drew was the youngest member of the Ontario Chapter of Showmen's League of America in Toronto. Eula Louise Whitworth Drew was born June 6, 1916 at Kings Mountain, North Carolina. Her son, James H. Drew III was born June 21, 1945 in Cincinnati, Ohio and her daughter, Doris Malinda Drew was born November 2, 1946 in Shelby, North Carolina.

Always working for the advancement of clean outdoor entertainment, the Drews and their huge midway are a credit to the collective amusement industry. Although "Georgia Boy" has been ill for some time with a heart ailment, much of his work has been taken over by Jimmy; the big show is going ahead on its course as charted by James H. Drew, Jr. and his wife, Eula, over twenty years ago.

EULA DREW (MRS. JAMES H. DREW). Being installed as president of the Showmen's League of America Auxiliary, 1964. Courtesy Amusement Business Photograph.

THE HILLIGOSS FAMILY. They own and operate the Fun Fair Shows and the Foley & Burk Shows. Latter is oldest active title in America. Courtesy Lloyd Hilligoss.

C. J. SEDLMAYR, JR. Courtesy Royal American Shows.

C. J. SEDLMAYR III. Courtesy Royal American Shows.

For over ninety years the title "The Greatest Show on Earth" has been used by a circus in which the name of Barnum was prominently displayed. Since 1919 the circus using this descriptive subtitle has been the Ringling Brothers and Barnum & Bailey. Although this title is the property of that great circus organization, it has not been exactly correct since the late nineteen thirties. For over thirty years there has been a larger outdoor show touring the United States and Western Canada. After the strike on the Ringling show in 1938, the Royal American Shows required more actual space to set up on than did the circus, as the latter never again was as large.

The Royal American Shows travelling on its ninety all-steel railroad cars is now the largest travelling amusement organization on earth, and it is likely to hold this position for the next thirty years. It is now being managed by the second generation of a family dynasty and the third generation is well trained and working on the showgrounds every day. This show has not had the complete family participation in operations as so many of the small shows have. The show's business is so great and office tasks so complex, that it would be impossible for the

manager's wife to be office manager. High salaried competent people must be employed for the heavy work load carried by them in the show's offices. Top management, however, is strictly a family affair, and has been ever since Carl J. Sedlmayr bought Sam Soloman's interest of their holdings in the middle forties.

Carl J. Sedlmayr was sole owner of the Royal American when he first started using that title in 1923. Two years later, he sold an interest in the carnival to the Velare Brothers, and this partnership continued until the early 1940's. The partnership was dissolved and the equipment divided. Sedlmayr was a partner with Soloman in buying and operating the Rubin & Cherry Shows for two years, but when World War II ended, he launched the Royal American as his own show without partners. This he continued to do until his death in 1966.

Carl J. Sedlmayr, Jr., C.J. as he is known to everyone on the show, operates the show almost exactly as his father had managed it for so long. Carl J. Sedlmayr, Jr., was born in Kansas City, Missouri, May 19, 1919 and attended schools there. He graduated from Rollins College at Winter Park,

Florida, and went into the U.S. Air Corps for two years' service. After this service he returned to the Royal American as assistant manager until his father's death. C. J. has inherited all his father's tact and ability in handling people whether they be fair board members or extra help on a riding device. In addition, he has brought onto the job his own ability with mechanical things.

C. J.'s father never worried too much about the mechanical departments of the big enterprises as Elmer Velare and the capable men hired by him handled all such work prior to breakup of the partnership. The greatest team of carnival mechanical department heads ever assembled by any show stayed with Sedlmayr as the Velares never again operated another complete midway. As those old-time mechanical department men began retiring in the late forties and early fifties, C. J. was ready to step in and handle that end of the midway management. Many of the labor and time-saving devices built on trucks and tractors around the Royal American midway are C. J.'s own creations.

He goes to the Octoberfest in Munich, Germany, and buys new riding devices that he thinks may have possible appeal for the Royal American patrons. Before that ride is ever used by the public on the Royal American midway, C. J. and his crew have reworked and in some cases redesigned it for ease in handling and for added safety for the riders. As general manager of the mammoth midway, he doesn't have the time he once had to actually work with his own hands, but he knows what he wants and can direct the work he wants done. The mechanics gladly perform the tasks laid out by the boss man as most of them have seen him do such work himself.

C. J. III is now his father's assistant on the great midway, the only traveling show so large that it has its own Shrine Club. This club, with around one hundred members with the show itself and several hundred additional members not working with Royal American meets each week in joint meeting with the local clubs. As the carnival has played every town on the route, except Milwaukee, Wisconsin, every year for over thirty years, these meetings are actually reunions for old friends and brothers.

Had there not been a capable, well-trained son to take over the management of this complex amusement organization, it is doubtful if it could have continued operations. The making of the manifests for entry into Canada for all of the people and equipment would be an impossible task for one without prior experience, and the laying out of the showgrounds would be just as impossible for a man who had not been trained by that master of them all, Carl J. Sedlmayr. Around May 1st the long trains will leave Tampa, Florida, for the show's first date of the season, guided by the hands of two men carefully trained by their predecessor to handle the show as he handled it for so long.

SEDLMAYR FAMILY. Courtesy John Colville, Calgary Journal.

FRED A. THUMBERG
CO-OWNER

FRED A. THUMBERG. Taken from 1969 Key City Shows ad in Amusement Business.

FRED C. THUMBERG
CO-OWNER

FRED C. THUMBERG. As shown in 1969 Key City Shows ad in Amusement Business.

The Key City Shows is not the largest collective Amusement Organization, and it doesn't book any of the big state fairs; but it is the perfect example of a small show framed to carry clean and pleasing midway entertainment to the county fairs in its territory. This territory extending from Michigan through Indiana, and Ohio to Alabama and Georgia, gives the show good business on its six months' season, and the fair-goers along this route all enjoy visiting the midway as many of them are now friends of the owners. The Thumberg family bought the show in 1960 and have built a solid reputation along their route.

Fred A. Thumberg was born in Medford, Oregon, June 7, 1902. His parents were farmers. He graduated from Benson Polytechnic School in Portland, Oregon, and went to Silverton, Oregon, as maintenance mechanic for the Silver Falls Timber Company's fleet of lumber carriers. He joined Martin's United Shows July 4, 1935, with his own riding device, and for the next twenty-five years toured with his rides and equipment with such shows

as Hildebrand's United, W. G. Wade, Jones Greater and Gooding Amusement Company. He and his son, Fred C. Thumberg, bought the Key City Shows April 1, 1960, and have operated it ever since.

Fred C. Thumberg was born September 8, 1930 and began to help his Dad as soon as he was old enough to work around a show. He worked for his father until 1952 when he joined Gooding Amusement Company as an independent operator. He is now president of the Key City Shows, and his father was vice-president until his death. Since acquiring the carnival, they have increased the number of riding devices carried from nine to eighteen. They also carry seventeen office-owned concessions which gives them control of that branch of their operations. The show is a family operation catering to the family patronage. Fred A.'s wife, Betty, runs one of the confection trailers while Mrs. Fred C. handles the show's office. Fred C.'s sister works in the confection trailer and her husband is the show electrician; during summer vacation, Fred A. II operates the fun house as his sister helps her mother in the office.

Both the older Thumbergs, father and son, have been outdoor men and sports lovers. Both have been airplane pilots for past twenty-three years. Fred C. served in the Navy. Golf has been the number one sport of the father ever since his early days in Oregon where he held the number one button in that sport at the Country Club in Silverton. His other great pleasure has been being able to work with his wife, children and grandchildren on the family enterprise. Recently, he has been a willing "baby sitter" for his grandchildren as their parents have taken trips during the winter months.

Fred C. says that it takes all winter to get rested up after a tough six-month season on the road with a labor-short midway. His idea of a good rest is en extended cruise along the coast of Florida, a seventeen-hundred mile trip down the Ohio and Mississippi Rivers or a voyage from the West Coast of Florida to the Bahamas and back. All of this in his own cruiser with his wife as mate. The family all spend the winter in the Tampa Bay area of Florida.

They came East from Arizona in 1942 and lived one winter in Dearborn, Michigan. Since 1943 they have had a permanent home in Columbus, Ohio, where they have a winter quarters for their equipment. After the Fair Meetings are over, they all go to Florida for rest and recreation. At this writing, Fred C. and Jannie are just getting back from the Bahamas with their boat. He has a ride booked for a string of Florida fairs with Specs Groscurth's Blue Grass Shows, but has a capable foreman to handle it while he is away.

The Thumbergs believe that many carnivals will not be able to continue during the next decade because of labor shortages, high costs, restrictive laws and other problems. They believe also that more and more fairs will have to operate without carnival midways if conditions do not change soon. Fred C. says aptly the carnivals that do survive for the next decade will be " the cream of the crop," and that is exactly what the Thumbergs have with their Key City Shows.

A visit to the Key City midway will be different as Fred A. Thumberg died March 10, 1970. The show will go on though as Fred A., II is helping his father on the lot and the family has "closed ranks" to carry on the work their husband, father and grandfather started over thirty-five years ago.

FRED A. THUMBERG
CO-OWNER

BETTY THUMBERG
TREASURER

FRED A. III, BECKY JO, PATRICE THUMBERG

FRED C. THUMBERG
CO-OWNER

JANNIE THUMBERG
SECRETARY

OUR 3rd GENERATION SERVICING OTHER MIDWEST FAMILIES 32 YEARS

KEY CITY SHOWS AD, 1969. Courtesy Amusement Business.

MISCELLANY
ROUTES

ROUTE   SEASON
1970

ROYAL
AMERICAN
SHOWS, INC.

Winter Quarters—Florida State Fair Grounds
Permanent Mail Address:
P. O. Box 512, Tampa, Florida 33601
CARL J. SEDLMAYR JR.
President and General Manager

MAY 9—16	*Cotton Carnival* Memphis, Tennessee
MAY 20—JUNE 7	*Annual Spring Festival* St. Louis, Missouri
JUNE 10—21	*Annual Shrine Jubilee* Davenport, Iowa
JUNE 26—JULY 4	*Red River Exhibition* Winnipeg, Manitoba, Canada
JULY 9—18	*Calgary Exhibition & Stampede* Calgary, Alberta, Canada
JULY 23—AUG. 1	*Edmonton Exhibition* Edmonton, Alberta, Canada
AUG. 3—8	*Regina Exhibition* Regina, Saskatchewan, Canada
AUG. 14—23	*State Fair of Wisconsin* Milwaukee, Wisconsin
AUG. 28—SEPT. 7	*State Fair of Minnesota* St. Paul, Minnesota
SEPT. 11—16	*Mid America Fair* Topeka, Kansas
SEPT. 19—27	*Kansas State Fair* Hutchinson, Kansas
OCT. 2—11	*Arkansas Livestock Exposition* Little Rock, Arkansas
OCT. 13—20	*State Fair of Mississippi* Jackson, Mississippi
OCT. 23—NOV. 2	*State Fair of Louisiana* Shreveport, Louisiana

CLOSE OF SEASON

ROYAL AMERICAN SHOWS ROUTE, 1970. Courtesy Royal American
Shows.

GASKILL CARNIVAL COMPANY ROUTE 1899

CHILLICOTHE, OHIO . . . . MAY 30 — JUNE 3

NEWARK, OHIO . . . . JUNE 5 — 10

SPRINGFIELD, OHIO . . . . JUNE 12 — 17

ZANESVILLE, OHIO . . . . JUNE 19 — 24

DAYTON, OHIO . . . . JUNE 26 — JULY 2

COLUMBUS, OHIO . . . . JULY 3 — 8

AKRON, OHIO . . . . JULY 10 — 15

FRANKLIN, PENNSYLVANIA . . . . JULY 17 — 22

NIAGARA FALLS, NEW YORK . . . . JULY 24 — 29

ROCHESTER, NEW YORK . . . . JULY 31 — AUGUST 5

SAGINAW, MICHIGAN . . . . AUGUST 7 — 12

LANSING, MICHIGAN . . . . AUGUST 14 — 19

DURAND, MICHIGAN . . . . AUGUST 21 — 26

BATTLE CREEK, MICHIGAN . . . . AUGUST 28 — SEPTEMBER 2

AKRON, OHIO (return) . . . . SEPTEMBER 4 — 9

PARKERSBURG, WEST VIRGINIA . . . . SEPTEMBER 11 — 16

NORWOOD, OHIO . . . . SEPTEMBER 18 — 23

MIDDLESBORO, KENTUCKY . . . . SEPTEMBER 25 — 30

KNOXVILLE, TENNESSEE . . . . OCTOBER 2 — 7

ATLANTA, GEORGIA . . . . OCTOBER 9 — 14

COLUMBUS, GEORGIA . . . . OCTOBER 16 — 21

SAVANNAH, GEORGIA . . . . OCTOBER 23 — 28

HOME RUN BACK TO CANTON, OHIO

NOTE: Above information supplied by an article in Billboard, March 21, 1925 by Mrs. Frank W. Gaskill. Information shown in another section of Billboard shows that the show actually played Columbus, Georgia, November 6 — 11. It is known that the show was in Akron, Ohio, for a return date Labor Day, so there are three weeks unaccounted for between September 4 and November 6.

Listings are for current week unless otherwise specified.

Carnivals

A-1 Ams.: De Soto, Mo.
Alamo Expo.: Brownwood, Tex.; Kermit, 18-23.
Allen Am. Co.: Indianapolis, Ind., 11-23.
Amusements of America: Orange, N.H.; Totowa, N.J., 18-23.
B & E: Bartlesville, Okla.
Barstow Ams.: Kenlock (Kensington) Pa., 15-23.
Bee Am. Co.: Somerset, Ky.; Williamsburg, 18-23.
Belle City Ams.: (2700 S. Chase) Milwaukee, Wis., 11-13.
Blue Grass: Owensboro, Ky., June 1-6.
Boling Am. Co.: Gainesville, Ga.
Brodbeck & Schrader: McPherson, Kan.
Brown, Al: Madison, S.D., 18-23.
Camack, Ray: Rapid City, S.D., 11-17; Miles City, Mont., 21-24.
Capital City: Dalton, Ga.; Dayton, Tenn., 18-23.
Caravan of Am.: Pueblo, Colo.
Cardinal State: Springfield, Tenn.
Carl, A. J.: Center Line, Mich., 11-17; Grand Rapids, 18-23.
Carnival Time: Half Moon Bay, Calif., 11-17; Pleasant Hill, 18-24.
Carolina Ams.: Travelers Rest, S.C.
Carroll's Greater: Northside, Minn., 11-17; St. Anthony, 18-24.
Cetlin & Wilson: Norfolk, Va.; Camden, N.J., 18-23.
Chanos, Jimmie: (Gateway Plaza Shop. Center) Richmond, Ind.
Cherokee Am. Co.: Broken Arrow, Okla., 14-16; Henryette, 18-23.
Citizen State: Broken Bow, Okla.; Sallisaw, 18-23.
Clark's Greater: Drexel, Mo., 12-16.
Coleman Bros.: Norwich, Conn.; New London, 18-23.
Collins, Wm. T.: (Golden Valley Shop. Center) Golden Valley, Minn., 18-23.
Continental: Arlington Heights, N.Y.; Hudson, 18-23.
Crystal United: Swainsboro, Ga.
D & D: Muscatine, Ia., 14-23.
Davis Am. Co.: Sweet Home, Ore., 12-17; Florence, 20-24.
Deggeller Am. Co. No. 1: Marietta, Ga.
Deggeller Am. Co. No. 2: Charleston, S.C., 11-17.
Dell & Travers: S. Philadelphia, Pa.; Roxborough (Philadelphia) 18-23.
DeLuxe, Inc.: Amherst, Mass., 14-16; Rockville, Conn., 18-23.
Dine Ams.: (Wooster & Hawkins Rd.) Akron, Ohio, 13-23; (Coventry Plaza) Akron, 25-30.
Drago Am. Co. No. 1: (No. Park Plaza) Marion, Ind.
Drago Am. Co. No. 2: (Shopping Center) La Porte, Ind.
Drew, Jas. H. Expo.: Mount Airy, N.C.
Dudley, D.S.: Wichita Falls, Tex., 15-23.
Dyer Bros.: Okmulgee, Okla., 11-23.
Endy, David B. Ams.: (Parkway Plaza Shop. Center) Winston-Salem, N.C.; (Cum-Park Shop. Center) Burlington, 18-30.
Evans United: Kirksville, Mo.; Booneville, 18-23.
Fair Time: Santa Fe Springs, Calif., 11-12; Escondido, 13-24.

Fanelli Ams.: Whitman, Mass.; Mansfield, 18-23.
Farrow Am. Co.: Memphis, Tenn.
Foley & Burk: Santa Rosa, Calif., 13-24.
Frankie's Rides: Washington, Pa.; McDonald, 18-23.
Fred's Playland: Atlanta, Ga., 11-30.
Funland Ams.: Isle of Palms, S.C., 16-31.
Gala Expo. No. 1: Bald Knob, Ark.
Gala Expo. No. 2: Marshall, Ark., 18-23.
Gentsch, J.A.: Greenwood, Miss.
Georgia Am. Co.: Dahlonega, Ga.
Gillette: Brewster, N.Y.
Gold Medal: Boomer, W.Va.
Grand American: Newton, Ia.; Ft. Dodge, 18-23.
Gregory Ams.: Shawano, Wis., 14-17; Sheboygan, 21-24.
Griffiths, Wm. A.: Williamsport, Pa.; Jersey Shore, 18-23.
Hale's Shows of Tomorrow: Lee's Summit, Mo.; Shawnee, Kan., 18-23.
Hames, Bill: Hillsboro, Tex.; Pleasant Grove (Dallas), 18-23.
Hammontree Am. Co.: Summerville, Ga.
Hannum, Morris: Plains (Wilkes-Barre), Pa.; Nanticoke, 18-23.
Haywood: Antlers, Okla.; Atoka, 18-23.
Heart of America: Kansas City, Mo., 11-23.
Heth: Albertville, Ala., 17-23.
Holiday Am. Co.: Independence, Mo., 14-23.
Holiday: Fayetteville, N.C.; Garner, 18-23.
Home State: Trumann, Ark., 18-23.
Johnny's Comb. Expo.: Foley, Ala.
Key City: So. Bend, Ind.
Kissel Bros. Am. Co.: St. Bernard, Ohio, 29-31.
Kraft: Sparks, Nev., 11-18.
Krekeler Ams.: Point Pleasant, W.Va.; Oak Hill, Ohio, 18-23.
Lone Star: Amarillo, Tex., 11-June 6.
M.D. Ams.: Hazleton, Pa., 11-12.
Marvel: (Town & Country Shop. Center) Springfield, Ill., 11-17; White Hall, 18-23.
Maryland Am. Co.: Chapel Oak, Md., 11-17.
Megerle & Ffile: Reynoldsburg, Ohio, 18-23.
Merriam's Midway: Denison, Ia., 13-16; Tama, 18-23.
Midland Empire: (Liberty Corners) Liberty, Mo., 12-16.
Midway of Mirth: Belleville, Ill.
Mo-Ak: Mansfield, Mo., 13-16; Piedmont, 18-23.
Monarch Expo.: Columbia, Mo.; Fulton, 18-23.
Moore's Modern: Del Rio, Tex., 13-23.
Motor State: Taylor (Detroit), Mich., 13-24.
Mundy, Jos. P. Ams.: N. Utica, N.Y., 18-24.
Murphy's Northern State: Fremont, Neb., 11-14; Blair, 15-17; Schuyler, 18-21.
P & J: Morton, Ohio, 11-17; Cadiz, 18-23.
Palmetto Expo.: No. Wilkesboro, N.C.; Thomasville, 18-23.
Penn Premier: Lynchburg, Va.; Charlottesville, 18-23.
Playtime Am. Corp.: Woonsocket, R.I.; Marlboro, Mass., 17-23.
Rainier: Spokane, Wash.
Reithoffer: Wappinger Falls, N.Y.
Robbins Expo.: Paragould, Ark. Mounds, Ill., 18-23.
Rohr's Modern Midway: Champaign, Ill., 18-23.
Rose City: O'Fallon, Mo.; Poplar Bluff, 18-23.
Royal American: Memphis, Tenn.; St. Louis, Mo., 20-31.
Royal United: Sioux City, Ia.
S & W: Bolivar, Mo.
Siebrand Bros. Cir. & Car. No. 1: Flagstaff, Ariz., 18-24.
Siebrand Bros. Cir. & Car. No. 2: Silver City, N.M., 11-17; Gallup, 18-24.
Smiley's Ams.: Lexington, Va.
Smith, Geo. Clyda: Saxton, Pa.
Smith Wonder: Canton, S.D., 13-16.
Southland Ams.: Sopchoppy, Fla.
Spencer, H.B. & Son Am. Co.: Deep River, Conn., 13-16.
Steele City: Derby, Colo.
Steele's Ams.: Valparaiso, Ind., 12-17; E. Gary, 19-24.
Strates, Jas. E.: Wilmington, Del.

Thomas, Art B.: Grand Island, Neb.; Hastings, 18-23.
Thomas Joyland: Beckley, W.Va.; Smithers, 18-23.
Thompson, Jack: Plano, Ill., 13-17; Joliet, 20-24.
Toby's Am. Co.: Chanute, Kan., 11-15.
Trailway: Waggoner, S.C.; St. George, 18-23.
Victory: (59th & S. Penn) Oklahoma City, Okla.
Wabash Valley: Lebanon, Ind., 15-23.
West Coast No. 1: San Pablo, Calif.
West Coast No. 2: (Fair) Angels Camp, Calif., 14-17; (Fair) Chowchilla, 18-24.
Whaling City: Milton, Mass., 18-23.
Wonderful World No. 1: Oswego, N.Y., 26-30.
Wonderful World No. 2: Wampsville, N.Y., 29-30.
World of Tomorrow: Ardmore, Okla.
Wright's Nov. Expo.: (Sunset Shop. Center) Kansas City, Mo., 11-June 2.
Wrigley's Novelty: (Wyandotte Plaza Shop. Center) Kansas City, Mo.

Circuses

Atayde Bros.: Guaymas, Son., Mex., 9-12; Hermosillo, 13-18; B. Hill, 19; Caborca, 20-21.
Beatty-Cole Bros.: Long Branch, N.J., 11; Red Bank, 12; Bayonne, 13; Dover, 14; Elizabeth, 15; Newark, 16; Asbury Park, 17; Vineland, 18; Cherry Hill (Camden), 20.
Clyde Bros.: (Arena) Sudbury, Ont., 11-12; (Arena) North Bay, 13; (Arena) Pembroke, 14; (Aud.) Ottawa, 15-16; (Centre) Kingston, 18-19.
Dailey Bros.: Winter Park, Fla., 11-16; Eau Gallie, 18-23.
Dobritch International: Winnipeg, Man., 16-23.
Graham Bros.: Vacaville, Calif., 11; Woodland, 12; W. Sacramento, 13; Fairfield, 14; Rancho Cordova, 15; Citrus Heights, 16; Sutter, 17; Colusa, 18; Grass Valley, 19.
Hagan-Wallace: Portsmouth, Va., 11-16; Fredericksburg, 18-23.
Hamid Morton: Pittsburgh, Pa., 12-16; Montreal, Que., 18-24.
International Hippodrome: (Memorial Centre) Cobourg, Ont., 11; (Community Centre) Bracebridge, 12; (Community Centre) New Hamburg, 13; (Arena Gardens) Galt, 14-15; (Arena) Georgetown, 16.
James Bros.: Albuquerque, N.M., 12; Santa Fe, 13; Pueblo, Colo., 14; Colorado Springs, 15; Denver, 16-17; Boulder, 18.
Kelly, Al G. & Miller Bros.: Mt. Pleasant, Pa., 11; Greensburg, 12; Latrobe, 13; Irwin, 14; Arnold, 15; McKeesport, 16; Cannonsburg, 18.
King Bros.: Reedsport, Ore., 11; Eugene, 12; Corvallis, 13; Oregon City, 14.
Mills Bros.: Fenton, Mich., 11; St. Johns, 12; Lansing, 13; Eaton Rapids, 14; Jackson, 15; Brighton, 16; Albion, 18; Marshall, 19; Pleasant Lake, Ind., 20; Syracuse, 21; Elkhart, 22; South Bend, 23; Wyoming, Mich., 25.
Polack Bros.: (Field House) Tacoma, Wash., 15-17; (McArthur Court) Eugene, Ore., 22-23.
Rudy Bros.: Los Angeles, Calif., 15-17.
Sells & Gray: Lansdale, Pa., 11; Phoenixville, 12; W. Chester, 13; Wrightstown, N.J., 15; Point Pleasant, 16.
Von Bros.: Pennsville, N.J., 11; W. Collingswood, 12; Media, Pa., 13; Haverford, 14; Folcroft, 15; Springfield, 16; Blackwood, N.J., 17; Brooklawn, 18.

Ice Shows

Shipstads & Johnson Ice Follies: Portland, Ore., 12-17.

Miscellaneous

Allen's Bears: Winnipeg, Man., 16-23.
Allen, Rex.: Brandon, Man., 15-18; Denver, Colo., 25-28.
Burnette, Smiley: Moosejaw, Sask., 18.
Hanneford, Geo. Family: (World's Fair) New York, N.Y., 11-Oct. 18.
Ring-A-Ding the Clown: Hudson, N.H., 13; Andover, Mass., 16; Marlow, N.H., 23; Laconia, 24.
Youngman's, Al, Music: Pittsburgh, Pa., 12-16; Montreal, Que., 18-24.

CARNIVAL ROUTES. Amusement Business, May 16, 1964. Only the leaders in midway business sent their routes in for this listing.

MORRIS & CASTLE SHOWS
The Show That Shows!
Compiled by Art Doc Miller

Permanent Address
c/o State Fair of La.
Shreveport, La.
P.O. Box 1100
Town

Official Route
Season 1923

Milton M. Morris
John R. Castle
Managers

April 14–21	Shreveport, La.		
April 23–28	Fort Smith, Ark.	Kansas City Southern	233
Apr. 30, May 5	Little Rock, Ark.	Missouri Pacific	164
May 7–12	Cairo, Ill.	Missouri Pacific	254
May 14–19	Decatur, Ill.	Ill. Central	205
May 21–26	Rockford, Ill.	Ill. Central	211
May 28, June 2	Kalamazoo, Mich.	Ill. Central 98 miles, Grand Trunk 145 miles	243
June 4–9	Detroit, Mich.	Grand Trunk	174
June 11–16	Detroit, Mich.		
June 18–23	Port Huron, Mich.	Grand Trunk	57
June 25–30	Saginaw, Mich.	Grand Trunk	120
July 2–7	Sault St. Marie, Mich.	Michigan Central 196 mi. D. S. S. & A. 98 mi.	290
July 9–14	Traverse City, Mich.	D. S. S. & A. 98 mi. Penna. 81 mi.	179
July 16–21	Muskegon, Mich.	Pere Marquette	137
July 23–28	Lansing, Mich.	Pere Marquette	115
July 30, Aug. 4	Battle Creek, Mich.	Grand Trunk	46
Aug. 6–11	Racine, Wisc.	Grand Trunk 176 mi. Chic. & N.W. 62 mi.	238
Aug. 13–18	Madison, Wisc.	Chic. & N.W.	91
Aug. 20–25	Wausau, Wisc.*	Chic. & N.W.	237
Aug. 27, Sept. 1	Ironwood, Mich.*	C. M. & St. P. 47 mi. M. St. P. & S. S. M. 121 mi.	168
Sept. 3–8	Superior, Wisc.*	M. St. P. & S. S. M. 52 mi. No. Pacif. 71 mi.	123
Sept. 10–15	Chippewa Falls, Wisc.*	M. St. P. & S. S. M. C. St. P. M. & Omaha	145
Sept. 17–22	LaCross, Wisc.*	C. M. & St. P.	124
Sept. 24–29	Beaver Dam, Wisc.*	C. M. & St. P.	140
Oct. 1–6	Batesville, Ark.*	C. M. & St. P. 77 mi. Ill. Cen. 450 mi. Mo. Pacif. 195 mi.	722
Oct. 8–13	Pine Bluff, Ark.*	Mo. Pacif.	156
Oct. 15–20	Shreveport, La.	Mo. Pacif. 168 mi. K. C. S. 74 mi.	242
Oct. 22–27	Shreveport, La.		
Oct. 29, Nov. 3	Beaumont, Texas		209
Nov. 5–10	Beaumont, Texas		
Nov. 12–17	Orange, Texas	So. Pac.	22
Nov. 19–24	Port Arthur, Texas	So. Pac.	44

Total miles traveled — 5089

* indicates fair date
R. D. Lohmar, Gen. Representative
(route sheet gone to press: other winter dates to follow)

Courtesy Art Doc Miller

COLLECTED MATERIAL

CIRCUSES, MENAGERIES AND A FEW RELATED ATTRACTIONS THAT HAVE PLAYED COLUMBUS, GEORGIA.

(Researched by Bob Brisendine — CFA — CHS)

NOTE: This material furnished by Mrs. James H. Drew. Complete files start in 1840 and end in 1927. We start with the 1899 Columbus Street Fair as it was played by Gaskill's Carnival Company on its first tour. This first organized collective amusement company selected Columbus as one of the twenty-one towns to be played that season. Also note the item in 1915 concerning the Con T. Kennedy Shows wreck.

All dates pertaining to carnivals are circled.

1899— GENTRY BROS. — Wed. March 23
(1899)— Columbus Street Fair — Nov. 6—11, Had Leota, the Lion Queen; William Worthington, lion
1st   trainer; Philion on spiral tower; balloonists and Gaskill Carnival on the midway. Also the Bicketts, aerial act.
1900— GENTRY BROS. DOG & PONY SHOW — Thurs. Oct. 11
1900— FOREPAUGH-SELLS — Mon. Oct. 29, Lot: Indersoll's hill in north part of Phenix (City). Forepaugh parade at 9 a.m.; Street Fair parade at 11 a.m.
(1900)— FRANK C. BOSTOCK WILD ANIMAL SHOW — (At Street Fair) — Oct. 29—Nov. 3
1901— GENTRY DOG & PONY SHOW — Wed, March 20
1901— GREAT WALLACE — Wed., Oct. 30
1901— GENTRY BROS. FAMOUS SHOWS — Sat, Nov. 2 (Lot: Third Ave. and 4th St.) (News story on Nov. 3 estimated 1300 attended afternoon, 1700 at night)
(1901)— DARLING'S DOG & PONY SHOW — Nov. 26—30 — At Girard, Ala. Street Carnival. J. S. Berger & Co.'s American Carnival Co. had midway. On Dec. 8, 1901, near Macon, Ga. the train carrying the Berger Carnival was in a wreck. No serious injuries.
1902— Al G. Field's Minstrels — Wed. Oct. 1 — In Springer's Opera House
1902— GENTRY BROS. — Tues., Oct. 7 — (Ran first ad on Oct. 2)
1902— WALTER L. MAIN — Thursday, Oct. 9 — (The Columbus, Ga. Enquirer-Sun on Oct. 7, page 2, quoted Main agent John D. Carey that the Main show might winter in Columbus (or Macon. Chattanooga, once under consideration, had been eliminated. Decision to be made when show played Columbus. No evidence found that it wintered in Columbus.)
(1902)— Columbus Fall Festival — Robinson Carnival Co. — Oct. 27—Nov. 1 — Free acts included: Prof. H. S. Record, loop the loop on bicycle; Nick Carter, high diver (90 feet into water 4 feet deep); M'lle Orocco, spiral tower and Kitaman's Jap troupe. Enquirer-Sun said Robinson went to Clarkesville, Tenn. after Columbus. Then Columbia, Tenn., Augusta, Ga. & Montgomery, Ala.)
1902— (Ala. State Fair, Birmingham — opened Oct. 23 — 101 Ranch Wild West there)
1902— FOREPAUGH-SELLS — Tuesday, Nov. 4 — Lot: on South Commons
1903— A. F. Allen's New Orleans Minstrels — March 9, 10 (under canvas, opp. C'house)
(1903)— Street Fair — Nov. 30—Dec. 5 — Girard, Ala. — Berger Exposition Co. — Nick Carter, high diver
1904— GENTRY BROS. SHOWS — Wed. April 6
1904— FOREPAUGH-SELLS — Tues. Oct. 18 — (first ad on Oct. 2)
(1904)— Business Men's Carnival & Race Meeting — Oct. 31—Nov. 5 — Layton Carnival Co. — with "Ben Hur," horse with human brain; horses & dogs of Mead and Schult.
1905— RINGLING BROS. — Fri. Nov. 3 (first time in Columbus) Lot: outside city.
1905— GENTRY BROS. SHOWS — Wed. Nov. 8 (Lot: at driving park)
(1905)— FERARRI BROS. ANIMAL SHOW — Nov. 6—11 — At Columbus Fall Festival — Robinson Amusement Co. on midway — also Nick Carter, high diver.
(1906)— Street Fair — April 2—7 at Phenix City — Weaver Amusement Co. — with balloon ascension and parachute drop. Also Prince, diving dog.

1906— GENTRY BROS. SHOWS — Thurs., Oct. 4 — (story said it was Big Eastern Co.)

1906— BARNUM & BAILEY — Thurs., Oct. 25

1906— PARKER AMUSEMENT CO. — Nov. 19—24 at Phenix City (had train of 12 cars)

1907— St. Louis Amusement Co. — April 1—6 at Phenix City, Ala.

1907— Street Fair — Dec. 16—21 — Phenix City — Wonderland Shows — had free trapeze act, snake show

1907— Chas. H. Yale presents "Devil's Auction" — Tues. Sept. 29 in Springers Opera House. Company had 4 baby elephants. Paper gave bad review.

1908— GENTRY BROS. UNITED SHOWS — Tues., Oct. 13. No matinee, late arrival from Macon (Oct. 12)— gave two night shows to straw houses.

1909— Street Fair — Jan. 4—9 — at Phenix City — St. Louis Amusement Co.

1909— Barkoot Amusement Co. — March 1—6 — in Columbus at foot of Broad St. under auspices of the Eagles — Matt Gay, high diver. "Mazeppa," trained horse.

1909— Cosmopolitan Shows — March 1—6 — Phenix City — had "wild animal Circus" (no name given. Also tightrope walker.

1909— At Elite Theatre (vaudeville) — March 16—21 — Prof. Lewis, 20 trained dogs and a monkey. Gave a parade on March 20.

1090— Y.M.C.A. Society Circus — Fri., April 3 — local talent — at Springer Ope House

1909— GENTRY BROS. SHOWS — Wed. Nov. 3 — (ran first ad on Oct. 30)

1909— SEIBEL'S DOG & PONY SHOW — Nov. 1—6 — at W.O.W. Carnival — also had Big Otto's wild animal show.

1909— HOWE'S GREAT LONDON SHOWS — Wed. Nov. 10 — had Marion Sheridan and troupe of performing lions; Prof. Buckley's elephants; Ty-Bell Sisters.

1909— MIGHTY HAAG SHOWS — Thurs. Dec. 2 — paper gave show bad review (Griffin)

1909— Robinson Carnival Co. — Nov. 22—27 at Girard, Ala. (Phenix City) — had Mme Loie and octette of leopards. (One story called it Famous Robinson Shows, Circus and Wild Animals.)

1909— G. W. CHRISTY CIRCUS — no evidence found it actually played. Story on Dec. 2 said the Ancient Order of Gobblers had contracted for show to play December 13, 14 and 15. No ad or other mention of the show was found. Checked local paper through December 31, 1909.

1910— SIG. JOSEPH FERRARI WILD ANIMAL SHOW — Feb. 28—March — Carnival under auspices of Eagles — with Barkoot Amusement Co. — Also Harding's Wild West; Matt Gay, high diver; Geo. Jannie on flying perch.

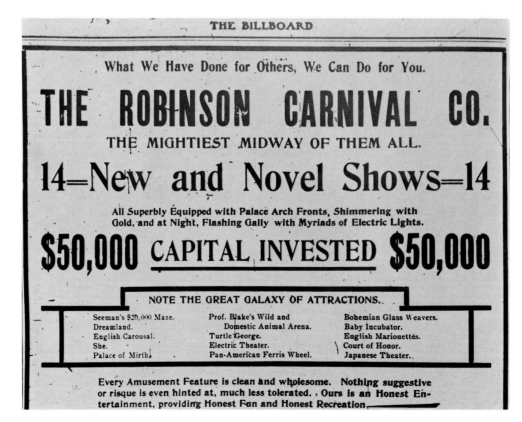

BILLBOARD AD. Robinson Carnival Company, 1903. Courtesy Billboard Publishing Co.

1910— SUN BROS. GREATER PROGRESSIVE SHOWS — Wed., April 6 — bill crew in Columbus March 23. Paper said show went to Lafayette, Ala. after Columbus. Poor matinee because of baseball game. Fair at night.

1910— Y.M.C.A. Society Circus — May 2 — local talent. At Springer Opera House

1910— Backman's Trained Animal Circus — Oct. 17—22 — At Confederate Vet. Carnival — United Fairs Booking Co. on midway — Had Capt. White's act of tiger riding a horse; Paul Johananing, animal trainer (head in lion's mouth); Toki, slide for life.

1910— K. G. Barkoot's World's Greatest Shows — Dec. 5—9 — Street Fair, Girard, Ala.

1911— Nix's Comedy Circus (vaudeville), ponies, dogs & mule — March 26—31 — Majestic Theatre.

1911— BARNUM & BAILEY — Fri. Oct. 6.

1911— Fall Festival — Oct. 9—14 — Barkoot Amusement Co.

1911— BUFFALO BILL — PAWNEE BILL — Tues., Oct. 17

1912— W. L. Swain Shows — May 6—11 — dramatic company under canvas

1912— Y.M.C.A. Society Circus — Wed., May 24 — local talent — Springer Opera House

1912— RINGLING BROS. — Wed., Oct. 9

1912— Street Fair — Nov. 18—23 — Girard, Ala. — St. Louis Amusement Co.

1912— Ga.-Ala. Fair — Nov. 27—Dec. 7 — Krause Greater Shows on midway — Dion's Animal Show. Payne's Fireworks.

1912— Street Carnival — Dec. 2—7 — Girard, Ala. — Nat Reiss Carnival Co.

1913— Red Men's Carnival — March 25—30 — Nat Reiss Shows — with Capt. Hoffman's wild animal act of pumas, panthers, hyenas and dogs.

1913— SANGERS GREATER EUROPEAN SHOWS — Tues., April 1

1913— Y.M.C.A. Society Circus — April 24, 25 — local talent — Springer's Opera House

1913— W. L. Swain Show Co. — April 28—May 2 — dramatic company under canvas with different play each night: Girl of Sunny South; Jason in New York; Hazel Kirk; The Cowgirl and the Indian; At the Mercy of Tiberius; Sat. Matinee — East Lynn; Sat Night — Deadwood Dick. Lot — Hammond Ave. & 17th St.

1913— BARNUM & BAILEY — Sat. Oct. 25 — Matinee only — tent (big top) caught fire near end of afternoon show. Approx. $1,000 damage. Night cancelled.

1913— De Alma's Dog and Pony Show — Nov. 10—15 — at street carnival in Girard, Ala. St. Louis Amusement Co. on midway.

1913— Metropolitan Shows — Nov. 10—15 — Girard, Ala. (This carnival and the one above were three blocks apart.)

1913— GENTRY BROS. FAMOUS SHOWS — Mon. & Tues, Nov. 17 & 18 — during Columbus Fair & Poultry Show that ran Nov. 17—22. Lot: entrance to fairgrounds.

1913— Fall Carnival — Dec. 1—6 — Tropical Amusement Co. — K. G. Barkoot, mgr.

1914— Elk's Spring Festival — March 30—April 4 — Johnny J. Jones Exposition Co. (had train of 16 cars) — Prof. Owens, parachute leaps from balloon; Thomas & Magaret Quincy, double high-divers; wild animal arena & mammoth menagerie.

1914— Redpath Chautauqua — May 19—25.

1914— RINGLING BROS. — Wed., Oct. 14

1914— Johnny J. Jones Expos. Shows — Oct. 26—31 — Girard, Ala. — Had Quincy's, high divers; and Capt. Wilson's wrestling lion.

1914— 101 RANCH REAL WILD WEST — Mon., Nov. 9

1915— Metropolitan Carnival Co. — March 22—27 — at Lower Girard, Ala. — Nelson & Nelson, aerial act and Prof. Smith, high diver.

1915— Y.M.C.A. Society Circus — Thurs. April 15 — Local talent — Springer Opera House

1915— Redpath Chautauqua — May 17—24 — Had Francesco Pallaria's band.

1915— GENTRY BROS. FAMOUS SHOWS — Monday, October 18

1915— ROBINSON FAMOUS SHOWS — Thursday, November 11 — press stories used the above title but ads used only Robinson's Circus.

1915— Brown & Leggette's Shows — Nov. 15—20 — At Lower Girard, Ala.

1915— Con T. Kennedy Shows — scheduled to play Girard, Ala. Nov. 22—27. Show train enroute Atlanta to Columbus in head-on collision with Central of Ga. passenger train 6 miles from Columbus. 7 killed, many injured. 9 show flats burned. Blew date. Went to Albany, Ga.

1915— Freedman's Great American Shows — Dec. 20—26 — at Lower Girard, Ala.

1916— Columbus Spring Festival — March 6—11 — Con T. Kennedy Shows — 15 big shows, 3 riding devices, 3 free acts and 2 air calliopes.

1916— Littlejohn Shows — April 3—8 at Girard, Ala.

1916— RINGLING BROS. — Saturday, October 21

1916— The Columbus Fair — Nov. 14—19 — Midway act: Mazeppa, the Wonder Horse.
1917— Y.M.C.A. Society Circus — Fri., April 20 — local talent — Y.M.C.A. Gym
1917— GENTRY BROS. FAMOUS SHOWS — Friday, April 20
1917— Redpath Chautauqua — May 17—24 — (with Creatore and band)
1917— SELLS-FLOTO CIRCUS — Monday, October 15
1917— BARNUM & BAILEY CIRCUS — Friday, October 19
1917— Chattahochee Valley Fair — Oct. 22—27 — Littlejohn Shows on midway. Acts: De val's Society Circus (dogs & ponies).
1917— Whiteway Shows — Dec. 10—15 — at Girard (Phenix City) Ala.
1918— Chautauqua — April 16—18 — At Phenix City, Ala. (Radcliffe Co.)
1918— Chattahoochee Valley Carnival — Dec. 2—7 — originally scheduled for October, postponed twice because of flu. H. W. Campbell Shows on midway.
1919— Metropolitan Shows — March 31—April 5 — with Milt Hinkle's Real Wild West. Newspaper stories report many gambling joints on midway.
1919— Redpath Chautauqua — April 24 — May 1 (with Kyrl and band)
1919— Chattahoochee Valley Fair — Oct. 6—11 — H. W. Campbell Shows on midway
1919— SPARKS WORLD FAMOUS SHOWS — Tuesday, October 14 — (ad claimed 33rd tour)
1919— RINGLING BROS. and BARNUM & BAILEY — Friday, Nov. 14 — no parade
1920— Redpath Chautauqua — April 15—22
1920— Kaplan's Greater 1920 Shows — April 12—17 — with Bristol's Trained Animal Circus. (Came to Columbus from Lagrange, Ga.)
1920— Chattahoochee Valley Fair — oct. 5—10 — Heth Shows on midway.
1920— HAGENBECK-WALLACE CIRCUS — Friday, November 5
1920— Metropolitan Shows — Nov. 1—6 — Ad claimed had "wild west," no name.
1921— Redpath Chautauqua — April 8—12
1921— Columbus Spring Festival (W.O.W.) — Miller Bros. Expos. Co. on midway
1921— Chattahoochee Valley Fair — Oct. 10—15 — Veal Bros. Shows on midway. Acts: The Duttons and the Casting Kays, aerialists.
1921— JOHN ROBINSON'S CIRCUS — Friday, October 28
1922— RHODA ROYAL CIRCUS — Billed for Sat., April 8. Closed 7th, Troy, Ala.
1922— Chattahoochee Valley Fair — Oct. 9—14 — L. J. Heth Shows on midway.
1922— RINGLING BROS. AND BARNUM & BAILEY — Saturday, October 21 1923 — SPARKS CIRCUS — Friday, April 6
1923— Chattahoochee Valley Fair — Oct. 15—20 — Johnny J. Jones on midway.
1923— JOHN ROBINSON — Wednesday, October 31
1924— Redpath Chautauqua — April 21—28 under canvas. Lott: Mott's Green
1924— MIGHTY HAAG SHOWS — Monday, March 24 at Phenix City, Ala. (Show arrived on Sunday the 23rd from Cottonton, Alabama.)
1924— Chattahoochee Valley Fair — Rubin & Cherry Shows on midway. With J. E. Ranch Wild West and Dolly Castle wild animal act.
1924— SELLS-FLOTO CIRCUS — Friday, November 14. (To Griffin 15th.)
1925— Redpath Chautauqua — April 20—27 under canvas.
1925— Chattahoochee Valley Fair — Oct. 19—24 — Rubin & Cherry on midway. Ad claimed Rhoda Royal Trained Wild Animal Circus was featured. Also "Muggins," trained elephant.
1925— MILLER BROS. 101 RANCH WILD WEST — Saturday, October 31 (Macon 30, Birmingham Nov. 2)
1926— Redpath Chautauqua — April 19—24.
1926— CHRISTY BROS. BIG 5 RING WILD ANIMAL SHOWS — Saturday, September 11 (at Carrollton, Ga. Sept. 10)
1926— SPARKS CIRCUS — Monday, September 27 — Sparks ran a "wait" ad on Sept. 10 saying it had no gambling or immoral acts. Enquirer-Sun of the 28th said over 1,000 were turned away for the night show.
1926— Chattahoochee Valley Exposition — Oct. 11—16 — Zeidman & Pollie Shows
1927— Barkoot Bros. Shows — March 31—April 9 — at Phenix City.
1927— KING BROS. RODEO WILD WEST — April 28—May 3
1927— SPARKS CIRCUS — Monday, September 26 (Newnan 24)
1927— SELLS-FLOTO CIRCUS — Saturday, October 8
1927— Chattahoochee Valley Exposition — Oct. 10—15 — Miller Bros. Shows

CON T. KENNEDY SHOWS. About 1915. Courtesy Albert Conover.

CON T. KENNEDY TRAIN. Mid-teens. Courtesy Albert Conover.

NOTE: Great Dominion Show coach in background. Con T. played his Southern dates next year after the wreck as the Great Dominion Shows. Author.

INVENTORY OF ASSETS, WALSH & WELLS GREATER SHOWS
Columbus, Georgia -- Oct. 21, 1925
Courtesy Art Doc Miller

2 68 ft baggage cars on lease from Hotchkiss-Blue RR Car Co.
    Lease and track storage Paid through Feb. 1926
1 36 ft. Hershell Merry-go-Round, band organ, LeRoi power unit, ticket cage, crates etc. . . $2300.00
1 No. 10 Eli, Eli power unit, ticket box, crates etc. 2200.00
1 Jones Merry Mix Up; 18 ft. tower, LeRoi power unit 800.00
1 Kiddie Seaplane, 1 kiddie chairoplane, fence, etc. 325.00
1 4-octave Una Fon and batteries 145.00
1 10x10 office top with awning, floor, poles etc. 82.50
1 Oliver typewriter 25.00
1 Army field desk, stock ticket box, 30 rolls misc. tickets 38.77
900 ft. (apx.) slugging cable, tape, switch etc. 90.00
1 Main Entrance Arch 62.85
1 bill trunk, apx. 200 sheets pictorial posters 1's, 3's, 9's — not crosslined 16.52
1 solid canvas 14x24 pictorial Oriental Theatre banner front 65.00
1 solid canvas 14x24 pictorial "At" show banner front 65.00
1 30x40 M. Kerr Co. top for Oriental Theatre, poles, stage 182.00
1 30x40 Martin Tent Co. top for "At" show, ring, poles, etc. 160.00
1 20x30 Baker, Lockwood top for Buel walk-thru Flanders Fields
    peep boxes & extra set pictures, Barbary Coast 245.90
1 12X18 snake show top, banner front, inside pit etc. 95.00
1 16x24 Plantation pictorial canvas front, bally, ticket boxes,
    30x40 top, stage, masking, plank seats 465.00
1 10—1 Beverly Bros. 20x60 top, string banner line, bally, boxes,
    inside pits and platforms, blow-off canopy 688.62
1 16x20 top, 3 banner front, Nelsons' Yolo & King Capakuli mummies 308.72
1 box tools, sledges, tapes, layout pins etc. 41.00
1 Deitz hand drive, gasoline floss machine 46.00

      All of above in storage at Youngblood's warehouse, River Rd.

      (Above compiled from data left in storage, uncalled for in 1928 at Roadhouse, Ill.)

CON T. KENNEDY TRAIN. Mid-teens. Courtesy Albert Conover.

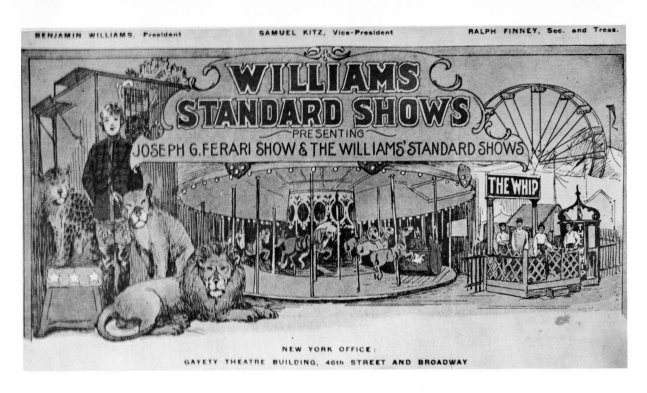

BENJAMIN WILLIAMS, President   SAMUEL KITZ, Vice-President   RALPH FINNEY, Sec. and Treas.

NEW YORK OFFICE:
GAYETY THEATRE BUILDING, 46th STREET AND BROADWAY

Another factual show data sheet from Art "Doc" Miller

M. J. Lapp Shows: This caravan operated with success for a number of seasons during the early 20's. It was built with funds supplied by Mrs. Lapp's father, a brewery owner at Ellenville, N. Y. The original wagons were rebuilt brewery and ice wagons. The original train was very old and in bad condition. To replace the train and some wagons, show routed into Bridgeport, Conn. where some cars were obtained, also many wagons. The discarded day coach and flats were run off a quarry spur track and dumped into a discarded quarry. Some old troupers claim this equipment eventually passed to the the Ketchum Shows. The Bill Woodcock photo of the loaded train leaving Bridgeport gave it a definite "circus" look. Later in quarters wagons were rebuilt for carnival use and the small type carnival wheels placed on all wagons. In its hey day, the wagons were painted orange, lettered in green, with blue shading. Coaches, dark green and flats yellow.

This information obtained in part from Lew Alter (his first carnival connection); a Mr. Zoppi, hoopla, hostler operator during the Bridgeport changeover; the Woodcock panarama photo and the writer's visit in 1922.

Semi Steel flat apx 50 ft	No. 30: 1¾ box wagon — Dangler boat swing, 18 ft; 1 box wagon 14 ft, fun house, 1 14-ft. roll-barrel
Wooden flat 45 ft	No. 36: 1 No. 76 wagon front "Oriental"; 1 No. 90 box circus; 1 power unit for ride
1 semi steel 62 ft	No. 40: 3 wagons No. 25, 26 & 27 Jenny, power unit.
1 semi steel 62 ft.	No. 41: No. 30, half box, No. 31 ¾ box, No. 32 box — Whip ride, power unit.
1 semi steel 62 ft.	No. 42: No. 33 half box Whip; No. 1 Office, No. 67 Pit Show, No. 68 snake show.
1 semi steel 62 ft.	No. 20 half box Eli, No. 21 half box Eli, No. 22 Box Eli & Kiddie ride, power unit.
1 semi steel 62 ft.	No. 45: 1 box water circus; (No. 60); 1 No. 7 mechanical city, 1 No. 71 Oriental; 1 No. 6 Wild West.
1 semi steel 58 ft.	No. 50: 1 No. 35 & No. 36, drome; No. 50 Hot Wagon; No. 66 Pit show, and Plant show.
1 semi steel 58 ft.	No. 51: No. 15, No. 5, No. 8, — Concessions
1 wooden 45 ft.	No. 25: No. 9 cookhouse; No. 3 utility; No. 37 box (???)
1 semi steel 50 ft.	No. 31: No. 65 Athletic show; No. 109 monkey Speedway; No. 100 "Single-O."

1 day coach; 1 combination car (compartment, day coach & stable car for draft teams, circus ponies, excess); 1 Jig coach

NOTE: As was the custom, some wagons were privately owned. These included the concessions, the Flying Horses (Jenny), mechanical village. A Whip ride was not always carried and during still dates some wagons were often empty. Billing usually was very weak, except awning streamers*, newspaper advertising was consistent. Auspices usually either The Redmen or Macabees.

* A form of billing now forgotten — these were muslin banners pinned on the valance of store awnings.

1929 SEASON'S ROUTE — PRINCESS OLGA SHOWS
Art Doc Miller

F. W. Wadsworth, Manager; Olga Wadsworth, Treasurer; Chas. Garthwaite, Asst. Mgr.; Eliza Wadsworth Garthwaite, Secretary; Eugene Hughes, Advance Agent; Fred Garrison, Ride Supt.; Harry Joyce, Electrician; Art Doc Miller, Trainmaster. Winter Quarters at Mounds City, Ill.

April 20th—27th — Opened at winter quarters lot. In spite of a bad "Hey Rube" the previous week at Mounds, business was fine and weather mild. At tear-down a heavy hailstorm hit the area. The Ohio River was at flood stage all week and the famous Frenche's New Sensation Show Boat was tied up at the boat works for major repairs. During the week drifting logs etc. further ruined this popular show boat.

April 29, Rosiclare, Ill. — Arrival at 3 P.M. on Monday and unloaded with farm wagons and teams. Lot jammed by 6 P.M. and empty by 9 P.M. Tuesday also big and balance of week completely lost due to heavy rain. The Cotton Blossom show boat tied up here on Thursday to nil returns.

May 6—11th — Remained over at Rosiclare and the flooded lot drained by hundreds of stake holes at all low points. Heavy rain continued all week except fine business on Tuesday. A blowdown here did considerable damage.

May 13—18, Carmi, Ill. — Rain all week, everything "gillied" on and off the lot. 18 carnivals and Christy Bros. Circus also "mud bound" in Ill. Business nil due to extreme cold and constant rain.

May 27 to June 1st, Odin, Ill. — Here we had everything from perfect weather to extreme heat, heavy winds and cold rain. Considerable damage to canvas from rain & hail. Strange enough, business was good. Enroute here our cars were on the same passenger train as the one-car Ben Wilkes Dramatic Show and the three-car W. A. West Shows. The Buck Jones Wild West Show advance car passed us on a siding. With a RR layover enroute we all watched the Harry Billock's Gold Medal Shows unload.

June 3—8, Dupo, Ill. — Weather fine and business fair. Visits exchanged with personnel of the Al C. Hansen Shows playing nearby.

June 10—15, Chester, Ill. — Summer was kind to us here and business Big.

June 17—22, Mt. Olive, Ill. — Lost Monday due to a heavy storm but balance of the week very good. Troublesome mining toughs visited here. A nightly visitor was Jockey Day, agent for the Mack Hale Circus.

June 24—29, Livingston, Ill. — This jump was made via Model T. Fords. Quite a novelty after the weekly jaunts by RR and farm wagons. Doc Miller opened a newly built platform pit show here — "Yojo," the double-bodied boy. Some rain but business big.

July 1—6, Sullivanville, Ill. — A beautiful grass lot in a park. The 4th was especially big, the Eli grossed $450, and Doc Miller's 5—1 topped the back end at $189.

July 8—13, Bluffs, Ill. — A RR lot and biz fair. J. T. McClellan Shows a short distance away.

WORKING BOYS. Princess Olga Shows, 1928. Second from left in the back row was Chick Franklin. Courtesy Art Doc Miller.

July 15—20 — Our spot booked cancelled as three large annual picnics in the area. The show split up to catch all three. Business as good for the particular days as the average full week spot.

July 22—29, Virginia, Ill. — Set up around the village square. A nice spot, friendly natives and business good. Several new arrivals and show increased to three baggage cars. Harry Joyce, show's electrician, built an elaborate platform snake pit show here.

July 31—Aug. 5, Astoria, Ill. — This was the bloomer to end all bloomers.

Aug. 7—13, Lewiston, Ill. — Moved here in royal style on 5 large Reo trucks. Considerable cook-house conversation on merits of a truck show against a railer. The rail fans won out. Our first fair and business terrific.

Aug. 14—19, Girard, Ill. — This spot claims the honor (?) of harboring more mosquitoes than Jersey and Texas Gulf combined. The midway was jammed with them while the natives stayed home in self-defense. Several ride boys decamped unable to swat them and still work a clutch.

Aug. 21—26, Albion, Ill. (Fair) — Usually a red one, but this time it rained from Tuesday on and the midway a sea of mud.

Aug. 28—Sept. 2, Carlinville, Ill. (Fair) — A new biller on this spot and most cards tacked on poles upside down. Even this didn't help   biz.

Sept. 4—9, Jerseyville, Ill. (Fair) — Always a nice spot and business good. Enroute here we passed the Barlow Big City Shows on a siding.

Sept. 11—16, Atlanta, Ill. (Fair) — Weather cool, business so-so. According to this week's Billboard, it was one of the wettest seasons in history. Many shows had folded, unable to cope with constant rain and hub-deep mud. With many fairs now lacking the midways   contracted, it was decided to split the show and pick the choicest spots suddenly available.

(Route sheet gone to press at Atlanta.)

The number One Unit was to continue to catch four more Ill. fairs, then barn as usual at Mound City.

The number Two Unit, usually known as the Winter Unit, with Miss Olga as manager, planned to stay out till late November as usual, playing through Tenn. and Miss. This as usual to be a one-car show. Staff and members as follows: Olga Wadsworth, Mgr; Gene Hughes, Agent; Harry Joyce, Electrician; Johnny (Roughhouse) Onafrey, Ride Supt.; Doc Miller Train Supt.

Line-Up: Grab Joint, Doc Miller; Popcorn, 'Liza Garthwaite; pitch-till-win, Pop Harrigar; String Game, Gene Glossick; corn game, Charles Garthwaire; One-Eyed Circus (Arcade), Miss Olga; High Striker, "Boots" Miller; blanket wheel, Gene Hughes; Jap Roll Down, Gene Hughes; Ball game, & juice, Doug (Novelty — Slim Womack); Dad White, Buckets; Platform freak pit show, Doc Miller; Platform snake show, Harry Joyce; Red and Chick Franklin, Merry Mix-Up; Roughhouse Johnny, twin kiddie rides.

Smart Concessionaires purchase all needs from N. SHURE CO. Chicago.

Baker-Lockwood Tent Co. supplies the circus and carnival world.

137

This list does not include all caravans that played in this area, but is a record of most of the railers, until about 1948.

Elks' Carnival, 1914. At that time organized carnivals were not too common. A promoter would "set" a date, and independent rides, shows and concessions would arrive from various celebrations far distant. This one ran several weeks on the lower end of the business section. Concession stands were hastily thrown-up wooden booths, sold for scrap lumber at the close of the event. The rides were a steam-powered track Jenny, a Conderman wheel, and a set of Venetian Swings. Wheels (60 number) worked for a nickel and a paper dressed kewpie or flash box of candy was tossed out each time enough players assembled to make the play worthwhile. As was the custom, the event ran until the crowds ceased, in this case it was big six weeks event.

In 1915 a flatcar carnival made the fair. Title was not remembered, except the wording Fairyland. Wagons were poorly painted and very old. Incidentally, for many seasons after this most county fairs were daytime only affairs. This show had a silo (or straight-walled drome). Again there were only three rides plus a long string of riding ponies. Incidentally these ponies were walked from fair to fair; in the case of leaving Elmira for the Bath fair, it was a good 50 miles. This string was owned by a wealthy farmer who "owned" a bound-out boy who helped on the fair circuit. At age 16 when he departed for over the hill, he told me he had never had any clothes except overalls, second-hand shoes, and a twice weekly thrashing.

One interesting note about the 1915 fair is the fact that George W. Christy of circus fame, made his first start at Elmira. From memory the writer recalls it as an educated horse exhibit and very good too. It was a sit-down show, the horse pulled a rope to a fire bell to warn the town of a fire (very realistic with a RR fuse), also holding chalk in his mouth and writing numbers on a slate. Another side show was the "Klondike" and included Eskimos in sealskins, bone harpoon tools, gold rush pans, etc. Both of these shows did capacity business and were highly entertaining. Along with a harem show that did not work strong, was a snake show and a large "working world," or mechanical world. The most popular grab joint was a stand selling steamed corn on the cob for 5 cents. What struck the writer as strange were the paint brushes on the counter to dip into the butter cans to smear on the corn. No name is recalled on the wagons of this show.

In 1916 on a city lot, a good-sized flatcar outfit played to big business. The name is not known, but the posters which plastered the city were very ornate showing an upper panel of an old man holding a whip and surrounded by lions. The balance of the poster showed a huge midway composed entirely of oriental style side shows. This was the first midway to be lavishly illuminated with electric bulbs that played the area. At that time most homes and stores were using gas lamps.

Perhaps the above show "closed" the city for a time as no carnivals are recalled until 1919 and 1920 when the Empire State Shows played the old Inter-State defunct fairgrounds south of town. This was a good-sized railer with nicely painted wagons. Advance publicity in the local papers stated that the show had been ordered out of the Albany-Troy N.Y. area, due to brazenly operated "red light" wagons behind the girl shows. The show bought all of the local snipe from the town billposter and then refused to pay off. As a result, the biller, an old Frank A. Robbins trouper, attached the office wagon. Payment was then promptly made to the sheriff but dire threats made to Dugan Clark, the billposter.

In '21 and '22, the M. J. Lapp Shows played the old Interstate grounds now known as the Driving Park. Sig Sautelle, the old circus owner, was with this midway working as a magician in the 10—1. During the '22 season he left and Lew Alter came on to replace him. Incidentally this was Lew's first carnival venture. Later he became very well known as a big time side show operator and tacking on the title "Colonel," to his moniker. This show had a strong back end but not too many concessions.

Following the Lapp Shows was a well-painted string of flat and wagons, about a 15-car show, but completely lacking on equipment as to title. This was billed locally as the Redmans' Carnival. This outfit was not as heavy on the back end but carried a long string of joints, most of which were sloughed a half hour after opening on Monday night. No doubt this one was on the order of the old Barlow Shows which used a different title at each spot (3 in all). However it ran "Sunday School" after the sloughing and did not incur the wrath of the local newspapers.

In 1923 the J. F. (or P.) Murphey Producing Co. played the Driving Park to good returns. This was a good-sized outfit and because the word carnival had become somewhat of a nasty term, Murphey had substituted "Producing Co." (As had Johnny J. Jones, using "Exposition.") This midway had a very strong back end, the flashiest being an elaborate Plantation Show. This was the term used prior to Minstrel Shows. Also recalled was the old broomstick bally illusion and Minnie Ha Ha, both on the 10—1. In those days Nelson mummified freaks were highly popular. The Murphey had a very flashy front picturing a jungle monster and the 6-legged Pollymaloozia, shown (on the banner) racing out into the ocean and destroying a dory of sailors. All Nelson freaks were nightmares to behold but sure did draw the crowds. They could stand close examination, always had celluloid fingernails etc. In damp, rainy weather they always started to mould and had to be carefully greased with lard. The secret of these wonderful fakes passed on with the inventor during the early 30's at South Boston.

Back in these days, many ride, concession and side show people owned their own wagons. Usually they would be designated as a living van, or gypsy wagon. These were often very fancy and had a vestibule on the rear end, much in the style of an old RR observation car. Inside they were fixed up in a home-like manner, once they were unloaded of side show etc. contents.

No doubt many have wondered why so many cars on the old shows, when only three or four rides were carried. Perhaps a 15-car show had a flat or two of these living vans.

To prove the point that many carnival wagons were owned by private showmen, the writer once hunted up the former owner of the famous Maple Shade Wagon Works in N.J. for an interesting evening of wagon building lore. In all of the years that they made carnival wagons, and they certainly built countless numbers over a 20-year period, all were for individual owners except for a string of wagons built for the George L. Dobyns Shows and for which, incidentally, the Maple Shade firm never received one penny from them. Perhaps this explains why the above-mentioned caravan lacked a title on the flats or wagons. It could have been the Dobyns Show on a hush-hush route.

Not far behind the Murphey Show came the Dobyns and Berger Shows. This must have been a switch date as they did not use any billing but used a full newspaper page. Various contests were held through the week to keep interest stirred up afternoons. This was a good-sized outfit and well painted. Minnie Ha Ha again appeared with this show, but not the same 10—1 and it's now forgotten whether it was in a Lapp, Murphey or Dobyns 10—1, was the old colored man, legless and armless, with huge brass rings in his ears. With just his tongue, lips and a set of wooden blocks, he could shake out tobacco from a Bull Durham sack, flip out a paper and roll a cigarette and light it. This drew considerable applause and the nickels and pennies were thickly tossed to him.

The big attraction on this show was a new ride, the Giant Sea Plane built by Travers of Beaver Falls. This was very high, and had rather large boats or sea planes with large electric motor-driven propellers on front. This slow-to-erect ride occupied a long flat on the train. Later that season one of the boat cables slipped, the passengers thrown out, and one man was killed. This case went to court where it was soon proved that "Riders assume all risk" was and is a bunch of hooey. The ride owner spent the next 25 years paying off that accident and when last visited, was running a small restaurant in western Penna.

Not much was noted about the Dobyns Show after '25 and perhaps this equipment passed on to Harry Copping Shows.

Previous to '23, a very popular athletic show always made the Elmira fairs and was owned jointly by one Frank Bacon, wrestler, Erie RR Dick, Nick Bozenis and Young Strgler Lewis, also wrestlers. The latter took the name James Strates and early in '23 they framed a small carnival out of Elmira. This was a gilly operation that year only, then going on huge solid-tired White trucks, discards from some trucking firm. The big feature of the midway was the "At" show, and all the popular upstate wrestlers came on for nightly bouts to help the show make a go of it. (Henry Pruess of Binghampton, Jack Albright, Slim Wolff, etc.) Many a week that first season, the At show moved their cars. Strates had purchased a beautiful three-abreast Spillman Jenny and they booked on an old Eli and a very high tower Smith and Smith Chair-O-Plane. Other attractions were a 10—1, monkey speed drome, snake show and arcade. It is interesting to note that for several seasons the show (titled Southern Tier Shows) did not carry any girl shows.

SOUTHERN TIER SHOWS TRUCKS. Courtesy Art Doc Miller.

JAMES E. STRATES. When he was wrestling as Young Strangler Lewis.

JAMES E. STRATES. With his long-time friend, Jack Dempsey.

A STRATES MIDWAY SHOW IN FIFTIES. Author's Collection.

No record has been kept for '24 and '25, but in 1926 and '27, the best show ever to play in Elmira appeared — The Brown & Dyer Shows. This was a beautifully framed and painted outfit with a strong back end. Included were Kelly Bros. 20—1, a Spillman Fun on the Farm, Tom Howard's Wild West Show, Stella, platform rep show, a platform fat gal show, snake illusion show, Burlesque, Hawaiian, Gay Paree and Plantation Show. The record of other back end attractions has long been mislaid. A sizeable string of joints was carried but none created any heat. This was about the last of the nicely maintained big railers to play Elmira except of course the Strates Shows which came back "home" annually for many seasons.

BROWN & DYER

Courtesy Art Doc Miller

SHOW, 1927.

Courtesy Art Doc Miller

Like many other fine shows, the Brown & Dyer outfit vanished off the face of the earth the following season and no troupers of that time seemed to have an inkling of how it ended or what became of the wagons and train. During the late 40's, rumor persisted that the owner, Al Dernberger, was operating a junk yard in the Richmond, Va. area.

The Carl Middleton Shows, a 2-car outfit, predated B & D in '27 and was a typical promoter's nightmare. All lumber etc. was crude, and protruding nails the rule and not the exception. As most everyone knows, nails, etc. left in lumber on a gilly show are absolutely taboo. This was an annual promotion for many years through New York and Penna., with headquarters in Dansville, N.Y. Carl had the knack to come out of a spending spree with a paltry two bits, use it to phone some fire chief and in a 3-minute conversation promote another winner.

In '28, the Melville-Reiss Shows wandered into the east, a complete stranger to the natives, and at fair time was still playing still dates. Easily the largest midway to visit Elmira, it presented a grand array of rides and also a strong back end, also plenty of joints. Nat had passed on and the outfit was operated by his widow and Melville. While still on 30 cars, it was badly in need of paint on both wagons and the train. This caravan also seemed to fade away at season's end, with no records of where the equipment eventually ended.

During all of these years, Southern Tier Shows, home based at Elmira, opened their season here and always returned for the late fall county fair.

The A. F. Crouse Shows on around 10 cars played the Elmira outskirts in either '28 or '29, as did O. J. Boch, a well-known gilly show for many years.

In 1930, the Kaus United Shows on ten cars limped into Elmira and the going was so rough that funds were lacking even to hire a team to unload the flats. As had evidently become the weekly practice, all of the ride boys tossed the hook rope over their shoulders, all leaned forward, and by brute strength inched the wagons across the flats. This sight was about as sad as can be imagined, but to make matters worse a bunch of Cornell college boys watching the unloading, started chanting "The Volga Boatman." Somehow the show crawled and staggered onward through the season.

MAN POWER. Loading wagons on Con T. Kennedy Shows, about 1915. Courtesy Albert Conover.

The material in the last several pages has been collected and compiled by Art Doc Miller. It is hoped that this book will stimulate interest in collecting such material and publishing it. Many old time carnival troupers have memories, papers and photographs that should be preserved and recorded. The Author thanks Art Doc Miller, Lou Dufour, Slim Kelly, Dick Best, Joe Pearl, Doc Cann (now deceased), Harvey Wilson, Nat Worman and all the others who have contributed. The "ball is rolling" now boys, let's keep our carnival history accurate.   Joe McKennon

That same fall four 72-ft. steel flats were switched onto the American Bridge siding, bearing the title A. F. Crouse Shows United and word leaked out Strates had picked them up from the Hershall Spillman firm and that the Southern Tier Shows would go out in the spring on rails. According to reports, the show (then changed to James E. Strates Shows), was the first to load flats with a truck, no horses needed.

Next summer Bruce Greater Shows limped into town on a 3-day billing of about 50 window cards. They had a long haul across town and the office wagon, a dandy wood scrolled ex-circus wagon, lost a front wheel rim on a downtown street car track, but continued, truck-drawn, to the lot. Long before the lot was reached that side was rolling on the wheel hub. This was a tough-looking outfit and opened with Big 6 wheels and Taylor cats etc. galore, but was promptly sloughed on the joints. Nothing seemed to get any money except the gal shows and at week's end the show was hauled crosstown to play another lot outside the city limits. Somehow the "wiggle shows" grossed enough to make the train "jump" onward and back into the dreary Penna. coal mining towns.

At the fall fair, the Otis L. Smith Shows were on the midway. This outfit clung to the old-time carnival theme of a featured wild animal show, which was Smith's pride. The show carried quite a variety of small cage wagons all non-related as to size. When the King Bros. Gentry Show went on the auction block, Smith had purchased the three bulls, along with a stock car, and two flats of wagons. All of the Gentry equipment still carried that title, though badly faded and no doubt convinced many natives that circuses always do split to play small towns. This was a very slow show to load and unload as the wagons were of various widths and the runs had to be continually changed back and forth.

In '33, the Glick show played Elmira, also a rough-appearing outfit, and the Bernardi Shows had the fair. The wagons and train of the latter were run down and sadly lacking on paint.

Following on the heels of the Glick Shows was the Travers Chautauqua Exposition, a four or five-car gilly show consisting of a large array of rides, no shows and no flat joints.

In '34 a Max Gruberg gilly show played the old Driving Park and carried the first Parker caged wheel seen in the area. The Coleman gilly show appeared for the fair, now changed into a day and nighttime event.

1935 brought the Strates Shows to Elmira, and by now it was a large outfit, everything painted a snazzy circus red. The show was carrying the cannon act, shooting Hugo over twin wheels, quite a novelty for those days. Along about this time, the Art Lewis Shows played the fair. This too was a fair-sized railer, neatly painted and wagons seemingly in good repair.

1936 the Marks Show, then partly a gilly and partly trucks played the Driving Park to a real bloomer. A season or two later Marks returned but played nearby Heights where the law was evidently not so fussy as to joints. Adolph Kaus played on the old circus lot with a small trucker. It was too small-looking after so many large outfits so the returns were nil.

Bantley's All-American Shows blew into town the following season. This was a neatly framed and rather large truck show, about the first to appear that gave the appearance of a 20-car outfit. Herman Bantley was the son-in-law of the well-known midway owner, Harry Copping.

In the late 30's O. J. Bach usually opened the season in either Elmira or nearby Sayre, Penna. During this same period Howard Potter's Buffalo Shows frequently appeared in the area. Firemen and other local organizations were beginning to learn of the profits on self-operated efforts and Potter supplied this idea, with the local sponsor operating all concessions. The only ride carried was an Eli, and that was usually erected in a very sloppy, loose-cable manner.

Totham's "baled hay wire" aggregation limped into town during the early war years and the natives had their first glimpse of kiddie rides made from bed rails and what have you, but everything got money like crazy.

Strates was returning every year, either for a still date or at the fair and the outfit was continuing to increase in size. One season the Strates show train included several Cole Bros. circus flats.

Although these were big money years, the familiar Bach show with a fine route that included the upper N. Y. loop, later long held by O. C. Buck, folded as it attempted to open in Elmira during the mid 1940's. At that time, all that Bach still owned was a hot wagon, some cable, side wall and a marquee.

This list is by no means complete; many outfits have been skipped as the writer was also trouping. Many of the shows mentioned, the date was forwarded to the writer by local old troupers. It is interesting to note that of all the older shows seen by the writer in Elmira, none except the 1916 outfit boasted of the fancy carved wagon fronts used by so many shows like J. J. Jones etc.

Many thanks to Lew Alter, Zoppi, Dugan Clark and all others who passed on "info" while I was trouping.

THIS IS A CIRCUS. Courtesy Ringling Museum of the Circus, Sarasota, Florida.

THIS IS A CARNIVAL. Courtesy of Harry Frost, Minnesota State Fair.

GLOSSARY OF CARNIVAL WORDS AND TERMS

NOTE: Many words have common usage between carnival and circus people. However, most words defined below are peculiar to carnival people only. DO NOT attempt to use these words on a carnival lot to gain acceptance among Carnies. A carnival trouper can "spot a phony a mile away," and words alone do not constitute the full vocabulary of the midways. The remainder of the sentence, gestures, facial expressions and such all contribute to the language of the carnival.

The same word may mean different things. The meaning may vary according to usage. The word "KIESTER" is used frequently among circus people. It is used four times in the following sentence, each with a different meaning: "Last night I cracked the 'Kiester' at the post office, went to the hotel and packed my 'Kiester,' was grabbed by the fuzz and kicked in the 'Kiester' before they threw me in the 'Kiester,'" Any old-time circus hand would understand this 'underworld'-derived sentence. Translation: I blew open the safe at the post office, went to the hotel and packed my suitcase, was picked up by the police who kicked my backside before locking me in the town jail.

—A—

ADVANCE: Ahead of the show. Everything pertaining to the show on its route before it arrives in a town.

ADVANCE AGENTS:

Contracting Agent: The person who gets all necessary contracts signed for a show's exhibition date.

General Agent: The person who lays out the route of a show and negotiates for the exhibit date. (On carnivals the general agent also acts as contractor).

Special Agent: The person who goes into town ahead of the show and makes final arrangements for the exhibition. On carnivals this person usually sold advertising banners to the local merchants. (On circuses one man sold the banners and a special agent called a 24-hour man handled the pre-exhibition details).

AHEAD: Advance of the show. "He was sent up 'ahead'."

AT SHOW: A carnival midway show featuring athletic contests between boxers and wrestlers carried by the show and local champions or contenders.

ARCH: The front gate of a carnival. Prior to the Thirties this term was used by all carnies for their midway entrance.

—B—

BACK-END: That portion of the midway consisting of rides and shows.

BALLYHOO: The free show given outside a midway attraction to attract a crowd (a Tip) of potential patrons. Usually shortened to BALLY.

BALLYS: See above. Also small gifts of merchandise placed in boxes of candy, Cracker Jack, etc.

BANNER: Canvas pictorial hung in front of midway shows. Also advertising signs of local merchants displayed on riding devices and rolling stock of show. (Latter not used as much now as in early years of the business.)

BANNER LINE: Line of banners in front of an attraction.

BARKER: (Not used by outdoor show people.) A writer's word for talker, lecturer, spieler, etc. Some "First of May" showman might use the word as he knows no better.

BELLY STICK: A person who works outside a game of chance to entice players for the game. He "bellys up" to the counter and pretends to play the game.

BIG TOP: The tent in which a circus performance is given. Never the circus as a whole. NEVER A CARNIVAL.

BLOWDOWN: Just that. Tents and portable equipment leveled by a storm.

BRASS: Coin-sized pieces of brass used by old-time carnivals in lieu of "White Money." Show's name was stamped on the brass.

BREAK THE ICE: First sale of the day.

BROAD TOSSER: A worker with a three-card Monte game in a circus side show. (Never worked on carnivals and always crooked. None left today.)

BUG: A chameleon. (Sold as pets by "Bug Board" salesmen.)

BULL: An elephant regardless of sex. (Most elephants in U.S. are female.)

BUSK: Show or give a performance on a street corner or vacant lot and pass the hat for a collection of coins.

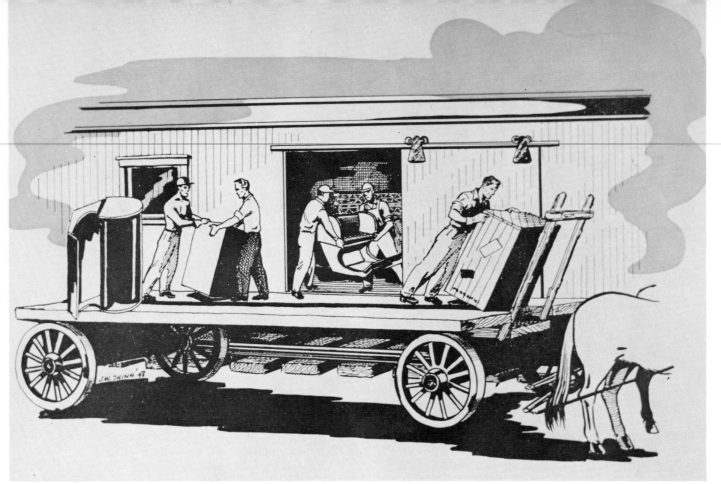

"GILLY SHOW" LOADING OUT. This sketch shows the system used by "Gilly" carnivals to load into railroad cars. Courtesy Gooding Amusement Co.

—C—

CARNIVAL: A collective amusement organization consisting of shows, riding devices, catering and gaming concessions. A circus may be just one of the shows on a carnival midway.

CARNY WEDDING: A union between carnival men and women without benefit of clergy. These common-law unions are usually of one season duration, but many of them have resulted in life-time arrangements. Many of them result in legal weddings.

CARS: (Railroad Show) The show's sleeping cars.

CARRY THE BANNER: Stay up all night because you have no bed.

CAT: Caterpillar or any other track-laying type tractor. (On Circus: any cat-type animal.)

CHUMP HEISTER: The Ferris wheel.

CHUMP EDUCATOR: The Billboard. A weekly publication devoted to amusement buisness. (Since 1960 a music magazine and no longer interested in outdoor shows.)

CIRCUS: A performance presented in a ring which is enclosed by tiers of seats. See Webster.

CIRCUS SIDE SHOW: Used by carnival freak show owners to designate their attraction. (Use the word CIRCUS in this way.)

COPS: Small prizes or "Ballys" placed in boxes of candy or Cracker Jack.

COOCH: (from Hoochy-kootchy) A movement of certain portions of their bodies by "dancing girls" in shows carried by some carnivals.

COOCH SHOW: A "dancing girl" show where the girls do the cootch.

COOKHOUSE: A show's dining facilities. The enclosure where show people eat their meals on the show grounds. Most carnival cookhouses also serve the general public.

CROSSING: (Railroad show) Railroad crossing where the show train is loaded or unloaded.

CHUTES: Same as Crossing. Refers to the inclined runs or chutes on which the wagons are loaded on and unloaded from the flatcars.

CUT UP JACKPOTS: A discussion of past events (often distorted) by showmen.

CUT or

CUT OF FLATS: Section of flatcars spotted in for loading or unloading.

CUT-INS: The fee the electrician collects for connecting electrical service.

CONCESSION AGENT: Operator of a sales or gaming concession.

CONCESSIONS: Merchandise, food or gaming booths.

—D—

DATE: A show's engagement in a town.

DATE BOOK: A book in which the show's route is listed.

DAUB: Advertising paper that has been pasted on some structure — a barn, fence or factory

RUBIN IN A MIXED GROUP. Another photograph of Rubin Gruberg in an unusual grouping. Author's collection.

building.

DIGGERS: A gaming device. A coin is inserted and a mechanical device scoops up merchandise (usually a ball of chewing gum) and delivers it to the player.

DONIKER: A toilet.

DONIKER LOCATION: A spot on the midway that isn't as good for business as other "locations" might be.

DRAG THE MIDWAY: An early day practice of some independent showmen on carnival midways of going to the front gate and enticing people down the midway to their attraction.

DUKEY: (Circus term only) A sack or box lunch given to the working men when the circus train had to make an extra long 'jump' between towns.

DUKEY RUN: A long move between towns.

DROME: A motordrome. A silo-like wooden structure where men and women ride motorcycles and small automobiles on the straight up and down wall.

—F—

FIRST OF MAY: (Mostly Circus) A newcomer on the show. A first season trouper.

FIXER: Legal Adjuster

FLASH: Merchandise on a gaming concession. Blankets, guns, radios, etc.

FLAT STORE: A gaming concession that has no winning numbers. The "gentlemanly agents" "sell conversation."

FLOP: A cheap bed or room.

FORTY MILER: A carnival trouper who never takes his concession, show or ride more than a few miles from his home base.

FRAME: To build a new concession, show or midway.

FRONT: The front of a midway show or attraction. An individual's personal appearance and clothing.

FRONT-END: That portion of the midway consisting only of concessions.

FRONT GATE: Main entrance to the midway.

FUZZ: Law enforcement officers.

—G—

GADGET: A device worn by certain girl show performers to enhance the illusion of their performance.

GAZOONIE: A young working man.

GEEK: A person who works in dens or pits of snakes and reptiles. They usually work as wild men or wild girls.

GLOMMING GEEK: Also called a "Glommer." A geek who eats live snakes, rats, chickens or other live animals and reptiles.

GIMMICK: The control on a crooked game of chance.

Courtesy Al Kunz

GILLY: Handle by manpower alone, or to move in a vehicle not built for the equipment being moved.

GILLY SHOW: A show that was moved between towns in boxcars or baggage cars. This entailed loading all equipment on "gilly" wagons or trucks and hauling it to the railroad yards where it was relaoded in the cars. Everything had to be handled four times on each move. In spite of what other writers may say, THERE HAS NOT BEEN A GILLY SHOW ON THE ROAD IN OVER TWENTY YEARS.

GRIFT: (Mostly used on circus lots) Crooked games of chance, shell games, short-change artists and the like.

GRIFT SHOW: A show that carried Grift. (A circus term but most early carnivals carried grift.)

GRAB JOINT: A lunch counter where the customer is served directly from the griddle and other appliances over the counter. Most are "stand up joints" but some do have a few stools. (Stools are usually occupied by carnies who are "cutting up Jackpots" as their wives work on the midway.)

GRINDER: A person who has a certain "set spiel" or sequence of words which he delivers on the front of a midway attraction as long as the show is open. If a show has "ballys," the spiel between them is the "grind." Ticket sellers "grind" as they sell tickets.

GRIND SHOW: A show that never "Ballys." Just "Grinds" all day.

GUNSEL: A young person. (A boy)

GUT: A circus bill poster's term meaning the main business street in a town.

GOES TO THE BARN: Show goes into winter quarters.

—H—

HANKY PANK: Also HANKY. A gaming concession that has winning numbers and gives prizes to the winners.

HEAT: Trouble with people who are not Carnies. Can be with the Law or people incensed over their losses on the games. Most of the 'heat' in the 'good old days' was generated by the games, the 'At' Shows or the 'strong' dancing girls.

HERALD: A piece of Outdoor Show advertising paper printed on colored newsprint. The herald was designed to be given to a person directly, placed in their automobile or front door, or mailed to their box number.

HEY RUBE: (Circus term) Many carnivals had more 'Hey Rubes' or 'Clems' with the local townspeople than did the circuses. A battle between showmen and the local people.

HIGH STRIKER: A long timber with a bell on top of it erected vertically. A weight which travels on a track fastened to the face side of the timber may be propelled upward by the player striking a hinged lever device with a wooden maul.

HOT WAGON: Electrical transformer wagons carried by most carnivals before generating plants were built compact enough to be feasible for midway use.

DWARFS AT GIBSONTOWN, FLORIDA. This special counter was installed at the post office for use of the "little people" who live in Gibtown each winter. Courtesy Amusement Business Photograph.

—I—

ILLUSION SHOW: A magic show that featured illusions such as the headless girl, etc., etc.

—J—

JAM: The act of turning everyone into a show on a reduced price ticket for a period of time after a 'bally' is ended.

JAM STORE: A sales concession that builds up the buyer's confidence in the salesman by giving away lots of 'slum' merchandise.

JOINT: a concession stand or booth.

JUMP: The move between towns.

JUICE: Electrical current.

—L—

LATIN, CARNY: A form of 'Pig Latin' used by some young carnies to impress the town 'Marks.'

LEFT HAND SIDE: Most Americans move to the right, so carnival midways are laid out to take advantage of this habit. Shows catering to children are always spotted on right hand side, if possible. Shows for the 'Sports' are in the back end, etc.

LECTURER: Inside talker. Emcee for circus side shows, illusion shows, etc. Lecturer in Unborn Shows, Crime Does Not Pay Shows, etc.

LOCATION: Space allocated to a concession, show or ride on the midway.

LOT: The Show Grounds.

LOT LICE: (Circus term) Persons who spend nothing but time on a showgrounds. Persons who stay on the grounds all day and spend nothing.

—M—

MAGIC CARPET: A Hyla F. Maynes riding device. The lobby of the Sherman Hotel in Chicago. Old-time showmen always went to the Sherman when in Chicago. There they met other showmen on the huge carpet in the lobby. This carpet became known by all showmen as the magic carpet.

MARK: (NEVER USED ON A CIRCUS) A carnival term for the townspeople.

MOVE: The 'jump' between towns on the show's route.

MUD SHOW: (CIRCUS TERM) There were no carnival 'mud shows.' The circus 'mud shows' travelled overland by horse-drawn wagon. All circuses were 'mud shows' prior to 1872, and some still travelled that way until the early Twenties. No record exists that any organized carnival ever moved any way other than by railroad or by motor truck. (A recent book has wrongly used the term in connection with carnivals.)

MULE: A rubber-tired tractor used to 'spot' empty wagons and load show train.

—N—

NUT: The expense of the show. (Daily Nut, Weekly Nut, etc.)

—O—

OFFICE: The carnival office wagon or trailer.

OFFICE SHOW or

OFFICE RIDE: Owned by the midway owner. Not an independent attraction.

—P—

PAPER: Advertising paper for the show. Also used for passes. You never say you have 'papered the town' for putting up advertising paper. You say, 'billed the town.' A 'papered town' has had a disproportionate number of passes given out. A 'paper house' means that almost all of the patrons are there on free passes.

PATCH: Legal adjuster or fixer.

PIG IRON: The riding devices. More particularly the heavy, flat type rides.

PIT: A small canvas enclosure in which acts are performed or animals, human oddities, snakes and reptiles are exhibited. The spectators stand around the four sides of the pit and look down into it.

PIT SHOW: A show in which the exhibits are shown in pits. A show with one pit is a 'Single-O,' while one with ten pits is a 'ten-in-one.'

PITCH: A sales concession where merchandise is sold outright after the salesman has given a demonstration.

PITCHMAN: A person who operates a 'pitch' concession. The candy salesmen in the 'Gal' shows are 'candy pitchmen.' A pitchman who works on an elevated platform is a 'high pitchman.' Pitchmen use the word 'Kiester' for the small case many of them worked from.

PICKLED PUNKS: Human fetuses preserved in glass jars. Two-headed babies and such are usually real human specimens.

PLANT SHOW: (No longer used) Old Plantation Show, or the colored minstrel show on early day midways.

PLATFORM SHOW: A small 'single-o' attraction presented on an elevated platform under a small canvas top.

PLAY: Show an engagement in a town or at a fair.

PLAY THE STREETS: Set up on the streets and sidewalks for an engagement.

PLAY A BLOOMER: Do no business on a date. Also 'Play a Blank.'

PRIVILEGE: The consideration paid for the rights to

operate on a show midway. Used in connection with concessions.

PRIVILEGE CAR: The dining car on a show train with slot machines and games for the show people only.

—R—

RAILROAD SHOW: A show which travels by railroad on its own train consisting of flatcars and sleeping cars.

RIGHT HAND SIDE: Preferred location for early opening shows that cater to children and the family trade.

ROUTE: (noun) List of towns and events played each season.
(verb) The laying out of a season's play dates. 'Route the show.'

ROUTE CARDS: Cards listing the show's play dates in advance.

RUN: The move between show dates or towns in which show exhibits.

RUNS: (Same as Chutes)

'GO TO THE RUNS': Go to the railroad crossing where the train is being loaded or unloaded.

REHASH: The practice of selling used tickets. The proceeds of this resale is kept by the ticket seller and split with the ticket taker.

—S—

SCUFF: Having a difficult time securing enough food for regular meals because of shortage of funds.

SHILL: One who pretends to play a game or to buy a ticket to an attraction in order to entice others to follow him.

SHEET: One-sheet, three-sheet, etc. A standard sheet of advertising paper is approximately 28" x 42". A standard billboard is 24-sheet.

SLOUGH: To tear down the show. To be closed by the Law. Billposters use the word for the side street areas off the main street of a town where they can 'sell-out a hod' (where he can hang all the paper he has issued).

STICK: Same as Shill.

SNIPE: A built-up billboard belonging to a local plant.

SNIPE PLANT: A company owning and servicing the billboards in an area.

STILL DATE: An engagement played that is not an annual fair, picnic or celebration.

STRING: A long line of horses, animals, objects, or things.

STRING SHOW: An open front show with a long line of canvas banners.

SUCKER: (Circus term) A townsperson.

SUNDAY SCHOOL: A clean show or operation. A carnival midway that never allows crooked games or dirty gal shows to operate on its midway.

STAND: The show date is referred to on circuses as a stand, i.e., one day stand. In billposting it refers to a location where paper has been posted.

STRIPPING: The practice of removing and loading decorative portions of fronts, rides and equipment before the engagement ends.

—T—

TALKER: **NEVER BARKER.** The man who does the outside talks and lectures in front of an attraction.

TEN-IN-ONE: A midway show with ten attractions. Usually a freak or illusion string show.

TEAR-DOWN: Dismantling the midway at the end of an engagement.

TIMBER: A stick or shill on concessions.

TIP: The crowd gathered in front of an attraction listening to the talker and watching the free attractions on the bally platform.

TOP: A tent.

TROUPER: A person who has spent at least one full season with some type of travelling amusement organization.

TURN: 'TURN THE TIP' The ones who are convinced by the talker that they must see the attraction are 'turned' when they purchase a ticket.

TUBS: The seats of many of the riding devices.

TOM SHOW: (Never with a carnival.) An Uncle Tom's Cabin Show. Such shows toured the Northern states for over fifty years. Many actors made life-time careers with 'Tom Shows.'

—U—

UP: Outdoor showmen are prone to add the word 'up' to other words without changing the meaning of the word added to. Example: An eight-horse team is referred to as 'eight-up.'

—W—

WHITE MONEY: Regular coins and currency of the United States or Canada with which old-time carnivals were apt to pay their employees only when they were doing good business.

WITH IT: An expression whereby Carnies may know one another, even though they have never seen each other before. **WARNING:** Do not attempt to use this 'word' unless you have been instructed in the proper way to deliver it.

THE OPERATION OF
A COLLECTIVE AMUSEMENT ORGANIZATION
or
"MOVING A CARNY"

Probably no other business man encounters as many problems in marketing his product as does the owner of a collective amusement organization. He not only has to sell his attractions to the carnival-going public but also must convince the possible bookers of the midway that his show can and will give them a better "deal" than any of his competitors. In addition, he must maintain good relations in the industry itself in order to insure that he will have reliable and experienced troupers on his midway when he does play the dates he has booked.

The booking of a new season's route starts long before the season ends. The best spots on the route are rebooked for the next season, if possible, before the show "goes to the barn." The fortunate ones who do have their show's route all booked before Thanksgiving cannot relax but must attend all the meetings that the other showmen do. The first and largest of these is the "Outdoor Meetings" held at the Sherman Hotel in Chicago and always starting the last Saturday in November. Here the amusement park men, the fair managers, the amusement device manufacturers and the outdoor showmen hold simultaneous conventions as they "wheel and deal" for sales and bookings. 1971 fair and showmen's meetings were held at the Star Dust Hotel in Las Vegas.

At these "Chicago Meetings" the show owners assisted by their agents, their family and some of their employees hold "open house" in their rooms or suites of rooms. There everyone is greeted cordially, but a special welcome is extended to the managers of the fairs played or hoped to be played by the carnival. The midway owner also entertains the managers and their wives by taking them to night clubs, theaters and the Showmen's League Banquet. The carnival showman's booking campaign doesn't end in Chicago though as he must attend the Fair Association's meetings with the attendant entertaining of managers in each of the states in which he plays. Then some managers may hold out on signing contracts and the owner or his general agent, if he has one, must go to the individual towns for more expensive coaxing before the date is firmly booked. All owners and their agents hope to have their route all set by February 1 so that they can attend the Florida State Fair in Tampa without worries about play dates for the coming season.

The "wheeling and dealing" in Tampa is no longer concerned with routing. There the hundreds of midway owners meet with the hundreds of independent ride owners, showmen and concession operators. The carnival owner with a good route booked has no difficulty in securing the rides and attractions he needs to make his midway "stronger;" but the one with only a few good dates must offer special concessions to the independents he hopes to book on his show. The meetings between these troupers take place in hotel and motel rooms, in the showmen's club rooms in Tampa and Gibsontown and in the showmen's cookhouse on the Royal American Midway. After the Tampa Fair is over, the show owners can start planning, building and rebuilding their midways for the new season.

All outdoor shows regardless of size must have an "Advance." On the smaller shows, the owner may

MINSTREL SHOW FRONT. Johnny J. Jones Exposition. Designed and built by Charlie Kidder in the mid-thirties, this was the last of the old style fronts built on any midway. Courtesy Albert Conover.

RUBIN & CHERRY? In Teens. Striping on wagon suggests Rubin Show, but not positive.
Courtesy Albert Conover.

do all the booking done by the general agent of the larger midways. He may also go "up ahead" and do all the work done by the special agents, but he usually does have someone connected with the show to do the billposting necessary to advertise the date to be played. On the larger shows, the owner, his manager or his "lot" man goes ahead and lays out the lot three days ahead of the show's opening. If the owner does this, the manager and lot man do their regular duties back on the lot; but if one of them lays out the new lot, the owner may handle the management while the other man "takes the show off the lot."

Most modern carnivals travel overland on the highways in their own fleet of trucks and semi-trailer units, but two of the large ones are still traveling on their own trains of flatcars and sleepers. The largest of them all, the great Royal American Shows is using ninety double-length steel railroad cars in 1972. When a truck-transported show arrives on the lot, the driver usually drives the truck directly to its location. The wagons of railroad shows must be unloaded from the flatcars and pulled to the showgrounds by trucks from a local cartage company. Police protection and traffic direction must be secured for the railroad crossing and the entrance to the grounds. Show-owned caterpillar tractors are used to "spot" these wagons on their locations on the lot. Regardless of the mode of transportation used though, the erection of the attraction is started as soon as the vehicle transporting it is "located" on the lot.

The erection of a carnival today is a scene of well-ordered mechanized confusion. Each show and each riding device has its own foreman and crew of men so that forty, fifty or even more individual tents, structures or riding devices are being raised simultaneously. While this is being done on the "back end" of the midway, scores of small tents and trailers housing direct sales, catering and gaming concessions are being erected on the "front end." Most all of these concessions are independently owned. The independent concession operator may have only one "joint," but many of them own a "string of joints" consisting of from three to twenty concessions. The independent concession operator pays so much per front foot rental for his location to the carnival office, or "Office." This rental or "privilege" varies with the dates played as the "Office" must pay a different amount per foot at each spot played. This "sale of real estate on the front end" often marks the difference between profit and loss for the show at some dates.

The independent ride and show operator works on a percentage of the gross with the 'Office." Eastern and Midwestern carnivals give a percentage of their gross to the local committee or fair. This gross is for the show and ride receipts. In addition, the carnival agrees to take a certain number of feet of concession space at a fixed price per foot, and the fairs are usually given guarantees of minimum amounts they will receive regardless of weather or business conditions during their dates. The Western Fair contracts are given out on a bid basis. The carnivals pay the fairs fixed amounts based on fair attendance. Usually the bid is made for so much per person attending the fair whether they go to the midway area or not.

The percentages of gross given the "office" by

independent ride and show owners pay for their "location" on the midway, their electric current and their transportation in an office-owned wagon if they are with a railroad show. They, as well as the concession owners, must pay the show's electricians certain fees for "cut-ins" or they are likely to find they have no "juice" when their business is biggest. So they all do pay the fees collected by the electrician. All persons who own living trailers must pay fees each week for locations on the lot, electrical and water connections and anything else that some person in the "office" may decide should be paid.

If a carnival is being erected on a fairgrounds on opening day of the fair, individual attractions and concessions open for the patrons as soon as they are ready; but after this first day the midway opens according to a "call" posted at the "office" each night for next day's opening. Ticket sellers for the rides and shows come to the office and are issued tickets and change by the show's secretary, who on many shows is the owner's wife. Owners or managers of independent shows and rides usually pick up the tickets for their attractions and issue them to their ticket sellers. Ticket takers for all attractions are furnished by the fair or local committee, but they are stationed at their posts by someone who works for the carnival. If there is any evidence of "rehashing" tickets, these ticket takers may be changed from post to post several times a day.

Each day's operations of a midway varies little except for different hours of opening which is determined by the type of crowd expected that day. Special "Kids Days" for school children at fairs may

have the midway all open and operating at 9:00 A.M. Other days may not have crowds that will require anything to open before afternoon. Once open, the attractions may remain open and operating until after midnight, if business and the crowds warrant it. Closing time (earliest) is usually determined by the "office" and not by the attraction's manager. Of course, an independent operator may close early, if he thinks his attraction will not get any more money by remaining open. Office employees on office-owned attractions must remain with the attraction on which they work until "official" closing time.

The routine does change a little on "slough night," as the foremen and their crews are likely to be dressed in their own working clothes by 10:00 P.M. On the shows that have "no stripping" rules from the "office," constant supervision is required to keep these men from taking down every piece of ornamental lighting, decorative paneling and other non-essential elements long before the crowd leaves the midway. On many shows, the foremen are allowed to "strip" these elements of rides and shows and load them on the trucks or wagons the night before closing night in order to expedite the "teardown" or "slough."

On the final night of an engagement, the midway remains open until usual closing time unless the weather has "sent the crowds home." At closing time the midway is darkened except for work lights on the attractions and one or two of the central lighting towers. Empty wagons or trucks are pulled onto the midway and spotted so that the ride equipment may be loaded into them as it is

RUBIN & CHERRY SHOWS, 1917. Gilly Cars. Courtesy Albert Conover.

dismantled from the device. Ornamental panels, lighting and ride "tubs" are loaded into closed, van-type vehicles. These first vehicles loaded will be the last ones required when the show sets up in the next town. On a railroad show these wagons are hurried to the show train and loaded onto a section of flatcars which will be the last cars unloaded the next day. As soon as these "light section" wagons are loaded, the "heavy" section of "work wagons" are loaded onto another cut of flatcars that will be the first unloaded in the next town.

Each show or ride which requires more than one vehicle for transportation, uses one of these conveyances as a "work wagon." On this wagon or truck is loaded the first equipment needed to set up the show or riding device, as well as all tools and working equipment. As nothing can be done towards setting up the attraction until this wagon is spotted on location, quite a lot of controversy is caused by them on railroad shows. As there may be as many as fifty major attractions, each with its own "work wagon," on such shows, the individual attraction owners, managers or foremen are all jealous of the attraction that gets its "work wagon" before they get theirs. Many good lot superintendents and trainmasters have left good jobs on good shows because of the beratings they received for being unable to unload all of the wagons at one time and drop them all on their locations simultaneously.

The superintendent who gets the show off the lot in the order it is supposed to be loaded on the train has the problem of foremen "stalling" on loading their wagons so that they will get them quicker on the set-up. The trainmaster has the problem of fitting those wagons of different lengths on seventy-two foot flatcars. Should he get an eighteen foot wagon when he has twenty-two feet of space on a flatcar, he must wait for a twenty-two foot wagon or he will not get the show all loaded on the cars.

On moves between towns, the truck shows move about the same as any fleets of trucks except they must follow a route laid out and "arrowed" by one of the show officials. These arrows were painted on utility poles, fences, etc. for many years. Now all shows have special printed "arrows" that are tacked to the poles, etc.. Even with plenty arrows on a route, some sleepy carnival hand is likely to "blow the route" and wind up in some town fifty miles from his show's new lot. Of course, railroad shows have no problem with lost drivers and broken-down trucks enroute. Once the show trains are loaded, they are transported to the next town as fast as the show's trainmaster can persuade the railroad employees to move it. If the show trainmaster is not as persuasive as he should be, the carnival trains can lay on side tracks as slow freights forge ahead of them, and the carnival will "blow" its opening day. Fortunately, the men handling the few carnival trains now in existence are not only persuasive boys, they are gentlemen.

Finally, no collective amusement organization is any stronger than its staff. Many of the smaller midways are owned, moved and operated by one strong rugged individual who needs very little staff to assist him on his twenty-hour per day job. Most of the larger midways do have full staffs of capable men. Briefly, a full staff of a carnival consists of: a manager (some have a general manager over the manager), a business manager (who is the. legal adjuster or "fixer"), a secretary (in many cases the owner's wife), a treasurer, a general agent (most owners do their own general agent work now), a special agent (does special promotions, etc.), a director of publicity (press agent), a superintendent (called lot man on some shows), a boss electrician, a boss mechanic, a ride superintendent, and foremen for each of the various office-owned rides and attractions. On many shows one man can handle several jobs through necessity, as capable men to fill all jobs open in the collective amusement industry today are not available.

SMITH GREATER SHOWS. "Tunnel Car" in Teens (about 1916 or 1917). Courtesy Albert Conover.

"GAL" SHOWS FROM LITTLE EGYPT TO GYPSY ROSE LEE

There is no record that any dancing girl shows existed in the outdoor amusement field prior to the Columbian Exposition. The Oriental Dances on the Midway Plaisance were not "wild" as they were reported to be, but they were new to American show goers. No dance inside the Exposition gates had the lustful impact of the mildest "strip-tease" of later years, and none of them were half as lewd as their imitators on the two midway areas outside Exposition gates. It was out on those midways that the "Little Egypt Legend" got its start.

It is doubtful that any girl calling herself Little Egypt appeared in Chicago on any midway in 1893. There are several stories concerning the first use of this name for a dancer, and few of them bear out the commonly accepted version of the genesis of this name. However, the "cooch" dancing done in the dirty little tents off the fairgrounds was the source from which this character developed. Those "cooch shows" were "wild" for that period, but none of them were as erotic as the ones that can be found on some midways today.

After the Columbian Exposition was over, all of the Street Fair promoters promised that they would bring in a "Streets of Cairo" with Little Egypt direct from the World's Fair. So, it was expected at all of these festivals. When Gaskill got his first carnival on the road, naturally, he carried a show of this type. In those early shows, the "cooch" girls were only a small portion of the performance. Jugglers, glass blowers, gun spinners, and all sorts of Middle Eastern entertainers worked along with the girls in the "Streets."

All big carnivals carried a "Streets of Cairo" type show until the early teens, when other shows took their place. The Cooch Girls stayed on the midways though. By 1915, some midway owners were experimenting with tented theatres in which they were presenting dancing girl revues similar to the ones still used on some of the larger midways today, but another type "girl orientated" show was being booked on all of the carnivals that season. The cooch girls were all working as hostesses and dancing partners in the '49 Camp Shows. These shows had "generated so much heat" and gotten so many towns "closed" to carnivals that they were no longer used in the twenties. By 1920, the girl shows had evolved into the patterns they have followed ever since.

The larger, more respectable, midways carried a tent theatre with a large dancing girl revue, and the others had from one to three cooch shows. The former have never been very profitable for the carnival owner, but they carried them as "committee" shows. Shows that they could escort fair managers and their wives to see. The latter with their two or three girls performing on a small bare platform with the "boys" standing around the platform are usually profitable, if they don't get the "midway sloughed by the fuzz." Very few of them get closed any more. Many of the county fair managers demand this type show on any midway they book for their fair. They know that a certain portion of their small-town "boys" wouldn't come to the fair unless there is a cooch show.

During the Thirties, the girl revues were built into production-type shows with eight and ten-piece stage bands, eight to twelve girls in line, four or five strippers and fan dancers, a couple of vaudeville acts and a comic or two. After the war, the big carnivals still had this type revue on their midways. The eight years starting in 1946 were noted for the "big name" stars on carnival girls shows. Many strippers from burlesque were featured by various carnivals. Sally Rand and her fans was featured on several shows, and Gypsy Rose Lee was the feature of one carnival "gal" show. Gypsy and Sally Rand were probably the highest-paid features any carnival ever carried; but they drew more than enough patronage to pay their salaries, and show a profit for the midway. Both were well-liked by all carnival people.

The advent of the spectacular rides in 1950 doomed big theatre-type shows on carnival midways. A few of the larger carnivals still have big girl shows, but dollarwise they do not pay. A riding device operated by four men, and costing no more than the girl show equipment, will gross as much on the season. So there is no profit in paying fifteen or twenty more people from the same amount of gross business. A well-run three-girl cooch show probably would outgross both the ride and the big girl revue, but it would have a degrading influence on the now respectable midway.

ROYAL AMERICAN CREST. Carl J. Sedlmayr asked Robert Wick, designer, decorator, and superintendent of the paint department to design a suitable crest for the world's largest outdoor amusement organization. "Bobby" Wick designed the crest pictured here. In color with gold, it is used on employees' uniforms, ticket boxes, wagons and trucks. Courtesy Robert Wick and the Royal American Shows.

CARNIVAL TITLES

NOTE: This listing of titles used by collective amusement organizations the past seventy-one years is not complete. It is doubtful that all titles used will ever be listed as many small shows were started every season; shows that played only a few dates and folded without leaving any written record. It is estimated that there are at least six hundred separate midway units in North America this 1972 season. A look at the listed routes in Amusement Business will show that not over twenty-five percent of them supply their route to the magazine.

All information in the following listing has been gathered from back issues of Billboard and its successor, Amusement Business. Dates following the show's title are not the complete lifespan of that title, but are the dates the author has confirmed that the show listed was on the road. Some shows known to be operating sent no routes in for publication for entire seasons.

It is hoped that this listing will be of aid to future students of carnival history, and that the average reader will gain some knowledge of the immensity of the collective amusement industry by browsing through them.

This list was compiled in 1969. No new shows are listed.

A & H Amusements (N.Y. & Conn.) . . . . 1965—66
A-9 Attractions (S.C.) .1963
A-1 Amusement Co. . . . . 1946—60
A-1 Amusements (III.) (John Hanson) . . . . 1961—69
A-1 Attractions (Conn.) 1961
A & P Amusement Co. . . . . 1944—51
A & P Shows (Wisc.) 1967
A T & T Shows . . . . 1967—68
A T & T Amusements (Tex.— Okla.) . . . . 1967—68
Abbott's Great Northern Shows 1910
Ace Amusements (Maine) .1969
J. F. Ackerman Bazaar Co. .1923
Acme Amusement Co. (Harry Heller) . . . . 1913—17
Acme Exposition 1939
Acme Shows 1919
Adams Amusement Co. . . . . 1911—12
Adams Greater Exposition Shows (Otis L.) . . . . . . 1913—15
Adams & Stahl Shows 1910
Otis L. Adams Exposition Shows 1916
Otis L. Adams Shows . . . . 1916—17
Admiration Shows 1948
Aeder Amusements (Mich.) . . . . 1965—69
Ague Amusements Co. 1929
Aiken Amusement Co. 1911
Aiken Famous Shows 1915
Ajax United Shows . . . . 1929—30
Akron Greater Shows 1930
Alabama Amusement Co. . . . . 1925—30
Alabama Carnival Company . . . . 1906—07
Alabama-Georgia Amusements 1939
Alamo Carnival Co. 1904
Alamo Shows 1928
Alamo Exposition (Southwest) (Jack Ruback) . . . . . 1926—69
Albion Amusement Co. 1913
Alexander & Foster Exposition Shows 1919
All American Amusement Co. . . . . 1942—50
All American Exposition .1942
All American Shows (Ky. & Va. to Ga.) . . . . 1962—69
All American Shows . . . . 1914—44
All American Shows Inc. .1963
Allen Amusement Co. (Ind. & III.) . . . . 1963—69
Allen Big League Shows .1921
Fred Allen Shows . . . . 1943—45

Tom W. Allen Shows . . . . 1915—19
All Fair Shows 1951
Allied Shows . . . . 1919—20
Allman Brothers American Shows 1913
Allman Brothers Big American Shows . . . . 1914—15
All Star Carnival Co. 1909
All Star Carnival & Midway Co. 1903
All State Shows (Pa. — N.C.) 1969
Al's Sooner State Shows .1947
Amalgamated Carnival Co. (E. M. Burk — Nat Reiss) 1902—04
American Amusement Co. (DeKrekos) . 1903—06, 1915, 1926
American Banner Shows . . . . 1946—47
American Bazaar Shows 1951
American Beauty Shows (Mo.) . . . . 1946—64
American Beauty Rides 1965
American Carnival Co. . . . . 1905—09
American Eagle Shows (Nebr.) . . . . 1950—69
American Exposition . . . . 1923—44
American Exposition Shows 1913, 1969
American Fiesta Shows (Kan. — Tex.) . . . . 1962—63
American Funland Shows (Ohio) . . . . 1964—65
American Midway Shows .1949
American Model Shows . . . . 1934—35, 1944
American Progressive Shows 1929
American United Shows . . . . 1935—48
A.M.P. Shows . . . . 1941—55
Amusement Co. of America . . . . 1953—59
Amusements of America (Vivona Bros.) . . . . 1961—69
Anderson Amusement Co. . . . . 1914—19
Anderson Greater Shows . . . . 1946—48
Anderson-Strader Shows . . . . 1921—48
Anderson-Williams Amusements 1928
C. W. Andreau's Amusement Co. 1907
Anthracite Shows . . . . 1925—26, 1948
Arcade Shows 1919, 1944
Arena Amusement Co. 1914—16
Arena Shows . . . . 1936—38
Argyle Shows . . . . 1916—19?
Ario Amusement Co. 1940
Matt Armstrong Shows (Wisc.—La.) . . . . 1968—69
Artdick's Greater Shows . . . . 1929—31
Arthur's American Shows .1942
Asal-Evans Shows 1919

M. J. LAPP EXPOSITION SHOWS, 1920. Courtesy L. Harvey (Doc)

Courtesy Circus World Museum, Baraboo, Wisconsin.

CETLIN & WILSON SHOWS. On a muddy lot. Author's Collection.

CENTURY 21 SHOWS MIDWAY. Courtesy Al Kunz.

WILLIAM T. COLLINS SHOWS, 1969. At Mower County Fair & Midwest Livestock Show, Austin, Minnesota. Courtesy Mower County Fair.

Courtesy J. W. PATTY CONKLIN.

163

Dana Thompson Dixie Carnival Co. 1903
Dandy Dixie Shows 1919–23, 1935
Dan Louis Shows 1947–49
Dano's Greater Shows 1917–18
Danville & Kasper Amusement Co. 1906–07
Danville & Wilson Shows 1919
Darnaby & Calkins Carnival Co. 1903
Dauberman's Amusements (Pa.) 1965
Davidson Amusements (Iowa) 1967
Davidson United Shows (Iowa) 1957–68
Davis Amusement Co. 1906–09
Davis Amusement Co. (Ore.) 1951, 1957–59
Davis, Evans & Wallace Combined Midway Attractions . .1919
Davis & Parrott Shows 1939
Davis United Shows 1932, 1953
Days of 49 Shows 1916
Dean & Flynn Shows . . . . 1969 (Dean killed)
K. Dee Greater Shows 1932
De Gaynor's Kiddieland 1956
Delgarian Combined Carnival Shows 1906
Deggeller Amusement Co. 1961–69
Dehnert Exposition 1929–30
Dehnert & Helm Shows 1925
Dehnert & Knepp Shows .1936
DeKreko Brothers Shows 1914–29
DeKreko Brothers Roman Carnival
& Exposition Co. 1902
Del Flore Amusements 1953–69
Dell & Travers Shows 1963–69
Delmar Quality Shows 1923–30
Delmar Shows (Tex.) (Dr. Shugart) 1918–32
Del Mar Shows 1948
Delmora Shows 1967
Delta Carnival Co. (T. Cannon) 1904
Deluxe Amusements 1947–48
Deluxe Rides, Inc. (Conn.) 1961–67
Deluxe Shows 1937–45
Deluxe Shows of America 1936
Dennis Rides 1946–47
Johnny J. Denton Shows 1942–48
Desbro Shows 1953–56
Deshelley Carnival Co. 1904
Devaux & Klein Shows 1916
Devak & Nelson Greater Shows 1914
Diamond Midway 1946
Diamond Sister's Shows 1932
Dick's Greater Shows 1948
Dick's Paramount Shows 1931, 1938–47
Dickson United Shows 1944–59
Raymond C. Dixey Shows 1959
Dine Amusements (Ohio) 1961–66
Dixie Amusements (S.D.–Okla.) 1955–63
Dixie Amusement Co. 1933, 1957–59
Dixie Belle Attractions 1937–44
Dixie Carnival Co. 1903–08
Dixie Exposition 1929–37, 1950, 1955
Dixie Model Shows 1931, 1937–39
Dixie Shows 1905
Dixie United Shows 1910
Dixieland Rides 1929–35
Dixieland Shows 1923–26, 1945
George L. Dobyns Shows 1922–24
Dobson's United Shows (Minn.) 1943–61
Dodson & Cherry Shows .1922
Dodson's Exposition 1928
Dodson's Worlds Fair Shows 1915, 1923–45
Dohrman Amusement Company 1914–15

Doris-Ferari Shows 1921
Douglas Greater Shows 1937–48, 1956
Dowland Shows 1948
Down East Attractions 1940
Down River Amusement Co. (Mich.) 1948–62
Dow's Coney Island at Home Shows 1923
Drago Amusement Co. (Ill.–Ind.) 1948–69
Dreamland Exposition Shows 1915–17, 1925
James H. Drew's Exposition 1961–69
James H. Drew's Shows 1951–60
James H. Drew's World's Fair Shows 1961, 1963, 1966
D. S. Dudley Shows 1935–69
Lou Dufour Shows 1921–1924
Dufour & Tilford Shows 1919
Duke's Exposition Shows .1919
Dumont Shows 1943–57
Romeo Dunn's Midway 1969
Jimmie Dupree Shows 1947–48
Dyer's Greater Shows 1937–58
Dyer's Lotta Hooey Shows 1956
Dykman & Joyce Shows 1922–23
E. J. C. Shows 1937–38
Eagle Carnival Co. 1905
Eakhart's Combined Shows 1918
Eastern Amusements 1917
Eastern Amusement Co. (Maine) 1951–64
East Coast Shows (Md.) 1969
Earle's Wonderland Shows 1932
Echlin, Harris Amusement Co. 1905
Ebersole Shows 1942
Ehring's Attractions 1920
Ehring Amusement Co. 1913, 1919
Otto F. Ehring Amusement Co. 1910, 1928
Otto F. Ehring Shows 1925
Eby Shows (Minn.) 1966–68
Eddie's Exposition (Pa.) 1943–61
Eddie's Rides 1929
Edgewater Amusement Co. 1929
Edwards & Allen Shows 1957
J. R. Edwards Attractions 1928–46
Edwards & Taggart Shows 1919–1920
Egyptian Carnival & Street Fair Co. 1902
Otto F. Ehring's Shows 1927–30
Elaine Amusement Co. 1937
Elaine Exposition 1936
Frank Elliot Shows 1937
L. W. Elliot Shows 1940
Ellis & Smithson Combined Shows 1912
Elite Exposition 1937–42
Ellman Amusement Co. 1924–25
Ellman Shows 1937–39
Ellman United Shows 1944–48
Elm City Shows (Ill.) 1968
Empire Amusement Co. 1917, 1942
Empire City Shows 1932–34, 1940
Empire Greater Shows 1923
Empire State Shows 1920
Empire United Shows 1931, 1943, 1957
Emshoff Shows (Wise) 1948–53, 1961–67
Empire State Shows 1964
Endy Brothers Shows 1931, 1936–48
David B. Endy Amusements 1961–69
Endy Exposition Shows 1919
Endy Shows 1923–34, 1940
English Amusement Co. 1917
Enterprise Shows 1923–36, 1944
Eureka Attractions 1920

FAIR TIME SHOWS FRONT GATE. This show owned by Olivia Waldron on the West Coast was photographed in 1964. Courtesy Amusement Business Photograph.

FOLEY & BURK SHOWS. Showing the ferris wheel with the "tulip design" lighting in the circle and the "wrong way" merry-go-round. Courtesy Lloyd Hilligoss.

DON FRANKLIN SHOWS. Mower County Fair and Midwest Livestock Show, 1950. Courtesy Mower County Fair.

GEM CITY SHOWS MIDWAY. Courtesy Mower County Fair, Austin, Minnesota.

JOHNNY'S UNITED SHOWS. Courtesy Johnny Portemont, Jr.

L. J. HETH SHOWS, about 1937. Note the SWOOPER riding device.
Only two of these rides were built. Courtesy Al Kunz.

Courtesy Albert Conover

MELVILLE-REISS SHOWS, 1930. This was the last season this show was on road as Harry Melville was too ill to put it out in 1931. Courtesy Earl Purtle.

MORRIS & CASTLE SHOWS, 1928. Courtesy Nat Worman.

PRINCESS OLGA SHOWS IN LATE TWENTIES. The wheel was the last Number 10 Eli manufactured. None made after 1928. Courtesy Art Doc Miller.

ROYAL AMERICAN SHOWS. Minnesota State Fair, 1935. Note the steel brake drum on side of ticket box for noisemaker. Courtesy Harry Frost, Minnesota State Fair.

Courtesy Joe Pearl

George T. Scott Shows 1923–30
Scott Greater Shows 1922, 1929–31
Turner Scott Rides (Fla.) 1955, 1964–66, 1969
Scottie Rides 1938
Scotty's United Shows 1948
H. T. Scarlock Shows 1909
Seccaium Park Rides 1937–40
Seeman Amusement Co. 1904
Seeman-Millicam Mardi Gras & Festival Co. 1904
Seeman-Millican Mardi Gras Co. 1905
Sehl's Northern Shows (Mich.) 1963–69
Seifer Greater Shows 1930
Shamrock Shows 1956
Shanan's Exposition Shows .1919
Shan Brothers Shows 1946–49, 1953–55
Shannon's Combined Shows 1929
Sheesley Greater Shows 1913, 1923, 1928–32
Sheesley Mighty Midway 1935, 1937–44
Sheesley Shows 1912
Sherman's Greater Shows 1919
Shipley Amusement Co. 1945
Shive & Christ Shows 1930
Shoemaker's Amusements (Pa.) 1968
Shorter's Greater Shows (Iowa) 1958–59, 1962–69
Shorty's Tri-State Shows 1959, 1962
Shop-O-Rama 1957
Doc Shugart Shows (Tex.) 1933–48
Walter K. Sibley's Shows 1915
Sibley's Superb Shows 1910, 1916–19
Siebrand Brothers Shows 1926–67
Siegrist-Silbon Shows 1920–22
Silk City Shows 1940, 1957
Silver Fleet Shows 1940
Silver Slipper Shows 1946–48
Silver Star Shows (Neb.) 1948, 1961–65
Silver State Attractions 1939
Silver State Shows 1935–40
J. C. Simpson's Greater Shows 1911
Simpsom Brothers Shows (N.Y.) . . . . .1926 (2 shows)
Sim's Greater Shows 1929–32, 1937–40
Sites & Gilbert Carnival Co. 1908
J. Harry Six Shows 1926–34, 1942
Skerbeck Amusement Co. (Mich.) 1934–69
Charles Skiver Shows 1928
SJM Fiesta Shows (Calif.) 1962, 1965–69
SJM Shows . . . . .1967?
Slocomb & Edwards United Shows 1919
Small & Bullock Shows 1935–36
Smiley's Amusement Co. (Pa.–N.C.) 1957–59, 1964
Smiley's Shows 1961–63
Smith Amusement Co. 1913, 1946–64
Smith Brothers Shows 1938–40
Casey Smith Shows 1945–48
Doc Smith Shows 1939
George Clyde Smith Shows (Pa.) 1942–64
Ed. J. Smith's Shows 1916–17
Smith's Funland 1956, 1959
Smith Greater Amusement Enterprises 1905
Smith Great Atlantic Shows 1934–36
Smith's Greater Shows 1906–1951
Smith's Greater United Shows 1919–27
J. Lacey Smith Shows 1926–38
Lexie Smith Amusement Co. 1926, 1939
Otis L. Smith Shows 1923–27
Roland Smith Amusement Co. (Okla.) 1947, 1966–69
Smith's Southern Shows 1919
Smith Wonder Show (N.D.) 1963, 1965–67

Smokey's Greater Shows . . . .?
Snapp Brothers Exposition Shows 1922–30
Snapp Greater Shows 1933–56
Snapp Model Shows 1947
Snapp Shows 1921
William R. Snapp Attractions 1931–32
T. L. Snodgrass Shows 1927–34
Snyder's Greater Shows 1947
Snyder's Greater United Shows 1912
Snyder's Greatest Shows United 1907–08
Sol's Greater Shows (Ark.) 1961, 1966
Sol's Liberty Shows 1929–42
Sol's United Shows 1917–20
Sol's & Rubin's United Shows (Gruberg) 1916
Sooner State Shows 1947
Sound Amusement Co. 1919
South Dakota Amusement Co. 1931
Southern Amusement Co. 1912–16, 1927
Southern Attractions 1939–40
Southern Carnival Co. (Nat Reiss) 1902–07
Southern Exposition 1920, 1930
Southern Exposition Shows .1919
Southern Fair Shows 1912, 1957
Southern Midway 1940
Southern State Shows 1930, 1942–48, 1956
Southern Superior Shows 1930
Southern Tier Shows 1926–33
Southern Valley Shows 1930
Southland Amusements (Ala.–Fla.) 1940, 1961–69
Southwest Amusements 1956
Space Age Amusements 1969
Spang Greater Shows 1931
Spangler Shows 1912
Sparks Brothers Shows 1945–46
J. F. Sparks Shows 1937–50
Sparks Shows 1907
Sparton Greater Shows . . . . .1954?
Bryan Spaun Carnival Co. 1906
Frank P. Spellman Shows 1909
Spencer Amusements 1969
C. L. Spencer Shows 1926–37
Spencer Celebrated Shows 1919–24
Spencer & Clark Shows 1937
Spencer Greater Shows (Tex.–Okla.) 1961–63
H. B. Spencer & Sons Amusement Co. (Conn.) 1962–64, 1966
Sam E. Spencer Shows 1923–39
Spencer Shows 1923
P. J. Speroni Shows 1929–42
Square Deal Shows 1934
M. A. Srader Shows 1944, 46–48, 1953
Stafford Shows (Ind.) 1957–58, 1962–65

SOUTHERN TIER SHOWS TRUCK, 1923. This was the first season of this first carnival of James E. Strates. Courtesy Art Doc Miller.

WEST'S WORLD'S WONDER SHOWS. Note the circus-type "turn-cages" (cage wagons that loaded cross-wise on the flatcars). These short wagons saved considerable space on the train. Courtesy Albert Conover.

FIRST ROLLOPLANE AT THE OTTAWA FAIR. World of Mirth Shows. Courtesy Earl Purtle.

Courtesy Circus World Museum, Baraboo, Wisconsin.

186

INDEX

SLIM KELLY. An all-around generally useful carnival trouper and a leading side show producer and operator. Courtesy Amusement Business Photograph.

ATTRACTIONS
SEASON, 1922

Merry-Go-Round	Bert Cobb, Mgr.
The Whip	L. T. McLaughlin, Mgr.
Ferris Wheel	Walter F. Hall, Mgr.
Seaplanes	S. B. Morey, Mgr.
D. M. Bristol's Equescurriculum	C. D. Bristol, Mgr.
O. K Hagger's Freak Animal Show	Harry Knowles, Mgr.
Hamond's Dog and Pony Circus	T. J. Barry, Mgr.
Hamond's Platform Show	Harry Hamond, Mgr.
Darktown Follies	W. J. Myers, Mgr.
Fun House	H. L. Masters, Mgr.
The Devil	E. P. Barker, Mgr.
Mamie Howard, Fat Girl	Geo. Brocket, Mgr.
Circus Side Show	Doc Hamilton, Mgr.
Museum of Wonders	Jack Walker, Mgr.
Hawaiian Theatre	Fred Culver, Mgr.
Jungleland Show	Beatrice Dungan, Mgr.
Noweka	Thomas Miller, Mgr.

LINE-UP OF ATTRACTIONS, Lou Dufour Shows, 1922. Courtesy Lou Dufour.

WALL TO WALL CROWDS. Another view of crowds at Canadian National Exhibition, 1968. Courtesy Amusement Business.

UNCLE THOMAS JOHN HENRY. This six year old gorilla pictured in 1963 sitting in his "Mommy's" (Mae Noell) lap. Courtesy Amusement Business Photograph.

A "WELL FLASHED" CONCESSION STAND. Some of the individuals out front of the joint were undoubtedly "shills." Author's collection.

Nevermore

WILL THE FORTY-CAR JOHNNY J. JONES TRAIN COME TO TOWN? Courtesy Albert Conover.

WILL THIS FRONT GATE BE SET UP ON A SHOWGROUNDS? It was designed and built by Joe McKennon for a midway show in 1938. Courtesy Albert Conover.

WILL THE RIDE BOYS LINE UP AT THIS WAG FOR THEIR NOON-TIME "DRAWS?" Courtesy Albert Conover.

JOHNNY PORTEMENT, JR. Owner Johnny's United Shows. He started own carnival in partnership with his sister and their father in 1946. He is now sole owner. His wife and children are all active with the show. His wife Marilyn is the show's secretary.

He was born August 20, 1921 in Brazil, Indiana. He has four children aged twelve to twenty-one. He is past president of the Miami Showmen's Club and of the St. Louis Chapter of Showmen's League of America. He is president of Showmen's League of America in Chicago. He is immediate past president of OABA and continues to work hard for this Outdoor Amusement Business Association. He has one of the cleanest, best-maintained midways in America. He gets things done for himself and for any organization to which he may belong. A real modern-day carnival man and midway operator.

It Has Been A Tough Job

END VOLUME TWO